DISCIPLINARY FUTURES

Disciplinary Futures

Sociology in Conversation with American, Ethnic, and Indigenous Studies

Edited by

Nadia Y. Kim *and* Pawan Dhingra

NEW YORK UNIVERSITY PRESS

New York

NEW YORK UNIVERSITY PRESS
New York
www.nyupress.org

© 2023 by New York University
All rights reserved

Please contact the Library of Congress for Cataloging-in-Publication data.
ISBN: 9781479819034 (hardback)
ISBN: 9781479819041 (paperback)
ISBN: 9781479819065 (library ebook)
ISBN: 9781479819058 (consumer ebook)

New York University Press books are printed on acid-free paper, and their binding materials
are chosen for strength and durability. We strive to use environmentally responsible suppli-
ers and materials to the greatest extent possible in publishing our books.

Manufactured in the United States of America

10 9 8 7 6 5 4 3 2 1

Also available as an ebook

CONTENTS

Introduction

How We Got Here, Where We'd Like to Go Now

NADIA Y. KIM AND PAWAN DHINGRA

We felt the need to compile this volume on how sociology (and the social sciences) can be enriched by close engagement with other disciplines because we had not seen anything like it, yet we and our own work had long been yearning for it. These sensibilities and concerns sprang from our deep engagement of sociology—our home disciplines—as well as ethnic, Asian American, American, and gender and women's studies. But it also came from a nagging sense that the theories, models, and trends of mainstream sociology could partially, but not fully, capture the phenomena we were studying, whether it was Korean-US relations and Korean immigrants, South Asian immigrant motel owners, Asian and Latinx immigrant activists for environmental and school justice, or the academic pursuits of South Asian parents. This nagging sense—one of having long worked within paradigms and frames that just didn't quite fit or make sense, of getting questions and comments from other sociologists that were out of step with our aims, analyses, and lexicon—was also cast into relief by engaging with new ways of thinking and articulating gained from ethnic, Asian American, American, and gender and women's studies.

This nagging feeling when only within sociology, yet the intellectual freedom and richness when engaging within *and* without it, is what led us to edit and put together this rare volume. As we well knew, finding scholars to contribute original pieces for a special volume is one of the hardest feats an academic can undertake, but such was the power of our desire for this inter-and multidisciplinary collection that we were willing to undertake the challenge.

So as not to seem myopic, biased, and overwrought, we write this not because we view sociology categorically as a failed discipline or a lost cause—not in the least. We co-edited this volume because sociology is at the center of our life's work; as Enriquez and Ochoa similarly argue in this volume, these were the undergraduate classes that first stirred our hearts, the first discipline to give us the language and the frameworks that made unwieldy and normalized forces within and around us legible. Because of this near lifelong dance with sociology and how it has enriched us, we want to remain in the dance hall. But we also believe that it could be more inclusive, expansive, engaging, reflective about what has been going on inside, and more in touch with the goings on outside. In this spirit, we are prompted to ask questions such as how sociology's dance hall became the institution that it did in the first place, why it is on the land that it sits on, whether the dances have become repetitive, and which dancers may not have been invited in or offered the spotlight.

In this vein, we review the evolution of sociology and American and ethnic studies, which serve as windows into the strengths and limitations of all the disciplines. We argue that the limitations have been caused in large part by disciplinary siloing but also by sociology's belief in itself as a "hard" science when human behavior cannot always be packaged into formulas, experiments, and mathematical equations. We then turn to the ways in which we and our contributors have navigated disciplinary silos and mainstream sociology's institutionalization by forging our own paths within, across, between, and around disciplines.

Finally, we should make clear that this volume primarily comprises essays that push the boundaries of *mainstream* sociology. By mainstream, we are referring to what the majority of sociologists write about, what is most frequently published in the discipline's top-flight journals, what proposals garner the largest grants, what topics graduate students are encouraged to study, and what the majority of job postings ask for. As such, this does not at all mean that sociologists have never studied empire, settler colonialism, racial capitalism, or nation-states outside of the United States. It does mean, however, that these paradigms and methods are not a priori within the mainstream of the discipline. Simply put, these are decidedly more the exception than the rule. Furthermore, we highlight American studies and ethnic studies because of their strong cross pollination (notwithstanding important distinctions) and their inter- and multidisciplinary cores, in stark comparison to the more insular discipline of sociology. We critique sociology not because we believe it has little to contribute but because its contribution, especially to the study of systemic racism and to the fight for social justice, has not been fully realized. But for the discipline to remain vibrant and relevant to a generation of scholars not afraid to put their political projects front and center, it must reckon with its past and learn from scholars pushing it from the margins.[1]

Disciplinary Origins and Limitations

Sociology and American studies have more in common than either discipline typically acknowledges. In the middle of the twentieth century, both embraced an American exceptionalism and a focus on American culture. American studies originated in the research pursuit of how the United States was able to establish its vaunted system of democracy, progress, and liberalism. As such, hegemonic forces like the US state and the Carnegie Corporation underwrote the discipline of American studies. Only after the Vietnam War did this come to be questioned by academics.[2]

In parallel fashion, the hegemony of "hard science" was at the origins of sociology. The discipline was wed to a structural functionalism and preoccupied with consensus and order, often assessed through quantitative methods, as the discipline modeled itself as a science.[3] Sociology also grew out of the Chicago school, which had a major influence on the tenets of the discipline. The assumption was that of research based in value-free objectivity. The Chicago school was also marked by racist ideology.[4] For instance, the second-generation White American "fathers" of the Chicago school, including Ernest Burgess and Robert Park, popularized Orientalist notions of Asian groups and contributed to the racialization that until only very recently was unacknowledged or dismissed outright by mainstream sociology.[5] Although W. E. B. Du Bois and a few others, especially African Americans, focused on sociology's potential to address social problems and emphasized the role of race, this was not widely taken up.[6] In the 1960s, as Ben Carrington chronicles in this volume, the pioneering work of Jamaican British sociologist Stuart Hall in founding cultural studies by way of the Centre for Contemporary Cultural Studies (later, the Birmingham School of Cultural Studies) was ignored by mainstream sociology, a problematic dismissal that continues nearly sixty years later.

These were not the only ways that sociology missed major opportunities to pioneer and advance the study of race, racism, and White supremacy. The great social theorists of the nineteenth century conceptualized race/ethnicity as remnants of a preindustrial order and predicted its declining significance in modern society.[7] For example, the classical Marxist understanding that capital seeks "abstract labor" overlooks the ways in which capital has profited precisely from the flexible racialization and gendering of labor.[8] Furthermore, the Chicago school predicted that most non-White groups would assimilate just as the southern Eastern European immigrants did.[9]

Notably, in the classic book *Sociology and the Race Problem: The Failure of a Perspective*, James McKee underscores that owing to its White-delimited perspective, sociology of the 1950s failed to foresee the Black American racial protest movements of the 1960s. McKee found that the discipline's failure of the sociological imagination traced to an intellectual trend starting in the 1950s, whereby mostly White male sociologists began making predictions about US modernity. By way of such a paradigm, these scholars assumed that all non-White groups, including Black Americans, would assimilate into mainstream society and that this process would be gradual, nonviolent, and led by Whites (rather than by Blacks or other people of color). Biased by this Whiteness-bound, assimilationist, functionalist, and deracialized approach, sociologists failed to anticipate—perhaps even to conceptualize—the landmark civil rights and the revolutionary Black Power movements that were to define those times and that so profoundly and unalterably changed the cultural and social landscape of the country (though not, regrettably, sociology itself).

While sociology changed little, the study of racial inequality in the United States evolved in significant ways. Ethnic studies curricula and departments appeared in higher education. American studies followed ethnic studies' prioritization of engaged scholarship in relation to marginalized group struggles. This marked a major turnaround for American studies, given its original hegemonic question of what made American culture successful in supporting democracy, progress, and liberalism. The anti–Viet Nam War movement and the 1960s' race-based revolutions crystallized American studies' move toward progressive intellectual orientations. Following the lead of critical studies of ethnic and racialized communities, American studies gradually adopted in-depth theorizing of racial capitalism, imperialism, and White supremacy.

On the other hand, in the postwar decades, sociology succumbed to the growth of the research university and of funding sources for the social sciences. Both of these forces have served to "scientize" sociology.[10] To be sure, during the 1960s, the discipline also moved away from grand theories and toward a growing interest in situational studies, such as those pioneered by Erving Goffman and in interactionist subfields like ethnomethodology.[11] This greater emphasis on qualitative methods seemed like a natural fit with American studies and a marked move away from a standard scientific commitment.[12] Yet even the qualitative-methods approach of mainstream sociology was positivist in the name of being a hard science. It often ignored information that deviated from the standard findings in search of the "truth" and tended to look for causality and to fixate on human behaviors rather than on meaning and subjectivity, among other concerns.[13] By becoming more specialized and less engaged with nearby disciplines such as ethnic studies, sociology's claim to universal and objective knowledge also moved the field away from an explicit commitment to social justice.[14]

Given the major missteps McKee (1993) identified—the inability to predict the 1960s' racial justice movements owing to assimilation and modernity paradigms—sociology diverged from American studies by not integrating ethnic studies into its core.[15] Noticeably, it opted instead to treat assimilation like a natural process and to treat race like a variable. The notion that race declines in significance, as the title of William J. Wilson's classic 1978 text so directly asserts, symbolizes the problematic thinking that race can simply be measured rather than be treated as foundational.[16] Counterarguments were certainly made to this thesis.[17] Yet the terms of the debate remained framed by whether race matters, a stance that stalled real progress by the discipline in theorizing the underlying place of White supremacy in the construction of institutions and daily interactions.

The Contributions of American and Ethnic Studies to Sociology

In this volume, we contend that the strengths of American studies and ethnic studies cast into relief certain key limitations of mainstream sociology. For instance, since the 1960s, when American studies fundamentally incorporated ethnic, women's, and sexuality studies, it was defined by interdisciplinarity. American studies therefore pivots on the precept that interdisciplinarity leads to more thoughtful and encompassing research (though this point is at times challenged).[18] American studies fundamentally values research that combines textual analysis with archives and interviews (often with activists), typically within a context of political economy.[19] Much of the analyses draw on literary and archival sources rather than on qualitative methods such as ethnography, one limitation that this volume also explores.[20] And although ostensibly bound to the United States, the field has increasingly connected to global formations. It recognizes the United States as an empire that utilizes militarization, corporatization, and neoliberalism abroad, each of which creates the conditions for immigration and, therefore, racial capitalism.[21] This theorization extends far beyond the individual or family levels that is the limited hallmark of sociology's transnational turn.[22]

Although ethnic studies has become a core part of American studies, it is a distinct field with its own interdisciplinary formation.[23] In addition to its origins in the new social movements, ethnic studies responded to the post-1965 rise in immigrant of color populations, as both new movements and new migrations transformed the academy and ushered in new subjects of (critical) social knowledge, contested the separation of knowledge and politics, and posed new questions to that end.[24] This was quite a feat, given how underfunded and under resourced ethnic studies was from the beginning and especially during the 1980s.[25]

Yet ethnic studies, explicitly critical and oppositional even in the face of "university ghettoization," condemned the production of "objective" and "universal" knowledge and fostered inclusive, situated, and transformative knowledge, such as that of Gloria Anzaldua's borderlands theory.[26] Espiritu contends that these types of ethnic studies and other interdisciplinary paradigms "left the barest traces on sociology" until the 1980s, following Michael Omi and Howard Winant's *Racial Formation in the United States* (1986). This was a groundbreaking theory of race/racism that fundamentally drew on ethnic studies to theorize the social construction of race and to center resistance movements in racial formations.[27] In an era when mainstream sociology was treating race mostly as additive, a variable, and as declining in significance, racial formation transformed sociology and the sociology of race. Bonilla Silva later argued that the United States operates within a racialized social system.[28] Yet mainstream sociology has not, like ethnic studies, transformed itself by drawing on "the best work in the humanities and social sciences and from the burgeoning theoretical and methodological innovations in Feminist Studies, Queer Studies, Postcolonial Studies, Cultural Studies, and Communication Studies" to conceptualize race/ethnicity as a central element of culture (as well as structure).[29]

The Contributions of Sociology to American and Ethnic Studies

Sociology was founded in response to massive historical shifts and the need to address the social problems that ensued. In Europe, the founding theorists—Marx, Weber, Durkheim, and Simmel—responded to the crises of emerging industrial capitalism and intended to shape the course of historical events through their social theories.[30] Within American sociology, the Chicago school spoke powerfully to the social issues of industrialization, urbanization, and urban immigration into our cities, through its attention to everyday experience. Du Bois theorized the Black experience as being foundational to the American project. Using a sophisticated research program, he showed how the effects of the color line were both structural and psychological.[31] Although most of his 1950s' contemporaries were focused on assimilationist and "US modernity" paradigms, C. Wright Mills blazed another trail with his book *The Sociological Imagination*. In it, he advocated for sociologists to make a social justice critique and for the restructuring of society that is central to a critical social science. Yen Espiritu, one of the contributors to this volume, was trained in sociology but works primarily within ethnic studies; yet as her piece on critical immigration studies shows, she also draws from both disciplines. She writes, "From sociology, I learn to be attentive to lived social experience, to grasp the social constructions of social reality, and to link the study of individual lives with broader issues of political economy."[32] Indeed, sociology's legacy of grounded research and commitment to the lives of everyday people provides a needed approach to studying the complicated and sometimes contradictory ways that groups of color inhabit their positionality relative to the state (and capital) and to one another. Understanding how people of color resist, but also reinforce, existing inequalities within various institutions better reveals how power operates.

Yet sociology's historical study of race—its Whiteness, assimilationism, functionalism, US-centrism, and underappreciation or misrepresentation of racial and racist matters—continues to reverberate. Indeed, several of the authors in this volume have had firsthand experience with these dynamics. In their graduate school days in sociology PhD programs, for instance, Enriquez and Ochoa were chastised or excluded for insisting on the centrality of race, intersectionality, and Chicana/o/x Latina/o/x studies to sociology. Carrington and his colleagues were not able to get a panel focused on Stuart Hall, the founding scholar of cultural studies, accepted at an American Sociological Association meeting program whose theme was the study of culture. At the same time, the interstices and peripheries of the discipline are beginning to establish a more critical assessment of its own racist genealogies. This gradual move began with *Racial Formation in the United States*, joined later by works on US racism that gave primacy to diaspora, imperialism, postcolonialism, settler colonialism, and the foundational rereading of the discipline and its study of race using Du Bois, Collins, and Stuart Hall.[33]

Furthermore, sociology addresses the problems in disciplines like American and ethnic studies, where grand statements and generalizations about the social world are sometimes made from partial or solely discursive evidence. Sociological practice at its best involves clear questions that are addressed with careful research within the context of existing literature. This is not to say that sociology is methodologically or empirically unproblematic. As noted, its quantitative and qualitative methods embrace a positivist approach aimed at proving an objective reality through data points, often made up of survey results and interview quotations. Its research designs have been known to assume that racialized groups are a natural phenomenon, and it has tended to explore racial inequality by way of methods (e.g., surveys) that inadequately ascertain people's actual opinions and feelings.[34] Bridging interdisciplinary studies and sociology can allow for new epistemologies and methodologies (the guiding theme of part 4 of this volume). Under this theme, for instance, Hōkūlani Aikau integrates social science frameworks into her teaching of literature (in this case, Octavia Butler); in her essays, she provides the resulting interdisciplinary pedagogical prompts that she uses in her literature courses.

Toward Inter- and Multidisciplinarity

To be clear, this volume is more of a meditation on the many ways that ethnic and American studies expand the purview of, and enrich and complexify, mainstream sociological frameworks and research design; it is less about what sociology does for the former. In this vein, we argue that interdisciplinary perspectives cannot simply be added on alongside existing dominant approaches within sociology, for they challenge key assumptions within the discipline. That is, mainstream sociology would be more apt to predict and grasp social and global processes by dint of prioritizing American and ethnic studies work on various forms of colonialism, military interventions, geopolitics, racial capitalism, neo-liberalism, and similar social forces related to the United States but also vis-à-vis other advanced nations. Centering racial capitalism and neo-liberalism, for instance, Pawan Dhingra and Sunaina Maira (both this volume) chronicle how these systems profoundly shape South Asian Americans' educational choices (Dhingra, chapter 3) and Yemeni American politics and small business practices (Maira, chapter 2).

More than sociology, these disciplines are also attentive to history. Sylvia Zamora and Nadia Kim argue thus with respect to the limitations of cross-sectional survey research on race attitudes to understand watershed moments like the 1992 civil unrest in Los Angeles (chapter 12). American and ethnic studies have also contributed much more than sociology to the ways the state operates to affirm imperial and racialized hierarchies and to negate tribal forms of governance. Monisha Das Gupta (chapter 7), Yvonne P. Sherwood (chapter 6), Erich Steinman (chapter 5), and Melissa Horner (chapter 8) argue convincingly that the very foundation and knowledge production of sociology would have to be transformed to account for the fact that Indigenous and Native peoples are not racial/ethnic minorities fighting for rights, recognition, or respect within the US nation-state; they are sovereign nations with systems wholly distinct from the racial formations that most Asian, Black, Latinx, and Middle Eastern American groups face. Participatory democracy is no answer to social inequality if that democracy upholds settler-colonial forms of land and property ownership and of individual rights backed by military force. The distinct cultural epistemologies that spring forth must be reckoned with, as Hafoka and Tovo explain in chapter 13 with respect to another issue: first-generation Pacific Islander college students. In this way, sociology has primarily been defined by a belief in the general functionality of a singular, bounded, and liberal nation-state. In so doing, it elides some of the most powerful systems and social events that consolidate White American supremacy historically and today.

Another way that mainstream sociology has been constrained is by its stuffing of groups of color who are not predominantly Black—Asian and Latinx ethnics in particular—into theoretical, analytical, and methodological frameworks premised on the White-Black order. The key question animating these frameworks is why and how Black Americans do not fare as well as Whites within our social institutions. As such, it has largely underappreciated the primacy of national and citizenship hierarchies to racism, which is predominantly experienced by groups with large numbers, or majorities, of immigrants and refugees; Espiritu's, Maira's, Dhingra's, and Escudero's pieces in this volume bespeak sociology's underappreciation of the imperialist, capitalist, colonialist, and other macro-historical forces that define immigrants, refugees, US possessions, and the United States itself. At the same time, there is no way of understanding (or dismantling) White supremacy without examining anti-Black racism. What this volume argues, however, is that we must pursue how global and American White supremacy depends on overlapping, differentiating, and/or interrelating racisms against all racialized populations and nations. In this vein, Miliann Kang (chapter 11) and Salvador Vidal-Ortiz (chapter 10) each broadly argues for troubling mainstream sociology by interrelating it with American and ethnic studies in particular. Kang engages interdisciplinarity (including disability scholarship) to grasp how the model minority myth of Asian Americans (which affects mothers in particular) hinges on ableism. Vidal-Ortiz spotlights Latin American contexts and (post)colonialism to forge a queer of color critique, approximating the spirit of transdisciplinarity.

Although a small number of essays in this volume do not formally critique sociology and instead demonstrate the benefits of its tools, the core of the volume contends that engaging disciplines on the outside offers mainstream sociology concrete pathways for how to expand from the standard questions and frameworks it uses to study race and racism—its Black-White binary framework, its fixation on the US mainland, its privileging of the nation-state (as a singular formation), its underappreciation of postcolonial and settler colonial studies, its liberal assumptions (a focus on "rights," insufficient attention to racial capitalism), its avoidance of naming and dismantling White supremacy rather than just racial inequalities, and its limited conception of what constitutes data. In the vein of what are data and of how sociologists are professionalized to analyze data, Brittany Friedman and Michael L. Walker, for instance, push sociology to go well beyond its positivist foundation to consider intuition as offering methodological insights (chapter 15). We hope that readers will learn primarily how to do sociology by way of these interdisciplinary fields and secondarily how to do American studies and critical ethnic studies from a sociological perspective. This volume is necessary because we know of no other that has tackled these issues in as direct and thorough a fashion. We hope that this anthology will inspire many more whose goal it is to make both disciplines more intellectually expansive spaces while still maintaining—and amplifying—their distinctive characters and strengths.

Organization of the Volume

The anthology is organized in four themes that we posit are central for a revitalized sociology and American and ethnic studies: empire and racial capitalism (part 1); settler colonialism and Indigenous studies (part 2); race/racism, intersectionality, and White supremacy (part 3); and new epistemologies and methodologies (part 4). We prioritized the first theme based on the precept that the United States must be understood as an imperial nation whose economic development has also relied on a racial capitalism. Immigrants voluntarily entering the country today are better understood within this framework rather than that of a liberal democracy with a meritocratic class system. This flows into the second theme, insofar as part of the country's imperial past and present involve the genocide and (attempted) removal of its Indigenous peoples. Settler colonialism is therefore a necessary framework to understand the history, present, and ideology of the nation. Overall, imperialism, racial capitalism, and settler colonialism set the stage for the contemporary effects of racism and the reality that these are never experienced in a singular fashion—the inspiration for our third theme on White supremacy. In other words, to understand minoritized communities and their resistance and contradictions, an intersectional lens is necessary. We highlight the interconnections of race with sexuality, gender, (dis)ability, and other structural hierarchies. With the theme of new epistemologies and methodologies, we end the volume pointing forward. For scholarship to advance and better tackle the problems we face, it is necessary to have creative frameworks and methods. Here we draw from Indigenous and Oceanic theories and frameworks, Latinx/Chicanx studies, cultural studies, methodological emotionality/affect, and pedagogical tools, among others, to reimagine how our disciplines and inter-disciplines can go beyond their traditional constraints.

The essays that fall under the theme of empire and racial capitalism explain the imperial/colonial and racial capitalist efforts of the United States or chronicle their effects. Conceiving of the United States and other countries as imperial nations better explains historical and contemporary migration patterns, the racial capitalist system, embedded hierarchies (such as various, yet related, racisms), and forms of resistance within and across borders. Sociology is increasingly paying attention to empire as a useful paradigm in understanding the United States, but such knowledge production is still nascent and lagging behind that of American and ethnic studies. As nation-states build up resources and power through imperial efforts abroad, they do the same for their highest caste citizens through a domestic racial capitalism. The chapters will offer both big-picture thinking on the value of this perspective and research-based studies in this vein.

Part 2 offers dedicated attention to a fundamental aspect of White supremacy, that of settler colonialism and Indigenous studies. For too long, the lives of Indigenous and Pacific Islander persons have been either ignored within the social sciences or treated as problems to be explained. Indigenous studies has forcefully argued that the Indigenous perspective, broadly defined, offers a distinct set of assumptions and politics from that of Western imperial logics. It explains how the United States and other "nations of immigrants" perpetuate settler colonialism not simply in the past but in the present as well, through practice and myth making. As throughout the book, this section will offer theoretical and empirically based research that makes clear to readers how settler colonialism changes sociology and/or operates in people's lived experience.

Part 3—"Race/Racism, Intersectionality, and White Supremacy"— does not simply focus on the primacy of race but makes sure to critically examine or theorize race outside of White/Black-only approaches, as tied to other social categories, namely gender and sexuality, and as inextricable from various forms of nation. Mainstream sociology has a good track record of arguing an intersectional approach to race, which interdisciplinary fields can learn from. Still, it is common for sociologists to remain mired in debates about whether race or class matters more. The mainstream discipline also tends to conceive of race as an independent variable that is discretely measured. The four chapters in this section all draw from grounded research to explicate how White supremacy intersects with other caste-like divisions in the lives of people of color.

Part 4, the final section of this volume, provides readers with an epistemological way forward for conducting research at the intersection of sociology and these interdisciplinary fields, with special emphasis on critiquing sociology. Sociology benefits not just from broadening what it counts as data and exploring new ways of collecting information but from an openness to rethinking its epistemological traditions and tenets and questioning its positivist assumptions. At the same time, essays like Hōkūlani Aikau's show us the benefits of drawing both on social science and literary concepts when we teach students how to think. Scholars in this section offer clear approaches to the study of social issues that are not limited to standard sociological methods and ways of knowing.

As discussed earlier, although the majority of essays in this volume do not lay out a transdisciplinary paradigm that could be applied by myriad disciplines and to myriad topics and methodological approaches, we do take to heart Enriquez and Ochoa's recommendation that dismantling disciplinary divides would help dismantle some of the silos, hierarchies, injustices, myopia, and territoriality we witness in the academy. Extending from their sage advice, we think of Katharine McKittrick's book *Dear Science*, which seeks to destabilize the orthodoxy of how we do "science." McKittrick asks us not to fixate on doing "more rigorous" science as disciplines come together but to consider instead *undisciplining*, that is, being more creative, finding new areas to explore, seeing where the work takes us, and envisioning "less terrifying" futures. It is our hope, by drawing from more than a disciplinary construct and praxis, that this volume indeed takes that next step.

NOTES

1 Although we are aware that critical race studies has been profoundly influential and is currently in the right-wing hot seat, we also contend that sociologists built the foundation from which critical race studies emerged, such as from Omi and Winant's racial formation theory. To be sure, the many renowned legal scholars— namely, women of color—who popularized critical race studies have concretized the legal dimensions of intersectionality within sociology, for instance. Yet some months after Kimberle Crenshaw's pathbreaking 1989 piece "Beyond Racism and Misogyny: Black Feminism and 2 Live Crew" was published, sociologist Patricia Hill Collins's canonical text, *Black Feminist Thought: Knowledge, Consciousness, and the Politics of Empowerment*, made waves in sociology and beyond. Unlike American and ethnic studies, then, critical race studies is much more interwoven with, and subsumed under, sociology, though some of our authors make reference to it. In addition, we are aware of transdisciplinarity and the debates over it, yet most of the pieces in this volume do not propose a holistic new cross-disciplinary framework under which relevant social issues could be subsumed (see Lawrence, "Beyond Disciplinary Confinement"). That is a tall theoretical order, one that we hope future scholars will take up.

2 Dubrow, "Sociology and American Studies"; Gleason, "World War II"; Marx, "Thoughts on the Origin and Character of the American Studies Movement."

3 Förster, "Micro-Sociology on the Rise."

4 Yu, *Thinking Orientals*.

5 Ibid. Only in 2020, when thousands of Asian Americans were beaten, even killed, for supposedly infecting the US with COVID-19, did mainstream sociology finally begin to grapple in earnest with this issue. See Kim, "Critical Thoughts."

6 Williams and Maclean, "Studying Ourselves."

7 Espiritu, "Disciplines Unbound."

8 Ibid.; Lowe, *Immigrant Acts*; Omi, "Shifting the Blame."

9 Gordon, *Assimilation in American Life*; Park, "Race and Culture."

10 Long, "Engaging Sociology and Cultural Studies."

11 Fine, "The Sad Demise"; Förster, "Micro-Sociology on the Rise"; Kalenda, "Situational Analysis."

12 Dubrow, "Sociology and American Studies."

13 Kalenda, "Situational Analysis."

14 Sprague, "(Re)Making Sociology."

15 McKee, *Sociology and the Race Problem*.

16 Omi, "Shifting the Blame."

17 Massey and Denton, *American Apartheid.*
18 Jacobs and Frickel, "Interdisciplinarity."
19 Deloria and Olson, *American Studies.*
20 Ibid.
21 McCoy, *Policing America's Empire.*
22 Ibid.
23 Espiritu, "Disciplines Unbound."
24 Seidman, "Queer Pedagogy/Queer-Ing Sociology" cited in Espiritu, "Disciplines Unbound," 510.
25 Hu-DeHart, "The History, Development, and Future of Ethnic Studies."
26 Anzaldúa, *Borderlands/La Frontera*, 510–11.
27 Espiritu, "Disciplines Unbound," 512.
28 Bonilla Silva, "Rethinking Racism."
29 Espiritu, "Disciplines Unbound," 512.
30 Ibid.
31 These comments are not offered to dismiss the compelling critiques of Du Bois's canon and political orientations, such as his underappreciation of gendered dimensions of race/racism and of settler colonialism and his impassioned support for the Japanese empire despite its brutal racist treatment of its own minoritized groups, Koreans, Filipinx, Chinese, and countless other Asian ethnic groups.
32 Espiritu, "Disciplines Unbound," 513.
33 Omi and Winant, *Racial Formation in the United States.* For diaspora, see Gilroy, *The Black Atlantic.* For imperialism, see Espiritu, *Home Bound*; and Kim, "Critical Thoughts on Asian American Assimilation" and *Imperial Citizens.* For postcolonialism, see Go, "For a Postcolonial Sociology." For settler colonialism, see Glenn, "Settler Colonialism as Structure." Foundational readings include Morris, *The Scholar Denied*; Collins, *Black Feminist Thought*; and Carrington this volume.
34 Christian, Seamster, and Ray, *Critical Race*; see Zamora and Kim in this volume.

BIBLIOGRAPHY

Anzaldúa, Gloria. *Borderlands/La Frontera: The New Mestiza.* San Francisco: Aunt Lute Books, 1987.
Bonilla-Silva, Eduardo. "Rethinking Racism: Toward a Structural Interpretation." *American Sociological Review* 62, no. 3 (1997): 465–80.
Christian, Michelle, Louise Seamster, and Victor Ray. "Critical Race Theory and Empirical Sociology." *American Behavioral Scientist* 65, no. 8 (2021): 1019–26. doi:10.1177/0002764219859646.
Deloria, Philip J., and Alexander I. Olson. *American Studies: A User's Guide.* Berkeley: University of California Press, 2017.
Dubrow, Joshua Kjerulf. "Sociology and American Studies: A Case Study in the Limits of Interdisciplinarity." *American Sociologist* 42, no. 4 (2011): 303–15.
Espiritu, Yến Lê. "Disciplines Unbound: Notes on Sociology and Ethnic Studies." *Contemporary Sociology* 28, no. 5 (1999): 510–14.

———. *Home Bound: Filipino American Lives across Cultures, Communities, and Countries.* Berkeley: University of California Press, 2003.

Fine, Gary Alan. "The Sad Demise, Mysterious Disappearance, and Glorious Triumph of Symbolic Interactionism." *Annual Review of Sociology* 19, no. 1 (1993): 61–87.

Fishkin, Shelley Fisher. "Crossroads of Cultures: The Transnational Turn in American Studies." Presidential address to the American Studies Association, November 12, 2004. *American Quarterly* 57, no. 1 (2005): 17–57.

Förster, Rosalie. "Micro-Sociology on the Rise: The Changing Sociological Field in the 1960s and the Case of Conversation Analysis." *American Sociologist* 44, no. 2 (2013): 198–216.

Gilroy, Paul. *The Black Atlantic: Modernity and Double Consciousness.* Cambridge, MA: Harvard University Press, 1993.

Gleason, Philip. "World War II and the Development of American Studies." *American Quarterly* 36, no. 3 (1984): 343–58.

Glenn, Evelyn Nakano. "Settler Colonialism as Structure: A Framework for Comparative Studies of US Race and Gender Formation." *Sociology of Race and Ethnicity* 1, no. 1 (2015): 52–72.

Go, Julian. "For a Postcolonial Sociology." *Theory and Society* 42, no. 1 (2013): 25–55.

Gordon, Milton M. *Assimilation in American Life: The Role of Race, Religion, and National Origins.* New York: Oxford University Press, 1964.

Hu-DeHart, Evelyn. "The History, Development, and Future of Ethnic Studies." *Phi Delta Kappan* 75, no. 1 (1993): 50–54.

Jacobs, Jerry A., and Scott Frickel. "Interdisciplinarity: A Critical Assessment." *Annual Review of Sociology* 35, no. 1 (2009): 43–65.

Jung, Moon-Kie. "The Racial Unconscious of Assimilation Theory." *Du Bois Review* 6, no. 2 (2009): 375.

Kalenda, Jan. "Situational Analysis as a Framework for Interdisciplinary Research in the Social Sciences." *Human Affairs* 26, no. 3 (2016): 340–55.

Kim, Nadia. "Critical Thoughts on Asian American Assimilation in the Whitening Literature." In *Racism in Post-Racism America: New Theories, New Directions*, edited by Charles A. Gallagher, 53–66. Chapel Hill, NC: Social Forces, 2008.

———. *Imperial Citizens: Koreans and Race from Seoul to LA.* Redwood City, CA: Stanford University Press, 2008.

Lawrence, Roderick. "Beyond Disciplinary Confinement to Imaginative Transdisciplinarity." In *Tackling Wicked Problems through the Transdisciplinary Imagination*, edited by Valerie A. Brown, John Alfred Harris, and Jacqueline Y. Russell, 16–30. Abingdon: Taylor and Francis, 2010.

Lipsitz, George. *American Studies in a Moment of Danger.* Minneapolis: University of Minnesota Press, 2001.

Long, Elizabeth. "Engaging Sociology and Cultural Studies: Disciplinarity and Social Change." In *From Sociology to Cultural Studies*, edited by Elizabeth Long, 1–32. Oxford: Blackwell, 1997.

Lowe, Lisa. *Immigrant Acts: On Asian American Cultural Politics*. Durham, NC: Duke University Press, 1996.

Marx, Leo. "Thoughts on the Origin and Character of the American Studies Movement." *American Quarterly* 31, no. 3 (1979): 398–401.

McCoy, Alfred W. *Policing America's Empire: The United States, the Philippines, and the Rise of the Surveillance State*. Madison: University of Wisconsin Press, 2009.

McKee, James. *Sociology and the Race Problem: The Failure of a Perspective*. Champaign: University of Illinois Press, 1993.

McKittrick, Katherine. *Dear Science: And Other Stories*. Durham, NC: Duke University Press, 2021.

Mills, C. Wright. *The Sociological Imagination*. New York: Oxford University Press, 1959.

Morris, Aldon. *The Scholar Denied: W. E. B Du Bois and the Birth of Modern Sociology*. Berkeley: University of California Press, 2015.

Omi, Michael. "Shifting the Blame: Racial Ideology and Politics in the Post-Civil Rights Era." *Critical Sociology* 18, no. 3 (October 1991): 77–98. https://doi.org/10.1177/089692059101800305.

Omi, Michael, and Howard Winant. *Racial Formation in the United States: From the 1960s to the 1980s*. London: Routledge, 1986.

Park, Robert Ezra. "Race and Culture." *Social Forces* 29, no. 2 (December 1950): 212–13.

Seidman, Steven. "Queer Pedagogy/Queer-Ing Sociology." *Critical Sociology* 20, no. 3 (October 1994): 169–76.

Sprague, Joey. 1998. "(Re)Making Sociology: Breaking the Bonds of Our Discipline." *Contemporary Sociology* 27, no. 1: 24–28.

Williams, Joyce E., and Vicky M. MacLean. "Studying Ourselves: Sociology Discipline-Building in the United States." *American Sociologist* 36, no. 1 (2005): 111–33.

Yu, Henry. *Rethinking Orientals: Migration, Contact, and Exoticism in Modern America*. New York: Oxford University Press, 2002.

PART I

Empire and Racial Capitalism

1

Critical Immigration and Refugee Studies

An Interdisciplinary Approach

YẾN LÊ ESPIRITU

Introduction

Immigration is a key symbol in contemporary US culture, a central and powerful concept imbued with a multiplicity of myths and meanings capable of rousing highly charged emotions that at times culminate in violently exclusionary practices. As part of the founding myths of the United States, immigration has been a key area of research in the social sciences. With an overwhelming emphasis on the immigrants' "modes of incorporation," the social science study of migration is divided into two key research questions: why people emigrate, and what happens after they immigrate. As this chapter documents, the field of sociology of immigration conceptualizes immigrants largely as a problem to be solved, ignoring the complexity of immigrants' subjectivities and eliding the role that "U.S. world power has played in the global structures of migration."[1] Departing from the linear narratives of immigration, assimilation, and nationhood, this chapter draws on the critical and interdisciplinary tools of ethnic studies, Asian American studies, and critical immigration and refugee studies, and my own research on Filipinx immigrants and Vietnamese refugees, to illuminate migrants' rich, complex, and multidimensional lived worlds, and the role that US empire, militarism, and racial capitalism has played in precipitating global migration. The chapter ends with a discussion of the need for migration studies to adopt interdisciplinary approaches to global migration and to reconceptualize migrant lifeworlds as a site of social, political, and historical critiques that articulate new forms of immigrant subjectivity, collectivity, and practice.

Sociology of Migration: Departures
Migration, Assimilation, and Culture

In the United States, sociology was the first academic discipline to make the study of international migration a central topic of inquiry. The Chicago school's concerns with large-scale immigration in the early twentieth century, primarily from southern and eastern Europe, placed the study of international migration at the core of sociological investigation.[2] The belief in gradual assimilation, "the process by which immigrant groups and host societies come to resemble one another," as both a theory and desirable ideological goal, has anchored the sociology of immigration for almost a century.[3] In 2005, some eight decades after Robert Park's publication of the "race relations cycle," Richard Alba and Victor Nee published the well-regarded book *Remaking the American Mainstream*, the first systematic treatment of assimilation since the mid-1960s, in which they argue that immigrants' drive to improve their circumstances has propelled the continuing importance of assimilation in American society.[4] Relatedly, the most prominent modification of assimilation theory, segmented assimilation, which suggests that structural barriers can lead different immigrant groups to assimilate into different segments of society, still retains at its core the emphasis on immigrant absorption into American society.[5]

The longstanding focus on assimilation, as the eventual outcome of "all the incidental collision, conflict and fusions of peoples and cultures" resulting from migration, is premised on a priori assumptions of the migrants as bearers of cultural difference.[6] Early on, Chicago theorist Robert Park, "who has probably contributed more ideas for analysis of racial relations and cultural contacts than any other modern social scientist," linked "cultural differences" with the foreign origins of certain human bodies: Where one came from became an important element of one's cultural consciousness.[7] When Park appropriated the "stranger" as a spatial metaphor to describe "the problem of race relations," he advanced a project of knowledge that is "predicated on a definition of the exotic, of what is absolutely foreign and different about one place and another."[8] As an example, the Orientalist construction of Asian cultures and geographies as fundamentally antipathetic to modern US society, racializes Asian Americans as the "perpetual foreigner"—as being less

American than their White counterpart, even when born in the United States.[9] Park's assertion of the connections between and among race, culture, and space has profoundly marked sociologists' understanding of assimilation, effectively locking immigrants conceptually in bounded, timeless, and unchanging cultural "traditions." It also uncritically accepts US White middle-class culture, viewpoints, and practices as the norm, leaving uninterrogated the ideological and material power of these normative standards.

The social upheavals and racial movements of the 1960s underscored the centrality of race in US society and shattered the myth of the inevitability—and even the desirability—of assimilation. In light of the new social movements that exposed the material histories of racialization, segregation, and economic discrimination, the prescription of assimilation was revised into "multiculturalism," a new liberal vision that publicly affirmed and celebrated the kaleidoscope of cultures in American society. Cultural studies scholars such as Lisa Lowe have critiqued multiculturalism's aim to integrate differences as "cultural equivalents abstracted from the histories of racial inequality."[10] Departing from this depoliticization of culture, Lowe argues instead that the characterization of the United States as a "polyvocal symphony of cultures" levels important differences and contradictions within and among racial and ethnic groups, deploying the liberal promise of inclusion to mask the history of exclusion.[11] In short, the multiculturalism (or ethnic pluralism) model, even as it appears to challenge the inevitability and desirability of assimilation, constitutes ethnic cultures as immutable traits to the peoples within presumed cultural groupings, much like the assimilation model propagated by Robert Park. This conception of culture essentializes difference by assuming that "the link between race and culture is organic, rather than contingent and historical."[12]

The prescription of integration also dominates sociological studies of forced migration. In a 2019 overview of the major themes and scholarly debates in the sociology of international migration in the United States, Noriko Matsumoto concludes that the future research agenda on refugees will continue to focus on "incorporation, native reception, possible obstacles to inclusion, and how the experience of refugees may differ from that of immigrants."[13] The intense sociological interest in the integration of Vietnamese refugees who arrived in the late 1970s and 1980s exemplifies the field's enduring interest in assimilation and "foreign" culture. Viewing the refugees as coming from "a society so markedly different from that of America," the federal government, in collaboration with sociologists and other social scientists, initiated a series of refugee surveys to generate information on what was widely touted as a "refugee resettlement crisis." Government officials and scholars alike regarded the accumulation of data on Vietnamese economic and sociocultural adaptation as essential to "protect[ing] the interests of the American public."[14] Prescribing assimilation as the solution to the refugee "crisis," sociologists characterized Vietnamese as America's newest "model minority"—docile subjects who enthusiastically and uncritically embrace and live the "American dream."[15] At its core, the model minority moniker promotes cultural essentialism; Vietnamese Americans' purported achievement is said to be rooted in their culture, with its strong work ethic, high regard for education, and family values. As an example, in a well-cited case study of Vietnamese American students living in a poor, biracial New Orleans neighborhood, sociologists Min Zhou and Carl Bankston argue that the youth's relative academic achievement is rooted in their "core cultural values"—a presumed strong work ethic, high regard for education, and family values; that is, in their cultural difference.[16]

Explaining Migration: Why They Come

A second research emphasis in the sociology of immigration is why people migrate. Focusing on disparities in conditions between place of origin and place of destination, many sociological accounts of why people move tend to "share the same basic view of migration as a consequence of foreign destitution and unemployment" and of desirable opportunities for migrant labor in the host country.[17] In its most classical form, migrants are said to be pushed out by low economic prospects in their countries and pulled by better opportunities in more affluent countries.[18] At the individual level, the push-pull model casts the migrants as calculating agents who rationally assess the benefits and costs of migrating.[19] Departing from this model of rational individualism, network theory modifies the push-pull framework by calling attention to migrant networks—the migrants' most important resource—that pass along information on transportation, job opportunities, and housing, thus lowering the costs and risks associated with migration, spurring further migration.[20]

In a 2017 review of the sociology of immigration, Roger Waldinger concludes that "whether concerned with emigration or immigration, the sociological literature is fundamentally about 'them', not 'us.'"[21] While the "us" in Waldinger's statement refers to US politics and policy on migration, I take up his turn of phrase to argue that immigration studies scholars have indeed focused more on "them"—on the migrants' need to migrate—than on "us"—on the US role in inducing migration.[22] Alejandro Portes and Ruben Rumbaut's widely praised *Immigrant America: A Portrait* (third edition), published in 2006, provides an example.[23] Adopting a "modes of incorporation" approach, the authors assert that "most immigrants come to America to attain the dream of a new lifestyle that has reached their countries but that is impossible to fulfill in them" but say little about the global-historical conditions that have produced and solidified US wealth and opportunities.[24] To be sure, the authors are cognizant of the historical roots of today's migration, noting the historical ties between each of the major sending countries and the United States, forged during the latter's successive interventions and expansionism. However, by limiting this analysis to less than four pages of the book (353–56), the authors skip an opportunity to critically inform public discussion about the origins of immigration—to show that "border crossers" are not just desperate individuals migrating in search of the "land of opportunity" but also calculating US colonizers, the military, and corporations moving in search of raw materials, labor, and markets. As an example, the relationship between the Philippines and the United States has its origins in a history of conquest, occupation, and exploitation. A study of Filipinx migration to the United States must begin with this history. Without starting here, we risk reducing Filipinx migration to just another voluntary immigrant stream and naturalizing the gap in earnings opportunities between the two countries.[25]

Eliding the US role in inducing migration, the push-pull approach shores up the national narrative of US-bound immigration as a unidirectional and voluntary phenomenon, one in which the poor and desperate of the world descend en masse on a wealthy and benevolent nation. By portraying immigrants to the United States as individuals seeking opportunities, this approach disregards the fact that since at least World War II, migration to the United States "has been the product of specific economic, colonial, political, military, and/or ideological ties between the United States and other countries . . . as well as of war."[26] It is this push-pull story—of distressed migrants searching for the promised land—that has emboldened politicians, anti-immigrant groups, and media agencies to contend that the US borders are out of control and that immigration is overwhelming US public institutions and threatening US core values and identity. Calling attention to the US role in precipitating global migration would be the first step toward having an informed discussion on immigration locally, nationally, and globally.

Critical Immigration and Refugee Studies: Reformulations

Drawing on ethnic studies scholarship on racial formation, critical immigration and refugee studies challenges the myth of assimilation, showing that the focus on incorporation and integration downplays the fact that for most of its history, the United States has institutionalized exclusionary laws that barred immigration and citizenship systems that favored White European immigrants. This critical approach conceptualizes immigration and citizenship laws as a technology of racialization that puts European and non-European immigrant groups on different trajectories with different prospects for full membership in the United States. A key example: the US Naturalization Act of 1790 limited naturalized citizenship to "free white persons," thus conjoining Whiteness and citizenship at the very outset of the new nation. On the other hand, the 1924 Johnson-Reed Act, which excluded Asian immigration on grounds that they were "racially ineligible for citizenship," cast Asians as permanently foreign and unassimilable, which has continued to negatively affect their social and cultural citizenship in the contemporary United States.[27]

Critical immigration and refugee studies also insists that we study immigration not for what it tells us about the assimilability of the immigrants but more so for what it says about the racialized and gendered economic, cultural, and political foundations of the United States. That is, we need to conceptualize immigration not as a site for evaluating the needs and acceptability of the immigrants but for critiquing how imperialism, racial capitalism, and settler colonialism have colluded to consolidate and maintain settler colonial, imperial, and racialized hierarchies in the United States.[28] Today, when close to 90 percent of immigrants are from non-European countries, immigration is regularly presented in public debates and popular images as a problem to be solved and a flow to be stopped. All too often, Americans speak of migrants as if they simply show up from out of nowhere. But migrations don't just happen; they are produced. Since the 1980s, accelerated globalization processes have led to the enormous expansion of international migrations.[29] Globalization has also produced the climate crisis, widely recognized as a contributing and exacerbating factor in forced migration.[30] In an increasingly globalized world, more affluent countries cannot pretend that they can profit from the exploitation of labor, raw materials, or consumer markets of countries around the world without inducing or encouraging reverse migration. As award-winning writer Suketu Mehta reminds us, migrants "are moving because the rich countries have stolen the future of the poor countries. . . . They are coming here because we were there."[31]

Building on American and ethnic studies scholarship, critical immigration and refugee studies advances a critique of the braiding of militarism and imperialism that underlies migrations on a global scale, then and now. In so doing, it disrupts the myth of the West rescuing and liberating migrants and refugees and makes visible the connections between migrant displacement and US interventions in countries in the Global South, via empire building and proxy wars, counterinsurgency actions, anticommunist insurgencies, terrorism counteraction, and peacekeeping operations. Decolonization theory, politics, and approaches, which seek to undo colonial ways of doing and knowing that permeate all institutions and systems of government, are vital to expose militaristic representations and militarized practices and to build a new grammar, syntax, and language for displacement and migration.[32]

In particular, critical refugee studies names militarism as a "way of life" in the modern United States and establishes that war is central to the history of US expansionism. Indeed, military power was key for the conquest of lands in North America itself. As Native American studies scholar Roxanne Dunbar-Ortiz pronounces, the Indian Wars were a "one-sided robbery and murder" backed by US government armies, paving the way for US imperialist expansion into the Pacific and the Caribbean, the Banana Wars in Latin America, the Cold War's proxy wars in the Asia-Pacific and in Central America, and the ongoing global war on terror.[33] In the post–Cold War era in which US imperialism and globalized militarization have taken the form of endless wars, the displaced peoples produced by these wars, such as Syrian, Somali, and Central American refugees, are cast as threats to be excluded and eradicated and not as displaced human beings in search of safety. After the September 11 attacks, the United States launched a global military campaign—dubbed the war on terror—that engaged in direct military intervention in a number of countries, including the invasion and occupation of Iraq and Afghanistan, drone strikes in Yemen, Pakistan, and Somalia, and special forces operations in Pakistan, Syria, Tunisia, Somalia, Mali, Nigeria, and Yemen, among others. According to a 2020 report from Brown University's Costs of War project, since September 11, 2001, the US-led war on terror has displaced at least thirty-seven million people in and from Afghanistan, Iraq, Pakistan, Yemen, Somalia, the Philippines, Libya, and Syria, forcing them into the streams of global migration. While the United States is not the sole cause of the forced migration from these countries, it has played either a dominant or contributing role in these conflicts.[34]

An ethnic studies focus on the history of US imperialism and militarism also shows that immigrant and refugee lives are shaped not only by the social location of their group within the United States but also by their home country's relationship with the United States.[35] In the case of immigrants from the Philippines, a US colony for more than half a century and that continues to persist as "virtually an appendage of the US corporate elite," their formation as a racialized minority does not begin in the United States but rather in the homeland already affected by US economic, social, and cultural influences.[36] As such, US racism against Filipinx immigrants—represented variously as the little brown brothers, the monkeys, the prostitutes, the mail-order brides, the nurses—is not only a contemporary backlash against the influx of recent Filipinx immigrants but also part of a continuum that goes back to US racism in and colonization of the Philippines.[37] In the same way, the Vietnam War—and its attendant propaganda—has had racist and gendered consequences not only for citizens of Vietnam but also for Vietnamese in the diaspora. The popular and official discourse on Vietnam and its people during the Vietnam War established images—of inferiority, innate violence, and unassimilability—that traveled with Vietnamese to their new homes and prescribed their racialization there. In numerous news accounts during the war, journalists projected Vietnam, "a tiny tinhorn country half way around the world," onto anachronistic space, depicting it as "exotic," "sensual," "alien," and infected with "sweltering, insect-ridden jungles," a place of "horror," "madness," and "violence," replete with snipers, drugs, and prostitution—in short, "hell."[38] The Vietnamese case thus makes evident the global dimension of racism; Vietnamese refugee lives have been shaped not only by the racialization of Vietnamese in the United States but also by the status of Vietnam in the global racial order.

Toward Interdisciplinarity: About Ghostly Matters

Given its focus on modes of incorporation and push-pull factors of emigration, the field of sociology of immigration is largely positivist and data driven, with the research questions revolving around "migrant selectivity, integration, transnationalism, and dissimilation."[39] Immigration studies generally relies on large-scale quantitative data from the census, the Immigration and Naturalization Service, the Current Population Surveys, and longitudinal surveys such as the Children of Immigrants Longitudinal Survey (CILS).[40] Ethnographic and interview-based studies of migrants' social lives, while offering rich descriptions of how migrants create their worlds, make meaning for themselves, and resist existing inequalities, also report largely on things that are observable. In a generative critique of the "social sciences' empiricist grounds of knowing,"[41] Avery Gordon makes an impassioned case for accounting for ghostly matters, for the realities of social and political life that have been systematically hidden, erased, repressed. She urges scholars to invent "a different way of knowing and writing about the social world," and to consider the complications of social life that escape standard social science methodologies and interpretation.[42] Heeding Gordon's insights on haunting and ghostly matters, I discuss below the importance of listening for unsaid things, relying on other senses such as feelings and emotions, and attending to the site of intimate domestic and familial interaction. I argue that it is the intimacy of knowledge from these sites that allows a whole new field to open, connecting immigrant and refugee day-to-day practices to war, militarist, imperial, national, and transnational dynamics.

As an ethnic studies scholar whose doctoral training was in sociology, I continue to adhere to sociology's attentiveness to lived social experience, to the social constructions of social reality, and to the link between individual lives and political economy. But my interest in social life also relies on more critical interdisciplinary methods to trace what has disappeared and what remains, as well as what could or would have been. Taking up Gordon's call to account for unaddressed injustices and systematically hidden social life, I ask what happens to events that cannot be narrated. What lies just beneath the surface? Which memories are erased, forgotten, or postponed and archived for future release? Where and how do these "nonevents" fit into the narration of immigration to the United States? In short, how would migrants and refugees, not as objects of study but as a site of social critique, make visible abusive global systems of power and their ongoing impacts in everyday life. Below, I draw on my research on second-generation Filipinx Americans and Vietnamese Americans to illustrate the possibilities of a critical interdisciplinary study of social life.

Filipinx Daughters, Gender, and the Politics of Culture

As established above, the sociology of immigration has been greatly influenced by the historical production of immigrants as bearers of cultural difference. The dominant theories in the field conceptualize the immigrants' "original" culture as fundamentally opposed to Native and White "American" culture. In contrast to the static and binary approach to culture in sociology, the field of cultural studies—an interdisciplinary field of theoretically, politically, and empirically engaged critical analysis of the texts and practices of everyday life—conceptualizes cultural identities not as an essence but as a positioning: "the names we give to the different ways we are positioned by, and position ourselves within, the narratives of the past."[43] Drawing on my research with second-generation Filipinx American daughters, I argue that sociology's conceptualization of cultural identity, as innate and abstracted from unresolved histories of racial inequality, promotes a discourse of race in which "cultural difference" is used to explain or explain away historically produced social inequalities. Here, I challenge the authority and authenticity of the term *cultural identity*, asserting instead that culture—or more precisely, culture making—is a social, historical, and transnational process that exposes multiple and interrelated forms of power relations and that articulates new forms of immigrant subjectivity, collectivity, and practice.

In my in-depth interviews that I conducted with almost one hundred Filipinxs in San Diego on the relationship between immigrant parents and their daughters, I found that gender is a significant determinant of parent-child conflict, with daughters more likely than sons to experience strict parental control on their activities and movements.[44] While Filipinx immigrant parents do place undue expectations on their sons, these expectations do not pivot around the sons' sexuality or dating choices. In contrast, parental control over the movement and actions of daughters often begins the moment they are perceived as young adults and sexually vulnerable. For example, the immigrant parents I interviewed seldom allowed their daughters to date, to stay out late, to spend the night at a friend's house, or to take an out-of-town trip. This is not to say that parent-daughter conflicts exist in all Filipinx immigrant families. However, the interview data do suggest that intergenerational conflicts are socially recognized occurrences in Filipinx communities. Even when respondents themselves had not experienced intergenerational tensions, they could always recall a cousin, a girlfriend, or a friend's daughter who had.

My findings are not new. Sociologists, as well as social historians, have long identified strict parental control on daughters' activities and movements as the primary source of intergenerational conflict.[45] However, these studies tend to assume that these patriarchal practices correspond to a bounded and static set of practices imported from the home country into the host society. This conception of culture essentializes difference by assuming that "the link between race and culture is organic, rather than contingent and historical."[46] In contrast, drawing on cultural studies and ethnic studies critiques, I argue that Filipinx immigrants deploy cultural claims about gender as a vehicle to assert cultural superiority over White Americans; the virtuous Filipinx daughter is partially constructed on the conceptualization of White women as sexually promiscuous. Within the context of the dominant culture's pervasive hypersexualization of Filipinx women, both in the Philippines and in the United States, the construction of the "ideal" Filipinx daughter—as family-oriented and chaste—can be read as an effort to reclaim the morality of the community. By turning the tables of the colonial racial moral calculus against White Americans, these cultural claims—that Filipinx culture is more family-oriented and thus morally superior to White American culture—constitute a strategy of resistance against the colonial racial denigration of Filipinx culture, community, and women and a reaffirmation of their self-worth in the face of colonial, racial, class, and gendered subordination. But this strategy is not without costs. The elevation of Filipinx chastity (particularly that of young women) has the effect of reinforcing masculinist and patriarchal power in the name of a greater ideal of national/ethnic self-respect.

In sum, my research on Filipinx families engages the tools of sociology by focusing on the complexity of social life, culled from interviews with Filipinx immigrants and their families in San Diego. In prioritizing their voices and experiences, I present them as providing knowledge into systems of power rather than only as problems to be solved. At the same time, I depart from the (multi)culturalist understanding of immigrant culture as inherited and static to show that culture is a constantly negotiated strategy deployed by racialized immigrants to claim through gender the power denied them by racism. In so doing, I move away from what is said and observable to what is fabricated and fabled by immigrants to evade, move beyond, and even invert inscriptions and identifications made by state, capitalist, and patriarchal regimes of truth. My analysis thus underscores the ways in which Filipinx immigrants maneuver and manipulate meanings within the domain of culture in an effort to counter the alternative assumption of inevitable White American superiority. In so doing, I challenge the depoliticized version of (multi)culturalism that unproblematically denigrates or celebrates the survival and reinvention of "ethnic" practices. I also show that intergenerational tension is not only a private matter between refugee parents and their children but a social, historical, and geopolitical affair that exposes multiple and interrelated forms of power relations.

Vietnamese Refugees, Private Grief, and Public Achievements

This section asks, How do young Vietnamese Americans, born and/or raised in the United States, deal with the "memories" of a war that preceded their births or their consciousness? Most sociological research on second-generation Vietnamese has sidestepped the complexities, tensions, and uncertainties of their social world, focusing instead on the narrower question of their educational and economic attainment. By the late 1980s, scholars, along with the mass media and policy makers, had begun to depict Vietnamese as the newest Asian American model minority; "The success of the Indochinese refugees are, in a broad framework, also part of the overall achievement of Asian Americans."[47] Refugee studies scholars were particularly effusive about the "legendary" academic accomplishments of Vietnamese refugees' children who "came to America as boat people . . . survived perilous escapes and lost one to three years in refugee camps."[48] Drawing on in-depth interviews with sixty Vietnamese Americans about their academic achievements, this section moves away from the "modes of incorporation" approach favored by sociologists and situates the postwar generation's seeming drive to succeed within the ongoing costs of war for Vietnamese refugees and their children.[49]

While social scientists and the media often hold up the Vietnamese as an example of the quintessential American refugee success story, the socioeconomic conditions for most Vietnamese refugees, the majority of whom arrived between 1975 and the mid-1980s, were greatly insecure.[50] In 1990, the poverty rate of Vietnamese in the United States stood at 25 percent; in 2010, it was 12 percent. Both rates were higher than the national average of 12 and 10 percent, respectively. Reflecting these economic data, for the majority of the interviewees in my study, economic insecurities haunted their home life. Growing up, many of the respondents recalled being hyper-aware of and anxious about their dire economic circumstances. In recounting their family history, they would talk about "before" and "after" migration stories, often depicting migration to the United States—the "after"—as a move toward economic instability, replete with unstable, minimum-wage employment, lack of health insurance, and welfare dependency.

It is true that downward mobility and economic insecurity is an immigrant story, not a refugee-story specific one. However, our interviewees invariably traced their family's economic hardship back to war-related events and not only to migration. Here is a typical example:

> I think early on I recognized that my stories, my family, my culture are different. . . . I mean my family, they were refugees and they came from a country that was ravaged by war and their lives were endangered. There were broken families and my dad was born in 1950 and the country was at war in 1954 and then until 1975. So all of his life basically, there was war and that he had to grow up in. So it wasn't until I started to understand the context of what my family came from and when they were raised, that I began to understand their perspective and why they came here. And why they are so harsh on me and wanting me to excel and take advantage of the opportunities that I have. So it's a long process of understanding.

Many interviewees insisted that in discussing the Vietnam War, we need to pay attention to "what happened after the war" and "to know about the people and what happened to them when they came here." For these young Vietnamese Americans, when they think about the Vietnam War, they think most about what happened to their families—and their family life—after they came to the United States. This is the part of the war that they knew most intimately and shared most freely. Their insistence that we pay heed to family life is an important reminder that wars affect not only the realms of politics and economics but also the domains of the intimate. As such, Vietnamese family life constitutes a key site to register the lingering costs of war that often have been designated as over and done with in the public realm.

Having witnessed their parents' economic anxiety and experienced its tolls on all of their lives, many interviewees expressed feeling deeply and personally responsible for realizing their parents' dream of "making it" in the United States. Their sense of responsibility was palpable; it had cost their parents too much to get here, and it was their responsibility to fulfill their parents' dream of family success via intergenerational mobility. Below are two examples that express this sentiment:

> When the Communists came, there were no opportunities. There was nothing for my dad to do. When he talks about how he grew up, there is

a certain mentality that he has which is that there is a whole generation of young men like him whose futures were just wasted. . . . My dad came here in his late forties and he had to catch up with the rest. And he'd had a really hard time. So he kept telling me and my brother that you need to go to school, graduate, work, and have a great life. I feel that they came here for our future and so now it's up to us to make it happen.

I think that the only reason why I intended to be pre-med was because of my parents and what they went through. I thought that this was the only way that I would be able to repay them.

For the majority of the young people we interviewed, college and career choices are less, or not only, a sign of Vietnamese assimilation and social acceptance and more a sign of a complex and strategic response to their and their parents' forcible and "differential inclusion" into US society. As such, their investment in success and money is meant to improve the lot and status of their families; it is not only or primarily about the pursuit of personal achievements.

In this section, I have relied on sociology's focus on social life—on grounded research and commitment to the lived experience of everyday people—to better understand what appears to be economic assimilation on the part of the children of Vietnamese refugees. I have argued that this investment in intergenerational economic mobility is much more than a reflection of "Vietnamese core cultural values"; their alleged strong work ethic, high regard for education, and family values.[51] Rather, it exhibits the poignant and complex ways in which Vietnamese refugees and their children use public achievements to address the lingering costs of war, to manage intimacy, to negotiate family tensions, and to ensure their social position and dignity in the racially and economically stratified United States. In so doing, I draw on critical refugee studies to offer an alternative and more critical explanation for the postwar generation's seeming drive to succeed; what appears to be an act of economic assimilation on the part of the "generation after"—an act of moving beyond the war—is in actuality an index of the ongoing costs of war, not only for the witnesses and survivors but also for their children. In short, for the postwar generation, the Vietnam War has become a constant motivator that pushes them to assuage private grief with public achievements.

Conclusion

Immigration is regularly represented in public debates and popular images as "a problem to be solved, a flaw to be corrected, a war to be fought, and a flow to be stopped."[52] Conceptualizing immigration primarily as a problem, the US sociological research on immigration has focused on immigrant cultural and economic and political incorporation and adaptation and on responses by native-born Americans to the influx. This modes-of-incorporation approach, which privileges the nation-state model and treats state borders as geographical givens, assesses the assimilability of immigrants but leaves uninterrogated the connection between US foreign interventions and migration to the United States. Drawing on my research on Filipinx migrants and Vietnamese refugees, I have offered two main tenets that undergird the field of critical immigration and refugee studies: the first examines the role that US colonialism and militarism has played in displacing millions of people around the world and forcing them into the streams of global migration; the second conceptualizes immigrants and refugees not as a problem to be solved but as a site of social critique that makes visible not only vast structures of power but also small moments of action—indeed, of creation—as immigrants and refugees search for and insist on their right to more.

In sum, at this moment of reinvigorated US imperialism and soaring immigration to the United States, it is imperative that we link immigration—in all its forms—to US (neo)colonial, corporate, military, and governmental actions abroad and that we integrate these critical approaches to global migration with the stories of real people as they navigate their social worlds in displacement and resettlement. To engage in critical immigration and refugee studies, then, is to always look for the "something more" and the "something else" in order to see and bring into being what is usually neglected or made invisible or thought by most to be over and done with.[53]

NOTES
1 Mae Ngai, *Impossible Subjects*, 11.
2 Hollifield, "Is Migration a Unique Field."
3 Waters and Pineau, "Introduction," 19.

4 Alba and Nee, *Remaking the American Mainstream.*
5 Portes and Zhou, "The New Second Generation."
6 Park, "Human Migration," 881.
7 American Sociological Association, "Robert Ezra Park," www.asanet.org. Yu, *Thinking Orientals*, 47.
8 Yu, *Thinking Orientals*, 6.
9 Devos and Ma, "Is Kate Winslet More American."
10 Lowe, *Immigrant Acts*, 30.
11 Lowe, *Immigrant Acts.*
12 Mishra, *What Was Multiculturalism?*, 427.
13 Matsumoto, "Immigration," 353.
14 Dunning, "Vietnamese in America," 55.
15 Roberts and Starr, "Differential Reference Group," 52; Finnan, "Occupational Assimilation."
16 Zhou and Bankston, *Growing up American.*
17 Portes and Rumbaut, *Immigrant America*, 15, 17–18.
18 Sassen, *Globalization and Its Discontents*; Massey et al., *Worlds in Motion.*
19 Lee, "A Theory of Migration."
20 Massey et al., *Return to Aztlan*; Massey Goldring, and Durand, "Continuities in Transnational Migration."
21 Waldinger, "Immigration and the Election."
22 Waldinger, "Immigration and the Election," 1425. Waldinger argues that to address the political challenge posed by Trumpism, migration scholars need to study "how politics and policy shape migrant options, and how migrant reactions in turn feedback into politics and policy."
23 Portes and Rumbaut, *Immigrant America.*
24 Ibid., 19.
25 Espiritu, *Home Bound.*
26 Ngai, *Impossible Subjects*, 10.
27 Ngai, *Impossible Subjects.*
28 Indeed, contemporary immigrants from Asia—the Philippines, Vietnam, South Korea, Cambodia, Laos, Afghanistan, and Pakistan—come from countries that have been deeply disrupted by US colonialism, neocolonial capitalism, and war.
29 Morawska, *A Sociology of Immigration*, 1.
30 According to a 2018 World Bank estimate, Latin America, sub-Saharan Africa, and Southeast Asia will generate 143 million more climate migrants by 2050. Rigaud et al., *Groundswell*, 2.
31 Mehta, "Why Should Immigrants 'Respect Our Borders'?"
32 Smith, *Decolonizing Methodologies.*
33 Dunbar-Ortiz, *An Indigenous People's History*, 5.
34 US involvement in these wars included initiating armed combat, escalating armed conflict, or participating in combat through drone strikes, battlefield advising, logistical support, and arms sales.

35 US imperialism and militarism also bring US racial hierarchies and ideologies into countries that they dominate. For example, Nadia Kim has shown how the United States' post–World War II dominance of South Korea introduced racial inequalities and ideologies that shaped South Koreans' understandings of the US racial order and their place along these color lines. See Kim, *Imperial Citizens*.

36 San Juan, "One Hundred Years," 12.

37 Espiritu, *Home Bound*.

38 Espiritu, *Body Counts*, 89.

39 FitzGerald, "The Sociology of International Migration," 118.

40 The INS ceased to exist under that name in 2003 when it was absorbed into the newly created Department of Homeland Security as part of a major government reorganization following the September 11 attacks of 2001. Led by Alejandro Portes and Ruben Rumbaut, CILS followed for more than ten years a panel representing a sample of more than 5,200 youths, whose parents come from seventy-two different countries on both coasts of the United States.

41 Gordon, *Ghostly Matters*, 9.

42 Ibid., 21.

43 Hall, "Cultural Identity and Diaspora," 225.

44 For more information on this research, see Espiritu, "We Don't Sleep Around."

45 See, for example Waters, "The Intersection of Gender, Race, and Ethnicity."

46 Mishra, *What Was Multiculturalism?*, 427.

47 Caplan, Whitmore, and Bui, *The Boat People*, 56.

48 Freeman, *Changing Identities*, 69. See also Caplan, Whitmore, and Bui, *The Boat People*; and Caplan, Choy, and Whitmore, *Children of the Boat People*.

49 The in-depth interviews were with sixty Vietnamese Americans—thirty men and thirty women—in Southern California, conducted between 2005 and 2010. All of the respondents belong to the postwar generation; 55 percent of the respondents were born in Vietnam, 38 percent in the United States, and 7 percent in a refugee camp.

50 Unlike in the past when most Vietnamese were admitted as refugees, those who obtain permanent residence in the United States today largely do so through family reunification. In 1982, 99 percent of Vietnamese that were granted permanent residence were refugees, while today, that group constitutes a mere 1 percent of the Vietnamese population. See Alperin and Batalova, "Vietnamese Immigrants."

51 Zhou and Bankston, *Growing Up American*.

52 Mahmud, "Migration, Identity," 633.

53 Gordon, *Ghostly Matters*, 4–5.

BIBLIOGRAPHY

Alba, Richard, and Victor Nee. *Remaking the American Mainstream: Assimilation and Contemporary Immigration*. Cambridge, MA: Harvard University Press, 2005.

Alperin, Elijah, and Jeanne Batalova. "Vietnamese Immigrants in the United States." *Migration Information Source*, September 13, 2018. www.migrationpolicy.org.

Caplan, Nathan, John K. Whitmore, and Quang L. Bui. *The Boat People and Achievement in America: A Study of Family Life, Hard Work, and Cultural Values*. Ann Arbor: University of Michigan Press, 1989.

Caplan, Nathan, Marcella H. Choy, and John K. Whitmore. *Children of the Boat People: A Study of Educational Success*. Ann Arbor: University of Michigan Press, 1991.

Devos, Thierry, and Debbie S. Ma. "Is Kate Winslet More American Than Lucy Liu? The Impact of Construal Processes on the Implicit Ascription of a National Identity." *British Journal of Social Psychology* 47 (2008): 191–215.

Dunbar-Ortiz, Roxanne. *An Indigenous People's History of the United States*. Boston: Beacon Press, 2015.

Dunning, Bruce. "Vietnamese in America: The Adaptation of the 1975–1979 Arrivals." In *Refugees as Immigrants: Cambodians, Laotians, and Vietnamese in America*, edited by David W. Haines, 55–85. Totowa, NJ: Rowman and Littlefield, 1989.

Espiritu, Yến Lê. *Body Counts: The Vietnam War and Militarized Refuge(es)*. Berkeley: University of California Press, 2014.

———. *Home Bound: Filipino American Lives across Cultures, Communities, and Countries*. Berkeley: University of California Press, 2003.

———"'We Don't Sleep around like White Girls Do': Family, Culture, and Gender in Filipina American Lives." *Signs* 26, no. 2 (2001): 415–40.

Finnan, Christine. "Occupational Assimilation of Refugees." *International Migration Review* 15 (1981): 292–309.

FitzGerald, David Scott. "The Sociology of International Migration." In *Migration Theory: Talking across Disciplines*, edited by Caroline B. Brettell and James F. Hollified, 160–93. New York: Routledge, 2014.

Freeman, James. *Changing Identities: Vietnamese Americans 1975–1995*. Boston: Allyn and Bacon, 1995.

Gordon, Avery. *Ghostly Matters: Haunting and the Sociological Imagination*. Minneapolis: University of Minnesota Press, 1997.

Hall, Stuart. "Cultural Identity and Diaspora." In *Identity, Community, Culture, Difference*, edited by Jonathan Rutherford, 222–37. London: Lawrence and Wishart, 1990.

Hollified, J. F. "Is Migration a Unique Field of Study in Social Sciences? A Response to Levy, Pisarevskaya, and Scholten." *Comparative Migration Studies* 8, no. 34 (2020). https://doi.org/10.1186/s40878-020-00192-3.

Kim, Nadia. *Imperial Citizens: Koreans and Race from Seoul to LA*. Stanford, CA: Stanford University Press, 2008.

Lee, Everett S. "A Theory of Migration." *Demography* 3, no. 1 (1966): 47–57. https://doi.org/10.2307/2060063.

Lowe, Lisa. *Immigrant Acts: On Asian American Cultural Politics*. Durham, NC: Duke University Press. 1996.

Mahmud, Tayyab. "Migration, Identity, and the Colonial Encounter." *Oregon Law Review* 76 (Fall 1997): 633–90.

Massey, Douglas, Jorge Durand, Rafael Alarcon, and Humberto Gonzalez. *Return to Aztlan: The Social Process of International Migration from Western Mexico.* Berkeley: University of California Press, 1987.

Massey, Douglas, Luin Goldring, and Jorge Durand. "Continuities in Transnational Migration: An Analysis of 19 Mexican Communities." *American Journal of Sociology* (May 1994): 1492–1533. https://doi: 10.1086/230452.

Massey, Douglas, Joaquin Arango, Graeme Hugo, Ali Kouaouci, Adela Pellegrino, and J. Edward Taylor. *Worlds in Motion: Understanding International Migration at the End of the Millennium.* Oxford: Oxford University Press, 1998.

Matsumoto, Noriko. "Immigration." In *The Wiley Blackwell Companion to Sociology,* 2nd ed., edited by George Ritzer and Wendy Wiedenhoft, 340–57. Hoboken, NJ: Wiley, 2019.

Mehta, Suketu. "Why Should Immigrants 'Respect Our Borders'? The West Never Respected Theirs." *New York Times,* June 7, 2019. www.nytimes.com.

Mishra, Vijay. *What Was Multiculturalism?: A Critical Retrospective.* Carlton: Melbourne University Press, 2012.

Morawska, E. *A Sociology of Immigration: (Re)Making Multifaceted America.* New York: Palgrave Macmillan, 2009.

Ngai, Mae. *Impossible Subjects: Illegal Aliens and the Making of Modern America.* Princeton, NJ: Princeton University Press, 2004.

Park, Robert. "Human Migration and the Marginal Man." *American Journal of Sociology* 36, no. 6 (May 1928): 881–93. www.jstor.org/stable/2765982.

Portes, Alejandro, and Ruben Rumbaut. *Immigrant America: A Portrait.* 3rd ed. Berkeley: University of California Press, 2006.

Portes, Alejandro, and Min Zhou. "The New Second Generation: Segmented Assimilation and Its Variants." *Annals of the American Academy of Political and Social Science* 530 (1993): 74–96.

Rigaud, Kanta Kumari, Alex de Sherbinin, Bryan Jones, Jonas Bergmann, Viviane Clement, Kayly Ober, Jacob Schewe, Susana Adamo, Brent McCusker, Silke Heuser, and Amelia Midgley. *Groundswell: Preparing for Internal Climate Migration.* Washington, DC: World Bank, 2018. https://openknowledge.worldbank.org.

Roberts, Alden, and Paul D. Starr. "Differential Reference Group Assimilation among Vietnamese Refugees." In *Refugees as Immigrants: Cambodians, Laotians, and Vietnamese,* edited by David W. Haines, 40–54. Totowa, NJ: Rowman and Littlefield 1989.

San Juan, E., Jr. "One Hundred Years of Producing and Reproducing the 'Filipino.'" *Amerasia Journal* 24, no. 2 (1998): 1–33.

Sassen, Saskia. *Globalization and Its Discontents.* New York: New Press, 1988.

Vine, David, Cala Coffman, Katalina Khoury, Madison Lovasz, Helen Bush, Rachael Leduc, and Jennifer Walkup. "Creating Refugees: Displacement Caused by the United States' Post-9/11 Wars." Watson Institute for International and Public Affairs, Brown University. September 21, 2020. https://watson.brown.edu.

Waldinger, Roger. "Immigration and the Election of Donald Trump: Why the Sociology of Migration Left Us Unprepared . . . and Why We Should Not Have Been

Surprised." *Ethnic and Racial Studies* 21, no. 8 (2018): 1413. https://doi.org/10.1080/0 1419870.2018.1442014.

Waters, Mary C. "The Intersection of Gender, Race, and Ethnicity in Identity Development of Caribbean American Teens." In *Urban Girls: Resisting Stereotypes, Creating Identities,* edited by Bonnie J. Ross Leadbeater and Niobe Way, 65–84. New York: New York University Press, 1996.

Waters, Mary, and Marisa Gerstein Pineau. Introduction to *The Integration of Immigrants into American Society,* edited by Mary Waters and Marisa Gerstein Pineau, 15–58. Washington, DC: National Academies Press, 2016.

Yu, Henry. *Thinking Orientals: Migration, Contact, and Exoticism in Modern America.* New York: Oxford University Press, 2001.

Zhou, Min, and Carl L. Bankston III. *Growing Up American: How Vietnamese Children Adapt to Life in the United States.* New York: Russell Sage, 1998.

2

Between a War and a Pandemic

Yemeni American Corner Stores during COVID

SUNAINA MAIRA

Introduction

This chapter focuses on Arab/Muslim American small business owners during the COVID-19 crisis and explores how US empire and racial
capitalism are reflected in the particular struggles of Yemeni Americans
in Oakland who have been caught between a war and the pandemic. It
is based on a new ethnographic study of the impact of the pandemic,
Trump's Muslim bans, counterterrorism policies, and the war in Yemen
on Yemeni Americans in the Bay Area. In fall 2019, I began doing a
community-engaged research project, funded by a Mellon/American
Council of Learned Societies fellowship for public scholarship. The
original proposal was to do ethnographic research and public forums in
the Bay Area focused on the experiences of Arab immigrant and refugee
communities related to immigration, race, Islam, and sanctuary movements under Trump. After the lockdown in California in spring 2020, I
was forced to pivot and modify my research focus as well as my methods.
I began doing (limited) participant observation in essential businesses in
Oakland (mainly small grocery stores but also gas stations and mobile-
phone stores) that were open during the lockdown, combining grocery
shopping with conversations with Arab/Muslim American store owners
and their families who were essential workers on the frontlines of the
pandemic. After pivoting to focus on corner stores as a permissible site
of in-person ethnography, I was able to grapple with notions of community, safety, and the "public" at a time when all of these notions were
being rapidly transformed.

Yemeni Americans occupy a niche in corner stores in Oakland, owning an estimated two hundred small grocery stores, which are family-owned businesses where children, generally sons, work as well.[1] This community became the primary focus of my research and the stores a spatial entry point into larger issues impacting the community. In 2020–21, I conducted over thirty individual interviews and more than twenty informal interviews with Yemeni American store owners as well as family members, students, educators, community activists, and lawyers in the Bay Area. I visited Yemeni-owned stores in West and East Oakland, which are low-income Black and brown neighborhoods where many Yemeni Americans are concentrated, as well as corner stores in gentrified districts such as Temescal and Glenview. This research opened up new, interrelated questions for me about Arab-/Muslim-owned small businesses in urban areas, the impact of the lockdown on their work and families; their relations with the local, largely low-income, Black and brown communities in which they are situated; and the experiences of Yemeni Americans with neoliberal capitalism, gentrification, public health and safety, war, humanitarian crisis, surveillance, and policing. My study is not primarily one about the operation of small businesses but rather, how the corner store is a prism where many important and timely economic, political, and cultural questions converge.

This chapter also reflects on questions of crossing disciplines and tweaking methodologies. I was trying to use ethnographic methods during a time when "participant-observation" was curtailed due to the "social distancing" protocols of the pandemic. I had to adapt my community-engaged research to the exigencies of the lockdown, learning how to do Zoom interviews, and organized a virtual town hall in February 2021 about the struggles of Yemeni Americans under Trump and during the pandemic. In spring 2021, I also did a digital storytelling workshop with Yemeni/Arab American small business owners, youth, and community advocates to cocreate digital stories for community advocacy and education. I was forced to experiment with using digital research methods to generate public scholarship while also grappling with the digital divide embedded in class and racial inequities, especially in terms of creating "virtual communities." This "hybrid" research forced me to reflect on the very notions of "distance" and "crisis" that were being deployed during the global health crisis, and to interrogate how these illuminate larger questions of US imperialism, warfare, and global capitalism.

This interdisciplinary study of Yemeni Americans in Oakland contributes to work on US imperialism and racial capitalism by exploring the everyday experiences of empire in the lives of racialized groups that are targets of US military interventions, surveillance, and counterterrorism. Foundational scholarship in American studies on the everyday cultures of US imperialism (Kaplan 1993, 2002) has generated a rich body of work that connects racial formation in the US to empire and settler colonization, not just domestic race politics.[2] Earlier scholarship on US empire was based primarily on historical, literary, and cultural analysis; my work is part of an expanding body of research that has used ethnographic methods to foreground the daily experiences and material realities of US imperialism. Critical ethnic and race studies have infused American studies with theorizing of White supremacy, racial capitalism, and imperialism and with engaged scholarship in relation to the struggles of marginalized groups. Yet Arab and Muslim Americans have often been missing from these accounts, despite the targeting of these communities by regimes of policing, surveillance, deportation, and mass incarceration for decades, not just since September 11, 2001.

Furthermore, while Arab American and critical Muslim studies are growing interdisciplinary fields, there has been relatively less work on Yemeni Americans—other than in Detroit, Michigan, which is home to a large Yemeni community—despite the fact that Yemeni Americans have now lived in California for at least three generations. Yemenis migrated to California as early as the 1920s, and most came after the 1960s as farmworkers, some moving from the East Coast or Michigan. Yemeni farm laborers became involved with UFW organizing, although this history of labor activism is barely known; they later moved to urban areas to work in the service sector or open small convenience or liquor stores.[3] Historically, Yemeni migrants have sent remittances to families in Yemen, which is one of the poorest Arab nations and has long exported labor to Gulf countries as well as to the United Kingdom, United States, and Southeast Asia. Yemenis in diaspora have used migration strategies and transnational family arrangements for survival.[4] Their experiences thus reveal the struggles of diasporic communities with global capitalism or disaster capitalism, as they intersect with militarism and imperialism, issues which I hope to explore in greater depth in my future work.

Empire and Racial Capitalism: Canaries in the Coal Mines

Yemeni Americans have been at the crux of multiple crises of public health, confinement, and border closures on a global scale. However, their stories are generally missing in public discussions, despite the centrality of Yemen to the US-led war on terror and interventions in the region. Not enough attention has been paid to the US-backed Saudi bombing of Yemen since 2015—and the drone strikes begun earlier under Obama—that have devastated the country. The "forgotten war" in Yemen, in which over one hundred thousand people have reportedly been killed (at the time of writing this), has led to one of the world's worst humanitarian disasters.[5] The sea and air blockade of Yemen by the Saudi-led coalition has prevented food, fuel, and medicines from entering the country and deepened mass starvation and economic crisis. An estimated twenty million people are food insecure, over fifteen million people need safe water and sanitation, and the health-care system has been devastated, while cholera and other treatable diseases have led to mass deaths.[6] Furthermore, COVID-19 has spread with a fatality rate in Yemen that is five times the global average as of summer 2021.[7] This tragic crisis was amplified when COVID-19 entered Yemen, but it is a public health disaster with which the United States is complicit and that has been little discussed.

This "humanitarian crisis" was a man-made political, economic, and social disaster, highlighting the multiple crises of public health, lockdown, and violence that have made life precarious and posed an existential threat to Yemenis and Yemeni Americans—well before COVID-19 radically altered life for Americans and caused mass deaths in the United States. I argue that Yemeni Americans are the canaries in the coal mines for US empire, on the one hand as targets of the ongoing global war on terror and on the other as disposable subjects of neoliberal capitalism that has decimated brown and Black communities lacking health care, worker rights, and state resources, especially during the pandemic.

This chapter is structured around three interrelated themes that speak to new epistemologies of empire and racial capitalism and methods for engaged research, based on my preliminary findings: lockdown, crisis, and distance and digital community/activism.

Lockdown

Lockdown is a key concept that framed the narrative about the pandemic, locally, nationally, and globally, but it also must be situated in relation to the restrictions on mobility of Muslim and Arab immigrants by US imperial borders and warfare. Yemeni Americans in the Bay Area have struggled with the economic and social ramifications of the emergency lockdown in California in 2020–21 and have also been severely impacted by Trump's Muslim/Arab/African travel bans as well as the US-backed Saudi blockade of Yemen, so they have endured a *transnational lockdown*. The first announcement by Trump in 2017 of the travel bans targeting seven Muslim-majority Arab and African countries, including Yemen (which remained on the banned list throughout its various iterations) sparked protests, including in San Francisco, in solidarity with Muslims and Arabs denied entry to the United States. In addition to protests at US airports by immigrant rights and Black Lives Matter activists, there was a historic bodega strike in New York involving over one thousand mostly Yemeni-owned stores and a march by Yemeni store owners.[8] The Muslim/Arab/African travel ban was a pivotal moment in the politicization of the community, including of merchants, and of a younger generation of Yemeni American activists. Jehan Hakim, an antiwar activist from San Francisco who cofounded the Yemeni Alliance Committee (YAC), said, "After Trump was elected and the Muslim Ban was in place, that's when the Yemeni community was like, oh snap! This is real!"[9]

Mohamed Taleb, a Yemeni American activist from Oakland who is a community advocate with the National Security and Civil Rights Project of the Asian Law Caucus (ALC)/Asian Americans Advancing Justice in San Francisco, noted that Yemeni Americans have been one of the communities most impacted by the travel ban.[10] The ALC was part of the No Muslim Ban Coalition, with CAIR (Council of American-Islamic Relations), that mobilized to end the ban and highlight the suffering caused by this transnational lockdown. The travel ban was devastating for Yemeni families because for years, they had relied on transnational family practices, economic and social, with transnational marriages—

men working in the United States while wives and children remained in Yemen—and remittances to support relatives back home.

After the war in Yemen started, the United States closed its embassy in Sana'a, and Yemenis fled to Djibouti, Egypt, and even to Malaysia to escape the violence and US-backed Saudi siege of Yemen, sometimes on risky journeys by boat, since the airport in Sana'a was closed, as was, for a while, the port at Hodeida; they remained trapped for months overseas and were unable to travel to the United States or to reunite with families. Approximately 3.6 million Yemenis have been displaced by the war in Yemen, with one million living in makeshift camps in Yemen, leading to a massive crisis of forced displacement; yet Yemenis are not often categorized as refugees and most arrive in the US on family reunification visas rather than as asylum seekers.[11] Taleb also worked with the YAC and CAIR on the #BringThemHome campaign and lobbied the US government to allow Yemeni Americans to fly to the United States; they succeeded in allowing a few flights from Yemen in summer 2020.

I heard numerous stories of how the siege and lockdown in Yemen has created family separation for Yemeni Americans. Madenh Hassan, whose father was a migrant farmworker in the Central Valley and later a store owner in Oakland, is a teacher at Oakland International High School. She says many of the forty Yemeni immigrant students at the school arrived in the United States as unaccompanied minors to live with a parent who had been working in the United States while the other parent and children lived in Yemen; they struggle with traumatic experiences due to the war and with Islamophobia in the United States, especially that directed against hijabi (covered) girls. "The travel ban has split up a lot of families," notes Hassan, commenting that a few families travel to Egypt every year to visit mothers stranded overseas. While these Arab/Muslim families have not been in migrant camps on US borders, they have, in effect, been interned in Yemen and trapped in countries around the world due to the US-backed proxy war on their homeland.

Thooraya, a Yemeni American college student whose grandfather and father both owned corner stores in San Francisco and who grew up in West Oakland, says many Yemenis who have fled the war "don't really talk about it . . . maybe because of the trauma." She recalled that her grandmother was trapped in Sana'a during the war, forced to eat flour for almost six months, and suffered from malnutrition and lack of clean drinking water. Eventually, her grandmother traveled to Djibouti on a cattle ship in 2017 to apply for a US visa, since it was no longer possible to do so in Yemen, and flew to the United States; however, her daughters and grandchildren remained stranded in Djibouti. Hakim says trenchantly of Yemeni Americans caught between the war and the travel ban, "You're an American citizen and you have the world's largest superpower banning and bombing your country, so it's horrible on all fronts because the country that is banning them is the same country that's helping bomb them. . . . The US creates refugees, they create these circumstances and they're putting a lot of these [US] nationals in a situation where they can't leave." Hakim comments, "This Muslim Ban and this administration has really lifted the veil off this system which is inherently white supremacist in its ideology . . . and anti-people." Thus, some Yemeni Americans, who also support movements challenging dictatorships in Yemen, recognize the ban as a product of authoritarian policies and imperial racism in the United States.

After Trump's election, there was justifiable public outrage at the Latinx family separations at the US-Mexico border due to harsher immigration and refugee restrictions, but few know about the traumatic family separations and immobilization of the Yemeni community. Furthermore, Yemeni immigration had already slowed in the years prior to the ban, including under the Obama administration, and Yemenis were burdened with arduous immigration requirements and fees, effectively creating an unofficial travel ban.[12] Yemeni Americans were also impacted by the heightened nativist racism and Islamophobia stoked by the Trump regime and the fear of ICE raids and deportations. Munera Mohsin, a Yemeni American who works at West Oakland Middle School (whose student population is approximately 20 percent Arab/Yemeni American), helped organize Know Your Rights workshops at the school. She recalled the interracial solidarity that emerged in Oakland, which is a sanctuary city: "The African American parents showed up in solidarity with Yemeni families and told them that they were safe, that this is a sanctuary school and a safe place for your kids." But Mohsin also observed that many Yemeni American students were very anxious, as they had relatives trapped overseas and an "intense fear of being separated from their families." Her colleague in the Office of Equity for Oakland public schools recalls, "Many students stopped going to school after the

Muslim Ban. When the Muslim Ban happened, there were Muslim students holding onto their mom at the door of their elementary school telling their mom to not go outside. They were very afraid that their mom was going to get taken." The underdiscussed story of family separation of Yemeni and Muslim Americans is intertwined with US foreign policy issues and militarized borders—a precarious context in which sanctuary has been very difficult to provide, or even imagine.

There is also an invisible experience of lockdown of Yemeni Americans due to de-naturalization via passport confiscations, immigration delays due to secret national security blacklists, and surveillance. There have been passport confiscations of US citizens by the US embassy in Sana'a from 2012 to 2014; the US State Department Office of Inspector General investigated these cases that resulted in "the exile of dozens of American citizens in Yemen" during a period of "humanitarian crisis and violent chaos."[13] These Yemeni Americans' passports had sometimes been illegally held for up to two years, despite there being no arrests or official revocations of citizenship, leaving Yemeni Americans stranded overseas.[14] The additional vetting and documentation required of Yemeni visa applications have delayed reunification of families and made it an extremely costly process for immigrants already struggling with unemployment and debt.[15] These state policies have led to painful experiences of immobilization, separation, and financial hardship for Yemeni diasporic communities.

Yemeni Americans have been caught in the dragnet of several covert state programs that amplify the ongoing anti-Muslim/Arab policies of the war on terror, restricting their rights to migration and safety. The slogan at the antiwar protest and for many campaigns of the YAC is "Yemen: Banned, Bombed, Forgotten." US empire has for decades operated through covert or indirect military and political interventions, so the "forgetting" of the war on Yemen is a deliberate strategy intrinsic to US imperial violence and a painful example of the imperial amnesia addressed by critical refugee and empire studies.[16]

Crisis

The Yemeni American community is at the crux of converging crises of public health, Islamophobia/Arabophobia, warfare/militarization, counterterrorism, and policing, crises that operate at global, national, and local scales. Yet the concept of crisis suggests that there is a "stable" everyday that is ruptured by an exceptional moment of precarity, evading the permanent crises that some populations endure on a daily basis—preceding, during, and after the publicly visible "crisis."[17] For example, the ongoing Orientalist framing of Arab/Muslim Americans as a national security threat has created a chilling crisis of policing for Yemeni Americans but one not sufficiently integrated into the debate about police violence in the United States during the resurgence of the Black Lives Matter (BLM) movement and calls to defund or abolish the police.

The war on terror has increasingly relied on covert programs targeting Muslim and Arab Americans and on secret collaboration between immigration and law enforcement agencies. Counterterrorism cases that have erupted into the public sphere involving Yemeni Americans from Oakland illustrate the persistence of covert policing and surveillance of Arab/Muslim Americans twenty years after 9/11—the long war on terror, also largely forgotten. In 2010, San Francisco police chief George Gascon justified spending $400 million for a new police headquarters because of the "threat" of terrorism posed by Yemenis in the Bay Area.[18] This racist and Islamophobic statement was followed by the discovery of a secret agreement between the San Francisco Police Department and the Joint Terrorism Training Taskforce (JTTF) for covert cooperation between local law enforcement and federal intelligence agencies, which was later overturned in response to organizing by the Coalition for a Safe San Francisco, a grassroots alliance of Muslim American and civil rights activists. Taleb, who was involved with this campaign, said:

> The JTTF is COINTELPRO [version] 2.0. The FBI takes local police officers from across the US and cross-deputizes them as FBI agents, so they follow the weak (protection) rules of the FBI. The FBI is infamous for sting operations and informants within the community. There's a lot of psychological trauma, there were people who were not terrorists [who were targeted].

In 2020, the ALC and other activists from the coalition also overturned the JTTF in Oakland, ending police cooperation with the FBI for anti-Muslim/-Arab "counterterrorism" programs. Yet the psychological and social impact of policing and surveillance on the Yemeni American community and other Muslim and Arab Americans that Taleb observes is not widely known.[19] According to him, about 30 percent of Yemeni Americans in the Bay Area have been visited by the FBI but community members generally do not want to report interrogations and surveillance because they are afraid. The persistence of FBI entrapment and sting operations targeting Muslim Americans has led to a form of "mental entrapment" among Yemeni Americans, in Taleb's view, who fear the stigmatization of terrorism allegations, understandably, and the risks that come with challenging the police and state agencies.

I argue that inserting Yemeni and Arab Americans into the debate that has been raging about policing, anti-Black violence, prisons, and abolitionism would add a deeper layer to analyses of the workings of US imperial power and racial capitalism in the military-spy-police state. For example, Yemeni-owned corner stores have been on the frontlines of the BLM-inspired protests against police brutality that sprang up across the US during the "Summer of Discontent" in 2020. The looting of businesses led to the framing of protesters as disruptive rioters who posed a threat to community safety and local businesses. Yet the Yemeni store owners I spoke to insisted that while Yemeni-owned businesses in Oakland had indeed been targeted, those damaging and raiding stores were not part of the BLM movement. Hashem, whose small convenience store is in the largely Black and brown Dimond district, said, "During the protests I boarded up the window as a precaution. But I wasn't afraid of the BLM protesters. The looters came from different cities and instigated the people. I was a big supporter of Black Lives Matter! The looters were not part of the protests." His comment was echoed by other Yemeni store owners who did not think that attacks on stores were fueled by anti-Arab/Muslim sentiments. For instance, Ali Albasieri, who leads the Bay Area Small Merchants Association in Oakland, was involved with trying to provide assistance to store owners whose businesses were damaged and said emphatically to me, "Race got nothing to do with it." Furthermore, Albasieri also pointed out that the police did not protect corner stores, and their owners did not feel protected by the city or the curfew imposed during those weeks in the Bay Area. Albasieri has organized corner store owners to challenge the Oakland Police Department's harassment of "store owners who had no voice" and who have been suffering from punitive fees and regulations.

The less dramatic form of policing that has for years undermined Yemeni-owned stores and other small businesses is what Miriam

Zouzounis calls the "compounded effect of the Broken Windows-era policies" of policing and criminalization that framed corner stores as threats to community safety and public health. Zouzounis, whose Greek-Palestinian family owns a corner store in San Francisco, is a San Francisco city commissioner for small businesses and a community leader with the Arab American Grocers Association and the Neighborhood Business Alliance. She assists Arab-owned small businesses with applying for financial support and Paycheck Protection Program (PPP) grants and loans, in addition to helping them sell healthy foods in so-called food deserts.[20] Although small grocery stores were considered essential businesses during the pandemic, not a single store owner I interviewed in Oakland had received a small business loan or any kind of local or state financial support, other than the federal stimulus check of $1,200. As small stores with single proprietors and limited capacity to file paperwork and spend time on online applications, they were either ineligible or unable to file applications; some said that the aid ran out quickly so they were cut out of assistance.

Ali works at Jalisco Market in deep East Oakland, a largely low-income Black and Brown community with the highest rates of COVID-19 infection. His store is next to a bright orange church where elderly African Americans are hanging out the day I visit, and there are a couple of houseless people on the sidewalk, which is strewn with personal items. Ali's grandfather was a farm and ranch worker in California in the 1960s who returned to Yemen, where his son was born. Ali's father then came to the United States and bought a store in the 1980s in East Oakland; his son now has a store in the same neighborhood, which is about half Latinx, half African American. Ali said:

> We got no funds and no help from the city or anyone. I think they don't want to help small businesses, only the big stores. We applied to about four programs and we didn't get any funds. They said they ran out of funds. We just got the PPP. We applied for the stimulus check but it never came. Some weren't eligible because you had to have more than sixty workers. I have just three other workers.

In the first few weeks after the lockdown, people flocked to corner stores to buy essential items rather than standing in long lines outside big-box stores or visiting crowded supermarkets. This early flurry of customers led some Yemeni store owners to decide not to apply for small business loans, but as months went by and the lockdowns recurred, their businesses struggled, while unemployment rapidly increased.

Store owners have also struggled with the mask mandate, especially in low-income Black and Brown communities, which have been hit hard by the virus but where many customers did not routinely wear face masks. I noticed this at many stores in 2020, especially in west and east Oakland, and I witnessed Yemeni store owners asking their customers to mask up. The pandemic's racial disparities that have disproportionately impacted low-income communities are coupled with minoritized communities' varied experiences of state authority and histories of medicalized racism that leave many either distrustful of public health mandates or uninformed and unaware of the nature of COVID—including Yemeni Americans. Store owners began installing plexiglass shields in front of the cash register and putting up signs announcing the new masking and distancing protocols to comply with Alameda County orders. When I stopped by a Yemeni-owned corner store in my own neighborhood, there was a handwritten sign above the entrance with an added punch: "No mask, no service! Must wear mask! No excuses, no BS!" Class issues

Figure 2.1. Yemeni-owned corner store, Oakland. Photo taken by author.

add another layer to the inequity in health care and safety in the diverse communities served by Yemeni stores. For example, in Temescal, Ismat said the customers at his family store, who are majority White, offered masks and gloves to him and his brothers working at the store.

The economic crisis unleashed by the pandemic has severely impacted Yemeni Americans in general, who were already struggling to survive given the lack of affordable housing in the Bay Area. Albasieri points out that most Yemeni Americans work in the service sector, as janitors in office buildings or workers in restaurants that shut down as well as gig workers for Uber and Lyft; he observes that the unemployment crisis has had a "financial and also mental health impact on the community." Ahmed Abozayd, a Yemeni American labor organizer who came to the United States as a farmworker in 1969 and worked with the UFW, is vice president of the janitorial workers union, SEIU Local 87, in San Francisco. He says that it had two thousand Yemeni members (40 percent of their membership), but at the time we spoke in April 2020, one-third of their members had lost their jobs due to the pandemic; it is very likely that those unemployment numbers have increased since then. This economic crisis, both community organizers pointed out, has impacted families in Yemen who relied on remittances from relatives in the United States; in some cases, Yemeni Americans have had to sell their homes in Yemen because of financial hardship here. Yet Albasieri noted that the store owners' association had also supported the local community during the pandemic by donating gift cards for groceries to families of diverse racial backgrounds and that they had raised funds to help subsidize rent for Oakland residents.

Transnational mutual aid networks spanning the United States and Yemen have been eroded by the global ripple effects of the economic crisis and the US role in the war on Yemen. Wire transfer services such as MoneyGram and Western Union limited funds transfers to Yemen after the war, in some cases even refusing wire transfer requests by Yemeni Americans because of economic sanctions against Yemen. When I spoke to Abozayd in spring 2021, he was frustrated that he could no longer send funds to the community kitchen he had launched in his village, a result of the disruption of remittances to Yemen. This economic blockade led to a hearing of the Immigrant Rights Commission in the San Francisco City Council in March 2019 organized by the Yemeni

Community Association and immigrant rights attorneys. Community members testified to the hardship this posed for their families and a community already impacted by the war and the Muslim ban, trapped in Yemen yet unable to receive economic support. The City Council issued a resolution acknowledging their concerns, but the restrictions on wire transfers and delays persist. This problem has only compounded the strangulation of Yemen's economy due to the US-backed blockade and war on Yemen that have deepened poverty, starvation, and illness.

Distance and Digital Community/Activism

On January 25, 2021, a Global Day of Action for Yemen was organized by a coalition of antiwar groups to mark the sixth anniversary of the ongoing war there, featuring an online rally cosponsored with Code Pink, Stop the War, and the Democratic Socialists of America, among other groups that mobilized publicly in cities around the world. The Yemeni Alliance Committee (YAC) was one of the organizers of the international action and of a car caravan in downtown San Francisco. Hakim observed that the war in Yemen had galvanized an antiwar movement in the Bay Area that had been dormant since the mass protests against the US war on Iraq in 2003, commenting, "This is really an antiwar movement that is global so I'm just overwhelmed with how much support we're getting! I mean something about COVID is really bringing people together. . . . This is something we haven't been able to do for years." Hakim spoke about how hard it had been to build resistance to the US-backed Saudi bombing of Yemen; she spent years "waiting for there to be a Twitter storm for Yemen," and when it did not happen, she and other Yemeni American activists formed the national YAC in 2017 with chapters in New York and Michigan. Significantly, the organization has a strong Yemeni female leadership, including Hakim, who is Yemeni-Pakistani American and speaks frequently at webinars and uses digital social media to create awareness of the war and humanitarian crisis in Yemen. After Biden took office, he announced that US support for "offensive" operations in Yemen would end, but Hakim pointed out that this was an ambiguous position that still left room for other attacks on a blockaded country whose infrastructure was already devastated.

Figure 2.2. Car caravan at protest against the war in Yemen, San Francisco. Photo taken by author.

The antiwar action in San Francisco used the format of the car caravan developed by activists during the BLM protests in 2020 to avoid large gatherings but still politicize the public sphere. That cold winter day in San Francisco, approximately 150 cars drove and honked their way through the streets of the financial district, some with hoods draped with Yemeni flags or signs taped to their windows. Small "pop-up" rallies were organized at key locations, such as outside the Black Rock office, a corporation involved with the global war economy. I participated in the protest myself and as I drove by a downtown construction site, some workers spotted the antiwar sign in my car window and yelled, "Send the bombs there!" I am not sure if those men on the sidewalk even knew where "there" was and if the distance from the Gulf made it possible to support bombing other Brown people or if they simply lacked knowledge of the war in the first place. The car caravan illustrates how the production of space has been transformed by organizers in response to pandemic-related protocols for social distancing and through events that politicize urban space, challenging the erasure of certain communities and struggles from the public sphere. The movement of cars through the urban financial district is an example of "mobile spatial fields" and "transitory expressions" of Yemeni American political identity that claim the space of the city, injecting a public challenge to the imperial state and its collusion with militarized capitalism.[21]

In April 2021, some young Yemeni American activists from Michigan engaged in a hunger strike in Washington, DC, calling on the Biden administration to end US support for the war.[22] Their fast also politicized the public sphere and dramatized the starvation that has led to mass deaths in Yemen and the erasure of this forgotten war. As in all exiled and oppressed communities, the war is a contentious issue among Yemeni Americans, who are divided politically for a variety of reasons and grapple with the legacies of colonization, the history of civil war and division of north and south Yemen, US imperial interventions, the war on terror, the involvement of regional players (such as Saudi Arabia, the UAE, and Iran), authoritarian rule backed by the United States, and the Arab uprisings.[23] For Hakim and others I spoke to, the potentially unifying issue for Yemenis in the diaspora is that of Yemeni sovereignty and freedom from foreign intervention. Osman, a store owner from Oakland whose father migrated to the United States in the 1960s as a farmworker and later opened a store, said pointedly, "A lot of countries are involved there [in Yemen] doing their b—s—! . . . It's because of what happened after the Arab Spring—these monarchies, dictators, don't want prosperity or freedom." Omar also incisively critiqued the impact of the military-industrial complex on Yemen, a country that has for years been framed through the prism of counterterrorism by the US state.

While store owners and family members, especially their school-age children, struggled with the shift to Zoom life and virtual schooling, digital media can also be an opportunity to bridge distance in a time of disconnection. In March 2021, I hosted a digital story workshop on Zoom in collaboration with Amy Hill of the StoryCenter in Berkeley, which focuses on participatory media for public advocacy. In the Zoom workshop, five Yemeni/Arab American community members—including Taleb, a college student, a male therapist, and two Arab women business owners—shared powerful stories. The goal of this digital media project was to create awareness of the experiences of Yemeni Americans in the Bay Area and Arab/Muslim small business owners through stories that can be shared with educators, policy makers, media workers, and activists. This collective memory work is significant for a community that is rendered invisible, for as Taleb observed, "We don't have our own people telling our stories." The videos highlight Arab/Muslim women's experiences of displacement, war, patriarchy, and domestic violence—as well as resistance and resourcefulness—and offer alternative tellings of Arab/Muslim masculinities by Yemeni American men doing work not conventionally gendered masculine.

As I continue this research, I am forced to ponder questions about digital community building and "distance" that emerged during the pandemic. What does it mean to make digital life a norm when so many are unable to access technology or retool their rituals to live life online? What does "social distance" mean for a community that is constituted, but also separated, across national borders? How can one build solidarity despite spatial distance? It is also important to honor the resilience of the Yemeni American community, which has endured a collective threat to national survival in their homeland in addition to the crises in the United States, which the majority of Americans have not experienced in their lifetime. Our worlds were already divided before the pandemic, though Covid clearly deepened health, economic, educational, and also social disparities.

Conclusion

The struggles of Yemeni Americans with immigration restrictions, disruption of transnational mutual-aid networks, policing, surveillance, public-health risks, financial insecurity, layered over the ongoing suffering caused by the war on their homeland all constitute what could be called a community crisis, or a community in crisis. Yet I was struck by the ways in which the narrative about the COVID crisis, or even the crisis of racist policing or of democracy under Trump, was generally based on nationalist frames that erased these other, transnational struggles. This is not simply an issue of expanding the crisis narrative, however, for as Roozbeh Shirazi incisively argues, we must question the very deployment of the word *crisis*; the concept of emergency "obscures how seemingly normal conditions may produce their own impasse" and "which actors are able to name emergencies and mobilize resources to address them."[24] If a moment of crisis implies a temporal rupture of a normative stability, we must rethink the temporality of crisis and "trace which modes of living are assumed to constitute stability and what forms of stability are desirable."[25] Many critics of the dominant narrative about the pandemic have pointed to the ways in which it erased longer histories of suffering of vulnerable groups.[26] The experiences of Yemeni Americans force us to reckon with the transnational "state of emergency" and the permanent crisis and ongoing precarity of vulnerable groups due to empire and racial capitalism.[27] We need to think critically about using the notion of doing "crisis research" so that it does not reify temporal and spatial assumptions about *where* and *when* crisis is situated—and for *whom*.

My experiences of trying to do ethnographic research during the pandemic helped me understand that the limitations of our research methods are themselves revealing of the struggles of those impacted by the multiple crises produced by medical apartheid, racial capitalism, and imperial wars. Methods such as critical ethnography that prioritize dialogic research and challenge extractive models of community research, as well as digital media or digital interviews, highlight both the possibilities and the limits of what it means to work in times of crisis when ongoing racial violence and economic precarity are dramatically, and fatally, visible. Public scholarship has to be flexible in order to meet the needs of shifting political or cultural circumstances but also must interrogate the framework of emergency. It is important to emphasize that ethnic studies scholars have been doing community-engaged research since the field's inception in a moment of national crisis shaped by antiwar and civil rights struggles in the United States, though it has not received adequate institutional recognition or resources for its foundational models of engaged scholarship.

The experiences of Yemeni Americans during the pandemic shed light on questions of transnationalism, borders, surveillance, and policing that are key to US empire studies and deepen conversations about these issues in ethnic and American studies. The stories Yemeni Americans shared with me, either digitally or while chatting through a plexiglass shield at the store counter, illuminate ways of reimagining crisis, lockdown, distance, and digital life, and I believe they will help carry us through the not-so-normal post-pandemic world.

NOTES

The digital stories can be viewed at: https://www.youtube.com/playlist?list=PL2zMrq 22-Y2tdE81Uc3Ro3tjGKSl264uU.

1 Estimate by Ali Albasieri, president of the Bay Area Small Merchants Association.
2 Amy Kaplan, "Left Alone with America": The Absence of Empire in the Study of American Culture," in *Cultures of United States Imperialism*, eds. Amy Kaplan and Donald Pease (Durham, NC: Duke University Press, 1993), 3–21; *The Anarchy of Empire in the Making of US Culture* (Cambridge, MA: Harvard University Press, 2002).
3 Neama Alamri, "Yemeni Farmworkers and the Politics of Arab Nationalism in the UFW." *Boom* (February 2020), https://boomcalifornia.org; Ron Kelley, "The Yemenis of the San Joaquin," *MERIP (Middle East Report)* 139 (1986): 22–36; Jon C. Swanson, "Sojourners and Settlers: Yemenis in America," *MERIP (Middle East Report)* (1986) 139: 5–21. Currently, the estimate for Yemenis in the Bay Area ranges from eight to ten thousand according to community leaders; given the absence of census data for Arab Americans, other than through the ancestry question, reliable numbers are hard to come by.
4 Mary Bisharat, "Yemeni Farmworkers in California," *MERIP (Middle East Report)* 34 (1975): 22–26; Loukia K. Sarroub, *All American Yemeni Girls: Being Muslim in a Public High School* (Philadelphia: University of Pennsylvania Press, 2005); Alisa Perkins, *Muslim American City: Gender and Religion in Metro Detroit* (New York: New York University Press, 2020).
5 Yemen Relief and Reconstruction Fund. https://yemenfoundation.org.
6 Ibid.
7 Yemen Relief and Reconstruction Fund; Norwegian Refugee Council: "Ten Facts about the Deadly Crisis in Yemen." www.nrc.no.
8 Louise Cainkar, "The Muslim Ban and Trump's War on Immigration." *Middle East Research and Information Project (MERIP)*. https://merip.org.
9 The YAC has organized lobbying campaigns for legislation to end US military and political support for the Saudi-led coalition's war on Yemen and sales of weapons to the Kingdom of Saudi Arabia.
10 Asian Americans Advancing Justice and CLEAR Project, *Stranded Abroad: Americans Stripped of their Passports in Yemen* (2016).
11 International Rescue Committee. "Yemen Crisis Watch." July 20, 2021. www. rescue.org; Norwegian Refugee Council "Ten Facts."
12 Louise Cainkar, "For Yemenis Fleeing War, the US Muslim Ban Means a High Price and Dangerous Wait," *Religion and Politics* (October 15, 2019) https://religionandpolitics.org.
13 Office of Inspector General, "Review of Allegations of Improper Seizures of Passports at Embassy Sana'a, Yemen." United States Department of State: Office of Evaluations and Special Projects, 2018.
14 Asian Americans Advancing Justice and CLEAR.
15 Cainkar, "The Muslim Ban," MERIP, 2020.

16 Kaplan, "Left Alone"; Yến Lê Espiritu, *Body Counts: The Vietnam War and Milita-rized Refuge(es)* (Oakland: UC Press, 2014).

17 Roozbeh Shirazi, "When Emergency Becomes Everyday Life: Revisiting a Central EIE Concept in the Context of the War on Drugs," *Journal on Education in Emergencies* 6 no. 1 (2020): 57–83.

18 "San Francisco Police Chief Apologizes for Terrorism Comments," *East Bay Times*, March 27, 2010. www.eastbaytimes.com.

19 "West Oakland Man Indicted on Terrorist Charges." *ABC News*, July 21, 2017. https://abc7news.com.

20 Short, Anne, Julie Guthman, and Samuel Raskin. "Food Deserts, Oases, or Mirages? Small Markets and Community Food Security in the San Francisco Bay Area." *Journal of Planning Education and Research* 26 (2007): 352–64.

21 Setha Low, cited in Perkins, *Muslim American City*, 23.

22 Iman Saleh, "I'm on Hunger Strike until the U.S. Ends All Support for the Saudi-Led Blockade against Yemen," *Washington Post*, April 8, 2021. www.washington-post.com.

23 Isa Blumi, *Destroying Yemen: What Chaos in Arabia Tells Us about the World* (Oakland: University of California Press, 2018); Marieke Brandt, *Tribes and Politics in Yemen: A History of the Houthi Conflict* (Oxford: Oxford University Press, 2017).

24 Shirazi, "When Emergency," 57, 62.

25 Ibid., 62.

26 Arundhati Roy, "The Pandemic Is a Portal," *Financial Times*, April 3, 2020. www.ft.com/.

27 Walter Benjamin, "Theses on the Philosophy of History," in *Illuminations: Walter Benjamin—Essays and Reflections*, edited by Hannah Arendt, translated by Harry Zohn (New York: Schocken, 1988), 253–64.

3

Precarity and Privilege

Racial Capitalism, Immigration Law,
and Immigrants' Academic Pursuits

PAWAN DHINGRA

Asian Americans' educational outcomes have become a topic of popular interest, with politicized implications. *New York Times* columnist Nicholas Kristof wrote about their academic achievements in 2015 as follows: "Some disagree, but I'm pretty sure that one factor [in Asian American academic achievement] is East Asia's long Confucian emphasis on education. . . . To me, the success of Asian-Americans is a tribute to hard work, strong families and passion for education."[1] Kristof is a noted liberal who, like those on the political right, endorses a racialized thinking around Asian Americans' educational achievement.

Such rhetoric around Asian American educational achievement illustrates the model minority stereotype and foregrounds why it is so important to understand what is behind this educational trend, even as many Asian Americans experience academic challenges. The stereotype suggests the weak, even irrelevant, role of racism against people of color. The logic is that if Asian Americans can achieve, any group can do the same with enough hard work, family support, and commitment to education. The stereotype is premised on the notion of a meritocratic economy and society that reward people's skills and effort in a context that is free of bias. The school system and capitalist labor market appear as equitable institutions that fairly compensate academically trained individuals. The seeming success of Asian Americans in school also has political implications for the school system. Kristof's rhetoric can be weaponized to belittle concerns of both inadequate school funding and the harmful effects of curriculums that do not adequately represent non-White people. Structural critiques of schools as being pipelines to the prison industrial complex become more easily dismissed, and instead the problems facing communities of color appear to be their fault rather than a result of the education system's inequities and biases.[2]

Given what is at stake, sociologists have often studied why Asian Americans attain high achievement in school. As I will explain, sociologists effectively push back on culturally essentialist explanations that are popular in public discourse. But the analyses remain limited in their purview. As reviewed below, the scholarship considers immigrant parents' upbringing, class status, and views on explicit racism as explaining their motivations around their children's educational outcomes. This is important, and I support such analyses. But parents' subjective reasonings are not merely the result of their ethnic backgrounds and concerns around daily barriers they witness in front of them. Race and racial capitalism set the conditions of their daily experiences. In contrast to sociology's frequent depoliticized approach of asking and measuring whether race matters to individuals, it is necessary to understand people as acting within racialized structures.[3] My research focus in this chapter is to explain how parents' views of education sit within a backdrop of racial capitalism and immigration laws that together frame how parents arrived in the United States, experience work and mobility, and plan for the future within global capitalism. I will draw from in-depth interviews with South Asian immigrant professionals and discuss their parenting choices within the broader context of racial capitalism in relation to their immigration experience.

The Social Science Approach to Asian American Education

As sociologists, education studies scholars, and other social scientists study the academic achievements of many Asian Americans, they distinguish Asian Americans' parenting strategies from those of Whites.[4] Middle- and upper-class Whites routinely engage in a concerted cultivation parenting, which involves paying for structured, extracurricular opportunities so as to indulge children's interests and give them a leg up over others.[5] Sociologists frame Asian Americans' investment in extracurricular education differently, as stemming not from a standard middle-class practice but instead as tied to their ethnic backgrounds and their immigrant experiences. This section reviews this sociological literature on Asian American parenting.

Social science scholarship rigorously explains Asian immigrants' parenting choices as resulting from two possible sources: parents' upbringing in Asia prior to emigrating and/or parents' experiences with race and mobility in the United States. Structural conditions in one's homeland shape people's youth and then, years later, their parenting choices. For instance, these immigrants have experienced intense academics from a young age in their homeland.[6] They also come from countries that have an infrastructure of educational support, and these pre-migration factors give them an advantage in supporting their children post-migration.[7] They learn to see extra education beyond school as normal, even if they did not participate in it personally.[8] The premise is that after having children of one's own, parents return to these same tactics that they experienced and/or witnessed around them when young.[9] Children of such immigrants are told to study hard and see success as possible only through academics.[10] Given that many of these parents not only attained high levels of education but were able to secure coveted visas to migrate to the United States due in part to their educational achievements, they have strong reasons to believe that such an upbringing serves children well. Math and science are the preferred subjects for their children, because parents often majored in them and believe that these fields will have the least chances for discrimination.[11]

Once they are in the United States, their social experiences also contribute to the belief that education is a key tool for mobility. Sociologists operationalize the effects of race as encounters with racism in the white-collar workplace, such as being passed up for promotions and feeling that one's voice and contributions are not valued equally.[12] Immigrants often lack professional mentors and networks, and so they find it harder to navigate the workplace. Xie and Goyette, as well as Zhou and Kim, have surveyed parents about their concerns around social capital and racism and connect such concerns to parents' decisions to emphasize education for their children. Parents want their children to stand out as highly qualified among peers whose families have high social capital or who are White (and hence will not suffer racism), which leads parents to promote academics for their children even after school hours.[13] They, for instance, enroll their Asian American children in after-school education for enrichment purposes at higher rates than do other groups.[14] In summary, whether sociologists emphasize immigrants' upbringing in

Asia or their encounters with racism in the United States, the explanations focus on parents' ethnic background and direct encounters with racism.

Racial Capitalism

The sociological literature is useful in explaining how parents' subjective understandings of their upbringings and local environment drive their choices around children's academics. Yet the relevance of race in parents' past and current circumstances is not limited to their subjective impressions of racism that they may or may not have encountered. Such a level of analysis gives exclusive attention to what is observable and articulated by individual respondents, which is important but not all-encompassing. It relies on immigrants' observations around racism as evidence that race matters. Obscured as a result within sociological studies are the embedded processes that create the conditions for parents' immigration, their experiences in the workplace, and ultimately their approach to education. Race matters as a structuring principle, not merely as a social category that elicits biased behavior from others toward immigrants (which it also does and is included below).[15] It must be studied as such so as to recognize its overarching effects.

I elaborate here on racial capitalism and then connect it to immigration laws. I later refer to these structural processes in my ethnographic accounts from immigrant parents as they discussed their children's education. A racial capitalism has defined the United States' economic expansion.[16] Racial capitalism, as I use the term, works in the following way: the labor market has multiple industries and occupational categories, each of which typically has specific racialized groups within them. Race is central to how capitalism not only developed but continues to grow and connect labor to industries. Historically and ongoing, certain ethno-racial groups are sought after for particular work and framed in ways so as to extract their resources. The colonization of the United States by White settlers was justified through the racialization of Native Americans as undeserving of their own land.[17] The enslavement of Africans was an essential component to the growth of US agriculture, and US manufacturing and the rise of urban centers depended on the legalized secondary status of African Americans post-enslavement.[18]

Racial capitalism is also at play in the treatment of Latinxs, whose lands were colonized and bodies used in food, landscaping, manufacturing, and other labor-intensive industries.[19] Contrary to arguments of linear Latinx mobility in an unbiased labor market, Latinxs attain increasingly higher incomes across generations but have lower or stagnant wages over time relative to their educational level.[20] They also have been on the front lines of Covid infections given their precarious labor positions.[21] Asian Americans, too, have played a key role in racial capitalism in the United States.[22] Historically, they were recruited to work in railroads, mines, and mills.[23] Capitalists took advantage of multiple Asian American groups' labor in the nineteenth and twentieth centuries and still today in agricultural, manual laborer, and professional fields.[24] At the same time, Asian Americans were framed as foreigners in the media and government rhetoric, attacked in their homes and at work, and exploited with low wages.[25]

Immigration Law

Racial capitalism does not simply manifest in corporate practices, military attacks, or the labor market. Immigration law plays a fundamental role in facilitating it and is foundational to how immigrant parents understand their work and domestic conditions, as I will explain through my ethnographic findings below. Before turning to those findings, I want to frame immigrants' labor experiences within the context of immigration law and its connection to racial capitalism. For instance, given that the Immigration and Naturalization Act of 1965 helped further a racial capitalism, it should be seen as a labor bill rather than only understood as an immigrant and family reunification bill. One of the priority groups for immigration was those who could serve the country's urgent medical and scientific labor needs.[26] Instead of training domestic Black and Brown people to take these white-collar jobs, the country turned abroad. The US state recruited doctors, nurses, and engineers from China, India, the Philippines, and elsewhere. As this happened, new racialized expectations formed about them by employers. For instance, the more international doctors in a hospital, the worse its status rankings were, regardless of how well the hospital cared for patients or the hospital's level of resources.[27] Discrimination against immigrant doctors was so popular in the decades following the Immigration and Naturalization Act of 1965 that hospitals would overtly say that only US-born doctors need apply for some positions.[28] Immigrant physicians faced everyday obstacles as well, including in their licensing and promotion. The legislation that allowed in immigrant physicians placed them into a racialized, secondary labor market that utilized them for specific and limited purposes.[29] Immigrant nurses, too, found themselves in gendered and racialized labor positions. They were afforded limited mobility and respect from their coworkers and instead worked within a postcolonial medical system that maintained long-standing hierarchies.[30] Later changes to immigration law continue this same logic of racial capitalism and create the conditions for current immigrant parents' educational practices, explained below. Many of the Indian immigrant parents I interviewed arrived under H-1B visas. The H-1 visa originally was written into the McCarran-Walter Act of 1952, which was a slight revision of the Immigration Act of 1924. The H-1B visa grew in popularity after the Immigration Act of 1990, which in part created the H-1B visa designation popularly used today by immigrant professionals, particularly those from India and China. It is part of a larger visa system meant for immigrant laborers to fill gaps in US labor sectors. Certain industries with labor shortages have successfully lobbied the US government for temporary workers, including in agriculture, medicine, engineering, and more. Indians comprise the largest percentage of H-1B professional worker visas in the United States, often in software engineering, and are second to Chinese Americans in student F visas.[31]

The H-1B Visa Worker

What it means to be on an H-1B visa is essential to understanding how parents I interviewed experience the workforce and their place in the country, which I will later argue influences their parenting. As discussed above, sociologists correctly refer to immigrants' upbringing and current concerns of discrimination as influencing their parenting decisions. But to understand immigrants' emigration and positionality in their workplaces, it is necessary to place them in a broader context of their visa status within a racialized economy. While IT workers may seem completely different from agricultural workers, they are understood by the US government and their employing companies in similar ways, as racialized laborers who are here to serve an industry lacking in US-born personnel.[32] Once in the United States, these visa holders traditionally have very limited bargaining power relative to their employers.[33] While they earn more than the national average, more than 80 percent of H-1B visa holders are approved to be hired at wages below those paid to American-born workers for comparable positions.[34] For many years, it was impossible for visa holders to change jobs while in the United States without having to leave the country, thereby giving employers heightened authority over them. As a compliant workforce, these immigrants tend not to protest against their pay or work conditions. On top of this, as a group gets known for being in a line of work, employers seek them out for that work. The immigrants' status as compliant, feminized Asian workers naturalizes their subordinate status in their labor market. Employers come to see groups from certain countries as good for particular jobs, which reproduces the racial capitalism already in place. Wages tend to be set at below market value and have not increased in line with economic assumptions, which suggests that non-economic factors such as racial stereotypes about pliable Asian workers are at play.[35]

The visa program has evolved over time and places workers in an increasingly delicate position. Rather than working in an IT department at a major US corporation, such as Google or Microsoft, it is increasingly common for immigrants to work for a subcontracting firm. Major corporations needing IT personnel hire computer programmers with H-1B visas as contractors from an intermediary firm. Nicknamed "bodyshops," these subcontracting firms pay limited wages and allow major industries to circumvent the need to invest in personnel or sponsor immigrants for green cards.[36] The immigrant workers can be laid off when business opportunities for the subcontracting firms run dry. In addition, the terms of H-1B define the status of workers under the visa in ways that subject them to a range of exploitative practices and lead to their construction as a tractable and flexible workforce.[37] The H-1B visa is not a type of work permit that gets attached to individual workers and allows work in the USA for any employer on his/her own right. Rather, it is an employer-specific and employment-based visa, belonging to the company. This, in turn, adds to employees' insecure status. As capital moves, so do people. Indians are now migrating to Monterrey, Mexico, for instance, as Indian corporations set up shops in locations near the United States.[38]

It is in this context of racial capitalism and its immigration laws that immigrant professionals raise their children and conceive of education. Immigrant parents are not emphasizing education merely in response to their upbringings or in response to direct racism, as the sociological literature argues. They are not simply workers worried about a possible glass ceiling. Interviews I conducted with immigrant parents reveal the complexity behind their decisions. As I will explain after reviewing the research design behind the study, their positionality within a racial capitalism is one of the most important influences on their parenting choices. Conversations with immigrant parents reveal their thinking around education in relation to their unsettled place in the visa system and the global labor market.

Research Design

Between 2014 and 2018, I spent time with Indian American families and others who have committed extra resources to education for their children. They often arrived in the United States on work visas such as the H-1B after finishing their university degrees in India. Studying a group known for its educational achievement, such as Indian American professionals, helps us ascertain whether features of the model minority truly apply to a group so closely aligned with the stereotype.

The study concentrated on Indian American parents with children aged fourteen and below. These children took part in academic competitions and/or after-school math tutoring classes run by corporate franchise companies (e.g., the Kumon Institute of Education, Mathnasium). While tutoring has long been a major industry in certain Asian and European countries, it is a fast-growing enterprise in the United States.[39]

For this study, I have conducted in-depth interviews with sixty Indian American parents whose children took part in extracurricular education. Each interview lasted around an hour. These interviews were heavily supplemented with eight group interviews, which took place at academic competitions and mostly with only Indian Americans. Each group had fifteen or more families present who participated, leading to eighty more substantive interviews. Across these interviews, I asked parents about their philosophy around childrearing, their immigration backgrounds, their hopes and fears for their children, and more. Follow-up questions varied based on the interview, but the general themes of inquiry remained consistent. Families lived all over the country (Texas, California, Colorado, Florida, Mississippi, Ohio, and elsewhere). I met many of them at academic competitions that they had traveled to. Interviews took place at the competitions or later over the phone. About a third of informants lived in New England. Their towns frequently were well-resourced suburbs whose school districts were highly ranked by *Boston Magazine* and *U.S. News & World Report*. The Boston-area suburbs in which some participants lived, for instance, had a higher percentage of Asian Americans than the state average (of 6.3 percent in 2014) and fewer people living below the poverty level than the state average (of 8.3 percent in 2014).[40] I met these informants at academic competitions and at local after-school learning centers, and interviews took place at these spaces, in homes, in cafés, and on the phone.

Consistent with their residential locations, families interviewed were professionals. Practically all were married and had one spouse—and often both—in white-collar occupations with individual annual salaries above $100,000. As fitting their immigration status as arriving under the H-1B visa, all also had a college degree or higher, typically in STEM disciplines. I interviewed an equal number of mothers and fathers, and they all migrated to the United States as adults.

I want to stress that while I am focusing on Indian American professionals who fit popular stereotypes of the immigrant group, they are not representative of all Indian Americans. It is a diverse group, and an increasing number are undocumented and low income. Over 25 percent of Indian Americans ages five and above have limited English proficiency as of 2013.[41] Attention to immigrant professionals should not suggest that they are the only group within Indian or Asian Americans or that others do not deserve greater attention.

Precarity Despite Class Privilege

To be able to migrate to the United States, parents I interviewed had already attained high levels of human capital. They had bachelor's and master's degrees from competitive universities and had relevant work skills. They were able to beat out countless others to secure one of the few visa opportunities available in the United States. Such backgrounds and job placements gave them a financial grounding. Yet they reported finding it challenging to move up in their industry. Some of these challenges were apparent to them in their daily lives. For instance, they often lacked the cultural capital rewarded within White-run establishments. As to be expected within a racial capitalism, racial privilege greases the wheels that makes some people appear more eligible and relevant for managerial positions while others more readily are relegated to subordinate roles. As business owners in Ohio said,

> If you're class of '80 from Ohio State, you're on the [corporate] board. But you know, I am not a class of '80, I graduated in Mumbai. I am not from Ohio State. I never been from Ohio State, so I'm never going to make the secret handshake.

Immigrants may have high human capital, which puts them in the position for opportunities. But they lack the other forms of capital that actually help move people from candidacy for opportunities to actually securing those openings. Not knowing the secret handshake and other forms of cultural capital popular within the old-boy's network limits their mobility. For that reason, when Asian Americans are in managerial positions, they typically manage other Asian ethnics and are not seen as being qualified enough to manage staffs that reflect the corporation's dominant ethnic profile.[42]

But beyond the challenges they saw in front of them, immigrants were able to recognize background economic insecurities, which seeped into their parenting calculations. They did not need to experience discrimination or bias in order to become cognizant of disadvantages tied to their immigration and racialized status. Part of that disadvantage was their material conditions upon immigration. Beyond their everyday-level experiences in the workplace, immigrants did not have a personal or government-provided safety net, which made their shaky position within the labor market all the more stressful. As a father who immigrated on a H-1B visa said of himself and his fellow immigrants, "They probably don't have a lot of other kinds of assets. They don't have extensive landholdings and so on that can be passed onto their kids. The only advantage [their] kids can get is education." As immigrants, they worried about their financial circumstances despite their white-collar professional status. Parents understand education within the context of their economic precarity relative to others.

In addition to material concerns, Asian Americans were racialized in the public sphere as economic aggressors regardless of their own feelings of occupational insecurity. They were not seen as deserving sympathy or support. An Indian immigrant father paraphrased a White high school commencement speaker who spoke about Asian immigration with trepidation rather than optimism:

> I'm saying about seven years back I was attending a graduation ceremony. I remember a CEO was there, he was giving the commencement speech. He said only one thing, he said kids of America close your PlayStations and start studying because the kids from India and China are coming to compete with you. . . . What matters is who you are going to compete with. See, previously America was locked down, immigration was very little. America would only take people who would help them in innovation, things like that, but it's changing, right, the influx is totally different.

Immigration has long been a tool to grow an exploitable workforce for major industries in the United States, while the immigrants are demonized so as to affirm a national identity of "real" Americans who are under threat from these newcomers.[43] Commencement attendees are warned about the influx of immigrants from Asia. Implicit in the speaker's warning is the notion that Asians, even once they arrive, do not belong here and that everyday Americans have the power to stop their settling in. Asian Americans are presumed to be foreigners to the nation and excluded from civic incorporation, which in turn adds to their precarious place in the nation.[44]

Parenting out of Fear

Parents' sense of precarity and isolation in their industries—beyond any personal encounters with discrimination or bias—also limited their impressions of what was possible for their children and, in turn, guided their parenting. A father of two elementary-school children knew that they would need more than skill to get ahead. He said one son excelled in playing the piano. But he had no "career capital" in the arts:

> I know nobody in the music industry; I don't know how that industry works. I know my son has a tremendous music sense, but I really hesitate to encourage music as a career. Because I don't have the career capital, I cannot advise him. I'm advising my son to learn math because there I can really advise him. I can guide him. It helps some kids to kind of leverage the parent's career capital. And so that's one of the reasons why all these scientists or Indian doctors are sending the kids to math centers.

For those who grew up and attended college in the United States, there are multiple networks that one can access, such as from one's extended family, fraternity or sorority, neighborhood associations, and more. Immigrants of color, including Asian Americans, often lack those resources. Parents did not just need social capital to connect them to other fields, as often noted by sociologists.[45] They needed to know the ins and outs of how careers worked and wanted someone to give them a leg up, for otherwise they worried their children would be at a disadvantage. Without land holdings and deep knowledge of different industries, parents raised children in a defensive manner.[46] This defensive mindset involved enrolling children in extracurricular education, like math centers, so that children would be highly skilled in fields that parents themselves could then better guide them in, given that the parents worked in mathematic-based IT careers. Parents also turned to ethnic spaces, including cram schools, academic competitions, and home-organized tutoring sessions.[47]

A Chinese American immigrant mother worried about visa and other hurdles to advancement, despite having a white-collar career as an engineer and living in an affluent suburb of Boston. An anxiety shaped her parenting:

> We don't have the education here, so we probably cannot understand the way things are supposed to be. Also, when we were here for our first job, it is difficult. You don't have the visa status. If your English is not good, even if you have good grades, it takes [a] much longer time to get a job. The immigrant parents have experienced that, so they push their kids a little bit harder.

Uncertainty in one's legal status and employment set the conditions for parents wanting to control what they can for their children, namely how much they can help their children achieve academically. Such achievement felt necessary in order to navigate an opaque system that privileges some over others based on language skills, legal status, and other forms of non-financial capital.

Global Workers and Global Parenting

I sat in the modest living room of a mother who ran an after-school math center in the Boston area. She also was the mother of two boys, one in high school and the other in elementary school. Over chai, she noted that in India, one had to be highly competitive and that immigrants needed their kids to be ahead, especially if they returned to India but also so as to boost their US college-entrance chances:

> In India, Asia, you have to be the best of the best to get a job. So much competition for spots. Why did we come from India to here? To get a better life. Since you came here for a better life, you want to give your kid a better opportunity. God forbid if I have to go back to India; I need to make sure the kid won't fall behind. Many Indians who come to my center are on H-1B visas and might have to go back. . . . That's the whole point. Do more now so [you] stay good in math, get into [a] gifted program, get AP classes, get good SATs. It's all geared toward that.

She does not refer to individual-level prejudice against her as concern. Instead, she recognizes the precarity that she and her peers live with as visa-dependent workers who can become disposable to their employers. To her point about competition, the likelihood of entrance into the university system in India has gotten so low that students find themselves rejected from elite universities there but accepted into US Ivy League universities.[48]

She and others I spoke to communicate a binary of safety versus risk. The personal and professional worlds are full of risk. In the personal realm, there is intense competition around whom one marries, what outings one gets to go on, and the rest. Growing up, one gets used to having to distinguish oneself over others to get attention. The business owner and mother whom we just met refers to competition in the professional sphere. The fear of not making it in the United States and returning to India is palpable. And this fear may come true even if one is qualified and performs one's duties well, given the aforementioned precarity around the H-1B visa that her clients rely on. Children need to be overqualified so as to compete here or back in their homeland. The structural conditions that influence their original immigration do not end upon arrival to the United States, for they remain within a racial capitalism that moves people around the globe based on their presumed best fit and the degree of nativist pushback. Immigrant parents could not control in which country or continent they may end up and so needed to parent accordingly.

Given that parents immigrated in pursuit of economic opportunity, they believed they had to prepare their children to do the same. Their concern was not a glass ceiling blocking their children in their personal workspace but, instead, the broader context of the global competition for jobs. A father of two young teenage girls involved in math and spelling said,

> If they have to go to some other country eventually in search of their careers that's fine. So, I guess there is this mindset that they'll probably be competing against a national or an international student body at some point. So, the notion is to try and expose them to that sort of competition at this age. So that means with respect to words and math, which are kind of foundational, for words you have the Spelling Bee and for math you have the AMC, MATHCOUNTS, that whole track.

There is little allegiance to staying in a nation that saw them as foreigners and may not have jobs for them. Instead, parents realize that capital is flexible, and therefore so must they be as well. They prepare their children not by letting them venture into particular passions around the arts or the like, as mental health experts suggest, but through building up their capital for global competition.[49]

Conclusion

Social science analysts on Asian American educational achievement help direct our attention to parents' upbringing in Asia and on their worries around racism and a lack of cultural or social capital. This is useful and is corroborated with my research. But crucially, it is necessary to place these concerns within a broader context of racial capitalism, in particular the immigration laws that shape immigrants' positionality in the United States. Rather than asking if race is relevant, it is more productive to analyze how it influences the conditions that parents respond to. Racial capitalism explains how the superstructure of parenting strategies makes sense based on people's position within the global labor market.

Middle-class parenting has been described as concerted cultivation, opportunity hoarding, tiger parenting, and the like. Yet these explanations underappreciate the structural context around immigrant parents. This context consists of visa programs that set the stage for how immigrants can cross borders. Immigrant parents occupy uncertain positions in the white-collar workplace given their dependency on a legal system designed to serve employers. Racial stereotypes as the passive model minority or as the unwanted foreigner land on top of that positionality and help create the conditions of their employment.

Most research within sociology documents the effects of race and racism by revealing people's personal experiences with discrimination. While useful, this insufficiently recognizes how race sets the conditions of people's experiences as immigrant workers and parents. This chapter broke down the effects of racial capitalism and immigration through three parts: people's sense of unsteady economic grounding and racialization as economic threats in public discourse, the limits of personal skill accumulation and human capital, and the risk associated with global capitalism. Across each of these, their place within a global capitalism as racialized immigrants bears on their domestic decision making. It is not merely that they lack social capital or cultural capital but that they also must navigate their work and child rearing from a sense of precarity despite their white-collar stature. They have little confidence in their occupational longevity. From this perspective, they would be neglectful if they did not parent in an intentional fashion with supplemental education.

Immigrant parents have an uncertain sense of work and belonging, given that their ability to stay in the country depends on immigration rules governed by their employer and the state rather than themselves. While sociologists have been effective in beating back the model-minority stereotype, as articulated by Kristof and others, it has not fully grasped how such achievement represents reactions within a racial capitalism. Racial capitalism not only explains the stratification of people of color but also informs the legal and economic context of their personal decisions. Parenting choices cannot be adequately understood through discussions of family upbringings or individual-level fears around racism.

While we analyze the impact of racial capitalism on parenting, however, it is important not to lose sight of the effects of families' decisions. As these parents hoard opportunities, push to make their children stand out, and try to outcompete others, they take advantage of economic privileges that distance them from others, in particular the working class and poor of all races, including would-be allies. The goal here is not to applaud but to explain parents' choices. Only then can steps be taken to connect them to the conditions of others.

NOTES

1 Nicholas Kristof, "The Asian Advantage," *New York Times*, October 10, 2015, www.nytimes.com.
2 Kwon, "Good Immigrant, Bad Immigrant."
3 Bonilla-Silva, "Rethinking Racism."
4 Saw and Okazaki, "Family Emotion Socialization."
5 Friedman, *Playing to Win*; Lareau, *Unequal Childhoods*.
6 Park and Chie, *Asian American Education*; Pearce, "Effects of Cultural and Social Structural Factors."
7 Oh and Kim, "'Success Is Relative.'"
8 Schneider and Lee, "A Model for Academic Success."
9 Louie, *Compelled to Excel*.
10 Lee and Zhou, *The Asian American Achievement Paradox*.
11 Campbell, "The Roots of Gender Inequity in Technical Areas"; Dundes, Cho, and Kwak, "The Duty to Succeed."
12 Chin, *Stuck*.
13 Dhingra, *Hyper Education*.
14 Byun and Park, "The Academic Success of East Asian American Youth."
15 Omi and Winant, *Racial Formation in the United States*.
16 Melamed, "The Spirit of Neoliberalism."
17 Karuka, *Empire's Tracks*.
18 Johnson and Kelley, *Race, Capitalism, Justice*; Massey, "Residential Segregation."
19 Ortiz, *An African American and Latinx History of the United States*.
20 Livingston and Kahn, "An American Dream Unfulfilled."

21 Garcia et al., "The Color of COVID-19."

22 McClure et al., "Racial Capitalism within Public."

23 Takaki, *Strangers from a Different Shore.*

24 Jung, *Reworking Race*; Mathew, *Taxi!*.

25 Lee, *America for Americans.*

26 Ong and Liu, "US Immigration Policies and Asian Migration."

27 Verghese, "The Cowpath to America."

28 Bhalla, "'We Wanted to End Disparities at Work.'"

29 Ibid.

30 Reddy, *Nursing and Empire.*

31 Mary Hanna and Jeanne Batalova, "Indian Immigrants in the United States," Migration Policy Institute, October 16, 2020, www.migrationpolicy.org.

32 Rudrappa, "Cyber-Coolies and Techno-Braceros."

33 Banerjee, "Flexible Hiring."

34 Josh Harkinson, "How H-1B Visas Are Screwing Tech Workers," *Mother Jones,* February 22, 2013, www.motherjones.com.

35 Julia Preston, "Large Companies Game H-1B Visa Program, Costing the U.S. Jobs," *New York Times,* November 10, 2015, www.nytimes.com.

36 Stephen Stock, Julie Putnam, Scott Pham, and Jeremy Carroll, "Silicon Valley's 'Body Shop' Secret: Highly Educated Foreign Workers Treated like Indentured Servants," *NBC Bay Area,* www.nbcbayarea.com.

37 Banerjee, "Flexible Hiring."

38 Indians in Monterrey have even created their own Facebook group, www.facebook.com/groups/334564163419349/.

39 Park et al., "Learning beyond the School Walls."

40 US Census Bureau: State and County QuickFacts. Data derived from population estimates, American community survey, census of population and housing, state and county housing unit estimates, county business patterns, non-employer statistics, economic census, survey of business owners, building permits; Source: US Census Bureau, 2010–14 American Community Survey Five-Year Estimates.

41 Hanna and Batalova, "Indian Immigrants."

42 Takei and Sakamoto, "Do College-Educated, Native-Born Asian Americans Face a Glass Ceiling?"

43 Lowe, *Immigrant Acts.*

44 Kuo, Malhotra, and Mo, "Social Exclusion and Political Identity."

45 Li, "Social Capital and Economic Outcomes."

46 Raleigh and Kao, "Do Immigrant Minority Parents Have More Consistent College Aspirations for their Children?"

47 Dhingra, *Hyper Education*; Park, "It Takes a Village."

48 Suruchi Sharma, "90 Percenters Get Cornell, Ivy League, but Not DU," *Times of India,* June 18, 2012, http://timesofindia.indiatimes.com.

49 Ginsburg, "The Importance of Play."

BIBLIOGRAPHY

Banerjee, Payal. "Flexible Hiring, Immigration, and Indian IT Workers' Experiences of Contract Work in the United States." In *People at Work*, edited by Marjorie DeVault, 97–111. New York: New York University Press, 2008.

———. "Indian Information Technology Workers in the United States: The H-1B Visa, Flexible Production, and the Racialization of Labor." *Critical Sociology* 32, no. 2–3 (2006): 425–45.

Bhalla, Vibha. "'We Wanted to End Disparities at Work': Physician Migration, Racialization, and a Struggle for Equality." *Journal of American Ethnic History* 29, no. 3 (2010): 40–78.

Bonilla-Silva, Eduardo. "Rethinking Racism: Toward a Structural Interpretation." *American Sociological Review* 62, no. 3 (1997): 465–80.

Byun, Soo-yong, and Hyunjoon Park. "The Academic Success of East Asian American Youth: The Role of Shadow Education." *Sociology of Education* 85, no. 1 (2012): 40–60.

Campbell, J. R. "The Roots of Gender Inequity in Technical Areas." *Journal of Research in Science Teaching* 2, no. 8 (1991): 251–64.

Chin, Margaret M. *Stuck: Why Asian Americans Don't Reach the Top of the Corporate Ladder*. New York: New York University Press, 2020.

Dhingra, Pawan. *Hyper Education: Why Good Schools, Good Grades, and Good Behavior Are Not Enough*. New York: New York University Press, 2020.

Dundes, Lauren, Eunice Cho, and Spencer Kwak. "The Duty to Succeed: Honor versus Happiness in College and Career Choices of East Asian Students in the United States." *Pastoral Care in Education* 27, no. 2 (2009): 135–56.

Friedman, Hillary. *Playing to Win: Raising Children in a Competitive Culture*. Berkeley: University of California Press, 2013.

Garcia, Marc A., Patricia A. Homan, Catherine García, and Tyson H. Brown. "The Color of COVID-19: Structural Racism and the Disproportionate Impact of the Pandemic on Older Black and Latinx Adults." *Journals of Gerontology: Series B* 76, no. 3 (2021): 75–80.

Ginsburg, Kenneth R. "The Importance of Play in Promoting Healthy Child Development and Maintaining Strong Parent-Child Bonds." *Pediatrics* 119, no. 1 (2007): 182–91.

Johnson, Walter, and Robin D. G. Kelley, eds. 2018. *Race, Capitalism, Justice*. Vol. 1. Cambridge, MA: MIT Press.

Jung, Moon-Kie. *Reworking Race: The Making of Hawaii's Interracial Labor Movement*. New York: Columbia University Press, 2006.

Karuka, Manu. *Empire's Tracks*. Berkeley: University of California Press, 2019.

Kim, Claire Jean. "The Racial Triangulation of Asian Americans." *Politics & Society* 27, 1 (1999): 105–38.

Kuo, Alexander, Neil Malhotra, and Cecilia Hyunjung Mo. "Social Exclusion and Political Identity: The Case of Asian American Partisanship." *Journal of Politics* 79, no. 1 (2017): 17–32.

Kwon, Sarah. 2019. "Good Immigrant, Bad Immigrant: The Intersection between Model Minority Myth and the Good/Bad Immigrant Dichotomy for Undocumented Asian Youth." Master's thesis, California State University, Los Angeles.

Lareau, Annette. *Unequal Childhoods: Class, Race, and Family Life.* Berkeley: University of California Press, 2011.

Lee, Erika. *America for Americans: A History of Xenophobia in the United States.* New York: Basic Books, 2019.

Lee, Jennifer, and Min Zhou. *The Asian American Achievement Paradox.* New York: Russell Sage Foundation, 2015.

Li, Peter S. "Social Capital and Economic Outcomes for Immigrants and Ethnic Minorities." *Journal of International Migration and Integration/Revue de l'integration et de la migration internationale* 5, no. 2 (2004): 171–90.

Livingston, Gretchen, and Joan R. Kahn. "An American Dream Unfulfilled: The Limited Mobility of Mexican Americans." *Social Science Quarterly* 83, no. 4 (2002): 1003–12.

Louie, Vivian S. *Compelled to Excel: Immigration, Education, and Opportunity among Chinese Americans.* Stanford, CA: Stanford University Press, 2004.

Lowe, Lisa. *Immigrant Acts: On Asian American Cultural Politics.* Durham, NC: Duke University Press, 1996.

Massey, Douglas. "Residential Segregation Is the Linchpin of Racial Stratification." *City & Community* 15, no. 1 (2016): 4–7.

Mathew, Biju. *Taxi!: Cabs and Capitalism in New York City.* Ithaca, NY: Cornell University Press, 2008.

McClure, Elizabeth, Pavithra Vasudevan, Zinzi Bailey, Snehal Patel, and Whitney R Robinson. "Racial Capitalism within Public Health—How Occupational Settings Drive COVID-19 Disparities." *American Journal of Epidemiology*189, no. 11 (2020): 1244–53.

Melamed, Jodi. "The Spirit of Neoliberalism: From Racial Liberalism to Neoliberal Multiculturalism." *Social Text* 24, no. 4 (89) (2006): 1–25.

Oh, Christine J., and Nadia Y. Kim. "'Success Is Relative:' Comparative Social Class and Ethnic Effects in an Academic Paradox." *Sociological Perspectives* 59, no. 2 (2016): 270–95.

Omi, Michael, and Howard Winant. *Racial Formation in the United States.* New York: Routledge, 2014.

Ong, Paul, and John M. Liu. "US Immigration Policies and Asian Migration." In *The New Asian Immigration in Los Angeles and Global Restructuring,* edited by Paul Ong, Edna Bonacich, and Lucie Cheng, 45–73. Philadelphia: Temple University Press, 1994.

Ortiz, Paul. *An African American and Latinx History of the United States.* New York: Beacon Press, 2018.

Park, Clara, and Marilyn Mei-Ying Chie. *Asian American Education: Prospects and Challenges.* Westport, CT: Bergin and Garvey, 1999.

Park, Hyunjoon, Claudia Buchmann, Jaesung Choi, and Joseph J. Merry. "Learning beyond the School Walls: Trends and Implications." *Annual Review of Sociology* 42, no. 1 (2016): 231–52.

Park, Julie J. "It Takes a Village (or an Ethnic Economy): The Varying Roles of Socioeconomic Status, Religion, and Social Capital in SAT Preparation for Chinese and Korean American Students." *American Educational Research Journal* 49, no. 4 (2012): 624–50.

Pearce, Richard. "Effects of Cultural and Social Structural Factors on the Achievement of White and Chinese American Students at School Transition Points." *American Educational Research Journal* 43, no. 1 (2006): 75–101.

Raleigh, Elizabeth, and Grace Kao. "Do Immigrant Minority Parents Have More Consistent College Aspirations for Their Children?" *Social Science Quarterly* 91, no. 4 (2010): 1083–1102.

Reddy, Sujani. *Nursing and Empire: Gendered Labor and Migration from India to the United States*. Chapel Hill: University of North Carolina Press, 2015.

Rudrappa, Sharmila. "Cyber-Coolies and Techno-Braceros: Race and Commodification of Indian Information Technology Guest Workers in the United States." *University of San Francisco Law Review* 44 (2009): 353–72.

Saw, Anne, and Sumie Okazaki. "Family Emotion Socialization and Affective Distress in Asian American and White American College Students." *Asian American Journal of Psychology* 1, no. 2 (2010): 81.

Schneider, Barbara, and Yongsook Lee. "A Model for Academic Success: The School and Home Environment of East Asian Students." *Anthropology and Education Quarterly* 21, no. 4 (1990): 358–77.

Takaki, Ronald. *Strangers from a Different Shore: A History of Asian Americans*. Boston: Little, Brown, 1989.

Takei, Isao, and Arthur Sakamoto. "Do College-Educated, Native-Born Asian Americans Face a Glass Ceiling in Obtaining Managerial Authority?" *Asian American Policy Review* 17 (2008): 73–85.

Verghese, Abraham. "The Cowpath to America." *New Yorker* (June 23, 1997): 70–89.

Xie, Yu, and Kimberly Goyette. "Social Mobility and the Educational Choices of Asian Americans." *Social Science Research* 32, no. 3 (2003): 467–98.

Zhou, Min, and Susan Kim. "Community Forces, Social Capital, and Educational Achievement: The Case of Supplementary Education in the Chinese and Korean Immigrant Communities." *Harvard Educational Review* 76, no. 1 (2006): 1–29.

4

Education for Community Empowerment

Layered Histories of Colonization and the Ongoing Movement for Decolonization in Guåhan's Social Studies Curriculum

KEVIN ESCUDERO

Education and colonization are closely linked processes both in terms of how the colonial project has historically been implemented and ways that colonized communities have sought to engage in a process of decolonization. When asked about this topic, especially in light of the Guam Commission on Decolonization's charge, which includes an educational mandate to increase the public's awareness about the implications of decolonization for all members of the island's community, Melvin Won Pat-Borja, the commission's executive director, explained,

> And so when it comes to education, it's such a critical piece [of the work that we do] because in a lot of ways we have to unlearn certain things . . . I think that's also important in the experience of the Commission on Self-Determination [which preceded the Commission on Decolonization] . . . [Previously] there was a plebiscite where status quo with improvements was the most popular vote. . . . It didn't say what those improvements were, nobody knew. . . . I feel like if people were better educated [on the issue] that we would be able to make a choice, not only to make a better choice but that we would be more motivated to even participate [in a future plebiscite]. I think a lot of people on Guam are apathetic [about the issue] because, "What's the point, didn't we do that already? . . . We tried that already so don't waste my time."[1]

As Won Pat-Borja's quote highlights, public education initiatives are a central component of ensuring that Guåhan (Guam)'s current and future generations are well prepared to participate in an upcoming plebiscite regarding the island's future political status and relationship with the United States.[2] Such a vote would be an important step toward Guåhan's decolonization, as it would provide members of the island's community, those individuals who for generations have been subject to multiple colonial regimes, a choice in their political status and thus greater autonomy over their own lives and futures. Relatedly, a key component of this vote—and conversations surrounding it—is the centering of CHamoru perspectives, given their role as the Indigenous people of Guåhan, whose culture was directly impacted by the violence of the colonial process.[3]

A present-day US territory in the western Pacific Ocean, Guåhan is the southernmost island in the Mariana Islands archipelago. After more than two hundred years of Spanish colonial rule, the island was ceded to the United States in 1898 with the signing of the Treaty of Paris, which also separated it from the rest of the archipelago. Since 1898, Guåhan's people have been subjected to US and Japanese imperial rule, while their northern relatives were subjected to German, Japanese, and US colonial rule. Efforts to contest colonization have been ongoing from the Spanish colonial period through today. Examples include the CHamoru-Spanish wars in the late 1670s, petitions submitted to the US Congress advocating self-governance from the early 1900s, CHamoru underground resistance to the Japanese military occupation during World War II, and the establishment of two Commissions on Self-Determination in the 1980s and the Commission on Decolonization in 1997.

Given the role of education in the island's ongoing movement for decolonization and the complexity of the Guåhan's colonial history, in this chapter I ask: How has education in Guåhan shifted from a tool of exercising colonial power to a key strategy within Indigenous-led movements for decolonization and self-determination? Relatedly, how have educators in Guåhan's public schools approached the island's layered imperial histories as part of the curriculum in Guam history and other social studies courses? To answer these questions, I draw on secondary literature, archival research at the Government of Guam Archives in Hagåtña, an online survey I developed and that was administered by the Guam Department of Education to public middle and high school social studies teachers, and observations from a teacher training that I co-facilitated for Guåhan social studies teachers on approaches for incorporating discussions of Guåhan's quest for decolonization into the Guam history and social studies curriculum. In this chapter, I argue that sociological research methods can assist in illuminating the implications of key arguments regarding present-day US imperialism as discussed within American/ethnic studies scholarship. This can be seen in ways that teachers are working to develop innovative ways to assist students in imagining an alternative future for their island that provides for the reclamation of colonial tools and centers Indigenous knowledge.

This chapter draws on and contributes to research in American/ethnic studies by combining its increasingly layered approach for analyzing instances of US imperialism (in Guåhan and other US colonies) and with the use of sociological research methods to study how this plays out in the context of colonial and decolonial educational processes. Since the onset of colonization, the people of Guåhan began discussing its impact and ways to counteract its effects. In terms of academic scholarship on this topic, specifically by individuals from colonized groups, such work proliferated during the period leading up to and following the "era of decolonization." This was a period from the 1940s to the 1960s, when many European empires across the globe felt the pressure of colonized peoples' movements for independence and self-determination.[4] With regard to the case of US imperialism, this work has often focused on the so-called edges of the US empire state, namely archipelagic areas under US jurisdiction in the Pacific Ocean and Caribbean Sea. American Studies/ethnic studies scholarship (along with some interdisciplinary sociological research) has sought to contextualize the study of US imperialism in relation to the effects of US militarism, settler colonialism, and movements for decolonization.[5] Yet an important addition to this conversation that American/ethnic studies scholarship has brought to bear is an analysis of the layered and relational effect of different colonial regimes on colonized peoples and their movements for decolonization.[6] As I demonstrate in this chapter, the adoption of a layered approach allows for an understanding of the continued legacies of colonialism in the lives of Indigenous and other colonized peoples, the ways that colonial empires built on and adopted the practices of one another, and the strategies that colonized communities have utilized to engage in a process of decolonization and self-determination across generations. Sociological research methods, namely historical sociological, survey, and qualitative (ethnographic and interview-based) methods, complement this development by assisting researchers in unpacking the full reach of these processes and the ways that they have impacted (and continue to impact) the lives of Indigenous peoples.

In the sections that follow, I begin by providing an overview of the ways that education has shifted from its use as a tool of colonial administrations to assimilate Indigenous CHamoru people into an "American" lifestyle to one that supports community empowerment and Indigenous resurgence as part of the decolonization process. I then discuss the methodological approaches I employed to understand how teachers engage the legacies of Guåhan's multiple colonial regimes in the Guam history and other social studies classroom contexts. This is followed by an analysis of the ways educators balance addressing the impact of these layered colonial histories on the lives of Guåhan's people alongside discussions of education for community empowerment.

The Shift from Colonial to Decolonial Approaches to Education in Guåhan

The shift to a decolonial educational approach did not occur as a result of the benevolence of colonial administrators but rather through community-led advocacy efforts that came to a head in the 1960s and '70s. Given this chapter's focus on education's role as a tool for preparing and empowering the next generation of Guåhan's youth to participate in discussions about their island's future political status and about the layered nature of colonialism, it is important to understand how this shift came about.

Prior to the arrival of colonial powers to the Mariana Islands, CHamoru education systems were structured to facilitate knowledge sharing in an intergenerational manner such as seen in the *guma'uritao*, where young men in a clan were educated by their elders in the ways of daily life.[7] With the onset of colonialism, however, foreign powers—Spanish then US and Japanese—used education systems to assimilate and control CHamorus, as they did in other parts of the globe. During the Spanish colonial period (1668–1898), education in Guåhan was primarily linked to the Catholic Church's efforts to Christianize the CHamoru people.[8] The Spanish did so by drawing on local CHamoru cultural practices to spread their message: "Spanish missionaries . . . used the popular . . . customs of competition in games among villages as a means to teach the Christian faith."[9] Additionally, the missionaries sought to cultivate a new generation of CHamoru leaders who would spread the word of the church among the island's community, assisting in the conversion of other CHamorus to Christianity.[10] This process often entailed the training of CHamoru elites hoping that it would encourage others in the community to do the same.[11] These practices were codified by formal instruction in schools. Schools were also used to promote Spanish culture and language over that of the CHamoru culture and language. In 1820, the Spanish colonial administration decreed that schools were to teach the Spanish language and that CHamorus were forbidden to speak the CHamoru language.[12] In 1858, education was gradually made compulsory for "all children ages 4 through 10 years [of age]."[13]

As CHamoru historian Alfred Flores explains, in comparison to the Spanish colonial administration's approach to education, whereby it prioritized the education of the elites, education during the US colonial period (1898–1941, 1944–present) has targeted a broader cross section of the island's population, primarily to fast track the assimilation of CHamorus into the "American" way of life.[14] In doing so, the island's education system parallels programs across other parts of the United States, which historically targeted Indigenous peoples and immigrants. More specifically, the US government's educational policies drew heavily on the model of Native American boarding schools, which were set up across the United States and served to "eliminate Indigenous cultural identity through curriculum and policies intended to assimilate native children."[15] These schools were extremely violent in their treatment of Indigenous children, often inflicting physical and cultural harm that continues to be felt across generations of Indigenous communities in the United States. With the entire island of Guåhan being declared a US Naval base from 1898 to 1950, "the naval admiral or commander appointed other lower-ranking naval officers to oversee various island-wide institutions such as Guam's Department of Education. Thus, Guam's public school system was imbued with the same colonial and militaristic sensibilities seen in native boarding schools in the continental United States."[16]

Japan occupied Guåhan during World War II from 1942 to 1944. The Japanese colonial school system was "similar . . . to that of the United

States" in that it focused on transforming CHamorus into "good" colonial citizens through instruction in Japanese culture and language.[17] Japanese administrators also established "two boarding schools in Guam . . . to prepare Chamorro students who were advanced in the Japanese language for employment in offices and schools throughout the island."[18] Like the Spanish colonial administrators, the Japanese government sought to train local-level bureaucrats who would then assist in carrying out and enforcing their colonial agenda in Guåhan.

Throughout the Spanish, Japanese, and US colonial periods, language served as a key mechanism through which colonial rule was imposed upon CHamorus. Similar to the Spanish colonial government's promotion of the Spanish language and culture through the school system, the US naval administration implemented a series of English-only policies as part of its Americanization program that were first codified in Captain Richard Leary's issuance of General Order No. 12 in 1900.[19] Additionally, "in 1922 . . . Governor Althouse had all Chamorro-English dictionaries through the island's schools collected and burned."[20] As noted earlier, the Japanization process also entailed the imposition of the Japanese language as taught within the local school system accompanied by bans on speaking English and CHamoru in public places. Despite colonial administrators' efforts to suppress the CHamoru language, CHamorus repeatedly voiced their discontent with these laws and continued speaking their language in the household and other spaces that were outside the gaze of colonial rulers.

During the second half of the twentieth century, with greater representation of CHamorus in the Guam Legislature (I Liheslaturan Guåhan) following the establishment of a civil government with the signing of the Organic Act of Guam, CHamoru educators and activists successfully implemented significant changes to the island's education system, namely legislating the incorporation of the CHamoru language, history, and culture into the curriculum for Guåhan's schools.[21] In the 1960s and '70s, CHamoru activists launched a renaissance of the CHamoru language that later resulted in a renaissance of CHamoru culture more broadly.[22] As CHamoru politician, educator, and activist Pilar Lujan explained, "In the 1970s, Guam's legislators encouraged the use and teaching of the Chamorro language. The late Senator Frank G. Lujan sponsored Public Law 12–31, which authorized the Board of Education to initiate and develop bilingual/bicultural education program[s] emphasizing the language and culture of the Chamorro people. Senator Paul J. Bordallo authored Public Law 12–132, which made both English and Chamorro the official languages of Guam."[23] Though these policies were designed to remedy decades of colonial control of Guåhan's education system, these changes were not necessarily met with excitement by all members of the island's community. Debates ensued regarding the utility of speaking the CHamoru language to secure employment and about the best means by which to develop an accurate CHamoru orthography given that the language was primarily an oral one.[24]

In January 1977, Robert Underwood and Clotilde Gould, along with twelve other committee members, organized the Chamorro Studies Convention.[25] The two-day convening included a welcome by local political officials; keynote lectures by Dr. Laura Thompson, Dr. Donald Topping, and Dr. Fred Reinman; a series of workshops on the CHamoru language, history, and culture; and a fiesta dinner. Based on newspaper reports chronicling the convention's events from the personal archives of Dr. Robert Underwood and Dr. Michael Bevacqua, many local teachers attended to hear the presenters from Guåhan, the Commonwealth of the Northern Mariana Islands, and scholars from the United States who had previously spent time in Guåhan studying the island's history and culture.

Building on the momentum of Public Law 12-31 and events such as the Chamorro Studies Convention, in 1991 the Twenty-First Guam Legislature passed Bill No. 45, "An Act to Repeal and Reenact §8103, Chapter 8, Title 17, Guam Code Annotated, Requiring Mandatory Courses in the Chamorro Language and in the History of Guam in Public Schools." As a result, not only were additional plans developed for Chamorro language instruction but a "mandatory course [was provided] in all public middle schools and high schools on the History of Guam, inclusive of the Organic Act or the Constitution of Guam . . . and Guam's quest for political status, including the Commonwealth Act." The bill also mandated that "no student who completes his or her senior year on Guam will be allowed to graduate from high school without having completed a full year course on the History of Guam." The Board of Education then implemented these directives through a revision of the school curriculum beginning with the 1993–94 school year.

In addition to the greater inclusion of CHamoru language education and cultural history within the classroom context, government mandates for public-facing educational initiatives on self-determination and decolonization were included in recent bills passed by the Guam Legislature establishing the two Commissions on Self-Determination and the Commission on Decolonization in 1980, 1984, and 1997, respectively.[26] As compared to general knowledge about CHamoru history and culture, these educational initiatives were focused on preparing voters for their participation in a political status plebiscite to determine the island's future political status. In 2020, as part of these efforts, the Commission on Decolonization, with a grant from the Department of the Interior, commissioned a self-governance study. Led by professors Carlyle Corbin and Kenneth Gofigan Kuper, the study discusses the importance of the United Nations as a key international forum for holding the United States accountable regarding its ongoing colonization of Guåhan and the implications of a change in the island's political status concerning areas that would directly impact residents' everyday lives. Released in late 2021, the study will be accompanied by two interrelated educational components: an island-wide social media campaign to disseminate the study's findings to a broad cross section of Guåhan's population and a middle and high school social studies curriculum to support the ongoing educational activities of Guam history and other social studies teachers. The Guåhan government's use of educational outreach campaigns to ensure that community members are aware of the implications of decolonization and self-determination demonstrates an important departure from education's previous use by colonial administrators in Guåhan.

Early uses of education in Guåhan among the Spanish, Japanese, and US colonial powers often drew on the strategies of the previous colonial administration. The shift in education's role, however, from a tool of colonial assimilation to one which has helped facilitate processes of decolonization in Guåhan underscores the transformative role of Indigenous-led social movements in bringing about long-term social change. Using Guåhan's education system as a forum for raising the political and oppositional consciousness of young people today, activists during the post-1960s period developed CHamoru language and Guam history courses, which have helped lay the foundation for a reclamation of CHamoru culture and identity.

Examining Strategies Utilized in the Guåhan History and Social Studies Classroom

To understand how educators in Guåhan today not only celebrate the CHamoru language and culture but also engage students in discussions regarding the relational effects of Spanish, Japanese, and US colonial regimes, I utilized sociological research methods. In particular, I employed a mixed methods approach consisting of archival research to understand the context regarding the teaching of CHamoru history and culture in Guåhan public schools, an online survey with Guåhan middle and high school social studies teachers, and ethnographic observations over the course of a three-day workshop I co-facilitated on ways that teachers might incorporate discussions of Indigenous-led movements for decolonization and self-determination into their classrooms. By taking such an approach, I was also able to engage a broad cross section of teachers while following the Guåhan government's health safety protocols given the impact of the global coronavirus pandemic.

Archival research was carried out at the Government of Guam archives at the Nieves M. Flores Memorial Library in Hagåtña. The official repository of government agency materials, the archives contained agency records and topic-based vertical files on issues relevant to members of the Guåhan community. On education, the vertical files largely contained articles published by local newspapers about funding for public education, the development of culturally relevant curricula for CHamoru and other Pacific Islander students in Guåhan, and litigation pertaining to agency officials and teachers.

Moreover, to ensure that the project reached a broad cross section of social studies teachers in Guåhan's public school system, I partnered with the Guam Department of Education (GDOE) to administer the survey. In summer 2021, after receiving approval from GDOE deputy superintendent for curriculum and instruction, Joseph Sanchez, I worked with GDOE staff to send an introductory letter about the project and a link to the online survey to all middle and high school teachers. Eligibility to participate was determined by the courses that the teachers had offered during the previous year or were planning to offer in the coming year. Nineteen middle and high school social studies teachers across

Guåhan responded to the online survey. Survey questions covered topics such as the length of time that educators had taught in Guåhan, what social studies courses they currently offer and have offered in the past, what assignments they utilize in the classroom, and whether they discuss issues of Guåhan's current and past political statuses with their students.

In July 2021, informed by the responses I had received from the survey earlier in the summer, I partnered with GDOE, the Guam Commission on Decolonization, the Guam Museum, and Guampedia to develop a three-day workshop on approaches to teaching about decolonization and self-determination in Guåhan social studies classrooms. Following a welcome by Joseph Sanchez, the workshop was kicked off with a lecture by Dr. Kenneth Kuper, an assistant professor of political science, CHamoru studies, and Micronesian studies at the University of Guam, on the implications of Guåhan's political status as an unincorporated US territory. This was followed by two working sessions, one in which teachers became familiar with a decolonization curriculum developed by Melvin Won Pat-Borja, executive director of the Commission on Decolonization, and another in which they provided input into a series of lesson plans that I am currently in the process of developing on the topic for use in Guam history courses. We then provided a discussion of ways that teachers might utilize community cultural institutions such as the Guam Museum's permanent exhibit, *I Hinanao-ta, Nu I Manaotao Tano—I CHamoru Siha* (The Journey of the CHamoru people) and Guampedia, a public-facing community resource providing accessible academically peer-reviewed information about Guåhan's history. Teachers were recruited to participate in the workshop through outreach conducted by GDOE. GDOE staff first reached out to middle and high school principals who were then asked to nominate two or three social studies teachers from their schools to participate in the workshop. In exchange for their participation, teachers were provided with the option of receiving either continuing education units or graduate credits from the University of Guam. A total of nine teachers participated in the workshop over the span of the three days, with others attending for one or two days but not completing the entire program. These teachers came from middle and high schools across the island teaching Guam history and CHamoru language courses to CHamoru and non-CHamoru students. At the end of the workshop, teachers submitted reflection papers on what they learned from participating in the training and how they planned to implement the material covered into their own classrooms during the upcoming school year.

Emerging Approaches for Teaching about the Legacies of Guåhan's Layered Colonial Regimes and Ongoing Decolonization Movement

In this section, I highlight ways that GDOE middle and high school social studies teachers have begun to engage the layered histories of Guåhan's colonial regimes in their classrooms and to connect these histories with discussions of the ongoing movement for the island's decolonization. I argue that while teachers were very much aware of these layered colonial histories, with some involved in decolonization activism themselves, they encountered two challenges: emphasizing the connections between the layered imperial regimes in Guåhan in a way that was relevant to students' everyday lives, and having students adopt a nuanced perspective on US colonial rule. Though there was variation among teachers' approaches to engaging these topics with their students, these preliminary observations might assist in understanding the ways that such conversations are taking place in classrooms in Guåhan today.

Workshop Observations

Given that Guam history is a required component of students' educational experience at the high school level, it is a context during which to introduce them to the relationship between the different colonial regimes that have occupied Guåhan. This also dovetails nicely with the Commission on Decolonization's recently completed self-governance study, which provides a culturally relevant approach to the island's history and ongoing efforts in Guåhan's quest for self-determination. It has also served as a core resource and was provided to workshop participants for developing their own lesson plans on this topic.

In conversations with GDOE administrators leading up to the decolonization curriculum workshop, a common topic of discussion was the Guam District Level Curriculum Map and Guam History College and

Career Readiness Standards, which teachers were required to follow in delivering content to students. These concerns were related to recent efforts among GDOE administrators to align more closely the curriculum of Guåhan's public schools with that of the rest of the United States, a colonial act within itself.[27] As Guåhan is an unincorporated US territory, the concerns of Guåhan's youth are not necessarily the same as those of their peers in other parts of the country; they instead center around the island's subordinate legal status within the United States. In fact, this distinction and the need for greater local control over educational issues were concerns raised by community members as early as the 1970s.[28] As was evident in the schedule that one teacher provided, the material in Guam history courses today is broken into four quarters of the academic year.[29] During the first quarter, students focused on the geology of the Pacific region and Guam, as well as on ancient Chamorro society. This was followed in the second quarter by the Spanish colonial period and the US Navy's administration of the island. The third quarter continued with the US naval government and included Japanese occupation during World War II. The final fourth quarter was devoted to the era spanning the post–World War II period to today. Notably, the curriculum map did not use the term *colonial* to describe the Spanish, Japanese, or US presence on the island and instead used occupation for both the Japanese and US naval government eras. Additionally, the US naval government period spanned two quarters of the academic year though it only constituted fifty years of Guåhan's history as compared to the precolonial and Spanish periods, which constituted hundreds of years of the island's history. A parent of a child in the teacher's class, who introduced me to the school's Guam history teachers, remarked that some of the teachers did not even make it through the entire curriculum outlined in the GDOE's suggested schedule, which itself included a note clarifying that pacing of the material was at each teacher's discretion. When discussing efforts to complete the curriculum in addition to covering the relationships between the different periods, teachers shared how they often became competing priorities and that if they had additional resources and training on how to do so, they might be better able to complete both aims during the academic year.

As part of the summer workshop, on the third day teachers were placed into groups and asked to develop lesson plans for the Guam history curriculum, drawing on the recently completed self-governance study, to assist students in developing a critical lens for examining the island's history under Spanish, Japanese, and US rule. Teachers chose three overarching topics from the study—language, land, and governance—and then proceeded to collaborate on their lesson plan ideas. As a closing activity, teachers presented their groups' ideas to the rest of the workshop participants. They then completed the lesson plans on their own and submitted them as a requirement to receive credit for their participation in the workshop. The lesson plans on the CHamoru language and on land stood out as providing especially unique insight into ways that educators in Guåhan are presenting material regarding the impact of the island's layered colonial regimes as they affect the lives of CHamorus and others in Guåhan.

Members of the group who were focused on CHamoru language instruction began by recounting concerns expressed by some, pre-dominantly linguists, that the CHamoru language has been so heavily influenced by colonial languages such as Spanish and English that it is too mixed of a language to be considered an "authentically" Indigenous language. Teachers also shared how some students in their classes complained about learning CHamoru, claiming that it was not useful in everyday life. As part of their ideas for lesson plans, the teachers in the group commented on the role of language instruction not only in increasing students' fluency in CHamoru but also for providing a means from which to better understand CHamoru worldviews and epistemologies. They then proposed beginning with familiarizing students with the consequences that their family members faced for speaking the CHamoru language during the Japanese and US colonial regimes by having students interview *manaiña* (elders) in their family and/or in their village. These narratives could then be juxtaposed with an overview of the circumstances surrounding the establishment of the Kumisón i Fino' CHamoru yan i Fina'nå'guen i Historiata yan i Lina'la'i Taotao Tåno' (Commission on CHamoru language and the teaching of the history and culture of the Indigenous people of Guam) as part of what has become known as the CHamoru Renaissance. Providing students an opportunity to trace the processes through which members of the CHamoru community asserted their agency through the right to speak their Indigenous language on their own terms, the group's lesson plans offered a way to center Indigenous knowledge and draw comparisons with other Native Pacific communities that have sought to do the same, such as the Māori in Aotearoa and Kānaka Maoli in Hawaiʻi. It also highlighted the importance of understanding the layered effects of Japanese and US colonial rule while demonstrating to students the relevance of these practices to their lives today.

Along these lines, the group that developed lesson plans on the issue of land sought to assist students in learning more about the processes through which CHamorus in Guåhan have been dispossessed of their land across generations to a point where the US military now owns over a third of the island's overall territory. They planned to accomplish this by having students create a set of maps of the island and trace the shift in land use and tenure during different stages of US colonialism (e.g., during the US naval administration as compared to the post-1950 period). The workshop co-instructors and I took this moment to comment to the teachers that their lesson plan also offers an opportunity for teachers to highlight for students the nuances of US colonialism and the development of strategies to challenge it. While activists during the first half of the American period (1898–1950) were highly invested in seeking access to US citizenship, as part of the US military buildup in the post-1950 period, much of the land taken by the federal government was facilitated by CHamorus' status as US citizens (through the process of eminent domain). Though pointing out this tension would assist students in approaching US citizenship from a critical perspective, teachers mentioned having to navigate the multiple perspectives that students and their families hold about the federal government and their status as US citizens. This is particularly true for students whose grandparents were subjected to Japanese occupation during World War II and subsequent generations of family members who have served (or are currently serving) in the US military to honor the United States' efforts during the war. This conversation thus served as an important reminder to the teachers in the group of the ways that these layered colonial histories are useful in explaining the complex realities of everyday life in Guåhan and how the impact of each colonial regime is not necessarily as easily visible and resistance-inducing as one might imagine.

Survey Responses

From the online surveys I conducted with GDOE middle and high school social studies teachers in summer 2021, I learned how for many educators, the ways they approached teaching about decolonization was largely informed by their and their family's background, the demographics of the students in their classrooms, the academic training they received on contemporary movements for decolonization and Indigenous self-determination, and their involvement in these movements. Considering teachers' own explanations for making these choices in their classrooms illustrates the way they, too, are part of the social fabric of Guåhan and, given the need for additional curricular materials on the topic, are increasingly utilizing online, public-facing materials that also have the convenience of being updated much more quickly than printed textbooks.

Describing the importance of teaching about Guåhan's colonial past and connecting it to discussions of ongoing movements for Indigenous self-determination and decolonization, multiple teachers pointed to the importance of their own family histories, both as CHamorus and non-CHamorus, in motivating them to take on this task. As one social studies teacher explained, "I would say that my greatest source of information [on Guåhan's journey for decolonization and self-determination] was my family. My paternal grandfather was a Senator for several terms in the Guam Legislature and my grandmother, a public school teacher after World War II . . . There was always conversation regarding political status when there were family gatherings." These conversations at home stood in contrast to this teacher's own experiences during high school and the Guam history courses offered at that time: "In terms of formal education [about these issues], political status was not taught during the required Guam History class in high school. The discussions . . . were not in depth. Sad to say, I learned what happened historically in the Pacific from my family and when I attended college off island." For teachers such as this individual, whose primary exposure to the issue was at home and in college, their own experiences had an important impact on their decision to proactively teach about the topic rather than reproducing their own experiences in high school. In comparison to the CHamoru teacher, another social studies teacher who identified as Filipinx described their reasons for teaching about these topics: "I am Filipino born and raised in Guam and went to college in the US. [In college] I was part of a program where we taught a multicultural curriculum at the seventh-grade level, [and] I came back home and have participated in meetings with [a local organization of immigrant community members supporting CHamoru self-determination]." Informed by their positionality as a non-CHamoru educator but someone well-versed in discussions of race, identity, and culture from their undergraduate education, this teacher pointed to the connections between the experiences of Filipinx immigrants as colonized subjects as a means of building solidarity with CHamorus who have similarly been subjected to Spanish and US colonialism. Such an articulation of these connections provide insight into the way that educators teaching about the issue to a diverse classroom context might model for their students the practice of allyship and coalition building while still drawing on the power of one's personal lived experience.

When asked about connecting historical accounts of Guåhan's colonial history with present-day movements for greater inclusion, teachers recounted how online tools were essential for conveying this information to students and in fact were able to use shifts in the classroom format as a result of the coronavirus pandemic to their advantage. They shared: "The students . . . really enjoy the videos of people from Guam discussing Guam's political status. My grade level social studies class accesses articles available [online] from Guampedia.com and current local periodicals . . . [Also] with the implementation of the online model of learning, videos, web quests, research presented on Google slides, and the use of online graphic tools have been successful." Similarly, another social studies teacher wrote, "Sources I use [to inform students about these topics] include articles from Guampedia, [the] Pacific New Center and other sources [including] position papers from the year 2000, political cartoons, etc." Teachers' use of online resources and content in these examples allowed them to build from where the course textbooks, which were developed in the 1980s and '90s, stopped and to engage students further using a medium in which they were already well-versed.

Conclusion

As I have shown in this chapter, American/ethnic studies scholarship's discussion of a layered approach to colonialism and sociological research methods are co-constitutive in illuminating the full extent of colonial subordination as well as ongoing efforts to contest its harmful effects. This work highlights how rather than serving as a tool of colonial oppression, educators have reappropriated educational curricula as tools for decolonization in Guåhan, even incorporating it into the laws establishing government-supported entities such as the first and second Commissions on Self-Determination and Commission on Decolonization. This work also sheds light on how social science methods can be adapted, especially in online forms, in the face of global pandemics. As part of this shift, Guam history teachers are employing innovative, exciting approaches to incorporate analyses of Guåhan's layered colonial histories into their curricula and to engage in a critical analysis of US empire today.

NOTES

I would like to thank co-conveners Kristin Oberiano, Paula Park, and Yu-Ting Huang and the participants in the Northeast Pacific Island Studies Workshop for their helpful comments on this chapter.

1 Melvin Won Pat-Borja (executive director, Commission on Decolonization), interview with author, May 2021.

2 Throughout this chapter, I use the spelling Guåhan rather than the Anglicized term Guam when referring to the name of the present-day US territory in the western Pacific Ocean. I do so because as part of the orthography established by the Kumisón i Fino' CHamoru yan i Fina'nå'guen i Historiata yan i Lina'la'i Taotao Tåno' (Commission on CHamoru language and the teaching of the history and culture of the Indigenous people of Guam), it was determined that Guåhan most closely reflects the name for the island in the CHamoru language. With regard to the plebiscite, in 2000 I Liheslaturan Guåhan (the Guam Legislature) passed Public Law 25-106, which mandated that the island's government hold a political status plebiscite including three political status options—"independence, free association, or statehood"—for "the native inhabitants of Guam." The vote was scheduled to be held in 2000, then 2002; it is now delayed indefinitely due to recent litigation at the federal level.

3 Based on the official orthography established by Kumisión i Fino' CHamoru yan i Fina'nå'guen i Historia yan i Lina'la' i Taotao Tåno' (Commission on CHamoru language and the teaching of the history and culture of the Indigenous People of Guam), I use the spelling "CHamoru" when referring to the Indigenous peoples

of Guåhan. The spelling "Chamorro" is used when quoting or paraphrasing authors when this was the spelling and/or pronunciation used by them.

4 Getachew, *Worldmaking after Empire*; Mar, *Decolonisation and the Pacific*.

5 Alamo-Pastrana, *Seams of Empire*; Baldoz, *The Third Asiatic Invasion*; Fujikane and Okamura, *Asian Settler Colonialism*; Go, *American Empire and the Politics of Meaning*; Isaac, *American Tropics*; Kaplan and Pease, *Cultures of United States Imperialism*; Kim, *Imperial Citizens*; Lutz and Enloe, *The Bases of Empire*; Nakano Glenn, "Settler Colonialism as Structure"; Shigematsu and Camacho, *Militarized Currents*; Tuck and Yang, "Decolonization Is Not a Metaphor."

6 Blackwell, "Indigeneity"; Camacho, *Cultures of Commemoration*; Caronan, *Legitimizing Empire*.

7 Lujan, "Role of Education in the Preservation of Guam's Indigenous Language." For additional information on the guma'uritao and the education that CHamoru youth received there, see the Guampedia entry on the topic: www.guampedia.com/guma-uritao/.

8 Del Priore, "Education on Guam During the Spanish Administration from 1668 to 1899," 24.

9 Ibid., 27.

10 Ibid., 30.

11 Ibid., 58, 72.

12 Ibid., 44.

13 Ibid., 83–84.

14 Flores, "US Colonial Education in Guam, 1899–1950."

15 Ibid.

16 Ibid. Indigenous peoples in the United States and Canada have been fighting for decades to raise awareness about the atrocities that took place at these boarding schools and to seek redress for the actions of the church that ran these schools. In summer 2021, the *New York Times* reported that members of the Cowessess First Nation discovered graves of hundreds of Indigenous children at the site of the Marieval Indian Residential School in Saskatchewan. This resulted in continued calls by the tribe's chief, Cadmus Delorme, for a papal apology from the Roman Catholic Church and greater self-governance as Indigenous nations. For more information on this saddening discovery, see Ian Austen and Dan Bilefsky, "Hundreds More Graves Found at Former Residential School in Canada," *New York Times*, June 24, 2021, www.nytimes.com.

17 Ibid.

18 Ibid.

19 Campbell, "General Order No. 12."

20 Flores, "US Colonial Education in Guam, 1899–1950."

21 Such efforts were later furthered by the first and second Commissions on Self-Determination and the Commission on Decolonization's educational mandates in the 1980s and '90s respectively.

22 Lujan, "Role of Education in the Preservation of Guam's Indigenous Language."

23 Ibid.

24 Ibid.

25 "CSC draws over 500 teachers," *UNION*, February 2, 1977.

26 Guam Public Law 15–128 (May 31, 1980) and Guam Public Law 23-147 (January 23, 1997). Under the oversight of the Commission on Self-Determination's Political Status Education Coordinating Commission, the Hale'ta Book Series was developed and used by teachers in Guåhan's public school system during the 1990s and early 2000s.

27 Temkar, "Calvo Praises New Common Core Curriculum."

28 Tennessen, "Needed Local Control of Public Education."

29 The names of teachers who participated in the workshop are not included in this chapter to respect the privacy of individual teachers and because I did not request such permission when conducting this research.

BIBLIOGRAPHY

Alamo-Pastrana, Carlos. *Seams of Empire: Race and Radicalism in Puerto Rico and the United States.* Gainesville: University of Florida Press, 2016.

Baldoz, Rick. *The Third Asiatic Invasion: Empire and Migration in Filipino America, 1898–1946.* New York: New York University Press, 2011.

Blackwell, Maylei. "Indigeneity." In *Keywords for Latina/o Studies,* edited by Deborah R. Vargas, Lawrence La Fountain-Stokes, and Nancy Raquel Mirabel, 100–5. New York: New York University Press, 2017.

Camacho, Keith. *Cultures of Commemoration: The Politics of War, Memory, and History in the Mariana Islands.* Honolulu: University of Hawai'i Press, 2011.

Campbell, Bruce L. "General Order No. 12." *Guampedia.* Last modified on June 18, 2021. www.guampedia.com/us-naval-era-general-order-no-12/.

Caronan, Faye. *Legitimizing Empire: Filipino American and U.S. Puerto Rican Cultural Critique.* Urbana: University of Illinois Press, 2015.

Del Priore, Martiza R. "Education on Guam during the Spanish Administration from 1668 to 1899." PhD diss., University of Southern California, 1986.

Flores, Alfred. "US Colonial Education in Guam, 1899–1950." In *Oxford Research Encyclopedia of American History.* New York: Oxford University Press, 2019.

Fujikane, Candace, and Jonathan Okamura, eds. *Asian Settler Colonialism: From Local Governance to the Habits of Everyday Life in Hawaii.* Honolulu: University of Hawai'i Press, 2008.

Getachew, Adom. *Worldmaking after Empire: The Rise and Fall of Self-Determination.* Princeton: Princeton University Press, 2019.

Glenn, Evelyn Nakano. "Settler Colonialism as Structure: A Framework for Comparative Studies of U.S. Race and Gender Formation." *Sociology of Race and Ethnicity* 1, no. 1 (2015): 52–72.

Go, Julian. *American Empire and the Politics of Meaning: Elite Political Cultures in the Philippines and Puerto Rico during U.S. Colonialism.* Durham: Duke University Press, 2008.

Isaac, Allan Punzalan. *American Tropics: Articulating Filipino America*. Minneapolis: University of Minnesota Press, 2006.

Kaplan, Amy, and Donald E. Pease, eds. *Cultures of United States Imperialism*. Durham: Duke University Press, 1994.

Kim, Nadia. *Imperial Citizens: Koreans and Race from Seoul to LA*. Stanford: Stanford University Press, 2008.

Lujan, Pilar C. "Role of Education in the Preservation of Guam's Indigenous Language." *Guampedia*. Last modified on June 19, 2021. www.guampedia.com.

Lutz, Catherine, and Cynthia Enloe, eds. *The Bases of Empire: The Global Struggle against U.S. Military Posts*. New York: New York University Press, 2009.

Mar, Tracey Banivanua. *Decolonisation and the Pacific: Indigenous Globalisation and the Ends of Empire*. New York: Cambridge University Press, 2016.

Shigematsu, Setsu, and Keith Camacho, eds. *Militarized Currents: Toward a Decolonial Future in Asia and the Pacific*. Minneapolis: University of Minnesota Press, 2010.

Temkar, Arvin. "Calvo Praises New Common Core Curriculum." *Pacific Daily News*, May 22, 2012. Government of Guam Archives, Hagåtña, Guam.

Tennessen, Richard G. "Needed Local Control of Public Education." *Guam Recorder* 3, no. 2 (1973): 26. Government of Guam Archives, Hagåtña, Guam.

Tuck, Eve, and K. Wayne Yang. "Decolonization Is Not a Metaphor." *Decolonization: Indigeneity, Education and Society* 1, no. 1 (2012): 1–40.

Underwood, Robert A. "American education and the acculturation of the Chamorros of Guam." PhD diss., University of Southern California, 1987.

PART II

Settler Colonialism and Indigenous Studies

5

Crossing the Lines

Sociology, Indigenous Nations, and American Studies

ERICH STEINMAN

Introduction: Grounded in Conflict

Between 1987 and 1992, recurrent intergroup conflict erupted in Wisconsin and Minnesota as Anishinaabe fishers utilizing treaty rights were met by intense resistance led by White sports fishermen at boat landings on the shores of Northwoods lakes. About a decade later, the renewal of whaling by the Makah people of Washington State was similarly met by years of sustained animus and opposition spurred by primarily White animal-rights activists. In both cases, members of the respective Indigenous nations and their predominantly White opponents metaphorically—and sometimes literally—spoke past each other. These Whites' attacks on Indigenous fishers and hunters were highly racialized and also invoked notions of civilization, culture, and American identity. In contrast, tribal members and leaders emphasized their own nationhood, tribal sovereignty, and inherent rights acknowledged in treaties.

Seen through sociological and American studies lenses, respectively, these dual conflicts raise many scholarly questions. Sociology asks what social forces motivated and structured these assertions and reactions, including the use of particular strategies and tactics. American studies seeks to interpret the history-laden meanings of these episodes in terms of the ongoing construction of American identity and the contested terms of inclusion and exclusion. While both fields offer insights regarding these conflicts, each also has limitations. In this essay I will describe how an approach incorporating a third perspective, that of Indigenous studies, can draw upon—and draw out—the strengths of sociological and American studies frameworks. As conceptualized here, Indigenous studies centers not only Indigenous peoples but also Indigenous conceptions, as opposed to defining and interpreting Indigenous peoples' experiences and agency through other disciplines' categories and lenses. The analysis starts with sociology, the discipline in which I received my own training, and identifies productive tensions between its perceptions of American Indians' sociopolitical assertions and those generated by Indigenous peoples themselves. The second part of the essay incorporates American studies and identifies distinctive ways that its scholarship complements the products of a sociological analysis informed by Indigenous studies. The conclusion argues that the growing incorporation of Indigenous perspectives in both sociology and American studies has created new avenues of interdisciplinary borrowing and learning across these fields.

The essay incorporates my own experience as a participant observer in both of the above conflicts over Indian rights. As a White staff person for a social justice organization based in Minneapolis, Minnesota, I became part of an effort to train allies to support Anishinaabe fishermen. In response to a request by the Wa-Swa-Gon Treaty Association, organizers (such as myself) trained individuals to serve as "witnesses for nonviolence" by providing an embodied buffer between anti-Indian demonstrators and tribal fishermen at lakeshore protests. Later, as a graduate student at the University of Washington, I developed a relationship with the Makah Nation and taught a course that brought students to the Makah Reservation to hear tribal perspectives. Making sense of these conflicts has driven my intellectual journey and revealed both the strengths and limitations of predominating scholarly approaches. I draw on this history to illuminate the intellectual landscape shaping perceptions of these cases and to argue for the benefits and potential of rich interdisciplinary scholarship across the fields of sociology, American studies, and Indigenous studies.

Sociology and Indigenous Perspectives: Minorities versus Nationhood

Anishinaabe and Makah assertions and the strong resistance to them posed a fundamental question for sociological analysis: "What is this a case of?" The answer to this question suggests which theories and social forces are salient to understanding the social pattern being analyzed. This question was a very practical one for me, who as a graduate student was launching a dissertation to make sense of these conflicts. Aligned with a Weberian focus on deep understanding, or *Verstehen*, I sought to see these dynamics through Indigenous frameworks and interpretations. Trying to incorporate both scholarly and community based perspectives, I found it very difficult to figure out exactly what category of social phenomenon these conflicts represented. At this time (2001) and largely still today, the default framings within sociology cast Indigenous people as a racial or ethnic minority group and their struggles as paralleling those of the Black struggle for equal rights and inclusion. Similarly, the resistance to Indigenous rights was most readily understood as an expression of racism and, when taking into account protestors' framing of tribal spearfishing as a threat to the health of the walleye population, as environmental scapegoating.

However, while perceptions of anti-Indian racism were certainly prevalent among the Anishinaabe and Makah, the leaders and spokespersons of these respective Indigenous communities predominantly framed the dynamic through very different terms. They saw themselves as Indigenous nations who were distinct political entities, each with their own cultures, forms of self-governance, and the like. They emphasized that their existence, and that of hundreds of other Indigenous nations, preceded the United States. Furthermore, the new nation acknowledged and negotiated with Indigenous nations as fellow sovereigns, entering hundreds of treaties of "peace and friendship." Tribal leaders pointed out that in article 2, section 8 of the US Constitution, the founders reserved for the federal government the right to make treaties with Indian tribes and asserted that treaty rights were thus constitutionally enshrined.

As I sought to develop a theoretical framework to ground my dissertation research, the clash between sociological conceptions and Indigenous articulations was striking. They constructed or revealed almost two completely different realities. Over time I realized that the sociological frameworks were more aligned with the terms and discourses used by anti-Indian protesters. While the sociological conceptions were analytical and critical of the racialized discourse, they spoke the same language: race, minorities, equality, individual rights, inclusion. Both sociologists and anti-Indian protestors unproblematically conceived of American Indians as minority groups within American society. The protestors' discourse asserted that distinctive Indian rights violated notions of equal rights and treatment under the law. Sociologists approached such resistance, including highly offensive language and imagery, as expressions of racism and conflict between dominant (White) and subordinate (Indian) racialized groups. But these were not the primary frameworks that grounded the assertions or actions of the tribal people involved in these struggles. Concepts of minority groups, equal rights, racism, and racialized conflict did not incorporate or address the dimensions that Indigenous actors repeatedly emphasized: treaty rights, nationhood, and sovereignty. As my dissertation research advanced—still without a fully satisfactory theoretical framing—another complementary point was added by interviewees and archival documents: the insistence that American Indians tribal members were *not* a racial or ethnic minority. Here, the conflict between default sociological perspectives and Indigenous articulations became glaring.

Taking Indigenous perspectives seriously meant not trying to fit the data and case within a race and ethnicity sociological framework. Race, racism, and racial conflict were inadequate as concepts. If not these, however, then what kind of case was it, and what were more appropriate orienting analytical frameworks? Were sociological approaches to nationalism and sovereignty applicable? Should this case somehow be understood in relation to the literature on nationalism, the construction of imagined identities, and adjacent concepts? Social constructionist theorizations such as by Brubaker and Wimmer conceptually suggested that the notion of nations was highly elastic and that they occurred at various scales.[1] There wasn't a clear dividing line between what qualified as a nation and other types of groups whose members share culture, social institutions, collective interests, and are joined together by a common identity and shared history. Should social scientific studies of nationalism perhaps be incorporating American Indians tribes?

This theoretical possibility begged another question: Did sociology conceive of American Indians tribes as nations? Had the sociological literature treated or conceived of American Indian tribes as nations or through nationalism-centered analytical frameworks? And could sociology perceive of nations that did not take the shape of internationally recognized nation-states, or did its cognizance exclude preexisting nations or emerging national formations that existed within or across geographic boundaries of this globally hegemonic political form? The answer seemed clear; I could find no such conceptualization of Indigenous communities in the United States, particularly regarding the contemporary era. In sociological attention (or lack thereof) to Indigenous peoples, the implicit understanding seemed to be that Indian tribes or nations were clearly within the United States and therefore had fallen outside the category of nations in any serious way.[2] Nations, in default sociological practice, were apparently nation-states recognized by the United Nations. In practical terms, Indigenous nations were invisible as nations in sociological scholarship. Indians were studied as an assimilating population, but tribes as nation-bearing collectivities were absent. There was clearly a gap between the theoretical deconstruction of nationhood and the practical exclusion of Indigenous tribes from the realm of nations. So while one could make the case that perhaps Indigenous tribes were nations, doing so would be going against the full force of the scholarly precedent. As an uncertain graduate student working without guidance from any faculty familiar with Indigenous issues, this was a rather daunting task to even consider.

This uncertainty fueled an exploration of American Indians nationhood and sovereign status in the eyes of federal Indian law. My deep reading of scholarship about American Indian rights illuminated the inconsistent nature of federal interpretations of tribes and tribal members. Legal scholarship revealed that treaty rights were affirmed by the United States Supreme Court, although such rights were not always fully observed in practice by federal and state officials. I gradually realized that it was in this context that tribal leaders aggressively expanded their respective nations' governmental activity and creatively asserted that tribal rights and powers were not new but rather long standing. Tribes' sovereign or semi-sovereign status and rights were affirmed by some lines of legal rulings but were latent or had been denied in practical terms. Drawing on the law and society scholarship to interpret some of my dissertation data, I identified some forms of Indigenous agency as legal entrepreneurship that mobilized the law in innovative ways in the latter part of the twentieth century.[3] Through these efforts, tribes gained increasing acknowledgment by non-Native officials of their own governmental and (semi-)sovereign status, as well as associated rights and powers.

Neither the uncertain terrain of nations and nationalism or the delimited and state-centered landscape of legal mobilization, however, offered a clear theoretical framework for understanding the nature of the *social* conflict over tribal rights. The issue of Indigenous nationhood remained in the sociological shadows. Thinly veiled in the salient topical literature (on the United States, minorities, etc.) was the discrediting fact that tribes were internal to the United States. Their legal and sovereign status and their growing governmental presence was not incorporated in any clear or formally acknowledged manner within sociological conceptions of the United States. For example, nothing in the political sociological literature or the scholarship on diversity suggested that the existence of tribal nations made the United States a type of multinational political confederation or structure; Indigenous nationhood seemingly exceeded the scope of recognizable diversity.[4]

Thus my conceptual confusion continued. Federal legal interpretation suggested that tribal nations were interior to the United States yet had legal rights premised on their status as distinct nations that had entered into treaties with the United States. But in the eyes of sociology, tribes were not nations in any serious way, and nor were they an enduring and distinctive collectivity worthy of scholarly acknowledgment and attention. When each of these understandings were taken seriously, in combination, they were impossible to reconcile. If the Supreme Court and growing ranks of state and federal officials were to be taken seriously, sociological conceptions were not aligned with empirical reality. And nor were these disciplinary understandings aligned with Indigenous perceptions, the original source of my confusion. I lacked a framework to account for the discrepancy regarding Indigenous nationhood and to give insight into tribal nations' status in relation to the United States.

Colonialisms

Scholars have concepts for the domination of and incorporation of one society by another: colonialism. Yet in light of these particular conflicts, the predominating sociological conceptions of colonialism seemed ill fitting at best, conceptually and as applied to the United States. In

reviewing various disciplinary representations of Indigenous-US relations, a clear if implicit theme was that American expansion had taken
place in the past, thus placing the contemporary US case as outside of the
domain of colonialism. Selected exceptions offered other perspectives
or more nuanced characterizations. Du Bois's critical but long underappreciated contributions to twentieth-century social science included
not only empirical elucidation of how race structured social life but
assertions of an active and ongoing linkage between White supremacy
and colonialism.[5] The color line was global, involved collective political
domination as well as intra-societal intergroup domination, and located
the US racial state as clearly among the colonizing forces (1945).[6] But
while Du Bois did have a relationship with Indigenous scholars and
activists, his work understandably did not distinctly explicate American
colonial domination of North America's Indigenous nations.[7] Subsequently, the first edition (1986) of Omi and Winant's seminal book on
racial formation briefly referred to the notion of internal colonialism as
a contemporary American reality. However, this Marxian model also
seemed quite inadequate for generating insight regarding Indigenous
nations and the United States, as it emphasized intergroup economic
inequality, and especially labor exploitation, that didn't closely reflect
the underlying American Indian-US relationship.[8] Nor did postcolonial frameworks, such as later articulated within sociology by Julian Go,
readily map onto the case.[9] While postcolonialism identifies some salient
dynamics of power operating through discourse and representation, it
does not squarely acknowledge or take account of the fundamental relations of prior and ongoing settler dispossession of Indigenous land.[10]
This critique is directly expressed by rhetorical questions organically
posed by many Indigenous peoples in response to the *post* in postcolonial, such as, "Did the colonizers go home? Have they given back our
land?" Finally, nor did other later critical work, such as in Steinmetz's
edited volume on sociology and empire, provide a theoretical approach
to the case.[11] The latter text briefly acknowledges settler colonialism but
primarily to distinguish it from colonialism and empire, the clear focus
of the collection.[12]

   A theoretical advance by social movement scholars Armstrong and
Bernstein brought the set of original conflicts over Indian rights, and
with it the larger case of Indian nations in the United States, into clearer

view. In *Sociological Theory*, Armstrong and Bernstein argued that the goals and strategies of social movements are formed in response to the particular forms of domination they are resisting.[13] Expressively joyous, deviant, and defiant, gay pride, for example, was a response to stigmatization and as such was distinct from the prior legislative pursuit of legal rights by the homophile movement that sought to gain social legitimacy by emphasizing conformity. In this conceptual vein, tribal rights and tribal sovereignty did not simply oppose racism or racial inequality. Rather, they specifically opposed the historic denial of tribes' nationhood and the accompanying federal paternalism and control over reservation life. Claims and actions asserting tribal sovereignty countered the widespread perception that tribes, *as political entities*, were a thing of the past. Contemporary tribal nationalism simultaneously resisted the racialization of tribal members and rejected the notion that they were simply or completely incorporated within American society as another assimilating minority group.

Following this logic, it became apparent that what tribal leaders and activists were resisting was settler colonialism. In this particular form of colonialism, members of a colonizing settler society work to create an independent version of their home society in a different land. Rather than primarily exploit the labor of Indigenous populations, settlers seek to displace or eliminate Indigenous polities in order to build their own society in the same place. This realization greatly clarified my emergent analysis and enabled a satisfying conceptualization of what these Indigenous rights conflicts and tribal assertions were a "case of." Tribal efforts proclaiming sovereignty, asserting rights, and building tribal nations were refuting claims that they had already been assimilated and were revising how they acted and were treated. These actions resisted ongoing efforts to deny and erase tribal nationhood. Realizing this was a case of Indigenous resistance to settler colonialism became the theoretical foundation for my next decade of scholarship. As I gained greater familiarity with settler colonial scholarship, the applicability of the concept to the United States seemed more obvious. A settler colonial framework articulated in conjunction with social movement analysis helped identify and generate new insights regarding Indigenous sociopolitical agency, while also expanding the use of settler colonialism within the field of sociology.[14]

Settler Colonialism, Sociology, and American Studies

The fact that American sociology was not well versed in analyzing the United States as a settler colonial society is not surprising. Indeed, as settler colonial scholar Veracini writes and as Yvonne P. Sherwood's essay in this volume demonstrates, "Settler colonialism obscures the conditions of its own production."[15] For example, rituals such as the celebration of national independence from Britain function to declare that the United States is not a colonial entity itself. Indeed, national narratives and culture, broadly construed, function to naturalize the presence of American society in North America and conceal US settler colonialism as an ongoing process. The vast majority of US sociologists are socialized within this intersubjective reality. Neither their general academic nor their sociological education necessarily challenges the understanding that the United States represents a departure from colonialism or the perception that Indigenous peoples are fully incorporated as racial or ethnic minorities with American society. Dominant sociological theorizing and practice over the last century has focused less on the critical analysis of the foundations and boundaries of the US polity and has instead scrutinized inclusion into and inequality within the society. Stepping back, sociologists have pragmatically construed the United States as a clearly bounded context in which to conduct rigorous empirical research regarding intra-societal relations. The United States is ubiquitously and unreflexively categorized as a modern nation-state, with its legitimacy and the fact of closure regarding its people and territory taken for granted.

But if American sociology has an inability to perceive the settler colonial foundations of American society and its imprint on social relations—or disinterest in doing so—American studies seems well poised to help bring such phenomena into critical view. As Dubrow writes, "American Studies' potentially greatest contribution to American sociology is in its unique strength, namely the re-interpretation of American history via interdisciplinary research."[16] As American studies foregrounds and dissects that which the discipline of sociology largely treats as a context, American studies can complement sociology by generating new insights and suggesting new concepts that reorient scholarly approaches. This is most pointedly the case regarding history and culture. As I will argue further below, sociological methods can make reciprocal contributions to scholarship regarding topics of great interest to American studies. While drawing on contributions from either field in an interdisciplinary manner may require some translation, the potential benefits are significant. Before I return to such general issues I first identify and explore three concepts from American studies that are useful to analyzing American nationalism, American settler colonialism, and interpretations of Indigenous sociopolitical agency.

The first of these is settler colonialism itself. Humanities scholars, including those with positions in American studies, have been important voices in the gradual interdisciplinary development of the field and in applying the concept to the United States, including Goldstein and historians Pedersen and Elkins.[17] Such works were a source of my own growing exposure to settler colonial thought as I grappled with the "case" of Indigenous resistance. Because they were generally descriptive rather than causal in nature, it was not immediately clear how to incorporate them into my disciplinary practices. In general, American studies scholarship on American settler colonialism didn't identify variables, make causal claims, or suggest questions that were clearly amenable to being answered by empirical research. While they were suggestive, however, I struggled to know what to "do" with these understandings vis-à-vis sociological audiences that required contestable hypotheses and rigorous empirical support in order to recognize new knowledge claims. Nonetheless, their existence helped create the interdisciplinary landscape of settler colonial scholarship that I began to tentatively build on by utilizing settler colonial concepts to conduct identifiably sociological research.

The second notion that critically enlivened American nationhood and illuminates American settler colonialism is, as named by Philip Deloria's classic text, that of "playing Indian."[18] American settlers are confronted by a conundrum: they need to both displace prior Indigenous inhabitants while also differentiating themselves from their originating home society of Great Britain. They need to forge a new place-based identity and social cohesion in the name of anti-colonialism while justifying the colonization and dispossession of prior societies. As settler colonial scholar Veracini summarizes, "home there" has to be replaced by "home here," with home carrying a set of associations and claims.[19]

One type of solution to this dual problem is to "occupy" Native identities. Deloria argues that the Boston Tea Party protagonists drew on the discourse and symbols of "noble savages" to distance themselves from the English while asserting that such distinctions are rooted in the new land. Such efforts are always complicated and contain their own contradictions, often exposed by the continuing presence of actual Indigenous peoples (in place of Indians as malleable symbols). In various historical moments, Americans searching for elusive foundations of cultural identity and orienting values have "played Indian" for different specific purposes. Indigenous peoples have expressed great concern over such appropriation of their identities, both specific (e.g., Cherokee) and general, and the many types of harms caused by these actions.

Deloria's analysis was not integrated with an explicit identification of American settler colonialism, and various forms of playing Indian can be analyzed through other lenses, such as general cultural appropriation, racism, and the like. But this specific analysis and the broader framework can definitely be seen as identifying a cultural dynamic that deeply reflects settler colonialism. In playing Indian, settlers occupy Indigenous identities and cultural traditions in addition to occupying Indigenous lands. While the relationships between such material and cultural dynamics are nuanced and variable, playing Indian provides a framework for incorporating identifiable social patterns—Indian mascots, New Age wannabe Indians, plastic shamans, and so on—into a broader explanatory framework and sociological analysis. And it also provides an approach to understanding and addressing dynamics that frequently complicate interactions between American Indian people and others, including my students' collaborations with Indigenous leaders, elders, and communities.

A third American studies contribution to analyses of American settler colonialism is Mark Rifkin's notion of *settler common sense*.[20] This generative concept, also examined by Sherwood's piece in this volume, refers to distinctly settler subjectivities. Rifkin analyzes texts of American fiction, including canonical writings of Hawthorne, Thoreau, and Melville, to identify how they give evidence of how settler access to Indigenous territories "come[s] to be lived as given, as simply the unmarked, generic conditions of possibility for occupancy, association, history, and personhood" of settlers.[21] This phenomenological exploration of interior settler experience reveals "forms of affect . . . imbued with a sensation of everyday certainty" that "can be understood as normalizing settler presence, privilege, and power."[22]

Playing Indian and settler common sense are two examples of American studies scholarship that deepen the understanding of US settler colonialism and have the potential to contribute to distinctly sociological research and analysis. And as suggested above, the latter has the capacity to extend, deepen, and refine these concepts or the scope of their applicability and/or impact. However, working across the disciplinary divide may require some creative transposition. I explore some challenges and possibilities regarding doing so in the next section.

Disciplinary Methods and Interdisciplinary Transposition

Sociology and American studies share strong concerns with race, ethnicity and gender issues. They both are concerned with culture and interested in the understandings that motivate individuals' actions. But significant differences make working across the boundaries challenging. As discussed in previous considerations of the relationship between sociology and American studies, the disciplines differ in terms of the dominant emphasis and nature of their respective scholarly tasks, the substantive topics they address, methods for doing so, and the data they utilize.[23] Whereas sociological practices center explanation and causal analysis based on the type of case being analyzed, American studies starts with the empirical case and aims to generate holistic representations. Whereas sociology incorporates culture as both something to be explained and something that helps explain other specific phenomena, American studies is overwhelmingly focused on explicating and interpreting culture (and history). Finally, American studies scholarship utilizes various kinds of texts as primary data, whereas sociologists tend to incorporate surveys, interviews, and ethnographic observation involving live humans as part of an inclusive methodological toolbox.

As a sociologist considering first and foremost how to incorporate American studies research, my challenge in writing for disciplinary audiences is to show how such scholarship can help provide new sociological insight to phenomena of interest. I suggest the notion of *transposition* as one framework for drawing from across this disciplinary divide.

Transposition involves changing the order of elements or altering their place in a sequence. I contrast this to cross-disciplinary *translation*, or trying to make the same claim—or assess the accuracy of the claim—through another disciplinary language or method. Thus, my primary concern is not on assessing the legitimacy of the representations generated by American studies scholarship through sociological criteria. Because of differences in purpose and methods, this quite often simply does not compute. Again, the descriptive and interpretive thrust of American studies does not necessarily translate into testable hypotheses readily amenable to most conventional social science methods. While I originally sought such direct translation of the implications of salient American studies (and settler colonial scholarship more broadly), this strategy proved to be a frustrating experience. Based on this, it became clear that transposition rather than translation was a more promising cross-disciplinary strategy.

In transposition, the focus is twofold, as I sketch out in a practical application using the notion of settler common sense. First, how can I take some suggestive findings from American studies—such as the outcomes or representations generated by a research project—and introduce them into the earlier stages of a research process? How I can I utilize concepts such as settler common sense to expand and invigorate my sociological imagination—the precursor of (and continuing animating force for) any sociological study? Put differently, how can settler common sense or other concepts and insights offer new lenses for reinterpreting social phenomena or imagining new dimensions, types, or locations of social forces? In such more formative stages of research, any sociological mistrust of American studies methods is largely irrelevant.

Secondly, and more concretely, how can such imaginings be creatively turned into research questions that can be addressed by empirical data gathered through sociological methods? Doing so might involve identifying (and researching) new *outcomes* in need of explanation that have been overlooked because of theoretical lacuna. Or it might direct research to the influence of a hypothesized novel causal factor regarding an already established but imperfectly understood social pattern? Or transposition might involve re-theorizing the relationship among a set of variables or processes. To further flesh out the specific example, I will note that in its investigation of group subjectivities, the explication of settler common sense is reminiscent of Du Bois's analysis of how the Black experience of looking through "the veil" of race affects *The Souls of Black Folks*.[24] However, settler common sense is even more closely aligned with Du Bois's more speculative work on "The Souls of White Folks" and more recent critical work on Whiteness and its affective and cognitive dimensions.[25] To move toward an empirical study, one might develop an argument that the "souls of settlers" is itself a topic worthy of sociological study. Relatedly, one might explore how settler identity and conceptions are related to, but not identical with, Whiteness and are not limited to White-identifying Americans. Or one could hypothesize that settler common sense is a factor that could affect a variety of sociologically significant actions. For example, how did settler common sense affect the reactions by North Dakota officials to the #NoDAPL movement at the Standing Rock Reservation in 2017? How does it impede or otherwise affect potential Indigenous solidarity by ideologically aligned settlers? How, as Sherwood in this volume asks, does it shape our mainstream understanding of the January 6 Capitol riot? Or how might being socialized into settler society shape the sympathies and solidarity of African Americans and other people of color regarding Indigenous rights and mobilizations?

Such questions, derived from a rich interdisciplinary encounter, could be explored through distinctly sociological research that would simultaneously enliven and update applications of settler common sense. Through such a process of transposition, in which findings from American studies (or other fields) are turned into questions or hypotheses that can be addressed empirically, sociologists' methodological training and tools expand the locations and type of data that can be brought to bear on the concept. More specifically, rigorous disciplinary-based research with living members of the American settler colonial society could affirm, complement, further develop, revise, or update an understanding of settler common sense that is based on nineteenth-century literary texts. Work in this vein, but without drawing upon this exact concept, is already being done by sociologists, such as Bacon (2017), and I am myself preparing a study that draws upon settler common sense. An additional contribution that sociological approaches could make is in exploring possible variation in settler common sense, and in particular the influences of various structures. My own collaborative research on institutional constraints on Indigenization of higher education touches on such themes.[26] However, our study was conducted prior to our familiarity with settler common sense; using this concept to re-analyze institutional responses could possibly generate new insights. Without exaggerating or reifying the culture-structure binary, sociological practice is more foundationally oriented toward identifying structures and on explaining variation than American studies. There is room for much work, individually and collaboratively, by sociologists, as well as the potential for productive interdisciplinary dialogue.

Moving Forward

Sociological research and theorizing benefits from interdisciplinarity. American studies and settler colonial studies have provided rich concepts and approaches that have deepened and extended sociological insights into Indigenous sociopolitical agency, the nature of domination by and resistance to US settler colonialism, and American settler colonialism itself. Apart from such interdisciplinary infusions, US sociology has had difficulty fully incorporating the perspectives of Indigenous peoples. This was most pronouncedly the case regarding the discipline's inability to perceive and grapple with Indigenous nationhood, and due to that, to perceive the nature of action bolstering tribal sovereignty and nations. Reflecting default notions of nationhood premised on Westphalian nation-states, methodological nationalism, and relative blindness to the mythological nature of US national narratives (of settler society closure and coherency), sociology has primarily construed Indigenous peoples as racial or ethnic minorities. However, sociological methods and approaches that incorporate and grapple with—take seriously—the perspectives of Indigenous peoples and the meanings they make of their own resistance have served to counter these assumptions and omissions. In this case, I am suggesting, empirical research guided by a critical approach demonstrates how such interdisciplinary exchanges both prompt distinctly sociological research and can improve sociological theorizing.

There is great potential for further cross-fertilization of American studies and sociology regarding understanding Indigenous experience and American settler colonialism, which should be of great interest to both fields. Exploring deep understandings of the emotions and logics generated by settler colonial structures, as well as their impacts on norms and behaviors, would seem salient to many subfields in each discipline. A process of transposition, as distinct from seeking direct translation, suggests one method for sociologists approaching this task. However, such a fundamental recasting of the overall context or "case" of the United States is undoubtedly disruptive and complicating in large and small ways for many areas of sociological scholarship. Scholars attempting to incorporate this complication can perhaps take inspiration from Du Bois and his brilliant and sustained scholarly uplift of critical attention to deeply institutionalized White supremacy. While the dynamics Du Bois analyzed were pervasively normalized in sociology in his day, they now are clearly seen as invaluably puncturing taken-for-granted assumptions in the field.[27]

What are the implications of more cross fertilization with sociology for American studies and its grappling with American settler colonialism? While these are less clear to me, the sociological practices of examining variation and of gathering data directly from Indigenous peoples and settlers means the scope or adequacy of American studies conceptions may be constrained, amended, or challenged by empirical sociological research. How might particular structures or contexts shape the nature or consequences of cultural notions generated by or accompanying settler colonialism? How might broad claims need to be adjusted or revised? Another challenge or task seemingly presented to American studies scholars is that of listening more broadly—and contemporaneously—to Indigenous peoples. How can a field focused on documents and other material texts listen to peoples for whom oral traditions are a central cultural tradition and mechanism? More particularly, how can contemporary sentiments be fully incorporated if they don't produce some form of accessible textuality? Again, I make these observations and questions as a sympathetic scholar rooted in sociology but eager to develop further interdisciplinary projects bridging sociology and American Studies.

Both fields have much more to learn from settler colonial studies and from Indigenous peoples, including from American Indian and Indigenous studies scholars. Speaking somewhat impressionistically, my sense is that scholars in these various fields are becoming more conversant with work and scholars from other fields, reducing the gaps across approaches, orienting concerns, and so forth. If there are a sufficient number of scholars able to speak from and—importantly—listen carefully across disciplinary divides, this creates conditions for deepened relationships. Amid the ongoing challenges that non-Native scholars have in hearing and apprehending Indigenous realities on their own terms, this is a potentially fraught conversation. It involves not only dynamics that occur within the scholarly lines (theories and manuscripts, such as presented at a conference panel) but also power, misrepresentation, and wounds that are offstage and beyond the lines (historic and contemporary exclusions, privileging of White male scholars, etc.). But here, non-Native scholars might learn from and appropriately be open to the centrality of relationality detailed in Shawn Wilson's *Research Is Ceremony: Indigenous Research Methods*.[28] For Wilson, research is about exploring "relationships between ideas" and the people who carry and develop them; relationality involves multiple dimensions and their histories. Imagining such expanded and deepened encounters, I am passionately convinced that sociology, even with all its limitations, has important and urgent contributions to such relationships and to the understanding they can develop. I am equally convinced that the other fields have essential contributions to make. Together, such deepened dialogue can, I hope, produce disciplinary specific work as well as cumulatively generate more interdisciplinary insight into American settler colonialism and Indigenous survivance and resurgence.

I understand my recent work on Indigenization as trying to work from this intersection. While there is ample critical work advocating and providing guidance for the process of incorporating Indigenous people and perspectives in higher education (especially in Canada), there is still little empirical research systematically and critically analyzing the dynamics and effects of Indigenization. In response, our study merged familiar sociological research tools (i.e., interviews) with a substantive focus on the phenomenology of Indigenous relationships to the university. The study thus centered Indigenous perspectives while using social scientific methods and also foregrounding both the institutional and macro–settler colonial contexts to illuminate and make sense of those experiences. Both recent publications from this project draw on those situated experiences to provide "cautionary tales" that illuminate, among other things, the complex interactions between such inclusionary goals and operative settler institutional logics and their impacts on Indigenous students, faculty, staff, and community partners.[29]

A number of sociologists, Native and non-Native, are developing work at such intersections. Exemplary recent work includes that by Robertson, Norgaard, Bacon, Murphy, Fenelon, Rodriguez-Lonebear, Jacob, Dhillon, Sherwood, and a growing number of other Indigenous sociologists and non-Indigenous scholars of settler colonialism and Indigenous resistance. The cumulative body of work is expansive and penetrating, opening up new lines of research and offering refreshing new ways to see familiar topics as well as bringing new topics to the focus of scholarly attention. These scholars are heavily represented in the recently formed American Sociological Association section on Sociology of Indigenous Peoples and Native Nations, and the existence of this hub for scholarly exchange and support will undoubtedly amplify such efforts. While sociology is somewhat of a latecomer to acknowledging and incorporating settler colonialism and Indigenous perspectives, the transformative and interdisciplinary potential of this growing network of scholars is quite exciting. Soon, one aspect of the work will turn from exploring what are obviously Indigenous-related topics to making claims about how other topics are pervasively informed by settler colonialism and Indigenous agency. It should continue to be lively and disruptive and cross additional boundaries of scholarly inquiry.

NOTES

1 Brubaker, "Ethnicity, Race, and Nationalism"; Wimmer, "The Making and Unmaking."
2 Cornell, *The Return of the Native*; Champagne, "From Sovereignty to Minority."
3 Steinman, "Legitimizing American Indian Sovereignty"; Steinman, "American Federalism and Intergovernmental Innovation."
4 Hartmann, Douglas, and Gerteis, "Dealing with Diversity."
5 Morris, *The Scholar Denied*; Du Bois, "The Souls of White Folk."
6 Du Bois, *The Color and Democracy*.
7 Mays, "Transnational Progressivism."
8 Gutiérrez, "Internal Colonialism."
9 Go, *Postcolonial Thought and Social Theory*.
10 Tuck and Yang, "Decolonization Is Not a Metaphor," 5.
11 Steinmetz, *Sociology and Empire*.
12 Ibid., 11.

13 Armstrong and Bernstein, "Culture, Power, and Institutions."
14 Steinman, "Settler Colonial Power"; "Decolonization Not Inclusion"; "Standing Rock."
15 Veracini, *Settler Colonialism*, 41.
16 Dubrow, "Sociology and American Studies," 313.
17 Goldstein, "Where the Nation Takes Place"; Elkins and Pedersen, *Settler Colonialism in the Twentieth Century.*
18 Deloria, *Playing Indian.*
19 Veracini, *Settler Colonialism*, 21–24.
20 Rifkin, *Settler Common Sense.*
21 Ibid., xv.
22 Ibid.
23 Dubrow, "Sociology and American Studies"; Jacobs, "American Studies."
24 Du Bois, *The Souls of Black Folks.*
25 Du Bois, "The Souls of White Folks."
26 Steinman and Scoggins, "Cautionary Stories"; Steinman and Kovats, "Magnifying and Healing Colonial Trauma."
27 Morris, *The Scholar Denied.*
28 Wilson, *Research Is Ceremony.*
29 Steinman and Scoggins, "Cautionary Stories"; Steinman and Kovats, "Magnifying and Healing Colonial Trauma."

BIBLIOGRAPHY

Armstrong, Elizabeth A., and Mary Bernstein. "Culture, Power, and Institutions: A Multi-institutional Politics Approach to Social Movements." *Sociological Theory* 26, no. 1 (2008): 74–99.

Bacon, J. M. "'A Lot of Catching Up', Knowledge Gaps and Emotions in the Development of a Tactical Collective Identity among Students Participating in Solidarity with the Winnemem Wintu." *Settler Colonial Studies* 7, no. 4 (2017): 441–55.

Brubaker, Rogers. "Ethnicity, Race, and Nationalism." *Annual Review of Sociology* 35 (2009): 21–42.

Champagne, Duane. "From Sovereignty to Minority: As American as Apple Pie." *Wicazo Sa Review* 20, no. 2 (2005): 21–36.

Cornell, Stephen. *The Return of the Native: American Indian Political Resurgence.* Oxford: Oxford University Press, 1988.

Deloria, Philip Joseph. *Playing Indian.* New Haven, CT: Yale University Press, 1998.

Du Bois, W. E. B. *Color and Democracy: Colonies and Peace.* New York: Harcourt, Brace, 1945.

———. *The Souls of Black Folks.* Chicago: AC McClurg, 1903.

———. "The Souls of White Folk." In *Darkwater: Voices from Within the Veil,* 29–52. New York: Verso, 2016.

Dubrow, Joshua Kjerulf. "Sociology and American Studies: A Case Study in the Limits of Interdisciplinarity." *American Sociologist* 42, no. 4 (2011): 303–15.

Elkins, Caroline, and Susan Pedersen, eds. *Settler Colonialism in the Twentieth Century: Projects, Practices, Legacies.* New York: Routledge, 2005.

Go, Julian. *Postcolonial Thought and Social Theory.* Oxford: Oxford University Press, 2016.

Goldstein, Alyosha. "Where the Nation Takes Place: Proprietary Regimes, Antistatism, and US Settler Colonialism." *South Atlantic Quarterly* 107, no. 4 (2008): 833–61.

Gutiérrez, Ramón A. "Internal Colonialism: An American Theory of Race." *Du Bois Review: Social Science Research on Race* 1, no. 2 (2004): 281–95.

Hartmann, Douglas, and Joseph Gerteis. "Dealing with Diversity: Mapping Multiculturalism in Sociological Terms." *Sociological Theory* 23, no. 2 (2005): 218–40.

Jacobs, Jerry A. "American Studies: Interdisciplinarity over Half a Century." In *In Defense of Disciplines,* 153–87. Chicago: University of Chicago Press, 2014.

Mays, Kyle T. "Transnational Progressivism: African Americans, Native Americans, and the Universal Races Congress of 1911." *American Indian Quarterly* 37, no. 3 (2013): 243–61.

Morris, Aldon. *The Scholar Denied.* Berkeley: University of California Press, 2015.

Omi, Michael, and Howard Winant. 1986. *Racial Formation in the United States: From the 1960s to the 1980s.* New York: Routledge.

Rifkin, Mark. *Settler Common Sense: Queerness and Everyday Colonialism in the American Renaissance.* Minneapolis: University of Minnesota Press, 2014.

Steinman, Erich. "American Federalism and Intergovernmental Innovation in State-Tribal Relations." *Publius: The Journal of Federalism* 34, no. 2 (2004): 95–114.

———. "Decolonization Not Inclusion: Indigenous Resistance to American Settler Colonialism." *Sociology of Race and Ethnicity* 2, no. 2 (2016): 219–36.

———. "Legitimizing American Indian Sovereignty: Mobilizing the Constitutive Power of Law through Institutional Entrepreneurship." *Law & Society Review* 39, no. 4 (2005): 759–92.

———. "Settler Colonial Power and the American Indian Sovereignty Movement: Forms of Domination, Strategies of Transformation." *American Journal of Sociology* 117, no. 4 (2012): 1073–1130.

———. "Why Was Standing Rock and the #NoDAPL Campaign So Historic? Factors Affecting American Indian Participation in Social Movement Collaborations and Coalitions." *Ethnic and Racial Studies* 42, no. 7 (2019): 1070–90.

Steinman, Erich, and Kovats Sánchez, G. "Magnifying and Healing Colonial Trauma in Higher Education: Persistent Settler Colonial Dynamics at the Indigenizing University." *Journal of Diversity in Higher Education* (2021). https://doi.org/10.1037/dhe0000215.

Steinman, Erich, and Scott Scoggins. "Cautionary Stories of University Indigenization: Institutional Dynamics, Accountability Struggles, and Resilient Settler Colonial Power." *American Indian Culture and Research Journal* 44, no. 1 (2020): 73–96.

Steinmetz, George, ed. *Sociology and Empire: The Imperial Entanglements of a Discipline.* Durham, NC: Duke University Press, 2013.

Tuck, Eve, and K. Wayne Yang. "Decolonization Is Not a Metaphor." *Decolonization: Indigeneity, Education & Society* 1, no. 1 (2012): 1–40.

Veracini, Lorenzo. *Settler Colonialism: A Theoretical Overview.* Houndmills: Palgrave Macmillan, 2010.

Wilson, Shawn. *Research Is Ceremony: Indigenous Research Methods.* Winnipeg: Fernwood (2008).

Wimmer, Andreas. "The Making and Unmaking of Ethnic Boundaries: A Multilevel Process Theory." *American Journal of Sociology* 113, no. 4 (2008): 970–1022.

6

Unsettling the Spectacle of Settler Sovereignty

Democracy and Indigenous Justice

YVONNE P. SHERWOOD

The Scene and Spectacle of Settler Sovereignty

On the cold morning of January 6, 2021, hundreds of American citizens smashed their way through security and breached the entrance to the US Capitol.[1] Their goal was simple that day: to stop the certification of the next democratically elected US president. According to many views of and responses to the scene, former president Donald Trump's White supremacist leadership, his incitement of the riot, and the crowd's dynamics were all outside of usual American political conduct and a direct threat to democracy. Senator Bernie Sanders lamented, "It was a sad, sad day for American Democracy."[2] Representative Brenda Lawrence declared, "This is not the America I know and love."[3] The former homeland security adviser, Tom Bossert, decried, "This is beyond wrong and illegal. It is un-American."[4] Elected officials of a bipartisan and bicameral group asserted, "The behavior we witnessed in the US Capitol is entirely un-American."[5] In addition, hundreds if not thousands of people across the political spectrum echoed the sentiments and posted across social media sites urging a lawful response to the rioters' attempts to disrupt American democracy.

Some might read the calls to protect American democracy as suggesting that politicians spanning the right and left who were united in their condemnations of the scene affirm an anti-racist national consciousness, refusing White supremacy and affirming the protection of inclusive democracy. However, to propose that White supremacy exists outside of, and was an affront to, state democracy is to invisibilize the settler colonial and capitalist projects at its foundation. Thus, our collective critiques of White supremacy and assertions of anti-racist futures must extend the analysis of the scene beyond rioters flooding the doors of the US Capitol to include the liberal narratives that buttress the settler state. Chickasaw scholar Shannon Speed similarly argues that framing the resurgence of White supremacy as a reaction to multicultural progress assumes "that white supremacy can be voted out or voted back in." Instead, she urges, it should be understood as a response to the changing needs of White settler capitalist power.[6] The dominant mediations on the January 6 event that presume that White supremacy exists outside of the state demonstrate well how commodified images of democracy have long served to mask the larger reality of the spectacle of settler sovereignty.[7] As Speed asserts, Trump's violent rhetoric and policies were "an extreme extension of the logics already at play under previous administrations while the discourse of the United States as postracial flourished."[8]

To refuse the too easy assertion that White supremacy exists outside of American democracy, hailed as a gift by the state despite the details of Indigenous and Black genocide, this chapter places the scene of the January 6 insurrection back into the sociopolitical context of the settler colonial capitalist state.[9] Placing the scene of the riot, including the dominant narrative that surfaced to frame the actions, back within our current conditions is essential because White supremacy—what Gerald Horne calls the "handmaiden" of slavery, colonialism, and capitalism—is co-constituted through networks of power that buttress capitalism through the dispossession of Indigenous lands and exploitation of the racially marginalized. Speaking of the spectacle and Indigenous justice is not to abstract the scene. Instead, I hope to show that asserting anti-colonial frameworks and critical Indigenous analysis is an embodied praxis that draws on Indigenous lifeways that refuse the invisibilization of Indigenous justice. Indigenous justice, rooted in Indigenous lifeworlds, challenges the spectacle's mediation of scenes of threat, extractive development, and the policing of property by way of self-congratulatory liberalism.

The Spectacle of Capital

Rather than defining the spectacle as a singular image, event, or scene, French philosopher and artist Guy Debord defined it as the product of commodified images that mediate social relations.[10] Similar to the experiences of alienation from the worker and worker's self, product, and others, the spectacle, he argued, detaches scenes from their conditions of production, and thus these scenes, to use Marxist language, become fetishized commodities of the capitalist state. From this process, the spectacle of capitalism abstracts the material condition of accumulation through dispossession targeting Indigenous peoples. It presents itself as an accepted system where spectators as "classes or sections of classes" come to "accept that system and strive to carve out a role for themselves within it."[11] In other words, the commodification of scenes, the doubling of alienation in all its forms, is a process by which the spectacle is normalized, and spectators come to accept their conditions. The spectacle, he urges, "is *real*."

Too often, however, dispossession and alienation are discussed in ways that fail to address the relation between capitalism and settler colonialism and, no less, Indigenous presence. As Indigenous and Black scholars point out, the logics of settler colonialism and capitalism, underwritten by patriarchal White supremacy, transform land and bodies into property.[12] The sovereignty of the state, and thus its bourgeois democracy dependent on accumulation and dispossession, are dependent on veiling this truth while providing a seemingly prospective future for the lands and bodies it actively manages and targets.[13] Thus, to speak of the spectacle of capitalism in the settler colonial context begs the question of anti-colonial refusal, ongoing resistance to the techniques of state-sanctioned genocide, and persistence of Indigenous modes of life.

The spectacle of settler sovereignty made its appearance in the commodification of the scene that caught the world's attention on January 6, 2021. Having accepted the state and its assumed sovereignty, many spectators understood this scene to demonstrate a White supremacist assault on American democracy. However, rather than dominant narratives of democracy under threat or calls for increased police response unsettling White supremacy, these pro-US mediations of the scene instead foreclosed conversations of ongoing settler colonialism and the police state, and Indigenous modes of life that challenge the legitimization of both. To further elaborate on the contours of the spectacle, it seems necessary to first briefly explain what I mean by Indigenous justice before I turn to my analysis of the scene.

Lifeworlds of Indigenous Justice

While not necessarily drawing a strict binary between colonial and Indigenous laws, Indigenous legal scholars assert that Indigenous legal principles are foundationally different from liberal constitutional rights regimes, particularly in the logics that inform our relations to land. As I have suggested, an overwhelming majority of spectators couch their calls for justice and equality in an assumption of American sovereignty and liberal democracy that orient us to narrowly consider "sustainable development" and "democratic processes" without fully considering the underpinnings of structural genocide.[14] Critical attention to settler colonialism complicates a legal analysis that relies on "expanding" democracy to include "difference" into legal structures to address social and economic inequality. As historian Roxanne Dunbar Ortiz argues, everything about US history "is about the land—who oversaw and cultivated it, fished its waters, maintained its wildlife; who invaded and stole; how it became a commodity ('real estate') broken into pieces to be bought and sold on the market."[15] With this in mind, Ortiz shifts the narrative that the settler government needs to deal with its racist or discriminatory policies: "US policies and actions related to Indigenous peoples . . . often termed 'racist' or 'discriminatory,' are rarely depicted as what they are: classic cases of imperialism and a particular form of colonialism—settler colonialism." The government, in short, cannot resolve the dispossession of Indigenous lands through so-called democratic inclusion.

To put this differently, it is not only "law" that constrains Indigenous peoples' constitutional orders, but capitalist, White supremacist, and settler colonial modes of being that exist beneath settler law.[16] Aaron Mills (Anishinaabe) asserts that law, including constitutional law, is part of colonialism's operation. Moreover, the "efforts to articulate Indigenous law within the forms of liberal constitutionalism ignore or trivialize the ongoing significance of Indigenous lifeworlds."[17] Using the concept of *lifeworld*, Mills conveys how legal institutions, settler or otherwise, are "grounded in something beyond." That is, as he puts it, all law "has a home." For example, as he shared, in contrast to the lifeworld of liberal democracy, Anishinaabeg language and ceremony carry a lifeworld rooted to the Earth by conveying a set of understandings that situate the

Anishinaabeg in relation to all creation.[18] This relation guides what is considered proper behavior and relations to others, including more-than-human relatives and the land. Liberal constitutional orders are grounded in a different set of relations and responsibilities. The broad tenets of Indigenous "grounded" relations and responsibilities, the sacred and material underpinnings of Indigenous legal orders, are reflected across what Secwépemc leader George Manuel called the Fourth World.[19]

Informed by critical Indigenous legal analysis and Indigenous feminism, I thus understand Indigenous justice as a lived praxis of caretaking and "making kin" with human and more-than-human relatives that re/constitutes Indigenous nationhood and diplomacy in and across territories.[20] Indigenous approaches to justice signify an understanding of justice that values traditional teachings, stories, and ceremonies that, as John Borrows has put it, "make life worth living."[21] Commitment to Indigenous justice asserts relations and futures different from those enacted through and within the spectacle of settler sovereignty. The nature in which specific understandings of earth, land, and treaty-making with our relatives inform Indigenous political orders is vital, especially in addressing the dis/order that settler colonialism has wrought (see also Das Gupta this volume).

Settler colonialism is not only the conditioning of relations between and among Indigenous peoples, lands, and settlers; it is a structuring mechanism that undergirds issues of White supremacy and patriarchy more broadly.[22] For Indigenous nations broadly, settler colonialism attempts to disrupt our ability to fulfill our specific directives to care for our first mother and relatives, human and more-than-human kin.[23] Furthermore, as Asian American sociologist Evelyn Nakano Glenn argues, settler colonialism simultaneously structures the relationship between Indigenous peoples and democracy as much as it informs understandings of race, class, sex, and gender for *everyone* within the nation-state.[24] Thus, collectively, we must attend to settler colonialism and consider Indigenous justice to unsettle our acceptance of the spectacle of settler sovereignty. Having established a broad concept of and orientation to Indigenous justice and the spectacle, I now turn back to the scene.

The Image of the Riot

In 2020, throughout his reelection campaign, Trump told US citizens that his opponents would use the global pandemic and fraudulent mail-in ballots to "steal" the presidential election. Along with social media organizing, Trump's false statements, vicious remarks, calls to action, and political victories led thousands to march on the United States Capitol. As the crowd spread throughout the chambers, rioters eagerly captured images of each other with United States, Trump, and confederate flags, "Stand By and Stand Down" shirts, and tactical gear. Several individuals lost their lives. An image of a single note left on Nancy Pelosi's desk that afternoon echoed Trump's speech just hours prior: "We Will Not Back Down."

Rebuking the violent actions of January 6, politicians, activists, and scholars across the political spectrum narrated the siege on the Capitol as a threat to American democracy and political freedom. A quick online search of Trump and the insurrection reveals that sociological investigations echoed much of these sentiments and pointed to a preoccupation with framing the riot as "a crisis" for democracy because of Trump's overt racism, hyper-masculinity, political polarization, and authoritarianism. Though I find each of these points extremely important in articulating the effects of neoliberalism and White supremacy, what is clear from a critical Indigenous studies perspective is the normalization of the redeemable nature of the state and its assumption of sovereignty on Indigenous lands.

Through the case of the January 6 scene, the spectacle of settler sovereignty commodified an image of American democracy and broke it off from its lifeworld of colonial doctrines. Within the spectacle and its legitimated "just wars" against Indigenous peoples, the image, scene, or moment of the insurrection and the response to protect American democracy become commodities detached from the lived conditions and experiences of Indigenous nations and all others who have a relation to settler colonialism. The spectacle appears neutral and separate from its modes of production and makes its appearance through a false sense of choice in bipartisan politics. Speaking of the spectacle of capitalism, Debord wrote that whether choosing between clothing brands or political parties, the spectacle has made the choice possible and normal.[25] In the US capitalist settler state, citizens are encouraged to choose between presidents, lean left or right, and protect American sovereignty against the "Other" that threatens American freedom. As Dunbar-Ortiz writes:

> The most revered presidents—Jefferson, Jackson, Lincoln, Wilson, both Roosevelts, Truman, Kennedy, Reagan, Clinton, Obama—have each advanced populist imperialism while gradually increasing inclusion of other groups beyond the core descendants of old settlers into the ruling mythology. All of the presidents after Jackson march in his footsteps. Consciously or not, they refer back to him on what is acceptable, how to reconcile democracy and genocide and characterize it as a freedom for the people.[26]

The spectacularized struggle for power and freedom has included a range of state tactics across government administration, but what remains consistent is the assumption of state sovereignty over Indigenous lands and laws. Therefore, a part of putting into motion anti-colonial worlding is refusing the scene's detachment from its roots of dispossession, accumulation, and structural genocide.

In contrast, to problematize dominant mediations of such scenes, Joye Braun (Cheyenne River Sioux) and other water protectors (Native and non-Native relatives) cast into relief the structural genocide advanced through American democracy and settler sovereignty when they question the state-sanctioned attacks on Indigenous bodies and land.[27] For example, on the same day that media focused attention on the Trump-led insurrection, Joye Braun publicly called for viewers to pay attention to what was happening at the state capitol in opposition to Oceti Sakowin Territories.[28] In a later conversation with me, Braun asserted that Indigenous governance across the globe continues to be terrorized, attacked, and undermined by corporations and governments pushing through extractive industrial projects.[29] Indigenous governance, from her perspective, includes the sacred right to protect land and water as spiritual, life-giving beings from the onslaughts of imperial and settler colonial extraction.[30]

From Democracy to Constituting Our Relations

When I began drafting this chapter, Jasilyn Charger (Cheyenne River Sioux) was facing criminal charges for allegedly trespassing (on her nation's homelands) and tying herself to a pump station. On January 6, Joye Braun sat outside the Haakon County, South Dakota, jail under the biting January sky and reported on the situation. From this space, she updated viewers on the jailing of water protectors and a slew of issues that she referred to collectively as a big water war. Braun, who was attending the arraignment of Charger, explained to spectators that Oscar High Elk (Cheyenne River Sioux) was also arrested the same day for protesting the construction of the Keystone oil pipeline. While Charger negotiated a deal to avoid imprisonment and High Elk still faces charges, from an Indigenous justice perspective, Charger's and High Elk's removal and detainment for protecting Indigenous modes of life and for embodying Indigenous legal orders was and remains an affront to Indigenous justice.

In addition to raising awareness about these two water protectors who were facing charges for protecting lands and kin assaulted by the US state-sanctioned extractive industry, Braun discussed the federal government's violation of its laws, particularly of the Winters Doctrine and the National Environmental Policy Act, during the scoping process for the Keystone XL Pipeline. As she laid out the issues and constructed her reading of the frontlines, she connected the scene of insurrection back to the state-sanctioned extractive terrorism experienced by Indigenous nations. Her analysis of the scene of the January 6 riot punctuated her coverage of the water war, and as she fought back the tears, Braun implored viewers to make the connections: "All of these things are violating our democratic rights. People think they can just push through whatever. They can't! They need to stop. They need to stop violating our people's rights. And they need to stop violating our natural rights."[31]

Braun utilizes and shapes the concept of democracy to call our attention to state-sanctioned energy projects continually violating Indigenous constitutional, natural, and sacred rights. By understanding the spectacle as a social context, we can understand Braun's assertion of democracy as being too mediated through Indigenous lifeworlds or grounded normativities, although she does not use those terms. Her and others' modes of life centered around the defense of waters and territories impact her use and conceptualization of democracy in a way that calls into question the spectacle of settler sovereignty and its scenes. Her words and her physical presence outside the South Dakota jail serve as a force that challenges the spectacle of settler sovereignty and its violation of Indigenous legal orders, lands, and lives.[32] As Braun and other water protectors put their bodies on the line to uphold Indigenous laws, they expose the performance of the spectacle, highlighting the processes by which settler colonialism attempts to hide its violation of our relations, treaties, and obligations with our human and more-than-human kin.

Conclusion

For those of us who assume that social justice is foundational to sociology, the construction of the discipline without settler colonialism as an analytical framework is particularly problematic for a sociological imagination, as colonizing frameworks have remained normative in the theorization of justice.[33] With capitalism, settler colonialism and its intersecting oppressive logics are part of enfolding individuals into the spectacle of settler sovereignty that invests us in particular understandings of justice. To demonstrate this claim, I showed that the mediation of the January 6 riot as a threat to democracy drew our attention away from the sociohistorical spectacle of empire and the specific nature of settler colonialism. Moreover, Indigenous womxn's embodied knowledges on the frontlines of water wars unsettle the scene of democracy while being practical forces in motion toward placemaking through Indigenous lifeworlds and justice.

NOTES

1 Naylor, "Graphic Video."
2 "Sanders: A Sad, Sad Day for American Democracy," WCAX, January 8, 2021, https://www.wcax.com.
3 Brenda Lawrence, "U.S. Rep. Lawrence Statement on the Attacks on the U.S. Capitol." Congresswoman Lawrence Media Center, U.S. Federal Government, January 06, 2021. https://lawrence.house.gov. Quoted by Ibram X. Kendi, "Denial Is the Heartbeat of America," 2. Ibram X. Kendi argues that "the heartbeat of America is denial." For more on American dreaming and its particular relation to the elimination of Indigenous Peoples, see Kim TallBear "Caretaking Relations."
4 Thomas P. Bossert (@TomBossert), "This is beyond wrong and illegal. It is un-American," Twitter, April 6, 2021, 1:06 p.m., https://twitter.com/tombossert/status/1346926112496996353?lang=en; Forgey and Niedzwiadek "'For Our Country!' See general coverage of calls to stop the insurrection.

5 "Bipartisan, Bicameral Group Issues Statement on Capitol Insurgence | U.S. Senator Joe Manchin of West Virginia," Representative Joe Manchin, January 6, 2021, https://www.manchin.senate.gov. Quoted by Kendi, "Denial Is the Heartbeat of America," 2.

6 Speed, "The Persistence of White Supremacy."

7 Mediation, as Couldry describes, is a non-linear transmission and reception of story shaped under social conditions, including social expectations and demands of making narratives "ready for broadcast." Following Couldry, I understand mediation "as the result of flows of production, circulation, interpretation and recirculation" ("Mediatization or Mediation?," 383). While Couldry is discussing mediation to theorize the potential for digital storytelling, for my purposes here, I am using "dominant mediation" to highlight the production, circulation, interpretation, and recirculation of narratives within the social conditions of settler colonialism.

8 Speed, "The Persistence of White Supremacy," 78.

9 Horne, *The Apocalypse of Settler Colonialism*.

10 Debord, *The Society of the Spectacle*, thesis 37, 12.

11 Debord, thesis 56, 16.

12 Moreton-Robinson, *The White Possessive*; Horne, *The Apocalypse of Settler Colonialism*.

13 Horne, *The Apocalypse of Settler Colonialism*; Simpson, "The State Is a Man."

14 This point was similarly made in a tweet, Resist Line 3. 2021. "I love democracy" @VP @KamalaHarris said—while standing idly by. Twitter, October 21, 2021, 9:09 p.m. https://twitter.com/resistline3/status/1451354955881791489?s=21.

15 Dunbar-Ortiz, *An Indigenous Peoples' History*, 1.

16 For more discussion on modes of being and how law is "grounded," see Coulthard and Simpson, "Grounded Normativity"; see also Coulthard, *Red Skin, White Masks*; Simpson, *As We Have Always Done*; Coulthard, "Place against Empire," 80.

17 Mills "The Lifeworlds of Law," 847. See also Borrows, *Freedom and Indigenous Constitutionalism*; and, specifically to Indigenous legal protocols around cultural heritage, Gray, "Rematriation."

18 Mills, "The Lifeworlds of Law," 847; see also Hill, "Traveling down the River of Life"; Stark, "Respect, Responsibility, and Renewal."

19 Manuel, *Fourth World*; Ryser, Gilio-Whitaker, and Bruce, "Fourth World Theory"; Sherwood, "Toward, with, and from a Fourth World."

20 TallBear, "Caretaking Relations." See also Wilson,. "Our Coming in Stories"; Driskill et al., *Queer Indigenous Studies*; Byrd, "The Transit of Empire"; Barker, "Critically Sovereign."

21 Borrows, *Freedom and Indigenous Constitutionalism*.

22 Glenn, "Settler Colonialism as a Structure."

23 Jacob, "Indigenous Cultural Values." For a discussion on how settler colonialism is bent away from Indigenous and Black justice and toward Black and Indigenous

genocide and enslavement, see Tuck and Yang, "Born under the Rising Sign of Social Justice."

24 Glenn, "Settler Colonialism as Structure," 54; see also Arvin, Tuck, and Morrill, "Decolonizing Feminism."

25 Debord, *The Society of the Spectacle*, "The Culmination of Separation," thesis 6, 7.

26 Dunbar-Ortiz, *An Indigenous People's History*, 108.

27 Wolfe, "Settler Colonialism."

28 Joye Braun, "Oscar High Elk Arrested Water Protector on Major Charges." Facebook, January 6, 2021, 3:58 p.m., www.facebook.com/Indigenousrisingmedia/videos/812558005962135. Although I don't focus on the case here, it's important to note that Berlinda Nibo, a Black woman, was assaulted on the same day in California by Trump supporters.

29 Personal communication.

30 Ibid.

31 Braun.

32 As Nick Estes and Jaskiran Dhillon argue, the voices from the Water Protector movement assert the practice of "being a good relative," and this is a kinship practice, "a recognition of the place-based, decolonial practice of being in relation to the land and water." "Introduction: The Black Snake," 3.

33 Romero, "Sociology Engaged in Social Justice."

BIBLIOGRAPHY

Alexander, Susan M. "Social Justice and the Teaching of Sociology." *Sociological Focus* 38 (August 1, 2005): 171–79. https://doi.org/10.1080/00380237.2005.10571263.

Alexiou, Gus. "Donald Trump's Disregard for Disabled Americans under Scrutiny Twice in One Week." *Forbes*, October 8, 2020. www.forbes.com.

Arvin, Maile, Eve Tuck, and Angie Morrill. "Decolonizing Feminism: Challenging Connections between Settler Colonialism and Heteropatriarchy." *Feminist Formations* 25, no. 1 (Spring 2013): 8–34.

Atlantic Council's DFRLab. "#StopTheSteal: Timeline of Social Media and Extremist Activities Leading to 1/6 Insurrection." *Just Security*, February 10, 2021. www.justsecurity.org.

Barker, Joanne. "Confluence: Water as an Analytic of Indigenous Feminisms." *American Indian Culture and Research Journal* 43, no. 3 (August 2019): 1–40. https://doi.org/10.17953/aicrj.43.3.barker.

———. "Critically Sovereign." In *Critically Sovereign: Indigenous Gender, Sexuality, and Feminist Studies*, 1–44. Durham, NC: Duke University Press, 2017.

———. "Gender, Sovereignty, and the Discourse of Rights in Native Women's Activism." *Meridians* 7, no. 1 (2006): 127–61. www.jstor.org/stable/40338720.

Borrows, John. *Freedom and Indigenous Constitutionalism*. Toronto: University of Toronto Press, 2016.

———. *Recovering Canada: The Resurgence of Indigenous Law*. 1st ed. Toronto: University of Toronto Press, 2002.

Byrd, Jodi A. *The Transit of Empire: Indigenous Critiques of Colonialism*. Minneapolis: University of Minnesota Press, 2011.

Centers for Disease Control and Prevention. "Disability Impacts All of Us Infographic | C.D.C." www.cdc.gov.

Couldry, Nick. 2008. "Mediatization or Mediation? Alternative Understandings of the Emergent Space of Digital Storytelling." *New Media & Society* 10, no. 3: 373–91.

Coulthard, Glen. "Place against Empire: Understanding Indigenous Anti-colonialism." *Affinities: A Journal of Radical Theory, Culture, and Action* 4, no. 2 (2010): 79–83.

———. *Red Skin, White Masks: Rejecting the Colonial Politics of Recognition*. 1st ed. Minneapolis: University of Minnesota Press, 2014.

Coulthard, Glen, and Leanne Betasamosake Simpson. "Grounded Normativity / Place-Based Solidarity." *American Quarterly* 68, no. 2 (2016): 249–55. https://doi.org/10.1353/aq.2016.0038.

Cox, Alicia. "Settler Colonialism." *Oxford Bibliographies*, 2017. doi:10.1093/O.B.O./9780190221911-0029.

Debord, Guy. *The Society of the Spectacle*. Translated by Donald Nicholson-Smith. Brooklyn, NY: Zone Books, 2020.

Driskill, Qwo-Li, Chris Finley, Brian Joseph Gilley, and Scott Lauria Morgensen, eds. *Queer Indigenous Studies: Critical Interventions in Theory, Politics, and Literature*. Tucson: University of Arizona Press, 2011.

Dunbar-Ortiz, Roxanne. *An Indigenous Peoples' History of the United States*. Reprint ed. Boston: Beacon Press, 2014.

Estes, Nick, and Jaskiran Dhillon. "Introduction: The Black Snake, #N.O.D.A.P.L., And the Rise of a People's Movement." In *Standing with Standing Rock*, edited by Nick Estes and Jaskiran Dhillon, 1–10. Minneapolis: University of Minnesota Press, 2019.

Finley, Chris. "Decolonizing the Queer Native Body (and Recovering the Native Bull-Dyke): 'Bringing Sexy Back' and Out of Native Studies Closet." In *Queer Indigenous Studies: Critical Interventions in Theory, Politics, and Literature*, edited by Qwo-Li Driskill, Chris Finley, Brian Joseph Gilley, and Scott Lauria Morgensen, 31–42. Tucson: University of Arizona Press, 2011.

Fong, Sarah, Rebekah Garrison, Macarena Gómez-Barris, and Hoesta Moe'hahne. "The Indigeneity and Decolonization Research Cluster of American Studies and Ethnicity at the University of Southern California." *Amerasia Journal* 42, no. 3 (2016): 129–41.

Forgey, Quint, and Nick Niedzwiadek. "'For Our Country!': Trump World Pleads with the President to Condemn Storming of the Capitol." *Politico*, January 6, 2021. www.politico.com.

Glenn, Evelyn Nakano. "Settler Colonialism as Structure: A Framework for Comparative Studies of U.S. Race and Gender Formation." *Sociology of Race and Ethnicity* 1, no. 1 (January 1, 2015): 52–72. https://doi.org/10.1177/2332649214560440.

Go, Julian. "Postcolonial Possibilities for the Sociology of Race." *Sociology of Race and Ethnicity* 4, no. 4 (October 1, 2018): 439–51. https://doi.org/10.1177/2332649218793982.

Gray, Robin R. R. "Rematriation: Ts'msyen Law, Rights of Relationality, and Protocols of Return." *Native American and Indigenous Studies* 9, no. 1 (Spring 2022): 1–27.

Hardt, Michael, and Antonio Negri. *Empire*. Cambridge, MA: Harvard University Press, 2000.

Harris, Cheryl I. "Of Blackness and Indigeneity: Comments on Jodi A. Byrd's 'Weather with You: Settler Colonialism, Antiblackness, and the Grounded Relationalities of Resistance.'" *Critical Ethnic Studies* 5, no. 1–2 (2019): 215. https://doi.org/10.5749/jcritethnstud.5.1-2.0215.

Hill, Susan. "Traveling down the River of Life Together in Peace and Friendship, Forever: Haudenosaunee Land Ethics and Treaty Agreements as the Basis for Restructuring the Relationship with the British Crown." In *Lighting the Eighth Fire: The Liberation, Resurgence, and Protection of Indigenous Nations*, edited by Leanne Betasamosake Simpson, 23–45. Winnipeg: Arbeiter Ring, 2008.

Horne, Gerald. *The Apocalypse of Settler Colonialism: The Roots of Slavery, White Supremacy, and Capitalism in 17th Century North America and the Caribbean*. New York: Monthly Review Press, 2018.

Jacob, Michelle M. "Indigenous Studies Speaks to American Sociology: The Need for Individual and Social Transformations of Indigenous Education in the U.S.A." *Social Sciences* 7, no. 2 (December 21, 2017): 1. https://doi.org/10.3390/socsci7010001.

———. *The Auntie Way: Stories Celebrating Kindness, Fierceness, and Creativity*. Whitefish, MT: Anahuy Mentoring, 2020.

Jacob, Michelle M., Kelly L. Gonzales, Deanna Chappell Belcher, Jennifer L. Ruef, and Stephany RunningHawk Johnson. "Indigenous Cultural Values Counter the Damages of White Settler Colonialism." *Environmental Sociology* (December 28, 2020): 1–13. https://doi.org/10.1080/23251042.2020.1841370.

Johnson, Hayley. "#NoDAPL: Social Media, Empowerment, and Civic Participation at Standing Rock." *Library Trends* 66, no. 2 (2017): 155–75. https://doi.org/10.1353/lib.2017.0033.

Johnson, Taylor N. "The Dakota Access Pipeline and the Breakdown of Participatory Processes in Environmental Decision-Making." *Environmental Communication* 13, no. 3 (2019): 335–52. https://doi.org/10.1080/17524032.2019.1569544.

Kandaswamy, Priya. "Gendering Racial Formation." In *Racial Formation in the Twenty-First Century*, 23–43. Berkeley: University of California Press, 2012.

Kendi, Ibram X. "Denial Is the Heartbeat of America: When Have Americans Been Willing to Admit Who We Are?" *Atlantic*, January 11, 2021. www.theatlantic.com.

Kreis, Ramona. "The 'Tweet Politics' of President Trump." *Journal of Language and Politics* 16, no. 4 (October 26, 2017): 607–18. https://doi.org/10.1075/jlp.17032.kre.

Longman, Nickita, Emily Riddle, Alex Wilson, and Salma Desai, eds. *The Land Back Issue*. 5th ed. Regina: Briarpatch Magazine, 2020.

Lopez, German. "Don't Believe Donald Trump Has Incited Violence at Rallies? Watch This Video." *Vox*, March 12, 2016. www.vox.com.

Maddow, Rachel. "Escalating Aggression Marks Trump's Rally Rhetoric." *MSNBC*, March 11, 2016. www.msnbc.com.

Manuel, George. *Fourth World: An Indian Reality*. New York: Collier-Macmillan Canada, 1974.

Marx, Karl. "Commodities." Chapter 1 of *Capital*, vol. 1, pt. 1, *Commodities and Money*. In *The Marx-Engels Reader*, edited by Robert C. Tucker. 2nd ed. New York: W. W. Norton, 1867.

McAdam, Sylvia. *Nationhood Interrupted: Revitalizing Nêhiyaw Legal Systems*. Illustrated ed. Saskatoon: Purich, 2015.

Mills, Aaron. "The Lifeworlds of Law: On Revitalizing Indigenous Legal Orders Today." *McGill Law Journal* 61, no. 4 (December 22, 2016): 847–84. https://doi.org/10.7202/1038490ar.

Mills, C. Wright. *The Sociological Imagination*. New York: Oxford University Press, 1959.

Moreton-Robinson, Aileen. *Critical Indigenous Studies: Engagements in First World Locations*. 1st ed. Tucson: University of Arizona Press, 2016.

———. "Locations of Engagement in the First World." In *Critical Indigenous Studies: Critical Issues in Indigenous Studies*, edited by A. Moreton-Robinson, 3–18. University of Arizona Press, 2016.

———. *The White Possessive: Property, Power, and Indigenous Sovereignty*. Minneapolis: University of Minnesota Press, 2015.

Naylor, Brian. "Graphic Video of Capitol Insurrection Opens Trump's Impeachment Trial." NPR, February 9, 2021. www.npr.org/.

Nichols, Robert. "Theft Is Property! The Recursive Logic of Dispossession." *Political Theory* 46, no. 1 (February 2018): 3–28. https://doi.org/10.1177/0090591717701709.

Pasternak, Shiri. "The Fiscal Body of Sovereignty: To 'Make Live' in Indian Country." *Settler Colonial Studies* 6, no. 4 (October 2016): 317–38. https://doi.org/10.1080/2201473X.2015.1090525.

Robertson, Dwanna L. "Decolonizing the Academy with Subversive Acts of Indigenous Research: A Review of Yakama Rising and Bad Indians." *Sociology of Race and Ethnicity* 2, no. 2 (April 2016): 248–52. https://doi.org/10.1177/2332649216628804.

Rodgers, Lucy, and Dominic Baily. "Trump Wall: How Much Has He Actually Built?" *BBC News*, October 31. 2020. www.bbc.com.

Romero, Mary. "Sociology Engaged in Social Justice." *American Sociological Review* 85, no. 1 (February 2020): 1–30. https://doi.org/10.1177/0003122419893677.

Ryser, Rudolph Carl, Dina Gilio-Whitaker, and Heidi G. Bruce. "Fourth World Theory and Methods of Inquiry." In *Handbook of Research on Theoretical Perspectives on Indigenous Knowledge Systems in Developing Countries*, edited by Patrick Ngulube, 50–84. Hershey, PA: IGI Global, 2017.

Sherwood, Yvonne P. "Toward, with, and from a Fourth World." *Fourth World Journal* 14, no. 2 (Winter 2016): 15–26.

Simpson, Audra. *Mohawk Interruptus: Political Life across the Borders of Settler States*. Durham, NC: Duke University Press, 2014.

———. "The Chief's Two Bodies: Theresa Spence and the Gender of Settler Sovereignty." Keynote presented at the R.A.C.E. Network's 14th Annual Critical Race and Anticolonial Studies Annual Conference . https://vimeo.com/110948627.

———. "The State Is a Man: Theresa Spence, Loretta Saunders and the Gender of Settler Sovereignty." *Theory & Event* 19, no. 4 (2016). http://muse.jhu.edu/article/633280.

Simpson, Leanne Betasamosake. *As We Have Always Done: Indigenous Freedom through Radical Resistance.* Minneapolis: University of Minnesota Press, 2017. https://doi.org/10.5749/j.ctt1pwt77c.

Smith, Linda Tuhiwai. *Decolonizing Methodologies: Research and Indigenous Peoples.* New York: Zed Books, 2007.

Speed, Shannon. "The Persistence of White Supremacy: Indigenous Women Migrants and the Structures of Settler Capitalism." *American Anthropologist* 122, no. 1 (2020): 76–85. https://doi.org/10.1111/aman.13359.

Spice, Anne. "Fighting Invasive Infrastructures: Indigenous Relations against Pipelines." *Environment and Society* 9, no. 1 (September 1, 2018): 40–56. https://doi.org/10.3167/ares.2018.090104.

Stark, Heidi. "Respect, Responsibility, and Renewal: The Foundations of Anishinaabe Treaty Making with the United States and Canada" *American Indian Culture and Research Journal* 34, no. 2 (January 1, 2010): 145–64. https://doi.org/10.17953/aicr.34.2.j0414503108l8771.

TallBear, Kim. "Caretaking Relations, Not American Dreaming." *Kalfou* 6, no. 1 (May 30, 2019): 24–41. https://doi.org/10.15367/kf.v6i1.228.

Toobin, Jeffrey. "Ending Trump's Assault on the Rule of Law," *New Yorker*, October 5, 2020. www.newyorker.com/.

Trimikliniotis, Nicos. "Public Sociology, Social Justice and Struggles in the Era of Austerity-and-Crises." *International Social Work* 63, no. 1 (January 1, 2020): 5–17. https://doi.org/10.1177/0020872818782324.

Tuck, Eve, and K. Wayne Yang. "Decolonization Is Not a Metaphor." *Decolonization: Indigeneity, Education & Society* 1, no. 1 (2012): 1–40.

———, eds. "Born under the Rising Sign of Social Justice." In *Toward What Justice?: Describing Diverse Dreams of Justice in Education.* 1st ed: 1-17. New York: Routledge, 2018.

Wilson, Alex. "Our Coming in Stories: Cree Identity, Body Sovereignty and Gender Self-Determination." *Journal of Global Indigeneity* 1, no. 4 (2015).

Wilson, Shawn. *Research Is Ceremony: Indigenous Research Methods.* Illustrated ed. Halifax: Fernwood, 2008.

Wolfe, Patrick. "Recuperating Binarism: A Heretical Introduction." *Settler Colonial Studies* 3, no. 3–4 (November 2013): 257–79. https://doi.org/10.1080/2201473X.2013.830587.

———. "Settler Colonialism and the Elimination of the Native." *Journal of Genocide Research* 8, no. 4 (2006): 387–409. https://doi.org/10.1080/14623520601056240.

Wunder, John R. "'Merciless Indian Savages' and the Declaration of Independence: Native Americans Translate the Ecunnaunuxulgee Document." *American Indian Law Review* 25, no. 1 (2000): 65–92. https://doi.org/10.2307/20070651.

7

In the Present Tense of Indigenous Politics

Lessons Learned from Hawaiʻi

MONISHA DAS GUPTA

I study migrant-led social justice movements in the United States. Trained as a feminist sociologist, I have lived my academic life in the last two decades in the critical and interdisciplinary spaces of ethnic studies and women, gender, and sexuality studies. As a sociologist, my work has been profoundly shaped by Michael Omi and Howard Winant's game-changing theory of racial formation and by Patricia Hill Collins's theorization of intersectionality. The theory of racial formation has been increasingly used in sociology to understand immigration to the United States and the processes through which immigrants are positioned in the US racial landscape. Likewise, I have learned from feminist scholar Priya Kandaswamy how useful it is to combine the theory of racial formation with the theory of intersectionality. The combination allows us to recognize the state itself as a site of conflict (rather than amelioration) over the co-constitution of race and gender.[1]

However, neither racial formation nor intersectionality is able to articulate the distinctive analytical tools required to grasp settler colonialism and assertions of Indigenous sovereignty that challenge settler politics. Since I moved from the US East Coast to teach at the University of Hawaiʻi at Mānoa in 2002, I have been thinking about the conceptual shifts required when bringing immigrant-led liberatory politics into conversation with Indigenous politics. The latter demand decolonial practices and visions of all movements for social transformation.[2] This thinking has been informed by my involvement in several Kanaka Maoli (Native Hawaiian)–led sovereignty movements as an Asian American settler in US-occupied Hawaiʻi. I discuss two such struggles—one to protect kalo (taro) and the other to protect Mauna a Wākea—below.

I want to note that the American Sociological Association (ASA) will have its first ever section dedicated to the sociology of Indigenous peoples and Native nations in 2021, 115 years after its establishment. This ASA section holds the promise of an emerging field of Indigenous sociology. Unlike anthropology, sociology has yet to see the kinds of interventions made by Indigenous scholars like Audra Simpson (Kahnawake Mohawk) and Ty Kāwika Tengan (Kanaka Maoli), who have offered new analytics and methodologies to their discipline. Their scholarship parts ways from those ethnographic frameworks that continue to culturalize sovereignty politics. They reframe Indigenous efforts to revive language and cultural practices and to restore the relationships between humans and other-than-humans as political acts that advance decolonial projects, which are centered on land-based governance rather than on the settler state.[3] Such projects can be neither equated with civil rights–based equity struggles nor contained within the US nation-state framework. Consequently, the questions about settler colonialism and the Indigenous politics of self-determination will require scholars to draw on theories, methodologies, and texts that are far outside of sociology.

My engagement with Indigenous politics to write about migrant justice represents a theoretical effort to grapple with these on-the-ground contradictions, as well as with connections between the two political projects—migrant rights and Indigenous sovereignty. In doing so, I build on my first book's critique of the modern (Westphalian) nation-state and its projection of territorial sovereignty, which comes with the legal division between citizens and non-citizens.[4] My current ethnography on anti-deportation activism in the United States and Hawai'i has been an experiment in writing about immigrant-led movements with the present tense of Indigenous politics in mind. This has led me to a line of inquiry about the extent to which migrant justice can move away from an investment in the settler state. I found that the coalitions and organizations I write about produce new narratives that depart from the settler myths of belonging and the promise of civil rights. This happens because they confront the combination of state-crafted crime control with immigration control. As a result, they sometimes, although not always, directly engage with the *settler* carceral nature of the US state, opening up possibilities for coalitional politics that question the United States' sovereignty.[5] In this essay, I share some lessons from Hawai'i to unpack the conceptual shifts I have had to make to account for Indigenous sovereignties as they operate today and the consequent disruptions to the territorial integrity of the United States.

I begin with the theoretical implications of reckoning with Indigenous sovereignty for some of the basic, taken-for-granted categories of sociological analysis that also cross over into ethnic studies. In line with the aims of this volume, I draw on the insights of settler colonial studies and critical Indigenous studies (CIS). These interdisciplinary fields offer two interrelated and foundational concepts: land-centered concepts of sovereignty, and Indigenous self-determination, which cannot be collapsed into civil rights–centered justice claims of racial minorities in the space we call the United States. I use the two Kanaka Maoli–led sovereignty struggles to protect kalo and Mauna a Wākea to illustrate the ʻŌiwi (Native Hawaiian) concepts of sovereignty that a racial formation and intersectional approach cannot adequately explain. The Kanaka Maoli mobilizations that I discuss below focus on relations of care for the elements, land, sources of fresh and saltwater, and plants (referred to as Aloha ʻĀina movements). The analytics are different from the race-class-gender framework usually used by sociologists and ethnic studies scholars to understand such uprisings. Just as ethnic studies scholars have been wrestling with the implications of settler colonialism and Indigenous sovereignty, so too will sociologists need to unlearn the very categories that organize knowledge in that discipline.

The first foundational concept is land.[6] American Indian studies scholar Mishuana Goeman (Tonawanda Seneca) points out that land is a keyword in Indigenous studies and is used "to invoke responsibility, rights, sovereignty" in contemporary Indigenous scholarship and self-determination movements.[7] Land attracts political, cultural, and ethical commitments. Settler colonialism is a very specific process that undercuts these commitments because it operates through land dispossession that severs Indigenous people from their genealogical and cultural ties to land in genocidal ways. Exercises of Indigenous sovereignty restore the relationships between humans and other-than-humans as political acts that advance decolonial projects. Such a project poses a further epistemological challenge for sociology, which as sociologist Erica Cudworth observes remains tethered to its foundational preoccupation with humans and social relations despite its critical direction.[8]

The second core concept is that Indigenous peoples are *not* racial or ethnic minorities. Racial and ethnic minorities do not have the right to self-determination as is the case for Indigenous peoples whose ongoing sovereignty is recognized in international treaties or treaties with the United States. Traditionally, US sociology has applied theories of ethnicity and race to discuss Indigenous people and their social formations. This tendency to privilege racial formations continues to inform recent efforts in sociology to engage settler colonialism as a process. Settler colonialism is put in the service of understanding heteropatriarchal White supremacy, as I elaborate below. The two critical Indigenous studies concepts decenter the approaches that sociology and ethnic studies have adopted to understand state sovereignty and struggles for social justice.

Land-Centered Concepts of Sovereignty

Indigenous studies calls attention to the dynamic link between the social and the natural (land, water, and elemental forms). These realms are not placed in a developmental hierarchy. This provokes a rethinking of how sociologists and those of us who study immigration theorize social relations and modern nation-state sovereignty. Indigenous studies insists on the intertwinement of politics, religion, arts, and culture in contemporary everyday interactions and intimate relations. In the context of sociology, such an insistence challenges the Weberian account of modernity, which unfolds with the separation of these spheres. The nation-state becomes the privileged site for politics. To define modernity (even as a lament) through the separation of the spheres is anti-Indigenous, since it puts Indigenous people in the past, representing them as unable to conform to and survive the demands of modernity. Thus, Indigenous studies necessarily generates critiques of Eurocentric knowledge. They expose the Western markers of modernity, which in effect disappear Indigenous people from the present.

Moreover, restoring the links between the social and the natural realms lies at the heart of Indigenous sovereignty struggles over territorial rights. The critical strain of CIS articulates concepts of sovereignty that diverge from state-centered and human-centered notions. Such an interrogation of state power disentangles understandings of Indigenous sovereignty from questions of state recognition and rejects state-endorsed proprietary definitions of land. CIS scholars name the very many technologies of continuous settling, desecrating, and toxifying Indigenous lands. These are settling practices geared toward eliminating Indigenous people and attacking their genealogical ties to the land and the elements. In my work, these redefinitions provoke me to ask what I can grasp about the US nation-state's sovereignty claims that I would not otherwise. To account for settler colonial power in anti-deportation activism, I focus not only on US sovereignty exercised in the form of border controls; I also frame deportation, which entails incarceration and removal, as a settler state technology to maintain control over the interior space, which, in fact, is disrupted by the realities of Indigenous nations. Deportation entrenches and legitimates US settler colonial power.

Only recently has settler colonialism been taken up in sociology. In a 2015 article, feminist sociologist and ethnic studies scholar Evelyn Nakano Glenn issues a rare invitation to sociologists to engage with scholar Patrick Wolfe, who argues that settler colonialism is an ongoing structure rather than an event in the past.[9] While she engages land dispossession as a central process, she continues to use racial-gender formation as the master frame by focusing on how those processes underpinned the settling of Indigenous lands. Building on Wolfe, Glenn asks sociologists to adopt settler colonialism as a framework that "can encompass racisms and sexisms affecting different racialized groups—especially Native Americans, blacks, Latinos and Asian Americans—while also highlighting structural and cultural factors that undergird and link these racisms and sexisms."[10] Thus, Native Americans, in this analysis, constitute another racialized group subjected to racist-patriarchal ideologies used to occupy their land rather than members of nations, not just in the past but today, with the distinct right of self-determination.

Glenn puts the framework of settler colonialism in the service of a better understanding of racial-gender formations. She shoehorns settler colonialism into structures of White supremacy and patriarchy to discuss US state strategies of removal, containment, exclusion, and deportation suffered by racial minorities. For Glenn, the framework of settler colonialism, then, serves its theoretical purpose to enable "a fuller incorporation of the role of Native Americans in how racism and gender oppression have developed and continue to operate."[11] Thus, her intellectual project is to investigate what US settler colonialism directed at Native Americans can say about variations in racism and sexism regionally and over time. I am suggesting a more robust approach that would attend to the dual importance of racial-gender formation and CIS paradigms. Indigeneity and Indigenous politics must be dealt with on their own terms while marking patriarchy and racism to understand how Indigenous people, settler migrants, and Indigenous migrants are positioned in distinct and intersecting systems of power.[12]

Distinctions between Indigenous Politics and Struggles for Racial Justice

The absorption of Indigenous self-determining polities (whether they are federally recognized or not) into a race relations model forecloses any serious engagement with settler colonialism. The interdisciplinary field of ethnic studies emerged out of a powerful social movement that initially saw racial minorities and Indigenous people fighting the same fight against capitalism, racism, and imperialism. In the last two decades, the field has increasingly responded to Indigenous studies by accounting for the fact that Indigenous people are fighting for sovereignty, with land and water protection at the center of these struggles. In distinguishing between the inception of ethnic studies and that of Indigenous studies, Lenape scholar Joanne Barker states that ethnic studies came out of struggles "for citizenship, voting rights and labor rights *within the state*" while the American Indian movement sought to exercise self-determination "*in relation* to the state."[13]

In the context of Hawai'i, Kanaka Maoli nationalist Haunani-Kay Trask names "genocide, land dispossession, language banning, family disintegration and cultural exploitation" as the ongoing mechanisms that erode Kanaka Maoli self-determination.[14] She argues that these injustices cannot be addressed through race-based civil rights remedies. She offers a sobering insight for scholars of race, racism, and immigration when she says, "In settler societies, the issue of civil rights is primarily an issue of how to protect settlers against each other and against the state."[15] In my own work, this realization has meant exploring intellectual and political alternatives that point away from the intra-settler negotiations over full US citizenship, a main goal of the mainstream immigrant rights movement. For Trask, landlessness and the resultant

impoverishment and criminalization of Native peoples and the exploitation of the land through tourism and the military continue to be central
to the Native Hawaiian movement, as will be evident from the examples
I give below.[16]

In Hawai'i, Kanaka Maoli struggles for sovereignty are an everyday
reality.[17] They represent steadfast and daily pushback against what Trask,
following Franz Fanon, has called "peaceful violence," or the normalization of US occupation of Hawai'i enacted through "historical dispossession, of racial, cultural and economic subjugation and stigmatization" as
well as overt acts of state violence.[18] The United States illegally occupied
Hawai'i in 1893 and annexed it in 1898. Hawai'i was a US territory until
it became the fiftieth state in 1959 through a plebiscite that was marred
by many irregularities. Unlike Native Americans, Kanaka Maoli do not
have a formalized trust relation with the United States. A 1993 Joint Resolution of Congress recognizes that the Hawaiian Kingdom was illegally
overthrown and Native Hawaiians "never directly relinquished to the
United States their claims to their inherent sovereignty as a people over
their national lands." This apology sits alongside US settler colonialism
operating under the guise of statehood, which has been challenged by
waves of Aloha 'Āina movements, through which Kanaka Maoli uphold
the sovereignty of the land and people.[19]

Sovereignty as expressed in Aloha 'Āina movements is a complex
concept. Kanaka Maoli scholar Noelani Goodyear-Ka'ōpua spotlights
the Hawaiian word ea. Ea constellates life, breath, and sovereignty.
Though ea is often used to declare political sovereignty, the three reg-
isters of ea are inseparable. She draws on Hawaiian language scholar
Leilani Basham's translation of King Kamehameha III's 1843 procla-
mation that sovereignty (ea) lay in the land, not the governance structure, and is perpetuated through righteous acts.[20] The daily practice
of ea against the assault on land, the ocean, and people through militarization and corporatization feeds the many Native Hawaiian–led
largescale mobilizations. In the time that I have lived in Hawai'i, I
have witnessed and participated in a number of highly visible and
large-scale struggles for self-determination led by Kanaka Maoli.
Many of these struggles have been successful. It is not difficult to see
the present tense of Indigenous politics here in US-occupied Hawai'i,
where I feel its daily throb.

Building Decolonial Movements 'Āina Up[21]

The two land-based struggles in Hawai'i I have selected explicate the analytical shifts that scholars looking to move beyond disciplinary boundaries need to make when examining oppression and social justice. Both struggles implicate the land grant university at which I work and the state of Hawai'i, which oversees its governance and, thanks to the neoliberal and entrepreneurial restructuring of public education, only partially funds. The struggles center the university's and state's monetization of land and life and their (failed) attempts to secure these interests. Kanaka maoli and kia'i (protectors) not only reframe arguments that privilege academic freedom and the advancement of scientific knowledge but also activate the reciprocal and caretaking relationship with the land as an assertion of ea in ways that cannot be grasped by theories of racialization or intersectionality. While racialized logics are certainly used to settle Indigenous lands, the exercise of sovereignty by restoring non-human and human connections requires the orientations and analytics proposed by CIS.

Patenting Kalo, Elder Sibling of Kanaka Maoli

The struggle against the patenting of kalo (taro) foregrounds notions of genealogy and 'Ōiwi epistemologies in the face of the university's efforts initiated in 2002 to monetize the use of three hybridized varieties of Hawaiian kalo by licensing these plants, more than three hundred varieties of which have been developed and tended through the centuries with Hawaiian knowledge. The example of this struggle orients sociologists and ethnic studies scholars to a CIS analytical frame, which hinges on the restoration of the relationship between humans and other-than-humans as political acts.

Under the patents, kalo farmers would have to enter an agreement with the university and pay royalties to use the patented cuttings (huli); the patents would prevent farmers themselves selling cuttings or breeding stock. The next year, the university in collaboration with the Hawai'i Agricultural Research Center began to genetically engineer kalo by inserting rice, wheat, and grapevine genes into three types of kalo, one of them Hawaiian (lehua). After a long and highly visible struggle with the university marked by Hawaiian protocol and the assertion of ea, the university dropped the patents in 2006.[22]

A powerful coalition of kalo farmers, Hawaiian charter schools, Hawaiian activists, and UH faculty and students called out the patenting efforts as a direct assault on the genealogical ties of kanaka (humans), who are younger siblings to Hāloa, the first kalo that grew from the burial site of a stillborn child of Wākea (representing the elemental force of the vast expanse of the sky) and his daughter, Hoʻohōkūkalani. The first human in Hawaiian tradition was the second child of Hoʻohōkūkalani. At a six-hundred-strong gathering at the university administration's offices at Bachmann Hall, Walter Ritte, a veteran of the Hawaiian sovereignty movement and a protector of the land and waters of the islands degraded by commercial and military development, declared, "The reason we are gathered is to honor Hāloa. We are Hāloa and Hāloa is us. No one can own us."[23] The conversion of plants that have flourished as a result of Indigenous knowledge into the intellectual property of non-Indigenous people in the service of profit is a flash point in movements worldwide. They have tenaciously resisted industrial agriculture's patenting of plant food sources and medicinal plants and the genetic modification of these food sources. In the case of Hawaiʻi, settler colonialism works to erase Kanaka Maoli presence and knowledge in the name of science. The appropriative actions masquerading as scientific innovation are driven by the university, which tried to sever the tie between Hawaiians and their relative, a plant, which in the settler world exists only to be instrumentalized.

The struggle to free kalo from the grip of privatization circulated the knowledge of elders (kūpuna) through the younger generations represented by the students at Hawaiian charter schools and those at the university. It challenged settler allies like me to grasp the significance of the ties between humans and other-than-humans as an epistemological (not anthropological) stance that Native Hawaiian feminist scholar Hōkūlani Aikau, a contributor to this volume, finds to be an essential orientation of settlers and Indigenous people alike in exercising their responsibility and obligations to the ʻāina.[24] To absorb the mutual and life-sustaining *familial* relationship between humans and land requires undoing the binary formulations on which the social sciences like sociology depend, such as humans/nonhumans, science/culture, and knowledge/myth. Native Hawaiian feminist scholar Noelani Goodyear Ka'ōpua undoes these binaries when she reminds us that "the health and well-being of Kānaka Maoli and of Hāloa, the kalo, are intimately tied. Through our cultural practices and propagating kalo, our kūpuna (ancestors) were able to sustain a population of approximately one million people in the islands with no imported foods. Hāloa, in turn, has enabled our ancestors to thrive for thousands of years. Together, they interwove a rich cultural heritage with ecological and social health."[25] This recognition would require those who study race and racism to do a different type of work. For example, it would require scholars to consider what it means for a plant to be related to humans through a sexual relationship between a father and daughter. It would require them to go beyond undoing the Black/White, woman/man, and normative/non-normative sexuality binaries even as we critique capital's relentless march toward commodification and examine the state as a site of conflict over stabilizing these binaries. Hawai'i and Asian American studies scholar Candace Fujikane, drawing on her immersion in land protection movements, argues that decolonial praxis requires the cultivation of knowledge and practice of Hawaiian protocols that ask not for a type of recognition that can be granted by the state but for a recognition from the land and elemental forms themselves to perpetuate the laws that govern dynamic relations of mutual care and responsibility.[26]

Kū Kia'i Mauna

Most recently, ea surges through the massive mobilization to protect Mauna a Wākea, a sacred site for Kanaka Maoli, from further desecration by the construction of a proposed thirty-meter telescope (TMT) to be built on state-designated conservation land on an existing complex of thirteen operating astronomy observatories managed by the University of Hawai'i.[27] In addition to astronomy research, the observatories also host a visitors' center and is a popular tourist site. The struggle on the part of Kanaka Maoli to stop the expansion of unpermitted observatories and the mismanagement of the lands by the university and by the state has spanned fifty years.[28] Analytically, I use this example to make cultural and language resurgence legible as a decolonial project. Such projects work in conjunction with the imperative illustrated above, in the case of Hāloa, that humans (kanaka) live in a relationship of responsibility to their other-than-human kin. I aim to expand the parameters of sociological approaches to facilitate a fruitful conversation with ethnic studies and Indigenous studies.

The struggle has upheld the cultural and ecological significance of Mauna a Wākea, a dormant volcano that rises 4,200 meters above sea on Hawai'i Island. It is sacred because it is the firstborn of Wākea and Papahānaumoku (the force that births islands) and, therefore, the oldest sibling of the kalo plant and Kanaka. Mauna a Wākea is the *piko*, both summit and umbilicus, that connects the people to their ancestors as well as future generations. Burial grounds where Hawaiian ancestors rest is located near the summit.[29]

Resistance to further development mounted in the last decade, once the state Board of Land and Natural Resources approved a 2010 Conservation District Use Permit application by the University of Hawai'i at Hilo to build the TMT. In a classic settler arrangement, the university has since 1968 leased the land from the state for one dollar a year, while the observatory generates tax revenues for the state—estimated to be $8.15 million in 2014, when the figure was last available—and extramural research dollars for the university.[30] The university and the state have pressed ahead with the TMT, an internationally backed $1.4 billion corporatized project, sparking a series of non-violent direct actions since 2013, when the ground-breaking ceremony for the proposed telescope was held.[31]

The stand to prevent the TMT construction in 2019 attracted thousands of kia'i across the islands, across Oceania, and across other Native nations. The momentum to stop construction built in the wake of a textbook settler ruling issued by the Hawaii State Supreme Court in 2018 to proceed with construction on the grounds that the TMT could not possibly cause further damage to an already degraded summit. As it became clear that state government, with the full backing of the university, would initiate another attempt at construction, the kia'i faculty and staff at UH declared in a January 2019 statement, "Our call to terminate the construction of the TMT is made in acknowledgment of the sovereignty of the Hawaiian nation and its unbroken claim to Mauna a Wākea as part of the Hawaiian national lands and to respect and honor Native Hawaiian spiritual and cultural beliefs, customs and practices."[32]

The unequivocal assertion of sovereignty illustrates the distinction be-tween such calls and demands of racial minorities for equality under the law and for the leveling of race-based disparities in socioeconomic out-comes. The assertion of sovereignty exercised with the discipline of kapu aloha—the sanction to always act with love, compassion, respect, and non-violence toward kiaʻi as well as aggressors to honor the sacredness of a particular place—fueled the mobilization in early July in response to the governor's order to move construction equipment up the mountain in yet another effort to build the TMT.[33] As of this writing, the Mauna Kea movement has effectively blocked the construction.

As kiaʻi gathered to confront the state and its use of force, they created a sanctuary space or puʻuhonua, which was established at Puʻuhululu. On July 17, thirty-eight elders, many of them in wheelchairs, put them-selves in the frontlines of the peaceful blockade and were arrested. Their public criminalization for exercising their sovereignty and defending the mountain from further desecration and degradation strengthened the steadfast resistance to the TMT. From July until March of 2020, Puʻuhonua Puʻuhululu served to hold the space and to teach and prac-tice the principles of aloha ʻāina, which are always intermingled with the exercise of ea, offering alternatives ways of living, relating, and knowing to the extractive and destructive technologies of settler colonialism.[34] These alternative framings bumped up against the overtly racist por-trayals by pro-TMT state actors of Native Hawaiians as primitive and anti-science in their invocation of the sacred.[35] Kanaka Maoli and other Indigenous people have long been racialized as backward and primitive, as in this case, and their resistance framed as an obstacle to modernity. The appropriation of their land and the destruction of their culture is justified in the name of progress. Racism certainly structured the pro-TMT discourse. The discourses and actions of kiaʻi contested these racist tropes to demonstrate ea at work, introducing and reaffirming principles that inform decolonial projects.

The decolonial learning and practice were not restricted to the Mauna but spread across the islands. Those who supported the movement at-tended ʻaha (gathering and ceremony) at different sites across the is-lands. Protocols were conducted three times a day—morning, noon, and dusk—and were led by kumu, Hawaiian teachers and practitioners, among them ethnic studies professor Ty Kāwika Tengan, who led them at the Mānoa campus. On the mauna, as singer and composer Kainani Kahauanaele observes, the daily ceremonies that drew on ancient and modern mele (song) had a regenerative effect: "As the lāhui [nation] learned the chants line by line, image by image, movement by movement, with repetition, reverence, intention, and application, our nation was rising more than ever." Kahauanaele, who is part of the Hawaiian language revitalization movement, underscores that mele encapsulates knowledge about place, times, gods (akua and aumakua), and people.[36] Such knowledge feeds the demand for self-determination and territorial rights.

This everyday dimension and spread of the multifaceted decolonial work, evident during the entire fall semester of 2019 at Mānoa campus, called on people of color and Black residents to practice allyship with Kānaka Maoli in embodied ways. It modeled the kind of commitments that are required of immigrant allies in Indigenous struggles. Through hula (dance), oli (chant) and mele, kiaʻi at Mānoa marshaled their strength to struggle, supported the efforts of those on the mauna, and reaffirmed the importance of place-based knowledge.[37] Native and non-Native students, staff, and faculty with different levels of language and protocol proficiency had the opportunity to join this daily practice to honor the elements and the land. These modes of teaching, learning, and practice represent a resurgence of ea, a reinvigoration of the ethic of care (mālama) extended to life-sustaining connections that people have with the land, sky, clouds, water, and people. For me as a settler ally, hearing and learning ʻŌlelo Hawaiʻi (Hawaiian language) in a public space outside of a formal classroom or lecture along with a large number of people dissipated the peaceful violence that Trask diagnoses in the "naturalness of hearing English on the street."[38] The performance of the protocols educated people about ʻŌiwi science, love of the land, the history of the Hawaiian nation, and the enduring spirit of resistance in the face of all odds.

The present tense of Native Hawaiian sovereignty is inescapable in both the examples I have offered. These examples of land-based struggles continue in the footsteps of those waged by the Hawaiian movement in the 1970s to assert their rights as sovereign people.[39] They embody expressions of ea to defy the settler state's instrumentalization of land and culture to prop up a capitalist economy. Land—taking care of it and protecting it against settler colonial destruction—is at the naʻau (gut, mind, heart, affection) of these Kanaka Maoli-led struggles. My account above highlights the dynamic and storied relationships between humans, places, and other-than-humans. These analytics destabilize the more familiar approaches of racial formation theory, which teaches us to trace the ongoing conflicts through which racial categories are invented, inhabited, and destroyed, and the racial projects that advance equity or entrench inequality.

Conclusion

These lessons from Hawaiʻi emphasize activist revitalization of Kanaka Maoli relations to land and ocean, steering those who study race, racism, and immigration through an intersectional lens toward critical Indigenous studies. Each struggle asserts Hawaiian independence. Each struggle resists the settler logics of monetizing land through public policy and the criminalization of Hawaiians under settler law. My colleague Ty Kāwika Tengan always emphasizes that these Aloha ʻĀina movements, easily translated apolitically as the love for the land, are in fact deeply connected to the expression and assertion of sovereignty instantiated in the people taking care of the land so that all life is sustained.

Questioning the securitization of the US national space, where Indigenous sovereignty in fact operates, allows me to see the limits of migrant struggles built on formal inclusion into a settler pact. The promise in the anti-deportation movement that I have been documenting elsewhere, led by folks who have been charged criminally or have criminal convictions, lies in their efforts to move away from appealing to the state for incorporation. They reach toward non-statist community based futures and the practice of mutual aid. Because the anti-deportation activists about whom I write directly engage the carceral state, they can move away from reinscribing settler scripts rife in the immigrant rights movement of the deserving law-abiding migrant ensconced in proper domestic arrangements.

Ethnic studies scholars Karen Leong and Myla Vincenti Carpio ask us to look for the linkages among differential state practices of carcerality that result in distinct outcomes of dispossession, displacement, rightlessness, and removal.[40] Putting pressure on the irreducibility of migrant and Indigenous politics illuminates a common object of analysis—how the production of US sovereignty has obscured the presence of sovereign Indigenous polities within and across bordered, policed, and contained space.

NOTES

1 Omi and Winant, *Racial Formation in the United States*; Kandaswamy, "Gendering Racial Formation Theory."

2 Das Gupta, "Rights in a Transnational Era"; Das Gupta and Haglund, "Mexican Migration to Hawaiʻi and US Settler Colonialism"; Lee-Oliver et al. "Imperialism, Settler Colonialism, and Indigeneity."

3 Simpson, *Mohawk Interruptus*; Tengan and Roy, "'I Search for the Channel'"; Tengan, Kaʻili, and Fonoti, "Genealogies"; Tengan, *Native Men Remade*. Decolonial visions depart from post–World War II decolonization projects, which aimed at capturing state power, and in their postcolonial form never achieved a clean break from colonial logics.

4 Das Gupta, *Unruly Immigrants*.

5 See also Walia, *Undoing Border Imperialism*.

6 In the Pacific, land and ocean together constitute an oceanic framework. ʻĀina, in Hawaiian language (Ōlelo Hawaiʻi), encompasses lands, freshwaters, and saltwaters.

7 Aikau et al., "Indigenous Feminisms Roundtable," 95.

8 Cudworth, "Killing Animals."

9 Wolfe, "Settler Colonialism and the Elimination of the Native."

10 Glenn, "Settler Colonialism as Structure," 52.

11 Ibid., 69.

12 For an example of this type of approach, see Fojas, Guevarra, and Sharma, *Beyond Ethnicity*.

13 Barker, "Introduction," 8.

14 Trask, *From a Native Daughter*.

15 Ibid., 25.

16 Trask, "The Color of Violence."

17 Some exemplary works are Silva, *Aloha Betrayed*; McGregor, *Na Kua ʻAina*; Goodyear-Kaʻōpua, Hussey, and Wright, *A Nation Rising*; Goodyear-Kaʻōpua, *Nā Wāhine Koa*; Kuwada and Revilla, "We Are Maunakea"; Tengan, "Hoa."

18 Trask, "The Color of Violence," 10.

19 United States Congress, United States Public Law 103–150.

20 Goodyear-Kaʻōpua, "Introduction," 3–7. King Kamehameha III presided over the return of sovereignty to the Hawaiian Kingdom after a rogue British naval effort to claim the islands for Great Britain in 1843. King Kamehameha declared, "Ua ma uke ea o ka ʻāina i ka pono," translated by Basham as, "The sovereignty of the land continues through justice and proper acts" ("Introduction," 4).

21 I am adopting the expression ʻāina up from Hawaiian activist Laulani Teale, who uses it in her interview with J. Kēhaulani Kauanui on Horizontal Power Hour, "Episode 38."

22 Ing, "Hawaiian Groups Voice Opposition to Taro Patents"; Hawaiʻi SEED, *Facing Hawaiʻi's Future*, 68, 75–76; Organic Consumers Association, "Native Hawaiians Protest Patent on the Sacred Taro Plant,"; Essoyan, "Activists Tear Up 3 UH Patents for Taro."

23 Ing, "Hawaiian Groups Voice Opposition to Taro Patents," 1.

24 Aikau et al., "Indigenous Feminisms Roundtable," 84–88.

25 Goodyear-Kaʻōpua, "Kuleana Lāhui" 149–50.

26 Fujikane, *Mapping Abundance for a Planetary Future.*

27 A substantial number of publications provide analyses of the 2019 stand on Mauna Kea. See "States of Emergency/Emergence: Learning from Mauna Kea," *Abolition Journal*; Kuwada and Revilla; hoʻomanawanui et al., "Teaching for Maunakea"; J. Kēhaulani Kauanui et al., "Mauna Kea"; Kaneaokana.net has curated resources about the struggle and the legal battles. The Facebook Puʻuhonua o Puʻuhuluhulu Maunakea page has a record of all the activities on the mauna as well as media coverage and kiaʻi analyses.

28 Kanaeokana, "50 Years of Mismanaging Maunakea." See "States of Emergency/Emergence: Learning from Mauna Kea"; Kuwada and Revilla, "Introduction: Mana from the Mauna"; hoʻomanawanui et al., "Teaching for Maunakea"; J. Kēhaulani Kauanui et al., "Mauna Kea."

29 Iwi kūpuna (ancestral remains) were buried in each of the many puʻu (cinder cones) across the mountain.

30 TMT, "TMT Supporting the Economy"; Associated Press, "University: Losing Hawaii Telescope Risks Billions in Funds."

31 Perry, "Court Decision on Mauna Kea Threatens Hawaiian Rights."

32 Faculty and Staff of University of Hawaiʻi System Campuses, "We Will Persist in Our Sacred Commitment to Protect Mauna A Wākea," January 31, 2019. Document in author's possession.

33 Goodyear-Kaʻōpua, "Protectors of the Future."

34 See hoʻomanawanui et al., "Teaching for Maunakea"; Kuwada and Revilla, "Introduction: Mana from the Mauna."

35 Aurora Kagawa-Viviani, "Maunakea"; Kuwada, "We Live in the Future."

36 Kahauanaele, "Mele and ʻŌlelo Hawaiʻi on the Mauna," 541, 545.

37 University of Hawaiʻi System News, "Maunakea Sit In."

38 Trask, "The Color of Violence," 10.

39 See Trask, *From a Native Daughter*; McGregor, *Na Kua ʻAina*; Goodyear-Kaʻōpua, Hussey, and Wright, *A Nation Rising.*

40 Leong and Carpio, "Carceral States."

BIBLIOGRAPHY

Aikau, Hokulani, Maile Arvin, Mishuana Goeman, and Scott Morgensen. "Indigenous Feminisms Roundtable." *Frontiers: A Journal of Women's Studies* 36, no. 3 (2015): 84–106.

Akaka, Moanikeʻala, Maxine Kahaulelio, Terrilee Kekoʻolani-Raymond, Loretta Ritte, and Noelani Goodyear-Kaʻōpua, eds. *Nā Wāhine Koa: Hawaiian Women for Sovereignty and Demilitarization.* Honolulu: University of Hawaiʻi Press, 2018.

Associated Press. "University: Losing Hawaii Telescope Risks Billions in Funds." *AP News*, April 21, 2021. https://apnews.com.

Barker, Joanne. "Introduction: Critically Sovereign." In *Critically Sovereign: Indigenous Gender, Sexuality and Feminist Studies*, edited by Joanne Barker, 1–44. Durham, NC: Duke University Press, 2017.

Byrd, Jodi A. *The Transit of Empire: Indigenous Critiques of Colonialism.* Minneapolis: University of Minnesota Press, 2011.

Collins, Patricia Hill. *Black Feminist Thought.* New York: Routledge, 1991.

Cudworth, Erica. "Killing Animals: Sociology, Species Relations and Institutionalized Violence." *Sociological Review* 63, no. 1 (2015): 1–18. https://doi.org/doi:10.1111/1467-954X.12222.

Das Gupta, Monisha. "Rights in a Transnational Era." In *Immigrant Rights in the Shadows of Citizenship*, edited by Rachel Ida Buff, 402–23. New York: New York University Press, 2008.

———. *Unruly Immigrants: Rights, Activism, and Transnational South Asian Politics in the United States.* Durham, NC: Duke University Press, 2006.

Das Gupta, Monisha, and Sue Haglund. "Mexican Migration to Hawaiʻi and US Settler Colonialism." *Latino Studies* 13, no. 4 (2015): 455–80.

Essoyan, Susan. "Activists Tear Up 3 UH Patents for Taro." GRAIN, June 21, 2006. https://grain.org.

Fojas, Camilla, Rudy P. Guevarra, and Nitasha T. Sharma, eds. *Beyond Ethnicity: New Politics of Race in Hawaiʻi.* Honolulu: University of Hawaiʻi Press, 2018.

Fujikane, Candace. *Mapping Abundance for a Planetary Future: Kanaka Maoli and Critical Settler Cartographies in Hawaiʻi.* Durham, NC: Duke University Press, 2021.

Glenn, Evelyn Nakano. "Settler Colonialism as Structure: A Framework for Comparative Studies of U.S. Race and Gender Formation." *Sociology of Race and Ethnicity* 1, no. 1 (2015): 52–72.

Goodyear-Kaʻōpua, Noelani. Introduction to *A Nation Rising: Hawaiian Movements for Life, Land and Sovereignty*, edited by Noelani Goodyear-Kaʻōpua, Erin Kahunawaikaʻala Wright, and Ikaika Hussey. Durham, NC: Duke University Press, 2014.

———. "Kuleana Lāhui: Collective Responsibility for Hawaiian Nationhood in Activists' Praxis." *Affinities: A Journal of Radical Theory, Culture, and Action* 5, no. 1 (2011): 130–63.

———. "Protectors of the Future, Not Protestors of the Past: Indigenous Pacific Activism and Mauna a Wākea." *South Atlantic Quarterly* 116, no. 1 (2017): 184–94.

Goodyear-Kaʻōpua, Noelani, Ikaika Hussey, and Erin Kahunawaikaʻala Wright, eds. *A Nation Rising: Hawaiian Movements for Life, Land, and Sovereignty.* Durham, NC: Duke University Press, 2014.

Hawai'i SEED. *Facing Hawai'i's Future*. Koloa, HI: Hawai'i SEED, 2006.

Horizontal Power Hour. "Episode 38: DeOccupy Honolulu." *Horizontal Power Hour*, March 27, 2012. https://horizontalpowerhour.wordpress.com/2012/03/.

ho'omanawanui, ku'ualoha, Candace Fujikane, Aurora Kagawa-Viviani, Kerry K. Long, and Kekailoa Perry. "Teaching for Maunakea: Kia'i Perspectives." *Amerasia Journal* 45, no. 2 (2019): 271–76.

Ing, Matthew K. "Hawaiian Groups Voice Opposition to Taro Patents." *Ka Leo O Hawai'i*, March 6, 2006.

Kagawa-Viviani, Aurora. "Maunakea: Redirecting the Lens onto the Culture of Mainstream Science." *Medium*, November 7, 2019. https://medium.com.

Kahauanaele, Kainani. "Mele and 'Ōlelo Hawai'i on the Mauna." *Biography: An Interdisciplinary Quarterly* 43, no. 3 (2020): 541–50.

Kanaeokana. "50 Years of Mismanaging Maunakea." Puuhonua o Puuhuluhulu, 2019. www.puuhuluhulu.com/.

Kandaswamy, Priya. "Gendering Racial Formation Theory." In *Racial Formation in the Twenty-First Century*, edited by Daniel HoSang, Oneka LaBennett, and Laura Pulido, 23–43. Berkeley: University of California Press, 2012.

Kuwada, Bryan K. "We Live in the Future. Come Join Us." *Ke Kaupu Hehi Ale* (blog), April 3, 2015. https://hehiale.com/.

Kuwada, Bryan K., and No'u Revilla. "Introduction: Mana from the Mauna" for "We Are Maunakea: Aloha 'Āina Narratives of Protest, Protection, and Place, Special Issue." *Biography: An Interdisciplinary Quarterly* 43, no. 3 (2020): 515–26.

———, eds. "We Are Maunakea: Aloha 'Āina Narratives of Protest, Protection, and Place, Special Issue." *Biography: An Interdisciplinary Quarterly* 43, no. 3 (2020).

Lee-Oliver, Leece, Monisha Das Gupta, Katherine Fobear, and Edward Ou Jin Lee. "Imperialism, Settler Colonialism, and Indigeneity: A Queer Migration Roundtable." In *Queer and Trans Migrations: Dynamics of Illegalization, Detention, and Deportation*, edited by Eithne Luibhéid and Karma R. Chávez, 226–55. Urbana: University of Illinois Press, 2020.

Leong, Karen, and Myla Vincenti Carpio. "Carceral States: Converging Indigenous and Asian Experiences in the Americas." *Amerasia Journal* 42, no. 1 (2016): vii–xviii.

McGregor, Davianna P. *Na Kua 'Aina*. Honolulu: University of Hawai'i Press, 2007.

Omi, Michael, and Howard Winant. *Racial Formation in the United States: From the 1960s and the 1980s*. New York: Routledge, 1986.

Organic Consumers Association. "Native Hawaiians Protest Patent on the Sacred Taro Plant." Organic Consumers Association, May 19, 2006. www.organicconsumers.org.

Perry, Kekailoa. "Court Decision on Mauna Kea Threatens Hawaiian Rights." *Ke Kaupu Hehi Ale* (blog), February 15, 2019. https://hehiale.com/.

Silva, Noenoe. *Aloha Betrayed: Native Hawaiian Resistance to American Colonialism*. Durham, NC: Duke University Press, 2004.

Simpson, Audra. *Mohawk Interruptus: Political Life Across the Borders of Settler States*. Durham, NC: Duke University Press, 2014.

Tengan, Ty P. Kāwika. "Hoa: On Being and Binding Relations." *Amerasia Journal*, 2021. https://doi.org/10.1080/00447471.2021.1922235.

———. *Native Men Remade: Gender and Nation in Contemporary Hawaiʻi*. Durham, NC: Duke University Press, 2008.

Tengan, Ty P. Kāwika, Tēvita O. Kaʻili, and Rochelle T. Fonoti. "Genealogies: Articulating Indigenous Anthropology in/of Oceania." *Pacific Studies* 33, no. 2/3 (2010): 139–67.

Tengan, Ty P. Kāwika, and Lamaku M. Roy. "ʻI Search for the Channel Made Fragrant by the Maileʼ: Genealogies of Discontent and Hope." *Oceania* 84, no. 3 (2014): 315–30.

TMT. "TMT Supporting the Economy." *Maunakea & TMT* (blog). Accessed July 20, 2021. www.maunakeaandtmt.org.

Trask, Haunani-Kay. *From a Native Daughter: Colonialism and Sovereignty in Hawaiʻi*. Honolulu: University of Hawaiʻi Press, 1999.

———. "The Color of Violence." *Social Justice* 31, no. 4 (2004): 8–16.

United States Congress. "United States Public Law 103–150: 103rd Congress Joint Resolution 19," November 23, 1993. www.govinfo.gov.

University of Hawaiʻi System News. "Maunakea Sit In at Bachman Hall Part of Long History of Sit Ins." Accessed July 20, 2021. www.hawaii.edu.

Voices of Truth. *Law of The Splintered Paddle—A Visit With Laulani Teale*. YouTube video, Honolulu, 2012. www.youtube.com/watch?v=W5MaonyEuYs.

Wolfe, Patrick. "Settler Colonialism and the Elimination of the Native." *Journal of Genocide Research* 7, no. 2 (2006): 387–409.

8

A Healing Methodology

An Indigenous Research Process

MELISSA HORNER

In many [research] projects the process is far more important than the outcome. Processes are expected to be
respectful, to enable people, and *to heal* and *to educate*.
They are expected to lead one small step further towards
self-determination.[1]

Michi Saagiig Nishnaabeg researcher Leanne Betasamosake Simpson
states that "processing underlying trauma and abuse in a responsible
way" is one of the most radical moves Indigenous Peoples can make in
our being and doing within contemporary social, political, and cultural
domains.[2] I respond to this awareness by recognizing that I cannot be
a good researcher or good relative unless I am a healing researcher and
healing relative. Thus, my research seeks to find an honest and respectful way to think, feel, talk, and know about issues that are challenging
for some Indigenous Peoples to acknowledge and navigate, particularly
the myriad manifestations of intergenerational historical trauma that
still appear in our families, nations, communities, and selves.[3] I particularly keep in mind the meaning of this research for reconnecting
Native people (including Indigenous researchers) like me from families
like mine—individuals who have been disconnected in the last couple
generations from their Indigenous homelands, cultures, nations, ceremonies, and languages due to settler colonial policies and practices
of assimilation and erasure on Turtle Island.[4] Métis Anishinaabekwe
scholar Chantal Fiola shares a conversation she had with a Métis friend
in which "she emotionally referred to us—Métis people—as *the lost children*, but at the time was not able to articulate why."[5] Fiola goes on to

say, "Pitawanakwat (2008), a scholar with mixed Aboriginal ancestry, echoes this sentiment when he states, 'The trouble with being (almost) assimilated is that I know something is missing but I am not sure what' (161)."[6] In this spirit, I hope the research project glimpsed in this essay will be meaningful (to my family, tribal nations, Indigenous Peoples, and myself) by creating healing opportunities through the research process and methodology itself. Thus, this essay finds roots in my orienting questions: 1) How are Native individuals navigating and healing the effects of intergenerational historical trauma caused by past and present settler colonialism? and 2) As Indigenous individuals, how do I/we heal intergenerational historical trauma and (re)connect to our Indigeneity in relationship through the research process?

As a way to explore these questions, this chapter puts forth an Indigenous methodological framework I call a *Healing Methodology*. This methodology emerged as the most authentic for my research purpose as it keeps (re)connection to Indigeneity and Indigenous healing from intergenerational historical trauma (IHT) as its metaphoric north star. A Healing Methodology asks me and co-participants to consider: Which is the route to get to my/our healing? What decisions lead to the next best step toward individual, relational, and collective healing? How is movement toward healing anchoring each decision in this research project? How are my/our decisions, methods, and questions always working to create and support healing for me/us? Is the research methodology itself facilitating healing in real time? How do I/we know healing is happening? A Healing Methodology is also part of a growing contingency of Indigenous research including what Anishinaabekwe researcher Kathleen Absolon calls "'conscious Indigenous scholars' [which] refers to those Indigenous scholars who are aware of our cultural and colonial history and who are on a path of intentionally learning, recovering, and reclaiming their Indigeneity."[7]

A Healing Methodology attempts to learn how Indigenous individuals navigate and heal IHT in their lives independent from this research project, and it seeks to transform emotions, realities, and experiences through its aim to create healing within and among co-participants. A Healing Methodology contains two families of methods: the first, Methods for Healing, is intended to produce healing, not collect/produce data according to Western qualitative traditions; the second, Methods for Gathering, is designed to gather, process, and understand the healing that has been produced as a result of the research. Methods for Healing and Methods for Gathering are mutually constitutive.[8] As a result of integrating Methods for Healing, co-participants can experience healing, and within Methods for Gathering, healing can also occur. Methods for Gathering offer a way to gain a meta-perspective about what co-participants experience as a result of the Methods for Healing, including insights gained, emotions processed, and specific moments co-participants identify healing happened. As a result of this reflection process, continued healing can occur following experiences intended to produce healing. These two families of methods are in a constant constitutive relationship throughout this project.

I situate a Healing Methodology within a broader context of Indigenous methodologies. An important consideration I have learned from academic aunties and uncles whose research is guided by Indigenous methodologies (e.g., Kathleen Absolon, Shawn Wilson, Jaquetta Shade-Johnson, Chantal Fiola, Michelle Jacob, Leanna Betasamosake Simpson, and Jo-ann Archibald) is that Indigenous methodologies are often specific to Indigenous individuals, Native nations, and communities. In other words, Indigenous methodologies are research methods, approaches, and practices that stem from various unique Indigenous epistemologies, beliefs, values, and processes, and these methodologies are holistic, relational, and interdependent with Indigenous knowledge systems and ways of being. The application of these methodologies is not a one-size-fits-all for all Indigenous research(ers). For example, Absolon's Indigenous methodology is grounded in her identity and relationships as Anishinaabekwe from Flying Post First Nation, and she created the metaphor of a petal flower methodology to guide her research.[9] Absolon's Indigenous methodology is different from Shawn Wilson's Indigenous methodology, which comes from his familial and social position and experiences as a Opaskwayak Cree and Scottish Canadian person. Wilson's Indigenous methodology posits that for him, all research is a ceremony.[10] In these two examples, the researchers make methodological decisions based on their respective relational identities, cultural epistemologies, and research contexts, which contain different Indigenous ways of knowing and involve different Indigenous people and places. Concretely, when I examine my own research through Indigenous methodological considerations, I ask myself several questions. How/ why does it matter for my intended research that I am a reconnecting biracial/cultural Métis/Anishinaabe and White researcher? What kind of relationships do I have with the Native people I seek to do research with? What are my responsibilities (based on the relationships) to the Indigenous folks involved in my research? Finally, I recognize that a Healing Methodology is not a methodological prescription for all Native Peoples, researchers, and contexts interested in healing and is one version of an increasing number of Indigenous research methodologies.

Researcher in Relational Context

Before delving into my research project and a Healing Methodology, it is crucial to share how I am in relationship with the ideas shared in this essay, which means I need to share about my interconnected relatives, places, and languages. Transparency in who my family is, where I am placed, and how I am connected to this research is a common Indigenous methodological practice. Much of my research draws on Indigenous autoethnographic sensibilities that incorporate my own experiences, and since I arrive to this work not only as an individual but as part of a community, I acknowledge and name the generations who came before me, especially considering the foundation of this research and methodology is rooted in intergenerationality.[11]

I come to this chapter carrying within me tangles of Turtle Island's complicated imperial, Indigenous, and settler colonial past and present. I come from people who spoke French, Anishinaabemowin, English, Cree, German, Russian, and Michif. Through one part of my family, I come from immigrants of Germany, England, and Russia. They were teachers, learners, parents, children, and farmers. They settled in North Dakota and Wisconsin. They came to what is colonially known as the United States to fulfill purposes they imagined from across the Atlantic.[12] As immigrants benefiting from the established structure of settler colonialism, they lent their minds, bodies, and words to a nation continuously building on the genocide of Native Peoples. Through another family branch, I come from French trappers, woodspeople, and fur traders who meandered back and forth along the then nonexistent boundary dividing the plains between Canada and the United States. I come from the relationships between the French and the First Nations Nêhiyaw and Anishinaabeg, who established a new nation of people known as *wissakodewinmi* (half-burnt woodspeople) in Anishinaabemowin, and *otipemisiwak* (those who rule themselves) in Nêhiyawêwin—the Métis People. I also come from Anishinaabe farther south who journeyed west from the Great Lakes to the Turtle Mountains. I am the product of movement and journey, of displacement and disruption, of relationships. In many ways, I am a product of violent settler colonization and the Indigenous ways of knowing and being that antecede settler colonialism by thousands of years. More specifically, I am the daughter of Janice Kuhn and Daryl Horner. I descend from German, Russian, and English immigrants who now identify as White Americans. I am of Métis/Michif descent (Moreau, Desjarlais, and Montour families) with ties to lands in Saskatchewan and Manitoba—around Winnipeg/Red River Settlement. I am a first-generation unenrolled descendant of the Turtle Mountain Band of Chippewa Indians (Jerome family), where my mother, aunties, and uncles are enrolled tribal citizens. My grandmother, Irene Jerome, was born on Treaty 6 territory near the current seat of Muskeg Cree Nation in Marcelin, Saskatchewan, Canada, and was my last immediate relative to live on the Turtle Mountain reservation in North Dakota. I was born in and call my homeplace the southwest region of Montana on lands with whom the Apsaalooké (Crow), Séliš (Bitterroot Salish), Ktunaxa (Kootenai), Piikani (Blackfeet), Shoshone-Bannock, and Tsétsêhést'hese (Northern Cheyenne), among others, hold historic and enduring relationships.

For most of my life, I primarily experienced my Indigenous relatives through trauma, and when the trauma in my family became so entangled with our identities and behaviors, it begins to look like a part of our Indigenous culture. The settler colonial–imposed traumas of my ancestors slip into the DNA, the homes, the words, and the actions of my grandparents, parents, aunties, uncles, and me.[13] Historic traumas are passed down to the present and layered upon by new traumas kept alive by the old ones, readying the next generation to inherit the past again and again and again. In these ways, as a multiracial, multicultural product of settler colonialism, rather than simply thinking my history, I feel it. Tanana Athabascan scholar Dian Million most aptly describes this feeling when she writes, "Canada and the United States have resisted the truth in the emotional content of felt knowledge: colonialism as it is felt by those who experience it."[14]

The specific understandings I share in this chapter are the entangled result of many ancestors, places, and events that have come before me, and so it is not only me here writing about these ideas and realities. They are all here too.

Research Project Background

Researchers and non-researchers alike define and explain intergenerational historical trauma (IHT) in various ways. In their seminal article, Maria Yellow Horse Brave Heart and Lemyra DeBruyen say it is the "cumulative emotional and psychological wounding across generations, including one's lifespan," and it is the psychological, physical, social, and cultural aftermath of settler colonialism that has targeted Native Peoples for hundreds of years.[15] Historical trauma originates from genocide and cultural loss including decline in population, land, family, and cultural practices.[16] Sotero outlines three phases of historical trauma: 1) dominant culture perpetrating mass traumas on a population, resulting in cultural, familial, societal, and economic devastation for the population; 2) the original generation of the population responds to the trauma showing biological, societal, and psychological symptoms; 3) the initial responses to trauma are conveyed to successive generations through environmental and psychological factors, often compounded by social prejudice and discrimination.[17] Yakama Nation researcher, Michelle Jacob outlines Duran's concept of the "soul wound" for Native Peoples by describing how "genocide, warfare, traditional homeland loss, forced attendance at boarding schools, and compulsory Christianity were all sources of grief and suffering for contemporary Indigenous Peoples," and many contemporary Indigenous Peoples experience grief and suffering in their lives even though they have not experienced these colonial violences firsthand.[18] Additionally, Jacob states "the soul wound is an important concept . . . because it accurately explains that the root cause of many [current] social problems can be traced back to historical and ongoing forms of settler colonial violence."[19]

In my family, IHT manifests in myriad ways, from alcoholism and addiction, to prostitution and incest, varying forms of verbal, physical, and emotional abuse given and received, to suicides, incarcerations, cancers, and autoimmune disorders. These manifestations all have traceable lines to the boarding schools, racialized fragmentation from homelands, treaty negotiations made under duress, cultural discrimination, and many other assimilatory and genocidal practices and policies settler colonialism unleased on my family and many others over more than five hundred years and across multiple generations. Ohlone-Costanoan Esselen scholar Deborah Miranda calls this layered historical process of colonially produced trauma a "genealogy of violence."[20] To have multiple manifestations of unwellness and dysfunction in any one family is not probable, and yet empirical data confirms that Native Peoples suffer from disproportionately high rates of the above afflictions among others.[21] For generations, the members of my own family have been enduring poor health, misdiagnosed concerns, and general psycho-emotional, spiritual unwellness that are manifestations of present and historical traumas that began with the onset of settler colonization.

The focus of my research connects me and family to other Indigenous individuals seeking to heal the IHT existing in them and their own families, communities, and nations. I am a co-participant in my research project, and the relationship between myself and the other Indigenous co-participants hinges on our intersecting journeys as Native people striving to heal traumas created by settler colonialism; to meaningfully (re)connect to our cultures, our languages, and our lands; and to craft futures for ourselves aligned with our ancestral Indigenous ways of knowing and being in the world. Jacob's work extends these understandings when she writes, "To heal oneself is to help heal ancestors' soul wounds, and to help protect future generations from soul wound suffering."[22]

The manifestations of IHT I shared have the potential to frame Indigenous Peoples in "damage-centered" ways, but it is important to note these manifestations of IHT are not the totality of either these research co-participants or all Native Peoples.[23] It is additionally crucial to recognize "where Indigenous Peoples and communities are dysfunctional and/or in crisis, it is because of colonialism, not because they are Indigenous."[24] Furthermore, IHT as a framework has been critiqued for "defining Indigenous Peoples solely in terms of their relationship with colonizers," even though many Indigenous Peoples draw on the theory because it is helpful to create understandings between individual/group grief and suffering and structural violence.[25] This research strives to create shifts from the pathological "damage" narrative of Native Peoples by centering the ways in which Native individuals are already whole beings despite settler colonial violence, as well as how they are healing from the historical and contemporary effects of settler colonialism by (re)connecting to their Indigenous cultures, relationships, and sovereignties.

Evolving Research Design

The research study I am conceptualizing coheres around a group of approximately seven Indigenous people (including myself), all of whom share two key qualifications: all have some level of explicit understanding about the relationship between past and present settler colonial structures and intergenerational historical trauma as it exists in them/ourselves, families, and tribal nations and communities; and all identify themselves on a spectrum of Indigeneity that includes a serious disruption by settler colonialism in some way, including but not limited to dis/unenrolled tribal citizen, disconnected from/reconnecting to their Indigenous culture, living off reservation or ancestral homelands, and not having close and/or healthy relationships with their Indigenous family or community members. The second qualification attempts to focus on Indigenous people who exist with varying levels of disconnection from their Indigeneity as a result of settler colonialism. Of the seven people, I have preexisting relationships with three; the other three participants will be people who meet the two qualifications above and who are known to the first three and whom the first three would like to invite into the research project as contributors and co-participants. An initial aspect of the project will be my learning about each co-participant's background and story; this means spending one-on-one structured and informal time with each co-participant in person and/or on digital platforms (e.g., Zoom, social media).

Several topic questions would be explored during initial relationship building: Do you and/or your relatives have relationships with ancestral lands and waterways? Do you have non-Indigenous ancestry in your family? What is your tribe's creation story? Do you feel connected to this story? Which more-than-human relatives (e.g., animal, water, plant) have relational significance to you and to your tribe? How does cultural belonging and tribal citizenship work for your nation? In what ways do you feel that you belong to or do not belong to the nation? Do you know what ceremonies are important to your tribe? Do you feel connected to these ceremonies? What is the cultural-historical relationship between my tribal nations and the nations or communities you belong to? What is your tribal nation's specific history with the US federal government and settler colonial nation-state? How do you feel/see/understand how intergenerational historical trauma currently appears in your own life and family? How do you navigate these manifestations of historical trauma? How, when, where, and why do you provoke healing from these complex traumas? Have you experienced healing in yourself or your family? How can you tell? I will also share about these topics from my own experiences as co-participants and I get to know one another.

A primary portion of the project will be the co-creation of a collective experience in the form of a healing retreat. The healing retreat is what I will focus on in terms of methods in the remainder of this chapter. The retreat experience will occur in a co-selected meaningful place for multiple days and will be a space for co-participants to gather and spend time together visiting, eating, connecting through shared activities, and sharing experiences related to manifestations of IHT in our lives, families, nations, and communities. The seven co-participants will collectively plan the healing retreat. Each co-participant will contribute to planning the retreat, be that through location suggestions, the incorporation of cultural objects or texts, the inclusion of specific activities, ceremonies, and rituals, and requests for specific purposes of the retreat. In other words, my aim is to co-design, along with co-participants, a physical place and social container that can hold our stories, promote relational connectivity, and facilitate an emotionally healing experience that directly benefits each of us. The following sections outline how a Healing Methodology draws on two families of methods intended to provoke and understand healing that takes place during the healing retreat.

Methods for Healing

The key function of Methods for Healing is to create pathways and experiences for co-participants to actually heal intergenerational historical trauma. It is critical to understand how the structure of settler colonialism produced and continues to produce IHT through policies, sociocultural practices, and geopolitical norms. In other words, knowing what causes co-participants' IHT is also what allows co-participants to identify what can heal it. For example, for me and my family, one way settler colonialism created/s IHT is by disconnecting me and my Native relatives from our Métis/Anishinaabe lands and waters, cultural practices, spirituality, languages, and each other. In turn, Methods for Healing prioritize creating experiences that (re)connect Indigenous individuals to lands and water, cultural practices, ceremonies, languages, and each other. The specificities of Methods for Healing will primarily exist in the healing retreat portion of this project, will be determined in collaboration with co-participants and will vary based on the myriad Indigenous backgrounds and onto-epistemologies informing co-participants' contributions. In other words, in addition to the following specific Methods for Healing, there will be others included in the retreat that will be identified by co-participants. My particular Indigenous background is different from my co-participants', and to think about (theory) and do (methods) this research, I draw on Métis and Turtle Mountain Anishinaabe teachings, knowledge systems, languages, and cultures I am reconnecting to, while concurrently utilizing ways of knowing connected to the settler parts of my background (e.g., English, German). The fusion of these onto-epistemologies is unique to me and contributes to how I approach and fashion the practices that guide the Methods for Healing that I find valuable. Additionally, I acknowledge the distinct version of Healing Methodology that I engage is inherently Métis and Turtle Mountain Anishinaabe. Based on my cultural epistemological coordinates, what follows are three Methods for Healing, along with three associated cultural knowledges, that I can contribute to the healing retreat at the core of this project.

Method for Healing 1

The first Method for Healing is a storytelling activity among co-participants. As co-participants plan the multiday healing retreat, I intend to suggest that we bring with us to the retreat an item that represents our healing journey (e.g., song, art, ceremonial object, photo, clothing, book). Inspired by a uniting phrase in the Michif language, *mamawi aachimotaak*, which means "let's tell stories together," this retreat activity includes co-participants sharing the story of the item they each brought.[26] Possible sharing questions include the following: What is the item? Who created the item? How/why is this item representative of your healing journey? What emotions do you have about this item? How does this item connect you to a person, nation, idea, place, animal, and/or relationship?

Supporting Cultural Knowledge 1

The first Method for Healing is steered by an Indigenous methodology informed by a Turtle Mountain Anishinaabe cultural epistemology. A sacred law of my Anishinaabe ancestors is the teaching of *debwewin*, or "truth." In Anishinaabemowin, this word expresses a kind of truth encompassing a manner of speaking and doing without omission or embellishment, one that flows from the core, or heart, of personal knowing. Algonquin Anishinaabe-kwe scholar Lynn Gehl shares her understanding of *debwewin* as "a personal and holistic truth rooted in one's heart."[27] The dissection of this word also highlights *deb*, meaning "to a certain extent," which exposes the kind of truth this teaching uplifts—that a person can speak truths only to the extent of what they have experienced or lived. The knowledge held within *debwewin* also relates to Absolon's research when she writes, "one does not tell or inquire about matters that do not directly concern one,"[28] as well as within "the oral teachings and writings of Indigenous peoples of different nations the message is consistent—all we can know for certain is our own experience."[29] This method of storytelling creates a space for co-participants to share a specific truth about their healing journey based on one artifact while simultaneously experiencing belonging within the retreat relationships and setting.

Method for Healing 2

The second Method for Healing includes co-participants collectively building a sweat lodge and participating in a ceremonial sweat. The majority of the co-participants come from Plains tribal nations, for whom sweats are integral ceremonies, regardless of if co-participants have ever partaken in this ceremony. One co-participant is a carrier of the knowledge necessary to orchestrate and lead a ceremonial sweat, and he has expressed a desire to include a sweat in the healing retreat. Additionally, the specific ceremony he will lead was gifted to him by someone in his community and that person was gifted the ceremony from an Anishinaabe person, which feels meaningful as it illustrates intertribal sharing of ceremonies. This method provides an opportunity for co-participants to (re)connect to an Indigenous spiritual ceremony many of our relatives were banned from and punished for creating and participating in. Constructing and gathering in a sweat lodge and participating in ceremony together avails co-participants to not only (re)connect to a millennia-old ceremony that our ancestors carried, practiced, and healed within before and since the onset of settler colonial disruption but also to step into real-time possibilities for healing to occur amidst and between us within the container of this ceremony.

Supporting Cultural Knowledge 2

Method for Healing 2 connects specifically to my position and identity. Many of the Indigenous methodologies I have learned are firmly located within a specific place, Native nation, and/or tribal community, often with elders or knowledge carriers who work closely with the researcher. I do not have direct ties to Indigenous elders in my tribal communities asking me questions about my research; I am not held accountable by any of the Métis Nations or the Turtle Mountain Band of Chippewa Indians Nation and its community members in my daily life. I am still in the process of reconnecting with relatives who live on (and outside of) the Turtle Mountain Reservation or who are part of Métis Nations. I am still searching for missing slivers and chunks of my ancestral languages, ceremonies, cultural practices, homelands, and self that got damaged in the initial and lingering disruption that is settler colonialism. Although I sometimes feel excluded and alone as a first-generation unenrolled descendant of my family's tribal nations who actively works against settler colonial aims to erase my Indigeneity, I do not forget to remember despite all that I *am* still connected. Re-membering this connection is intimately informed by sharing ceremonies with Indigenous people who *have* been able to maintain their connection to ceremonies or who have been able to reconnect to them prior to my own reconnection—specifically people from Plains tribes and more specifically other Métis/Turtle Mountain Anishinaabe people.

Native Peoples constitute a unique diaspora, particularly folks who grew up in or live far away from their ancestral homelands and/or tribal reservations, Indigenous people who are dis/unenrolled due to colonially imposed frameworks of belonging (e.g., blood quantum), and all the Native individuals who are disconnected from or reconnecting to the seemingly scattered or nonexistent ceremonies, ancestral knowledges, and cultural practices of their immediate and extended Indigenous relatives. It is these Indigenous people, who travel paths parallel to mine, with whom I am in a specifically close relationship, accountable to, and want to remember my story and heal alongside.

Method for Healing 3

A third Method for Healing included in the retreat is an activity for co-participants to teach and learn the art of beading. This activity will entail co-participants spending time together in a beading circle wherein I (and others familiar with beading) will teach and learn specific beading stitches, culturally specific patterns, color theories, and cultural knowledges about beading. My Anishinaabe relatives believe that what we see, hear, think, and feel while we bead all penetrate the material product we create. In these ways, our beaded items (e.g., earrings, pin) will contain the healing we are co-producing that we can take with us as talismans from the healing retreat. Many Indigenous cultures include beading as a form of art, and although this particular cultural artform may not exist in every co-participant's culture, it can still be an opportunity that supports intertribal cultural exchange among co-participants in a way that connects us to cultural art and to one another.

Supporting Cultural Knowledge 3

The first time I visited the Turtle Mountain reservation—where my grandma was raised—I visited the cultural heritage center, and one of my cousins showed me dresses and moccasins in glass cases that some of my aunties beaded over several generations. Since that visit, I have sought out opportunities in person and online to learn beading skills and the significance of beading and beaded artifacts to Métis and Turtle Mountain Anishinaabe people. The Métis have often been referred to as the Flower Beadwork People by Dakota people because of the ubiquitous flower designs in their beadwork on coats, vests, bags, and moccasins, among other cloth and hide items. Métis people used beads procured from trading with Europeans and created intricate beadwork patterns by combining Anishinaabeg and Nêhiyaw beadwork with the floral patterns introduced by the French. Over time, bright florals represented Métis from the Red River region, and floral beadwork has become an enduring Métis symbol. Long-term learning about the convergence of history, art, utility, economy, and cultural significance of beadwork to my Métis relatives has been a space where I feel culturally and relationally connected to a specific material practice. In other words, since I have found belonging—and as a result, healing—in this artform, I want to share it with co-participants who may also find support in this experience.

Methods for Gathering

The second family of methods—Methods for Gathering—in a healing methodology are methods geared toward gathering and ascertaining any healing produced by the experiences, ceremonies, and activities that take place as part of the Methods for Healing. The Methods for Gathering may be indigenized versions of qualitative methods such as talking circles akin to focus groups; conversational, storytelling interviews related to personal narrative; photovoice; and journaling, among others. Methods for Gathering primarily take place after co-participants experience any of the Methods for Healing. These gathering methods identify the shifts that happened for co-participants as a result of contributing to and participating in various Methods for Healing. More importantly, Methods for Gathering attempt to pinpoint and collect co-participant perspectives about specific moments, materials, interactions, and activities where co-participants experience healing feelings, energetic changes, and/or realizations.

There are many Methods for Gathering that a Healing Methodology could include, and these methods will differ depending on the preceding Method for Healing and what method will be best suited to understand how a co-participant experiences healing from IHT. The prevailing Method for Gathering in this study is inspired by the Cree/Métis practice of *kiyokêwin*, or connecting through visiting—like sitting around a comfy kitchen table or hanging out in a meaningful place—as a way to create conversation, learn from each other, and build nourishing relationships. Specifically, Métis researchers Flaminio and colleagues articulate that the relationship-based process of *kiyokêwin* "can be distilled as a process of meeting together over tea, listening to, and talking with, one another, and understanding each other's point of view."[30] Another Métis researcher, Janice Cindy Gaudet, explains that "visiting is much deeper than the research concept of 'relationship-building' found within western research methodologies," and Nêhiyaw scholars Makokis and colleagues point out the visiting-related concept of "Mâmawi-kiyokeyahk is an essential protocol for building and maintaining loving relationships—it invites humility and openness into the learning environment and establishes a focused intensity and observation for learning and retaining information."[31] The *kiyokêwin* Method of Gathering attempts to learn where, when, and how healing occurs for co-participants. This method prioritizes learning information about co-participants' healing experiences in a way that is grounded in a Métis-specific way of visiting that is also inspired by other Indigenous conversational methods.[32]

Methodologically Healing

A Healing Methodology outlines considerations that can guide Indigenous-centered research across disciplines, and Native folks in non-academic settings can also draw on some of the underlying principles that center Indigenous healing and (re)connection to Indigeneity. A Healing Methodology also provides opportunities for *methodological healing* to occur within the academy and academic research. To methodologically heal asks researchers in the academy to pursue healing avenues for often harmful exclusionary ways of doing research on colonially targeted and marginalized individuals and communities (e.g., Indigenous Peoples). Academic disciplines, scholarly journals/books, and researchers need to generate transformative healing for the damage created by Western methodologies that have long been used *on* people and move toward methodologies that are not only neutral or less harmful, but that repair damage, and radically re-imagine and reciprocate healthy research relationships.[33]

As an Indigenous sociologist and I have not (yet) encountered a Western research methodology framed in terms of (Indigenous) healing or that has the bandwidth to do so. It is unsurprising that it is not possible for mainstream qualitative sociological research methodologies to stimulate, provoke, and strengthen Indigenous healing, regardless of how apt these Western methodologies may be in certain regards. A Healing Methodology for Indigenous Peoples requires Indigenous epistemologies because the power and practices needed to not only heal but to thrive and remember the health and wellness that Indigenous Peoples and Native nations experienced prior to the settler colonial apocalypse that began over five hundred years ago already exists within Indigenous Peoples and our homelands, ceremonies, knowledges, languages, and relationships with one another and our more-than-human relatives. Though some qualitative methods can valuably support a Healing Methodology, Indigenous epistemologies present in a Healing Methodology have the potential to be uniquely transformational by way of showcasing Indigenous orientations that recognize "knowledge arises from the intellectual realm of the mind, the affective domain of the heart, the kinetic domain of the body, and the spiritual domain of the soul. Knowledge is cognitive, embodied, instinctual, and spiritual."[34]

Continuing to uncover what a Healing Methodology means for Native Peoples (including myself), how it is operationalized in community and academic spaces, and what sociology might learn from this methodological tilt are as complex as the ways in which I arrive at this essay. By holding this reality, I sustain commitment to my research and to the people and places I am in relationship with. From this reality, I understand that my responsibility to heal always precedes my role as a researcher.

NOTES

1   Smith, *Decolonizing Methodologies*, 130.
2   Simpson, *As We Have Always Done*, 52. I use the terms *Native* and *Indigenous* interchangeably and identify tribal affiliations when speaking about specific

individuals, communities, and nations. I pluralize *Native/Indigenous peoples* to note the unique plurality and diversity of Indigenous nations and cultures and to emphasize that these nations and cultures have been practicing self-determination and governance long before colonization. My use of the capital *P* in *Peoples* signifies the respect with which I am addressing Native/Indigenous Peoples in North America as official *nations* (i.e., sovereignties, not just ethnicities). This capitalization is a growing trend among Native and Native-focused scholars as part of the politics of representation.

3 To define colonially produced intergenerational historical trauma, I draw on Nêhiyaw author Suzanne Methot: "The unresolved trauma of Indigenous peoples who have experienced, witnessed, or inherited the memory of horrific events creates an ongoing cycle of patterns and behaviors that are passed down from generation to generation. These intergenerational impacts are felt on a day-to-day basis by survivors and their families. Different communities experience different impacts and to differing degrees." *Legacy: Trauma, Story, and Indigenous Healing*, 28–30.

4 I define settler colonialism first as an event where European settler colonists arrived on Turtle Island, *then* as a five-hundred-plus year ongoing structure intended to control lands and construct a European-based society in place of the Indigenous societies who have been present on this continent since time immemorial. Settler colonial power is driven by the logic of eliminating (e.g., genocide, assimilation) Native Peoples, knowledges, and cultures so the settler society can claim physical lands and profit from them through settler colonial ideologies of acquisition and ownership. The contemporary structure of settler colonialism on Turtle Island is one that privileges European culture by systematically erasing Native bodies, cultures, histories, and knowledges through laws, popular culture, epistemicism, sciences, and so on. For more, see McKay, Vinyeta, and Norgaard, "Theorizing Race and Settler Colonialism within U.S. Sociology"; Wolfe, "Settler Colonialism."

   I choose the term *Turtle Island* as the name of the lands and waters that make up the "North American" continent as a way to prioritize converging Indigenous worldviews and creation stories while also linguistically decentering the colonial perspective and nomenclature of "North America."

5 Fiola, *Rekindling the Sacred Fire*, 80.

6 Fiola, 80.

7 Absolon, *Kaandossiwin*, 22.

8 I include the term *Western* not to describe any specific group, culture, or country, but instead to refer to knowledges and ideologies originating in Europe and brought to Turtle Island with the onset of settler colonialism. The adjective *Western* helps describe imperialistic legacies within cultural and academic thought and application that favor colonial practices of individualism, linearity, meritocracy, ownership/property, binarism, and objectivity.

9 Absolon, *Kaandossiwin*, 51.

10 Wilson, *Research Is Ceremony*

11 Michelle Bishop, "'Don't Tell Me What to Do.'"

12 I use "colonially known" here to disrupt normative settler colonial practices of naming places that already did and still do have place names based on Indigenous relationships to lands, waters, and more-than-human beings. Indigenous Peoples of many cultures and locations still refer to many places in Indigenous languages. For the remainder of the paper, I use the colonially imposed names of states and countries in order to ensure geographic clarity across audiences.

13 Myhra, "It Runs in the Family."

14 Million, "Felt Theory," 58.

15 Brave Heart and DeBruyn, "The American Indian Holocaust," 7.

16 Stamm et al., "Considering a Theory of Cultural Trauma and Loss."

17 Sotero, "A Conceptual Model of Historical Trauma."

18 Duran, *Healing the Soul Wound*. Jacob, *Yakama Rising*, 11.

19 Jacob, 11.

20 Miranda, *Bad Indians*, 2.

21 Wilk, Maltby, and Cooke, "Residential Schools."

22 Jacob, *Yakama Rising*, 12.

23 Tuck, "Suspending Damage."

24 Methot, *Legacy*, 3.

25 Jacob, *Yakama Rising*, 11.

26 The Mamawi Project (@themamawiproject), "We are a collective of young Métis people from across our homeland," March 17, 2019, www.instagram.com/p/BvHm6hJHBoY/; Lavallée, "Practical Application."

27 Gehl, "Debwewin Journey, 55.

28 Absolon, *Kaandossiwin*, 23.

29 Kovach, *Indigenous Methodologies*, 54.

30 Flaminio, Gaudet, and Dorian, "Métis Women Gathering," 58.

31 Gaudet, "Keeoukaywin," 59; Makokis et al., *mâmawi-nehiyaw iyinikahiwewin*.

32 Kovach, *Indigenous Methodologies*.

33 For more on the harm Western research has caused on Indigenous Peoples, see Smith, *Decolonizing Methodologies*, 58.

34 Kovach, *Indigenous Methodologies*, 69.

BIBLIOGRAPHY

Absolon, Kathleen E. *Kaandossiwin: How We Come to Know*. Halifax: Fernwood, 2011.

Bishop, Michelle. "'Don't Tell Me What to Do': Encountering Colonialism in the Academy and Pushing Back with Indigenous Autoethnography." *International Journal of Qualitative Studies in Education* 34, no. 5 (2020): 367–78.

Brave Heart, Maria Yellow Horse. "The Historical Trauma Response among Natives and Its Relationship with Substance Abuse: A Lakota Illustration." *Journal of Psychoactive Drugs* 35, no. 1 (2003): 7–13.

Brave Heart, Maria Yellow Horse, and Lemyra M. DeBruyn. "The American Indian Holocaust: Healing Historical Unresolved Grief." *American Indian and Alaska Native Mental Health Research* 8, no. 2 (1998): 56–78.

Dunbar-Ortiz, Roxanne. *An Indigenous People's History of the United States.* Boston: Beacon Press, 2014.

Duran, Eduardo. *Healing the Soul Wound: Counseling with American Indians and Other Native Peoples.* New York: Teachers College Press, 2006.

Fiola, Chantal. *Rekindling the Sacred Fire: Metis Ancestry and Anishinaabe Spirituality.* Winnipeg: University of Manitoba Press, 2015.

Flaminio, Anna Corrigal, Janice Cindy Gaudet, and Leah Marie Dorian. "Métis Women Gathering: Visiting Together and Voicing Wellness for Ourselves." *AlterNative: An International Journal of Indigenous Peoples* 16, no. 1 (2020): 55–63.

Gaudet, Janice Cindy. "Keeoukaywin: The Visiting Way—Fostering an Indigenous Research Methodology." *Aboriginal Policy Studies* 7, no. 2 (2019): 47–64.

Gehl, Lynn. "Debwewin Journey: A Methodology and Model of Knowing." *AlterNative: An International Journal of Indigenous Peoples* 8, no. 1 (2012): 53–65.

Jacob, Michelle M. *Yakama Rising: Indigenous Cultural Revitalization, Activism, and Healing.* Tucson: University of Arizona Press, 2013.

Kovach, Margaret. *Indigenous Methodologies: Characteristics, Conversations, and Contexts.* 2nd ed. Toronto: University of Toronto Press, 2021.

Lavallée, Lynn F. "Practical Application of an Indigenous Research Framework and Two Qualitative Indigenous Research Methods: Sharing Circles and Anishinaabe Symbol-Based Reflection." *International Journal of Qualitative Methods* 8, no. 1 (2009): 21–40.

Makokis, Leona J., Marilyn V. Shirt, Sherri L. Chisan, Anne Y. Mageau, and Diana M. Steinhauer. *mâmawi-nehiyaw iyinikahiwewin.* Alberta: Blue Quills First Nations College, 2010.

McKay, Dwanna L., Kirsten Vinyeta, and Kari Marie Norgaard. "Theorizing Race and Settler Colonialism within U.S. Sociology." *Sociology Compass* 14, e12821 (2020): 1–17.

Methot, Suzanne. *Legacy: Trauma, Story, and Indigenous Healing.* Ontario: ECW Press, 2019.

Million, Dian. "Felt Theory: An Indigenous Feminist Approach to Affect and History." *Wicazo Sa Review* 24, no. 2 (2009): 53–76.

Miranda, Deborah A. *Bad Indians: A Tribal Memoir.* Berkeley, CA: Heyday, 2013.

Myhra, Laurelle L. "'It Runs in the Family': Intergenerational Transmission of Historical Trauma among Urban American Indians and Alaska Natives in Culturally Specific Sobriety Maintenance Programs." *American Indian and Alaska Native Mental Health Research* 18, no. 2 (2011): 17–40.

Simpson, Leanne Betasamosake. *As We Have Always Done: Indigenous Freedom through Radical Resistance.* Minneapolis: University of Minnesota Press, 2017.

Smith, Linda Tuhiwai. *Decolonizing Methodologies: Research and Indigenous Peoples.* 2nd ed. London: Zed Books, 2012.

Sotero, Michelle. "A Conceptual Model of Historical Trauma: Implications for Public Health Research and Practice." *Journal of Health Disparities Research and Practice* 1, no. 1 (2006): 93–108.

Stamm, Beth Hudnell, Henry E. Stamm, Amy C. Hudnall, and Craig Higson-Smith. "Considering a Theory of Cultural Trauma and Loss." *Journal of Loss and Trauma* 9 (2004): 89–111.

Tuck, Eve. "Suspending Damage: A Letter to Communities." *Harvard Educational Review* 79, no. 3 (2009): 409–27.

Wiechelt, Shelly A., and Jan Gryczynski. "Cultural and Historical Trauma among Native Americans." In *Trauma: Contemporary Directions in Trauma Theory, Research, and Practice*, 2nd ed., edited by Ringel Shoshona and Jerrold R. Brandell, 167–205. New York: Columbia University Press, 2020.

Wilk, Piotr, Alana Maltby, and Martin Cooke. "Residential Schools and the Effects on Indigenous Health and Well-Being in Canada: A Scoping Review." *Public Health Reviews* 38, no. 8 (2017).

Wilson, Shawn. *Research Is Ceremony: Indigenous Research Methods*. Halifax: Fernwood, 2008.

PART III

Race/Racism, Intersectionality, and White Supremacy

9

The Souls of Sociology

Imaginative Sociology, Cultural Studies, and the Post/colonial Disruption

BEN CARRINGTON

Contesting canonical histories of the discipline requires not only highlighting the alternative traditions that were also present at the time in question, but also . . . using the intellectual resources of these alternative histories to think differently about sociology today
—Gurminder Bhambra

Serious interdisciplinary work involves the intellectual risk of saying to professional sociologists that what they say sociology is, is not what it is. We had to teach what we thought a kind of sociology that would be of service to people studying culture would be, something we could not get from self-designated sociologists. It was never a question of which disciplines would contribute to the development of this field, but of how one could decenter or destabilize a series of interdisciplinary fields. We had to respect and engage with the paradigms and traditions of knowledge and of empirical and concrete work in each of these disciplinary areas in order to construct what we called cultural studies or cultural theory
—Stuart Hall

The Danger of the Du Boisian Moment

We are in a moment of radical contestation when it comes to thinking about the relationship of critical race and ethnic studies to mainstream sociology, and vice versa. This moment is located within a broader set of discussions concerning, for example, the status and place of the work of W. E. B. Du Bois in US sociology, the relevance of cultural studies to contemporary analyses of the social, and the overdue reckoning with sociology's imperial racial unconscious.[1] This is a period of opportunity and cause for cautious celebration. It is also, at the same time, a dangerous moment.

It is now undeniable, in light of Aldon Morris's extraordinary work of scholarship that is *The Scholar Denied*, that US sociology, as a field, engaged in a systematic, deliberate, and until now largely effective campaign to marginalize and ignore the ideas, works, and groundbreaking intellectual contributions of Du Bois.[2] The exclusion of Du Bois by US sociology—what Reiland Rabaka labels "epistemic apartheid"—should be regarded as a shameful episode of scholarly marginalization, revealing the operation of anti-Black racism from a discipline that likes to imagine itself as at the progressive forefront of addressing social ills and problems.[3] The current move not just to add Du Bois to the sociological canon but more radically, to foreground his ideas and work as foundational to the discipline itself, has *the potential* to reshape not just how we understand sociology's past and its core concerns but how we (re)think and practice sociology today.

As Lawrence Bobo emphatically put it in his 2015 review of Morris's book for the *Du Bois Review* ("Bringing Du Bois Back In"), "Du Bois should be an obvious presence, speaking metaphorically, on the Mount Rushmore of American sociology."[4] Bobo discusses whether what he mockingly calls the Keepers of the Canon will in fact acknowledge the significance of the challenge that Morris laid down. "The great test here," Bobo suggests, "is whether the Keepers of the Canon come to fully acknowledge the profoundly distorting impact of the racism of the past on how we think about and do sociology even today and, especially, whether they too now work to undo both the shameful legacy and its enduring effect on the culture and practices of the discipline itself."[5] Bobo concludes his review by stating, "Aldon Morris's stentorian enunciation brings Du Bois back into the theoretical and methodological mainstream of the discipline, right where he has always belonged."[6]

This, then, is the opportunity accorded to us, namely, to place Du Bois in the mainstream of US sociology, that is, to add Du Bois, as it were, to the Boys—Marx, Durkheim, Weber *and* Du Bois—thus providing a new quartet of founding forebears. This would also have the effect of centering questions of race as axiomatic to sociology's core problematics rather than being a topic for week ten of the Introduction to Sociology, when students are typically introduced to "diversity and identity" questions, which is where, at best, Du Bois usually appears.

A change is clearly afoot within the conservative corridors of sociology. Developing this notion, Back and Tate suggest that a

> storm is brewing around questions of race and racism within the Republic of Sociological Letters. It is a gale that blows periodically through the journal stacks and conference colloquia when scholars of color and their allies are pushed to the limit. This storm can be found in the new critical writing on how academic authority is colonized by white somatic norms in the university and how class, race, and gender inequalities structure the academy.[7]

This gale has been accelerated by the impact of Morris's book and by other interventions, such as the establishment of the Du Boisian Scholars Network, led largely but not exclusively by sociologists, as well as the series of commemorative workshops, events, and conferences honoring Du Bois. The American Sociological Association has changed the name of its prestigious Career of Distinguished Scholarship Award to the W. E. B. Du Bois Career of Distinguished Scholarship Award. Since 2015, winners of the award have included Black scholars very much committed to a critical, broadly Du Boisian, form of sociology, including Patricia Hill Collins (2017), Elijah Anderson (2018), Morris himself (2020), and Eduardo Bonilla-Silva (2021). In his 2004 book, *The Social Theory of W. E. B. Du Bois*, Phil Zuckerman predicted that the canonization of Du Bois was imminent.[8] Surveying the academic field today, one could say that day has arrived. For reasons that should be obvious, this is a moment to celebrate.

And yet it is this very achievement that merits some caution and reflection. This "success" comes, potentially, at a cost that may undo some of the productive and transformative work the Du Boisian moment might otherwise accomplish. The danger, put simply, is one of cooption, that Du Bois's assimilation into US sociology does not in fact transform the field but that the field transforms Du Bois—the possibility that rather than opening up a space to include more engaged and radical works rather than broadening the sociological universe, we instead may see a closing of sociology's door behind Du Bois, especially to the ideas and insights from critical ethnic and racial studies, as well as from cultural studies more broadly. Without wishing to undermine the potential of the Du Boisian moment, we must at least reckon with three significant concerns.

First, in *some* of these discussions, there is a startling lack of reflexivity concerning canon formation itself. In other words, rather than questioning the idea of disciplinary canons, with all of the policing, patriarchal exclusions, and silencing that occurs in such moments, there seems to be an urge to simply add Du Bois to the sociological pot and stir; to add some darker water to the lily-white, profoundly western ingredients of mainstream sociological theory. Or, as I noted earlier, to add Du Bois to the Boys. Yet simply hoping that the addition of Du Bois to an earlier slot as we teach Introduction to Sociology, rather than his usual place later in the semester, will itself produce a disruption to the field is unlikely to be sufficient. Indeed, such an approach poses an additional danger in that it allows the veneer of disciplinary inclusion, canonical disruption, and pedagogical change that is purely performative: "OK, OK, we added Du Bois to the reading list and we give you awards in his name. We even created a professorship in his honor, what more do you want?" say the keepers of the canon.[9] There is a danger of a form of diversity inclusion that *appears* to listen, *appears* to change, even amends syllabi, readings, and citational practices, but one that does not substantively engage with the deeper challenge Du Bois's work could and should pose to the hyper-professionalized field of modern-day US sociology.

Sara Ahmed, among others, provides important insights into how the mainstreaming of even radical voices and the managerial language of diversity and inclusion too often end up serving the self-interests of the institutions themselves by the surface appearance of change that does not in fact change much at all.[10] The movement from margin to center, as bell hooks noted many years ago, comes at the risk of incorporation and the loss of radical and insurgent agency that the margin allows for.[11] This is not to naïvely celebrate marginality but to caution against the idea that simply "moving to the center" or having a place close to the center, especially if the center itself is not rethought, is not necessarily a progressive move.

A second concern is this: Which Du Bois gets incorporated? Which Du Bois will be let in? Du Bois was many things at different periods, his thinking developed and evolved over time, and above all, he was more than just a sociologist. The fear is that the Du Bois who will be allowed to become part of the mainstream of US sociology, the Du Bois permitted to be cited by graduate students, will be a carefully selected, partially read and de-politicized Du Bois. Much like Martin Luther King's subsequent neutering into a non-offensive, peace-loving, all-American hero by dominant US nationalist politics, we must similarly resist a Disneyfied version of Du Bois from entering into the sociological canon.

It should be stated emphatically that Du Bois was a pan-Africanist, he was an anti-colonialist, and he was a socialist deeply committed to international revolutionary politics, as much as he was a sociologist. Indeed, it was his *political* commitments, which arguably grew *more*, not less, radical over time, that shaped and influenced his best work and some of his more important ideas. It is that radical, socialist Du Bois, an internationalist and diasporic thinker who worked across disciplines and who had sharp words to say about sociology, that will almost certainly be stripped away and downplayed, if not outright denied, by the American keepers of the canon.

There is also a related though opposite risk that a sanitized and equally idealized Du Bois is presented by those wanting his canonization. A version of Du Boisian scholarship that fails to adequately interrogate Du Bois's omissions, both theoretically and politically, whether that be his underdeveloped considerations of gender in his work alongside his embodiment, as Hazel Carby, among others, has noted, of a masculinist and elitist "Race Man" identity, or the awkward facts of his embrace of Stalinism and his affection and admiration for Imperial Japan. Arguing *for* Du Bois must not be based upon hagiography.[12]

The third concern is an extension of the last two points. To include Du Bois's work and ideas with integrity can be achieved only if sociology itself is fundamentally reconfigured as a result. At the moment there is little evidence of any willingness to engage in such a rethinking on the part of sociology's dominant gatekeepers and the elite institutions where the hegemonic center of US sociology still resides. To put this another way, to commit to a Du Boisian sociology today is to also commit to a postcolonial sociology, which requires that sociology, and especially US sociology, relinquish its ongoing hostility to cultural studies and acknowledge the vital contributions of critical race and ethnic studies.

This would be a sociology that understands questions of empire and imperialism as central to the formation of modern liberal democracies, of the inherently racialized foundations of Western modernity, and a sociology that takes seriously the historical antecedents of what we now call "racial capitalism." As Du Bois himself put it, "It was black labor that established the modern world commerce which began first as a commerce in the bodies of the slaves themselves and was the primary cause of the prosperity of the first great commercial cities of our day . . . Black labor, therefore, . . . became an important part of the Industrial Revolution of the eighteenth and nineteenth centuries."[13] It would be a sociology that does not take the nation-state as the natural and sole unit of analysis but instead interrogates and reads the formation of nation-states, as David Theo Goldberg notes, as inherently *racial* states.[14] The core would become a postcolonial sociology—as the likes of Gurminder Bhambra, Raewyn Connell, and Julian Go, among others, have tirelessly argued for—that understands that modern sociology is far from being a neutral and disengaged science of the industrial age.[15] Rather, we would emphasize that the core concepts of the discipline—the nation-state, modernization theory, ideal types, and so on—are actually born from and of imperialist frameworks forged from highly racialized ways of seeing and understanding the world from the vantage point of the global north. Sociology, to paraphrase the geographer J. M. Blaut, has all too often been the colonizer's model of modernity.[16]

The postcolonial intervention, then, argues that sociology did *not* emerge, as it likes to self-narrate, as one of the children of the Enlightenment in order to make sense of the modern world (the self-declared "Queen of the social sciences") but was itself a product of and helped to shape a profoundly racialized, particular, and violent form of Western modernity. Precisely because it was so intimately tied to empire, Western modernity was from its inception a racialized and racializing project, and so too was sociology. Unlike, say, anthropology, sociology has failed to come to terms with its imperial racial unconscious and instead trundles along as if there were nothing to see concerning the specifically colonial entanglements of its European origins other than a coincidence of timing, somehow unrelated to its epistemes.

A postcolonial sociology, therefore, is not something that can be taught in the final weeks of Sociology 101, just after Du Bois and before the student evaluations. A postcolonial sociology, indebted to Du Bois and thoroughly grounded in the political, ethical, and intellectual convictions of cultural studies, usurps the entire intellectual edifice of sociology. This is why Du Bois was so mocking of bourgeois sociology's "blind allegiance" to that abstraction it invented called "society." Du Bois stood against everything modern US sociology has become— hyper-specialized, narrow in scope, often, to paraphrase the great C. Wright Mills, mindlessly empiricist when it is not hopelessly fetishizing concepts, and a sociology with little interest in power outside of "stratification studies" that too often fail to adequately theorize questions of domination, violence, and ideology.

Another Sociology Is Already Here

As we begin to imagine this alternative sociological world, I would suggest that the outlines of what a different model of sociology might look like already exist, especially if we look beyond the disciplinary state borders of the United States. There are many possible models, but I want to highlight one here that I have invoked earlier, namely, the critical and conjunctural sociological approach associated with the British sociologist and public intellectual Stuart Hall.

In 1996, Stuart Hall delivered the presidential address at the British Sociological Association (BSA) annual conference in Reading, England. Hall admitted that he was honored, if a little surprised, that he had been appointed BSA President as he had never formally studied sociology. Hall then outlined the starting point for the work done at the Centre for Contemporary Cultural Studies (CCCS) at Birmingham University during his time there. "We went to Parsons," he said, "and whatever he had rejected, we read."[17]

Though used as an amusing anecdote to situate the type of engaged, reflexive, and critical intellectual work done by the CCCS, at least as Hall recounts its history, the work of cultural studies in the 1970s was not driven to directly *engage with* the dominant American model of Parsonian sociology; rather, it attempted to de-center that model of socio-logical work altogether. Cultural studies addressed more urgent political questions focused on power, ideology, representation, and resistance, questions that could not easily be framed within the conventional so-ciological priorities given to studying norms and group behavior, find-ing causal mechanisms for social action, or assessing the integrative function of social institutions in the maintenance of value consensus. Crucially, rather than relegating culture to a discrete sphere within "so-ciety" or narrowing its definition to norms, values, and mores, it in-stead operated with a much expanded understanding of culture outside of which there was no society. Cultural studies subsequently produced a new, revised, and vigorous sociological project around those aspects of everyday life, and especially popular culture, that traditional sociol-ogy too often overlooked. Culture was where meanings were produced, where ideas circulated, and where the dialectics of individual biography and historicized social forces could be found. This cultural frame paid particular attention to *discourse* as constitutive of social practice and centered power (be that economic, political, or ideological) and identity (an active process of becoming, always in formation, never fixed) as con-tested domains. In so doing, Hall and others developed what has come to be understood as a *conjunctural* analysis of the social.

As noted in Hall's *Cultural Studies 1983: A Theoretical History*, cultural studies embarked on a radical rethinking of the very epistemic founda-tions of sociology. What Hall and others sought to retrieve from the Parsonian theoretical dustbin were those parts of Durkheim's analysis found in texts such as *The Elementary Forms of Religious Life* that would later also prove useful for French structuralism but that Parsons and his followers dismissed as Durkheim's "idealist texts." As Hall puts it, Parsons read selectively from Durkheim to establish a statistically based form of quantitative sociology as science, a legacy that continues to shape US sociology today. In contrast, Hall, and by extension cultural studies, took a broader view. Drawing on the ideas of critical deviancy studies writers such as Howard Becker, Hall extended the orthodox so-ciological discussion on social action, norms, and value consensus to study those who challenged such norms, to consider the ways in which rule-governed behavior was created and maintained (and by whom), and to reflect more critically on the underlying issue of social order itself—a social order understood as fundamentally shaped by historical changes in the structures of political economy and by the actions of the state in trying to "manage" the crises of capitalism.

We can see here how Durkheim's interests in crime, the symbolic order, and ritual acts of punishment, provided *part* of the theoretical apparatus for later texts such as *Policing the Crisis: Mugging, the State, and Law and Order*, arguably one of the most important sociological projects produced by the CCCS.[18] But these insights were put into conversation with other theoretical paradigms, most notably Foucauldian-influenced forms of poststructuralism and neo-Marxist scholarship, particularly the debates around ideology, the state, power, and resistance developed from readings of Antonio Gramsci and Louis Althusser and more recently the insights of radical Black scholars such as C. L. R. James and Frantz Fanon.

Of course, the interventions of cultural studies were met at the time with hostility from social scientists. Hall recounts the "blistering attack specifically from sociology" that was directed at the CCCS when it was first opened in 1964.[19] This was an attempt, Hall suggested, to put cultural studies back in its place. Notes Hall, "The opening of the Centre was greeted by a letter from . . . social scientists who issued a sort of warning: if Cultural Studies overstepped its proper limits and took on the study of contemporary society (not just its texts), without 'proper' scientific (that is quasi-scientific) controls, it would provoke reprisals for illegitimately crossing the territorial boundary."[20] We might suggest, then, that attacks on cultural studies from sociology are almost a tradition in and of themselves. However, as I have argued elsewhere, this "cultural studies versus sociology" framing denies the inherently symbiotic relationship between the two and fails to acknowledge the pivotal ways in which cultural studies has decisively reshaped the theoretical, methodological, and conceptual concerns of sociology since the 1970s in ways that have given sociology new impetus, energy, and relevance to the public issues of the day—even as this is still denied by some.[21] As Paul Gilroy forcefully put it many years ago:

> In the field of Sociology, as in many other places, there is a very strong current of resentment which suggests that all of these arguments around culture and its complexities were things that were already

known and already practiced by Sociologists. I think that's bullshit, but it's very interesting that this position represents itself as common sense. . . . What is more of an immediate issue for me is the kind of culturalisation, a novel sensitivity to the workings of culture that has been evident in the implosion and collapse of Sociology as a discipline. This disciplinary predicament has produced a political battle around culture and its workings.[22]

Sociology Still in a Straitjacket

At the start of his presidential address to the American Sociologi-cal Association (ASA) conference in Los Angeles on August 28,1963, Everett C. Hughes asked the assembled delegates a rhetorical question: "What is there new to say about race relations?" Hughes's address that year was titled "Race Relations and the Sociological Imagination," a clear acknowledgement of the legacy of C. Wright Mills, who had died just the year before. Hughes's paper that day was a painful acknowledgement of the failure of mainstream sociology, despite its newly developed sci-entific skills, experimental methods, and predictive theories, to foresee, let alone make sense of, the tumultuous social changes that were tak-ing place not just within US society but globally during the period of the early 1960s, changes that ranged from civil rights marches and pro-tests, to the collapse of the European empires in the face of anti-colonial movements, to the emergence of new nation-states and the break-up of others. As Hughes starkly put it, "Why did social scientists—and soci-ologists in particular—not foresee the explosion of collective action of Negro Americans towards immediate full integration into American society?"[23] Hughes delved into the work of Robert E. Park to make sense of "the nature of race relations." But without a theory of racism or a historicized account of the continuance of neocolonial modes of gov-ernance and the reproduction of White supremacy, Hughes struggled to make sense of the historical moment, except to realize that whatever was going on, sociology was ill-prepared for the task. The notion that the very model of "race relations" was itself part of the problem did not figure in Hughes's otherwise reflexive account.

The irony of history, of course, was that sociology's marginality was geographically inscribed on that very day, being in the wrong place at the wrong time and looking for answers using the wrong tools when the "action," so to speak, was taking place elsewhere. At the exact moment when US sociology's finest minds gathered in Los Angeles to listen to Hughes lament sociology's failure to spot the changes taking place within society, Martin Luther King Jr. was delivering one of the greatest speeches in US history on the steps of the Lincoln Memorial to hundreds of thousands in Washington, DC.

No doubt with Mills in mind, the question of method and its effect on developing the sociological imagination lay at the heart of Hughes's critique of where sociology was going wrong, when he noted, "Some have asked why we did not foresee the great mass movement of Negroes; it may be that our conception of social science is so empirical, so limited to little bundles of fact applied to little hypotheses, that we are incapable of entertaining a broad range of possibilities, of following out the madly unlikely combinations of social circumstances."[24] Hughes concluded his talk with the following:

> Our problem is not that we are too deeply involved in human goings-on but that our involvement is so episodic and so bound to the wheel of particular projects with limited goals; in short, that we are too professional. While professionalizing an activity may raise the competence of some who pursue it by standardizing methods and giving license only to those who meet the standard, it also may limit creative activity, by denying license to some who let their imagination and their observations run far afield, and by putting candidates for the license [PhD] so long in a straitjacket that they never move freely again. Our problem, as sociologists, in the next few years will be to resist the drive for professionalizing, and to maintain broad tolerance for all who would study societies, no matter what their method.[25]

Six decades after Hughes's warning about the narrow professionalizing tendencies of American sociology, the extent to which that "broad tolerance" exists today is a matter of some dispute, but the push to "professionalize" US sociology, as Michael Burawoy, has noted, is surely not. For some, like Eduardo Bonilla-Silva, and directly echoing C. Wright Mills, sociology in the United States has sacrificed its sociological imagination "at the altar of methodological correctness" with the result that

"American-made sociology tends to be boring . . . uninspiring, apolitical, badly written, and hardly relevant."[26]

Similarly, in prose that may have made even Mills wince, Richard Sennett, writing in the 1990s, has argued that:

> American sociology has become a refuge for the academically challenged . . . . The British Prime Minister Margaret Thatcher famously declared a generation ago, "There is no society, only individuals and their families." In an eerie way, much positivistic sociological research subscribes to this antisocial nostrum. . . . The 'dull science' as Michel Foucault called American sociology—legitimates dissociation from the entanglements, contradictions, and difficulties of actual social experience . . . . In the last twenty years, more interesting "hard" sociological research has been done in medical, planning and law schools, and better research on culture and society in the humanities departments, than in sociology departments. . . . Sociology in its dumbed-down condition is emblematic of a society that doesn't want to know too much about itself.[27]

It remains the case that what passes for sociology in the United States looks very different to how the discipline is practiced elsewhere in the world. Even a cursory glance through the pages of, say, the *American Journal of Sociology*, *American Sociological Review*, and *Social Forces* compared to the *British Journal of Sociology*, *Sociological Review*, and *Sociology* reveals a gulf in methodological, and theoretical approaches, and writing styles that underlie the major divergence of US sociology from its British counterpart since the 1960s.

Interestingly, there is also a strand of American sociological scholarship, often but not exclusively Bourdieuian influenced, that is seemingly committed to an apolitical sociology fixated on definitional issues of boundary-making as well as a sociology that is broadly neo-Weberian in approach, concerned with ideal types that rely on a neo-functionalist scientific positivism. Thus, although these scholars come from seemingly differing schools of thought, and at times may even contest each other's claims, they actually share a commitment to a deeply conservative vision of sociology and a general disdain for cultural studies scholarship, often with explicit attacks on Black studies and critical ethnic studies. This is how we might begin to explain the astonishing absence of a figure like

Stuart Hall from US sociology by the keepers of the canon. Let me use two brief examples to illustrate my point.

In the same year, 2014, that Hall passed away, the renowned historical and comparative sociologist Orlando Patterson published a key review article titled "Making Sense of Culture" in the *Annual Review of Sociology*.[28] Remarkably, this comprehensive state-of-the-art overview failed to cite a single contribution from Hall's extensive oeuvre and steadfastly refused to even acknowledge the relevance of cultural studies scholars to the study of culture. In other words, in the same year that eulogies to Hall's singular contribution to the critical sociological study of culture were widespread, both within academia and further afield, the once-a-decade summation of the key sociological works and ideas on culture, written by one of Harvard's most renowned sociological thinkers, simply refused to acknowledge even the existence of Hall and cultural studies as a field relevant to the sociological study of culture. Instead, Patterson put forward a neo-Parsonian framework for making sense of culture that consists of measuring values and norms and embracing behavioral psychology and cognitive neuroscience as the future for critical cultural analysis.

Second example: In 2015, I submitted a panel proposal to the American Sociological Association's annual conference with three other scholars, Sharmila Rudrappa of the University of Texas Austin, Jyoti Puri of Simmons College, and Roderick Ferguson of Yale. The panel was titled "Honoring Stuart Hall: Sociologists Engage Hall's Legacy." Hall had not long passed, and it seemed a fitting way to acknowledge his sociological legacy and contribution to the study of culture. What was more, the theme for the forthcoming conference was "Culture, Inequalities, and Social Inclusion across the Globe," a perfect fit, one would have imagined, for a panel on Hall. To our surprise, the panel idea was rejected. When we enquired as to why, we were told that due a large number of submissions, ours had not made the cut. We asked if there had been other panels on Hall that had been selected. We wanted ours, of course, but if another Hall panel was deemed better, that would have been fine. But there was not. When we directly contacted the ASA president-elect and therefore chair of the Program Committee for a fuller explanation, we were told to "try to submit a proposal to a regional meeting."[29]

In other words, Stuart Hall, in the year after his death, was not deemed significant enough of a sociological figure for a panel (a single panel, mind, not a plenary or number of sessions) at a conference on the topic of globalization, culture, and inequality. Instead, the ASA president-elect for that year implied, such a panel might work better at a smaller, regional conference.

Rather than dismissing these as being isolated, atypical examples, I believe they are in fact symptomatic of the current state of US sociology and the continuing power of the keepers of the canon to exclude work that might challenge the hegemonic model of what constitutes sociology as taught in the "leading" departments. Especially among some of the key figures who write broadly in the area of culture, there is a commitment to either a neo-Parsonian understanding of culture as "meaning making" framed as the socialization into norms and mores, patterned forms of behavior and value consensus, or a de-politicized and profoundly abstract interest in "boundary making," with a side set of questions focused on recognition, stigma, and stratification.

I would argue that mainstream US-based sociologists of culture too often define the object and field of study in this way not because it *makes sense* (to borrow Patterson's title) but because it makes culture *measurable* (within the standard methodologies of the discipline) and able to fit within preexisting frameworks—frameworks that are deemed to be appropriately scientific and therefore apolitical, a sociology, in other words, that remains profoundly anti-Du Boisian.[30]

Toward Imaginative Sociology

If we are to take up the Du Boisian challenge rather than being content with the ritualistic chanting of *The Sociological Imagination* as text whenever the field feels under threat, we need more sociologists with actual imagination and a desire to expand, not contract, the boundaries of the field. This would require retrieving and fighting for the more creative aspects of sociology. It would mean supporting sensual and open-ended sociological projects that may require more than a semester to complete, to embracing and recognizing the avowedly interdisciplinary as a sociological good, and an institutional commitment to experimental forms of *live* sociology (as the British sociologist Les Back puts it), in contradiction to the deadening Eurocentric hand of positivistic sociology, which, all too often, serves as a convenient disciplinary mask for the mundane, the repetitive, and the reactionary.[31]

It might be useful here to draw a contrast between *sociology* as an institutionalized discipline, committed to defending its particular methods and ways of knowing the world, and *the sociological*, defined as a broader, open-ended intellectual and, in some ways, political project. In thinking outside of the disciplinary logics of sociology, we should remember that sociology does not have a monopoly on the sociological.

In other words, truly wrestling with the postcolonial predicament, of understanding that Western modernity was also a colonial modernity and thinking through how we might start to rejuvenate the sociological imagination through decolonizing our field, as Gurminder Bhambra, Julian Go, and Raweyn Connell, among others, have urged, is a necessary first step. It is not enough to study imperialism and empire through a sociological lens. It is not sufficient to add "colonialism and slavery" as topics, although that is much needed, but rather to engage in a radically reflexive project of uncovering and reworking sociology's complicitous role in coloniality and race making. Part of this new sociological imagination, or what I would like to term instead, imaginative sociology, would prioritize imagination as a core component of the intellectual craft of our discipline and would help us, following Mills, to better identify the signal features of our period.

The warnings against the direction American sociology was heading, issued by Hughes back in 1963, were ultimately ignored. The truth is that until relatively recently, we would have concluded that the Parsonians won and that critical sociologists such as Mills lost. The legacy of Du Bois was largely buried, and the insights of scholars like Hall and more recently Gilroy were banished into the various "ethnic studies" centers far from the prestigious "scientific" corridors of sociology departments. To be clear, there is much brilliant, innovative, and engaged sociological work taking place today all across American campuses of higher education and beyond, often directly inspired by Du Bois and often influenced by Hall as well; it is just that such work rarely resides within departments of sociology.

Just as during the height of his academic career, although for different but related reasons, today Du Bois would not likely be employed by any leading US sociology department. Du Bois would be labeled a "social justice warrior," his broader "woke" politics would be held against him, his methods would not be considered scientific enough, his publications (beyond two or three examples) would be questioned, his engagement in cross-disciplinary work held against him, his interests in music, poetry, and popular culture would be deemed unsuitable, and he would definitely be asked about all this autobiographical stuff. In short, his sociological credentials would be questioned, and likely he would be accused—because in the eyes of many American sociologists, this is an accusation—of "doing cultural studies or critical race studies but not sociology." His visit, if he ever got close to a campus visit, would likely end with a thanks but no thanks and a recommendation that the Department of African and African American Studies might want to take a look at his CV. And with that, the sociology department would instead likely hire someone more competent in running regression analyses, especially if that involved comparing racial and ethnic groups in different countries (provided, of course, that one of the countries was the United States), with a preferred focus on measuring "stratification" in education, health, crime, or immigration, all decontextualized and without theorizing White supremacy, colonial domination, or racial violence. There is a certain irony listening to established sociologists now singing the virtues of Du Bois, knowing that these are the very same gate keepers who have worked to ensure that critical, cross-disciplinary scholarship, grounded in a politics of transformation that is actually more in tune with the intellectual spirit of Du Bois, is kept out of their version of what constitutes "proper sociology."

Rather than seeing the interdisciplinary turn, the engagement with critical theory from outside the narrow sociological canon and the challenge of taking (post)coloniality seriously as an opportunity to make sociology relevant again, especially at a time of radical social disruption, protests, and global social movements centered around race, US sociology instead sees such work as a threat to its standing as a science. A postcolonial sociology, in meaningful conversation with cultural studies, is something to be dismissed or banished, often rejected out of hand, if not ignored altogether. How else to make sense of US sociology's deliberate and purposeful exclusion of the work of Stuart Hall, to give just one example?[32]

I use Hall simply to highlight a certain intellectual hypocrisy on the part of those sociologists who want to add their names to the cause of reinviting Du Bois back into the sociological family but who have spent much professional energy in making sure that the contemporary scholar who most approximates the Du Boisian form of multidisciplinary, critically informed, anti-colonial scholarship, namely Stuart Hall, is kept outside of the discipline's borders.

In the spirit of Hall, who gave the W. E. B. Du Bois public lectures at Harvard in 1994, I would suggest that we are in a period of hegemonic struggle over the meanings and legacy of Du Bois and, related, a discursive battle around the legitimacy of sociology's disciplinary borders. Intellectually speaking, we stand at the edge of a conjunctural shift. As we know from our readings of Gramsci, the most dangerous moment is when you think you have won, that you have successfully wrestled some space from the dominant, only to find out, much later, that the moment of victory was in fact one of incorporation, of the reproduction of dominant social relations within the field, and therefore of defeat.

So with a cautious pessimism of the intellect but a necessary optimism of the will, while we should of course welcome and even celebrate this moment, let us do so on the understanding that to honor Du Bois, we need to go beyond the necessary but limited step of inclusion into the canon toward changing the souls of sociology. Moreover, we should perhaps question the very need for a sociological canon in the first place if we are to produce a radically different, postcolonial sociological field. This would be one that embraced critical ethnic and racial studies as sources of theoretical insight and intellectual renewal and would therefore be in keeping with Du Bois's intellectual, scientific, and, yes, *political* commitments, too. A truly Du Boisian sociology would enact a post/colonial disruption that challenged the current hegemony of the conservative professional gatekeepers and instead would create a more relevant, engaged and imaginative sociology.

NOTES

1 Morris, *The Scholar Denied*; Iltzigsohn and Brown, *The Sociology of W. E. B. Du Bois*; Hall, *Cultural Studies 1983*; Meghji, *Decolonizing Sociology*.
2 Morris, *The Scholar Denied*.
3 Rabaka, *Du Bois*.
4 Bobo, "Bringing Du Bois Back In," 461.
5 Ibid., 467.
6 Ibid., 468.

7 Back and Tate, *For a Sociological Reconstruction*.

8 Zuckerman, *The Social Theory of W. E. B. Du Bois*.

9 The keepers of the canon are tenured faculty, normally full professors with endowed chairs, at the leading American research institutions, overwhelmingly located in the self-reproducing (and often self-defined) "top departments" in the field that dictate the research agendas of graduate students, who are invested in a positivistic model of "scientific" sociology that dominates the "top journals." These keepers actively discourage alternative modes of sociological discourse (methodical, theoretical, and literary) and become disciplinary gatekeepers for their version of sociology. See Agger, *Sociological Writing in the Wake of Postmodernism*.

10 Ahmed, *On Being Included*.

11 hooks, *Feminist Theory*.

12 Carby, *Race Men*.

13 Du Bois, *The Gift of Black Folk*, 53; see also Du Bois, *The World and Africa*.

14 Goldberg, *The Racial State*.

15 Bhambra, *Connected Sociologies*; Connell, *Southern Theory*; Go, *Postcolonial Thought and Social Theory*.

16 Blaut, *The Colonizer's Model of the World*.

17 Carrington, *Decentering the Centre*.

18 Hall et al., *Policing the Crisis*.

19 Hall, *Cultural Studies*, 21.

20 Ibid.

21 Carrington, *Decentering the Centre*.

22 Smith, *On the State of Cultural Studies*, 20.

23 Hughes, *Race Relations and the Sociological Imagination*, 879.

24 Ibid., 889.

25 Ibid., 890.

26 Burawoy, *For Public Sociology*; Bonila-Silva, *The Many Costs of Racism*, 1240.

27 Sennett, *Sex, Lies and Social Science*.

28 Patterson, *Making Sense of Culture*.

29 Email, personal message to author, 2015.

30 As Hall notes, "Although sociology thinks it's a predictive science, it doesn't predict anything very much, very well," Carrington, *Remembering Stuart Hall*. In contrast to sociology, it is cultural studies' ability to center the political within its conjunctural analysis that gives a better ability to make sense of emerging trends and shifts in the social order, such as Hall's prediction of the emerging neoliberal period in the 1970s that became Thatcherism in the 1980s.

31 Back, *Live Sociology*.

32 I note here that Henry Louis Gates has called Stuart Hall "the W. E. B. Du Bois of Britain." If Du Bois was the scholar denied, perhaps Hall has been the scholar ignored.

BIBLIOGRAPHY

Agger, Ben. "Sociological Writing in the Wake of Postmodernism." *Cultural Studies Critical Methodologies* 2, no. 4 (2002): 427–59.

Ahmed, Sara. *On Being Included: Racism and Diversity in Institutional Life*. Durham, NC: Duke University Press, 2012.

Back, Les. "Live Sociology: Social Research and its Futures." *Sociological Review* 60, no. 1 (December 2012): 18–39. https://doi.org/10.1111/j.1467-954X.2012.02115.x.

Back, Les, and Maggie Tate. "For a Sociological Reconstruction: W. E. B. Du Bois, Stuart Hall and Segregated Sociology." *Sociological Research Online* 20, no. 3 (August 2015): 155–66. https://doi.org/10.5153/sro.3773.

Bhambra, Gurminder. *Connected Sociologies*. London: Bloomsbury Academic, 2014.

Blaut, J. M. *The Colonizer's Model of the World: Geographical Diffusionism and Eurocentric History*. London: Routledge, 1993.

Bobo, Lawrence. "Bringing Du Bois Back In: American Sociology and The Morris Enunciation." *Du Bois Review: Social Science Research on Race* 12, no. 2 (Fall 2015): 461–67.

Bonilla-Silva, Eduardo. "The Many Costs of Racism: Book Review." *Social Forces* 82, no. 3 (2004): 1240–42.

Burawoy, Michael. "For Public Sociology." *American Sociological Review* 70, no. 1 (2005): 4–28.

Carby, Hazel. *Race Men*. Cambridge, MA: Harvard University Press, 2000.

Carrington, Ben. "Decentering the Centre: Cultural Studies in Britain and its Legacy". In *A Companion to Cultural Studies*, edited by Toby Miller, 275–97. Malden, MA: Wiley-Blackwell, 2001.

———. "Remembering Stuart Hall: Socialist and Sociologist." *Racism Review* (2014). www.racismreview.com.

Connell, Raewyn. *Southern Theory: Social Science and The Global Dynamics of Knowledge*. Cambridge: Polity Press, 2007.

Du Bois, W. E. B. *The Gift of Black Folk: The Negroes in the Making of America*. Oxford: Oxford University Press, 2014.

———. *The World and Africa: An Inquiry into the Part Which Africa Has Played in World History*. New York: Viking, 1947.

Go, Julian. *Postcolonial Thought and Social Theory*. Oxford: Oxford University Press, 2016.

Hall, Stuart. "Cultural Studies: Two Paradigms." *Media, Culture and Society*, 2 (1980): 57–72.

———. *Cultural Studies 1983: A Theoretical History*. Durham, NC: Duke University Press, 2016.

Hall, Stuart, Chas Critcher, Tony Jefferson, John Clarke, and Brian Roberts. *Policing the Crisis: Mugging, the State, and Law and Order*. Basingstoke: Palgrave, 1978.

hooks, bell. *Feminist Theory: From Margin to Center*. London: Routledge, 1984.

Hughes, Everett. "Race Relations and the Sociological Imagination." *American Sociological Review* 38, no. 6 (1963): 879–90.

Goldberg, David Theo. *The Racial State*. Cambridge, UK: Wiley-Blackwell, 2002.

Iltzigsohn, Jose, and Karida Brown. *The Sociology of W. E. B. Du Bois: Racialized Modernity and the Global Color Line*. New York: New York University Press, 2020.

Meghji, Ali. *Decolonizing Sociology: An Introduction*. Cambridge: Polity Press, 2021.

Morris, Aldon. *The Scholar Denied: W. E. B. Du Bois and the Birth of Modern Sociology*. Berkeley: University of California Press, 2015.

Patterson, Orlando. "Making Sense of Culture." *Annual Review of Sociology* 40 (2014): 1–30.

Rabaka, Reiland. *Du Bois: A Critical Introduction*. Cambridge: Polity Press, 2021.

Sennett, Richard. "Sex, Lies, and Social Science: An Exchange." *New York Review of Books*, May 25, 1995. www.nybooks.com.

Smith, Marquard. "On the State of Cultural Studies: An Interview with Paul Gilroy." *Third Text* 49 (1999–2000): 15–26.

Zuckerman, Phil. *The Social Theory of W. E. B. Du Bois*. London: Sage, 2004.

10

A Queer of Color Critique for Sociology

The Mutual Constitution of Race and Sexuality

SALVADOR VIDAL-ORTIZ

Introduction

Sociological studies on systems of power more often than not recur to independent categories of analysis—be it race, class, gender, sexuality—to make the mechanisms behind power operational. Whether this urge for operationalization is or is not inherently a component of a disciplinary crisis in sociology, the distinctiveness of such singular categorizations determines the limits of disciplinary application and theorizing. To think race and sexuality together, for instance, still forms part of the excess in a sociological scholarship that intends to quantify social life and the impact of inequalities. A queer of color critique is a field external to sociology, created, in part, by sociologist Roderick A. Ferguson, whose work connected with political scientist Cathy Cohen, literature scholar Chandan Reddy, and performance studies scholar José Esteban Muñoz, among others.[1] (While sociologists have been marginal to the field, a number of scholars have produced race and sexuality scholarship with and apart from the queer of color critique.[2]) The queer of color critique established itself as a rupture from sociology and at the same time a USAmerican project, given its racial formations history.[3]

As a discipline, sociology has been foundational to the theorizing of racial formations and racialization, yet the mainstream of the discipline has underappreciated the interconnectedness of systems of mutual constitution such as racialized sexualities.[4] It has been important to push, at venues like the American Sociological Association, for scholarly work on racialized sexualities, which has happened, unequivocally, in race and ethnic minority sections and scholarly networks sooner than in sexual minority and sexualities studies ones. For instance, in 2007, I was able to organize a racialized sexualities panel as council member of the section on racial and ethnic minorities of the American Sociological Association, which was a rupture in the normative and one-dimensional lens for thinking sexuality, gender, and race as distinctive dimensions with no interconnectedness.

American studies, on the other hand, has been a fruitful space to think through power beyond notions of multiculturalism—even if those were some of the initial efforts in the field—and to connect culture and political economy with race, gender, and sexuality in ways not often interwoven before. For scholars in the study of racialized sexualities in either field, the experiences that flow from normative systems—such as Whiteness in terms of race and heterosexuality and heteronormativity in terms of sexuality—were and have always been interlocked, so that when thinking about conceptions of beauty, the relationship between race, gender, and sexuality are tied together in popular or discursive understandings, making it inherently impossible to separate these as distinctive categories of social analysis. Yet it might be more evident how to do so in American studies than in mainstream sociology—even in the latter's more "specialized" subfields—because of the inability of incorporating a more interdisciplinary, intersectional lens.

Most relevant to this chapter is Roderick A. Ferguson's *Aberrations in Black*. Ferguson insists on thinking through some canonical aspects of sociology—for instance, the geopolitics of racial-cultural difference as fascination and deficit from the racialized ethnographic analyses emergent from the Chicago school of sociology and the reification of a troubled and deeply pathologized Black family in sociologist Patrick Moynihan's *The Negro Family: The Case for National Action*, most commonly known as the *Moynihan Report*—and in doing so, goes through, but moves past, the sociological canon. Since the publication of this book in 2004, little has been done to sustain a connectivity between American studies and sociology through an analysis that reiterates how heteronormativity is articulated racially and in terms of gendered norms as well. Meanwhile, African American studies, ethnic studies, American studies, and women's, gender and sexuality studies are among the interdisciplinary fields where, increasingly, the queer of color critique is cementing. At its most elementary level, this chapter asks, What can sociology learn from a queer of color critique?

While the queer of color critique is balanced by, and depends on, both sociology's and American studies' critiques of each other, this chapter's goal is to bring forth the mutual constitution of race and sexuality in the queer of color critique from an American studies framework. I do this to enhance sociological theorizing.[5] I argue that the rupture and resulting distance from the break between the two disciplinary formations that emerges with the queer of color critique is a productive force to think sociologically in newer ways.

To situate a queer of color critique for the reader, this chapter first outlines the relationship between feminist, sexuality, and queer studies interdisciplinary formations. It then focuses on the contributions of Roderick A. Ferguson to the study of the field within and outside sociology. I then extend the chapter into a discussion based on a series of considerations for thinking about how sociology may successfully incorporate a queer of color critique. I close the chapter with a brief conclusion.

Multiple Articulations: Feminisms, Sexualities Studies, and Queer and Racial Studies

This section illustrates the importance of understanding the queer of color critique as the result of a three-decade long set of processes that wove together scholarly and activist work; through the racial criticism of second-wave feminism, which in turn focused on marginalized categories such as lesbian, sex worker, or woman of color, a (queer) feminist of color formation paves the way for a similar model—this time, the queer of color critique in response to the Whiteness of queer theory. This section articulates some of the basic elements to situate the process that gives form to the queer of color critique and allows it to make sense.

From the work of the Combahee River Collective in the 1960s and '70s or the impact of Stonewall, (now) trans activists Sylvia Rivera and Marsha P. Johnson (Ferguson 2018), feminist of color formulations such as the 1983 edited collection *This Bridge Called My Back*, and Audre Lorde's work have been highly influential. These contributions are important in how we then receive intersectionality in sociology and beyond.[6] Interestingly, they are not so central to the solidification of queer theory's own canonical authors (such theory is connected most often to Foucault and Butler). Moving from the exploration of difference and subcultural understandings of gender-specific gay male and lesbian women's sexual spaces and communities (DeLauretis, 1990), queer theory quickly evolved into a poststructural analysis that went beyond social institutions, diffusing any relation to heterosexism (for instance) and opting instead to focus on heteronormativity. Within these developments, there was a shifting of conceptual categories (e.g., from the term *heterosexism–foundational* in sociology to *heteronormativity*, central to queer theory's tenets), where sociological analyses of institutions recede from the social study of sexuality in queer studies, queer theory in particular.[7] Suffice it to say here that queer theory's main trajectory has unsurprisingly privileged a type of sexuality that is coherent with Whiteness, to the detriment of racialized analyses; the queer of color critique emerges out of the quest to produce queer theoretical formulations that do not ignore other axes of power in ways not unsimilar to those that Combahee, Lorde, hooks, Baldwin, or Moraga and Anzaldúa produced.[8]

As an approximate, it is within a decade of the recognition of queer theory as a field of study that a queer of color critique begins to emerge. Within the mid- to late 1990s, the queer of color critique began to be articulated in academic circles and outlets through the words of political scientist Cathy Cohen's critique of queer theory's Whiteness, race, and AIDS in her foundational "Punks, Bulldaggers, and Welfare Queens" article, although the queer of color critique was yet unnamed as such.[9] This might have happened through Chandan Reddy's 1998 book chapter partially centering the importance and impact of the documentary *Paris Is Burning*, in order to locate the place of queers of color in the formation of this nation-state during the last century.[10] Yet if a field is only considered so, based on book-length formulations, then José Esteban Muñoz's 1999 book *Disidentifications* is the book that articulated a space outside, although woven into, mutually constituted systems of heteronormativity and Whiteness to demonstrate how the markings of expulsion from both systems result in a third space of sorts, a reconfiguration (or more explicitly, a reconstitution) of their own lives as a distinctive space for queers of color.[11] In other words, the queer of color critique pursued an inter-articulation of race, gender, and sexuality that began with feminist of color formations—one that resisted, and made visible, discursive systems of compulsory heterosexuality and the centrality of Whiteness in USAmerican society.[12] Before these works, a handful of authors, activists, and movements such as the Combahee River Collective, bell hooks, Audre Lorde, Cherríe Moraga, Gloria Anzaldúa, and James Baldwin were centrally engaged in linking gender, race, and sexuality, bringing much needed visibility to non-White sexual minorities while resisting messages that negated the lives of queers of color.[13] In all these, the queer of color critique loops back to central critiques of queer theory's formulation to date, just as feminist of color critiques emerged in the late 1970s and early 1980s in response to the predominant middle-class White feminism of the 1960s and 1970s; that is, it is work that does not let go of the tenets of the troubling and intervening of categories and of noticing the systems impacting marginalized lives but adds layers of complexity to the analysis.[14]

The early proponents of the queer of color critique engage with the sociohistorical importance of the ways in which race, gender, and sexuality were co-constitutive of the nation-state, particularly for African American formations.[15] For instance, Chandan Reddy speaks to historical racialization processes and how those have impacted labor, gendered relations, the stipulation of minimum salary and how it benefitted White families (and White family formation), and sexuality. Roderick Ferguson as well evokes the internal migration of freed people of color to the northern and western parts of USAmerica in his book *Aberrations in Black*. Queers of color in the US context is rightfully rooted in the oppositional treatment of Blacks and Whites and how gendered and sexual readings impact these dynamics; still, today, scholarship tackling contemporary issues through the queer of color critique center African American populations and issues.[16] My noting of the Black centrality to the queer of color critique should not be read as diminishing; it is a strength from which to operate and inherently a reason why we are able to articulate a distinctive framework that is indebted to intersectionality but departs from it.[17] In comparative racialization scholarship, the historical, slippery place of Blackness as both outsiders to the nation's symbolic and material citizenship but also modern and thus separate from immigrants to the United States has been explored in what Jun called "provisional Black inclusion in relation to Chinese exclusion."[18]

Indeed, understanding the centrality of a USAmerican Blackness inter-twined with processes of US nation-state formation (in terms of a seem-ingly contradictory inclusion within a larger legal system of exclusion) is imperative to better situate this framework as a US racial formation one, which only complicates its applicability in other spaces and contexts. Ferguson helps understand how this happens, which is the reason for turning to his work next.

Ferguson's Queer of Color Critique

Ferguson's work is most relevant here, as his contribution to the queer of color critique, in his own words, "was born as a means of delivering a political and economic inquiry to the study of sexuality" and "was never about a multicultural response to queer theory."[19] As he has noted in *Aberrations* and elsewhere, a politics of diversity and inclusion does not decenter Whiteness in academe, nor does it become a barrier for struc-tural redistribution—because of the task that a queer of color brings, which is to rethink political and economic hegemony.[20] Indeed, his shift to understanding the role of academic complicity in the neoliberal deployment of diversity as a form of domination is connected to the formation of the queer of color critique as part of the larger project and enterprise of diffusing a focus on social exclusion and the channeling of the academic enterprise as interconnected with corporations.[21]

Roderick Ferguson's *Aberrations in Black: Toward a Queer of Color Critique* (2004) was, among other things, an incisive analysis that oblit-erated the foundational practice of ethnography central to US sociol-ogy (and the Chicago school in particular). In it, Ferguson uncovered a project that sharpened migration (and movement) within the nation and labor (and material conditions) with citizenship. For him, racial formations are already intertwined with sexuality—and always were; as a critical example of this, much of his work has concentrated on dem-onstrating the normative gendered hauntings, and the racial deficit, in family formations for African Americans.[22] White ethnographers went "slumming" to Black urban spaces in Chicago. In the creation of the most prominent school of ethnography, sociology replicated the study of racial otherness (through a lens of deficit) in the metropolis, not un-like how anthropology replicated similar notions of power, through its study of culture, in other countries. To establish his critique of canonical sociology, Ferguson argues for an understanding of disidentification of belonging to a nation and resists the uses of liberal capital. The queer of color critique is the mechanism that allows him to do so.

Ferguson's *Aberrations in Black* illustrates the historical blend of racial and heteronormative formations through migration, labor, and housing for marginalized populations in processes during the late nineteenth and twentieth centuries. *Aberrations in Black*'s cover depicts a defiant Black trans woman who is looking straight at the camera; in this regard, Ferguson acknowledges and follows the work of Cathy Cohen in "Punks, Bulldaggers, and Welfare queens," and as Ferguson notes, his focus is "the regulation of people like the transgender[ed] man, the sissy, and the bulldagger as part of its general regulation of African American culture."[23] Likewise, in his introduction, Ferguson connects historical materialism to queer formulations through culture, denoting a typical heteronormative lens in Marxist theorizing while simultaneously critiquing the discursive Foucauldian work of the proliferation of sexualities, which for Ferguson denote the non-heteronormativity of racial minority populations, African Americans in particular.

The three main chapters of the book connect sociology (in some form), literature, and policy-related aspects. Chapter 1 engages the questions of social (dis)organization and the center of cities, such as Chicago, as these urban spaces seduce the emergent sociological tradition of ethnography. Chapter 2 ignites an engagement with an unpublished chapter of Ralph Ellison's *Invisible Man*, where heteronorms are broken. Chapter 3 brings together the visibility of a male-centered Black Panthers Party against the critique of Black matriarchy in the *Moynihan Report* and how literature such as Toni Morrison's *Sula* brings to life non-White, non-heteronormative spaces of existence. These chapters all serve as interventions that call into question sociology's commitment for social justice, given its constant investment in the exotic lens that sexually racialized African Americans in the twentieth century.

Among the work's contributions, Ferguson's queer of color critique's interventions push sociology to think of the field of study outside of USAmerica, which is where American studies becomes beneficial. Similarly, an analysis of Ferguson's queer of color critique challenges the study of racial formations as heteronormative (or as foundationally anchored in heteropatriarchy), thus bringing critical race theory analyses to the center.[24] Lastly, queer studies, as squarely situated in a White gay and lesbian subjectivity, are troubled by the ability of the queer of color critique to push the boundaries of intelligibility.

Ferguson also bridged Marxist concerns of matter, life, and the exploitation of surplus populations to the service of both heteronormativity and White supremacy as a central inquiry of his work.[25] At a time when matters of social location and identity are separated from class (and political economic lenses), Ferguson insists on materialist practices and sexuality analyses in and through a population that we might make intelligible only through a racial lens. The cultural response to African American migration North and West from the South toward the end of the nineteenth century was one of the concrete models Ferguson utilized to demonstrate the inherent duality of race and sexuality for African Americans, irrespective of their sexual identity or experience, and the potential dangers or risks associated with their presence outside of the South. In this regard, *Aberrations in Black* argues that African Americans are rendered "queer" by virtue of the various ways they defy constructions of normative citizenship in USAmerican society. Ferguson's argument in this piece interlocks, through disidentification—a term he borrows from José Muñoz's book of the same title—Marxist arguments to those of the home, the nation, and ethno-racial minorities and their regulations, including sexuality and gender. In doing so, it "moves" the idea of queer as something connected to a sexual or innate identity and looped back to systems of exclusion that marginalize beyond mere identification.

Ferguson bases his work in *Aberrations in Black* and in publications leading to the book on a comparison of key texts (either on social movements or historical documents), novels, reports (invoking social policy), and other writing (connecting through literature with American studies), which he put in conversation with sociological discourses of exclusion. As an intervention into sociology, his aim is to show how canonical sociology framed the abject position of African Americans during at least the last hundred years. Sociological inquiry made African Americans become foreigners in their own "home" by virtue of the cultural distinctions set up by sociologists studying—and separating—gender and sexual "anomalous" populations from the "proper" ones, thus maintaining social order. *Aberrations* produces key examples to understand this—when African American women are masculinized, when the African American household is pathologized because women are heads of households, when African Americans' racial temperament "feminizes" them. But Ferguson also forces sociology—like feminist of color formations and intersectional scholarship did before his work—to illuminate how discursive practices are gendered, racialized, and hyper-sexualized simultaneously, in spite of how those discursive practices are consumed by us as being only about African Americans. By taking to the literary texts, policy reports (like the *Moynihan Report*, produced by a sociologist), and Black cultural formations foregrounding masculinist notions of Blackness (such as the Black Panthers Party), Ferguson moves past the ethnographic canonical sociology from the book's earlier pages into texts, corpus, and other forms that magnify the lens of lived experience and thus redefine constructs of truths based on the empiricism inherent in ethnographic engagement.

The USAmerican specificity (the racializing set of historical processes that constituted a Black and White binary foundational to the United States) is the very same specificity that forges the book to center the analysis of African Americans in relation to the queer of color critique. In other words, the Black and White binary endemic to USAmerican history—and different from other racial formations elsewhere—structures much of the queer of color critique; it also structures its application (or more specifically, the failure of an application) outside the United States. I am not suggesting that the queer of color critique remains committed to a racialized understanding of the United States as a specific nation-state. What I seek to unpack is the impossibility of this framework to be merely translated or applied to other settings. (Indeed, in this regard, the queer of color critique is as "American" as queer theory in how difficult it is to connect to other contexts, either transnationally or internationally; in addition, the common negation of Blackness as a reality in other countries exacerbates this response.)

However, Ferguson has connected the queer of color critique to "third world" formations elsewhere and in the United States, in order to insist on a queer of color critique that will be conceptually sound beyond the USAmerican borders.[26] While it is debatable that this constitutes the queer of color critique as transnational, it does offer an expansion, even when Blackness operates as an uninterrogated, Global North construct that may be superimposed elsewhere. This ought to be addressed in its own right and exceeds the influence of American studies' queer of color critique on sociology.

Queer of Color Critique's Influence on Sociology

This chapter extends Ferguson's work to show the particularities of how the queer of color critique is rooted in a USAmerican racialized system—with a US racial formation logic—not necessarily applicable or intelligible elsewhere.[27] American studies might hold the upper hand over sociology in that the training and scope of scholarly foundations allows American studies to see "American" and "studies" in inherently comparative ways—which cannot be said of mainstream sociology. How American studies, today, travels—with the ability to retain coherence as a field given the status and privilege coming from the Global North—influences other societies, and it is in turn influenced by the flow of ideas and the migration of other peoples and cultures returning to US society. Moreover, in the last couple of decades, American studies has turned its lens of analysis onto itself to consider the global reach and power of USAmerican culture elsewhere. Given how sociology, not unlike anthropology, pursued an understanding of "other" cultures not as mere difference but through a hierarchy (sociology needed no travel to other global sites; they enforced this in the metropolis with Black communities and "slumming"), American studies does provide a formidable model for sociology as a discipline to consider.

Just as American studies has offered a multifaceted sense of analysis of power in many potential articulations, settings, and relations, so too has the queer of color critique attempted to infuse sociology with markers of mutual constitution difficult to grasp for the macro and quantitative discipline. For Ferguson, the space created in the limits of connectivity between Black male social and activist mobilizations (Black Panthers) or the attentive figure that emerged from the pencil of a writer onto an ambivalent "queer" Black woman (Toni Morrison's character's name is *Sula*) or the policies that demonized Black matriarchy and the absence of Black fathers (in the *Moynihan Report*) all served a purpose to rethink "data"—perhaps converting it to "corpus" in sociology. As well, the telling of the formative and co-constitutive aspects of race and sexuality in how the Chicago school of sociology viewed racial and sexual difference still haunts sociology today. The Chicago school of sociology today remains recognized as the mainstream ethnography and sociological site of the early twentieth century, in spite of the recognition of the importance of the Atlanta school.[28] This becomes important and crucial to understanding the inherent contradictions of a twenty-first-century sociology that celebrates W. E. B. Du Bois and its women founders, while it inhabited a hostile environment for non-White male sociologists for decades, if not a century—if not, still, today.[29]

Ferguson's work not only brings together what might seem to some sociologists to be disparate sources for analysis; it does so with how it troubles the canon for the inherently central, overarching, and yet invisible Whiteness of both sociology and of queer theory. Ferguson's queer of color critique not only reproves of sociology; it disavows it from claiming a progressive past. Removing any chance of absolution, Ferguson's incisive critique renders sociology ill equipped. At the same time, and because Ferguson thinks from the borders of sociology and with American studies at its core, he tends to bring forth an analysis that is always already woven into heteronormativity (including gendered norms and regulations) and the overwhelming result of White supremacy to the study of USAmerican societies.

Conclusion

The queer of color critique has to be understood as a result of three decades of scholarly and activist work, which emerged through criticism of the second wave feminism, especially from lesbians and women of color (as well as lesbians of color). With the introduction of gay and lesbian studies and the "founding" of queer theory and its subsequent inability to address race but leave Whiteness untouched, the queer of color critique has established itself as an alternative to queer theoretical writings as a not-so-simple way to dismiss a queer theoretical project but to address the abject of queer subjects through its many marginal positions. While the epistemological assumptions of a queer of color critique may seem to rest on essentialist thinking (of who queers of color "are"), I would like to suggest—as I believe Ferguson does as well—that this critique has at its core a sort of essentialism that uses *queer* and *of color* as basic parameters of analyzing social life and not merely of experience. In the case of Ferguson's book, it does so in arguing that African Americans are, by their very placement and history in US society, sociological studies and social policy "queer"—regardless of same-sex sexual behavior. In this sense, it is important to understand the "queer" project (even the use of the term) in at least two ways: as both non-heteronormative and a destabilizer of identities. For a queer of color critique, one has to extend those meanings to include racialized, unstable, queer sets of social locations (and not merely experiences). How Ferguson did this was inherently through his dismissal and critique of canonical sociology and the White ethnographic project foundational to the Chicago school of sociology, in how the racial and sexual inter-articulation produced a practice of marking otherness inherent to the core of the design of not just ethnography but perhaps of the discipline. More importantly, that Ferguson did so attests to an unearthing of remains and propositions of disciplinary practice that in the twenty-first century promotes itself as social justice based while in the late nineteenth century and early twentieth century was constituting the very premise of difference and inequity that it attempts to change today.

This does not mean that Ferguson's queer of color critique does not have limitations; certainly, his engagement with a US West Coast education and a writing collective for this first book produced an absence of militarized territories—such as Puerto Rico—that he has subsequently addressed in more recent works.[30] In sociological migration studies, a "third" migration (not immigration) pattern or wave discussed is that of internal rural to urban migration, here in the United States, and most notably with two specific groups: African Americans moving from the South to the North (central to his book's argument) and Puerto Ricans moving from the Island to the mainland (altogether absent in the project).[31] *Aberrations in Black* starts with a geographical and historical premise about the migration of Blacks in the United States, but it omits discussions about Puerto Ricans or the relationship between these two second-class citizen groups of people of color, who are similarly positioned at the turn of the century, have been significantly pathologized by sociology, and continue to be case studies and exceptions to assimilation theories.[32] While Ferguson links his arguments to other populations—

making specific, necessary distinctions between Asian Americans and Asians, Mexicans, and Blacks—other populations, most notably Indigenous peoples and Puerto Ricans, are excluded from the discussions on surplus populations, migration, and their multiply minoritized relationship to the state. I bring this up to suggest that coalitions are impossible to produce as all-inclusive and that while the queer of color critique has advanced our thinking, it too has the potential to be framed in very specific ways in its moving forward. (This has practical implications in coalition building among academics of color, for instance as African American scholarship cannot systematically ignore Native American and other ethno-racial minorities' social mistreatment.)

If we assume that American studies' purview is not the unification of all humanities fields but the development of a field that supports the inherent thread of literature, history, philosophy, ethnic studies, and gender and sexuality, then the field is shaping itself as a parallel conversation along disciplinary fields of study such as sociology. Yet if we see the queer of color critique as a critical and continuous intervention into some of these more established fields of study, then the queer of color critique, like American studies, formulates a way to think theory anew, without the obsession for unit of analysis precision or the tenets of dead White men, the way mainstream sociology (still) does.

NOTES

1   To credit the foundation of a field to a certain set of scholars may elicit the omission of other scholars and works. I name but suspend the tripartite of foundational scholars that has been most recognized until now: a sociologically trained American studies scholar, Roderick Ferguson, who is African American; a performance studies professor, José Esteban Muñoz, who was Cuban American; and Chandan Reddy, an English/literature professor who is South Asian. Cathy Cohen precedes them in significant and important ways, even if she never called it a queer of color critique. Cohen, "Punks, Bulldaggers, and Welfare Queens"; Reddy, "Home, Houses, Nonidentity"; Muñoz, *Disidentifications*; Ferguson, *Aberrations in Black*. Other significant scholarship include Johnson, "'Quare' Studies"; Manalansan, *Global Divas*; Eng, Halberstam, and Muñoz, "What's Queer about Queer Studies Now?"

2   While outside the scope of this chapter, it is important to denote two interrelated points. First is the influence of these interdisciplinary scholars' scholarship in the work that sociologists were thinking with, about, and against and writing in tandem with between the 1980s and early 2000s—which is a point I return to briefly,

particularly in relation to Lionel Cantú Jr. Second, these emergent contributions to cementing a queer of color critique were themselves influenced by feminist of color formations, moving across intersectionality and cutting into the invisibility of Whiteness in queer studies; for more on this, refer to Moussawi and Vidal-Ortiz, "A Queer Sociology."

3 *American* references both the United States of America and the hemisphere, which is the Americas. To better situate the scope of American studies, when referencing the country or culture (and not the studies), I utilize the term *US-American* to address the geopolitical location and to resist the reproduction of ethnocentrist language.

4 Omi and Winant, *Racial Formation*. For two central examples of the absence of sociologists, see HoSang, LaBennett, and Pulido, *Racial Formation in the Twenty-First Century*; and Kyungwon Hong and Ferguson, *Strange Affinities*. Except for Ferguson's own training in sociology, and a trained sociologist teaching in Canada, USAmerican sociologists are conspicuously not contributing to the field.

5 Recent scholarship from sociologists has connected race and sexuality (with or without the queer of color critique). See, for example, Smith and Han, *Home and Community for Queer Men of Color*.

6 For sociology, see Collins, *Black Feminist Thought*; for scholarship beyond the discipline, see Crenshaw, "Demarginalizing the Intersection of Race and Sex."

7 Adam, "Theorizing Homophobia."

8 Combahee River Collective, *Combahee River Statement*; Lorde, *Sister Outsider*; hooks, *Black Looks*; Baldwin, *Native Son*; Moraga and Anzaldúa, *This Bridge*. For more on the co-constitution of gayness and Whiteness, see Guzmán, *Gay Hegemony*; refer also to Bérubé, "How Gay Stays White."

9 Cohen, "Punks, Bulldaggers, and Welfare Queens."

10 Chandan, "Home, Houses, Nonidentity."

11 Muñoz, *Disidentifications*.

12 Rich, "Compulsory Heterosexuality."

13 On the activist front, Barbara Smith has for over four decades been a monumental figure; she was a member of the Combahee River Collective, an author of several books, and more recently has produced op-eds critiquing the mainstream (White) gay and lesbian movement.

14 Combahee River Collective, *Combahee River Statement*; Lorde, *Sister Outsider*; Moraga and Anzaldúa, *This Bridge*.

15 With some exceptions, little scholarship explicitly using the queer of color critique (particularly by sociologists) points to the work of Asian Americans' participation in these historical processes, and when they do, sources often speak to the Western region of the country; similarly, Indigenous scholarship using a queer of color critique approach has only begun to be published in special issues of journals like *GLQ*. Of course, race and racial categorizations do not map out independent of one another—despite institutional works like the US Census forcing the split on us. As a case in point, Black and Latinx—not mutually exclusive

categories—are considered in relation to the queer of color critique in Johnson and Rivera-Servera, *Blacktino Queer Performance.*

16 For a brilliant recent example tackling the criminalization of Black male sexualization through anti-Black misandry and portrayals of Black men as potential vultures (in this case, readily able to expose others to HIV), see Smith, "'The Crime of Black Male Sexuality.'"

17 Moussawi and Vidal-Ortiz. "A Queer Sociology."

18 Jun, "Black Orientalism," 294.

19 Ferguson, "Authoritarianism."

20 In *Aberrations*, Ferguson states that another socialization institution, academia, especially in the West, "has historically worked to socialize its subjects into the state" (59). For more on how neoliberalism takes interlocking forms of sexuality and race and coopts related social justice projects, see Ferguson, "The Distributions of Whiteness"; and Ferguson and Hong, "Reflections." For more on the active steps to coopt minority needs in spaces like academia but also governance, see Lima, *Being Brown.* Lima connects to the queer of color critique through the thinking in Muñoz's "Feeling Brown."

21 Ferguson, "Authoritarianism," 282.

22 Ferguson, "The Nightmares."

23 A November 2021 talk by Jules Gill-Peterson, titled "Being Street: The Trans Woman of Color as Evidence," points to the momentary presence of this trans figure, which is not reconnected to the remainder of the text. Gill-Peterson is tracing the usage of the figure of the trans woman of color in ways that may produce a trans of color critique from within the queer of color critique, as did the queer of color critique, which emerged from resistance to queer theoretical formulations. Ferguson, *Aberrations*, ix.

24 Ibid., 29.

25 I return to a previous point about sociologists engaged with Ferguson's work. My own evaluation and editing of the work of the late Lionel Cantú Jr. suggests to me that he was engaged in parallel conversations with scholars we view as proponents of the "official" queer of color critique (i.e., Ferguson, Muñoz, Reddy) with those inherently influencing it, including Moraga and Anzaldúa. Using the work of the latter, Cantú coined the "queer political economy of migration" in ways like the discursive work that was based on materialism and historical political economy produced by Ferguson and Reddy. His untimely death in 2002 prevents us from knowing the full relationship between these scholars' work. For his published work, refer to Cantú, *The Sexuality of Migration.*

26 Ferguson, "Queer of Color Critique and the Global South."

27 I insist on the notion of US racial formation because racialization, as noted before, is not universally the same.

28 Morris, *The Scholar Denied.*

29 Ibid.; Lengermann and Niebrugge-Brantley, *The Women Founders.*

30 At the 2007 American Sociological Association "Author Meets Critics" session on the *Aberrations in Black* book, I posed this critique to Ferguson, and he graciously engaged with the roots, formulations, and networks that fueled his emphasis in the groups and issues that he did at the time of thinking and writing the book.

31 Samoans and other Pacific Islanders have experienced similar militarized strategies of survival to those of Puerto Ricans and thus began migrating to the United States in the late nineteenth century as well.

32 Oscar Lewis's the culture of poverty thesis was rehearsed with Mexican and Puerto Rican populations before it influenced the writing of the generational culture thesis with African Americans, spilling over onto the *Moynihan Report*.

BIBLIOGRAPHY

Adam, Barry. "Theorizing Homophobia." *Sexualities* 1, no. 4 (1998): 387–404.

Baldwin, James. *Notes of a Native Son*. Boston: Beacon Press, 1955. Reprinted 1984.

Bérubé, Allan. "How Gay Stays White and What Kind of White It Stays." In *The Making and Unmaking of Whiteness*, edited Birgit Brander Rasmussen, Eric Kinenberg, Irene J. Nexica, and Matt Wray, 234–65. Durham, NC: Duke University Press, 2001.

Cantú, Lionel, Jr. *The Sexuality of Migration: Border Crossings and Mexican Immigrant Men*. Edited posthumously by Nancy A. Naples and Salvador Vidal-Ortiz. New York: New York University Press, 2009.

Cohen, Cathy. "Punks, Bulldaggers, and Welfare Queens: The Radical Potential of Queer Politics?" *GLQ* 3, no. 4 (1997): 437–65.

Collins, Patricia Hill. 1990. *Black Feminist Thought: Knowledge, Consciousness, and the Politics of Empowerment*. New York: Routledge.

Combahee River Collective. *Combahee River Statement*. Boston: Combahee River Collective, 1977.

Crenshaw, Kimberlé. "Demarginalizing the Intersection of Race and Sex: A Black Feminist Critique of Antidiscrimination Doctrine, Feminist Theory, and Antiracist Politics." *University of Chicago Legal Forum* 1, no. 8 (1989): 139–67.

DeLauretis, Teresa. "Queer Theory: Lesbian and Gay Studies. An Introduction." *Differences: A Journal of Feminist Cultural Studies* 3, no. 2 (1991): iii–xviii.

Eng, David L. Eng, Jack Halberstam, and José Esteban Muñoz. "What's Queer about Queer Studies Now?" *Social Text* 23, no. 3–4 (2005): 1–17.

Ferguson, Roderick A. *Aberrations in Black: Toward a Queer of Color Critique*. Minneapolis: University of Minnesota Press, 2004.

———. "Authoritarianism and the Planetary Mission of Queer of Color Critique: A Short Reflection." *Safundi* 21, no. 3 (2020): 282–90.

———. "Queer of Color Critique and the Global South." *The Global Trajectories of Queerness: Rethinking Same-Sex Politics in the Global South*, edited by Ashley Tellis and Sruti Bala, 49–56. Boston: Brill, 2015.

———. *One-Dimensional Queer*. Cambridge, UK: Polity, 2018.

———. "The Distributions of Whiteness." *American Quarterly* 66, no. 4 (December 2014): 1101–6.

————. "The Nightmares of the Heteronormative." *Cultural Values* 4, no. 4 (2000): 419–44.

Ferguson, Roderick A., and Grace Kyungwon Hong. "Reflections: The Sexual and Racial Contradictions of Neoliberalism." *Journal of Homosexuality* 59 (2012): 1057–64.

Guzmán, Manolo. *Gay Hegemony/Latino Homosexualities*. New York: Routledge, 2006.

hooks, bell. *Black Looks: Race and Representation*. Boston: South End Press, 1992.

HoSang, Daniel Martinez, Oneka LaBennett, and Laura Pulido, eds. *Racial Formation in the Twenty-First Century*. Berkeley: University of California Press, 2012.

Johnson, E. Patrick. "'Quare' Studies, or (Almost) Everything I Know about Queer Studies I Learned from My Grandmother." *Text and Performance Quarterly* 21, no. 1 (2001): 1–25.

Johnson, E. Patrick, and Ramón H. Rivera-Servera, eds. *Blacktino Queer Performance*. Durham, NC: Duke University Press, 2016.

Jun, Helen H. "Black Orientalism: Nineteenth-Century Narratives of Race and U.S. Citizenship." In *Strange Affinities: The Gender and Sexual Politics of Comparative Racialization*, edited by Grace Kyungwon Hong and Roderick A. Ferguson, 293–315. Durham, NC: Duke University Press, 2011.

Kyungwon Hong, Grace, and Roderick A. Ferguson, eds. *Strange Affinities: The Gender and Sexual Politics of Comparative Racialization*. Durham, NC: Duke University Press, 2011.

Lengermann, Patricia M., and Jill Niebrugge-Brantley. *The Women Founders— Sociology and Social Theory, 1830–1930: A Text/Reader*. Long Grove, IL: Waveland Press, 2007.

Lima, Lázaro. *Being Brown: Sonia Sotomayor and the Latino Question*. Berkeley: University of California Press, 2019

Lorde, Audre. 1984. *Sister Outsider: Essays and Speeches by Audre Lorde*. Berkeley, CA: Crossing Press.

Manalansan, Martin. *Global Divas: Filipino Gay Men in the Diaspora*. Durham, NC: Duke University Press, 2003.

Moraga, Cherríe, and Anzaldúa, Gloria, eds. *This Bridge Called My Back: Writings by Radical Women of Color*. 4th ed. Albany: State University on New York Press, 2015.

Morris, Aldon. *The Scholar Denied: W. E. B. Du Bois and the Birth of Modern Sociology*. Oakland: University of California Press, 2017.

Moussawi, Ghassan, and Vidal-Ortiz, Salvador. 2020. "A Queer Sociology: On Power, Race, and Decentering Whiteness." *Sociological Forum* 35, no. 4: 1272–89.

Muñoz, José Esteban. *Disidentifications: Queers of Color and the Performance of Politics*. Minneapolis: University of Minnesota Press, 1999.

Omi, Michael, and Howard Winant. *Racial Formation in the United States*. New York: Routledge, 1986.

Reddy, Chandan. "Home, Houses, Nonidentity: Paris Is Burning." In *Burning Down the House: Recycling Domesticity*, edited by Rosemary Marangoly George, 355–79. Boulder, CO: Westview Press, 1998.

Rich, Adrienne. "Compulsory Heterosexuality and Lesbian Existence." *Signs* 5, no. 4 (Summer 1980): 631–660.

Smith, Jesús Gregorio. "The Crime of Black Male Sexuality: Tiger Mandingo and Black Male Vulnerability." In *Home and Community for Queer Men of Color: The Intersection of Race and Sexuality*, edited by Jesús Gregorio Smith and C. Winter Han, 149–71. Lanham, MD: Lexington Books, 2020.

Smith, Jesús Gregorio, and C. Winter Han, eds. *Home and Community for Queer Men of Color: The intersection of Race and Sexuality*. Lanham, MD: Lexington Books, 2020.

11

Cripping the Model Minority Mother

Race, Disability, and Reproductive Exclusion
in Asian American Families

MILIANN KANG

Able-bodiedness is a central condition for claiming model minority status. Intersections of disability and race show how easily Asian Americans fall out of their venerated position as model reproducers when their children do not conform to ableist standards of hard work, disciplined behavior, and high achievement. Drawing on scholarship in American studies, Asian American studies, feminist disability studies, and sociology, this chapter builds on my earlier framework of "reproductive exclusion" to bring greater attention to motherhood and reproduction as central sites of racialization.[1] Specifically, this chapter centers constructions of ability and disability to show how model minority status is contingent upon fulfillment of normative family structures and reproduction. Taking a multidisciplinary approach, it brings qualitative sociology together with historical, literary and cultural analyses, particularly those in Asian American studies.

Having a disabled child can challenge an Asian American family's already limited claims to belonging in the United States. Rather than assuming essentialized notions of ableism in "Asian culture," this study instead highlights historical and contemporary processes of model minority racialization that shape Asian American parenting in general, and specifically of children with disabilities. The desire of many Asian American families to project a sense of vibrant health and industriousness do not simply channel static views of disability grounded in ethnic culture but are molded by directives in US immigration laws that would exclude immigrants who appear otherwise. This chapter demonstrates the varied ways that Asian American mothers with disabled children respond to model minority standards and how these responses reflect but also resist ongoing legacies of reproductive exclusion.

Introduction

The timeliness and importance of this volume—and the larger project of bringing sociology and ethnic studies into closer conversation—was tragically driven home to me and many others who work at the intersections of these fields in the aftermath of the shootings of eight people, six of them Asian immigrant women, in Atlanta massage spas in March 2021. Speaking with journalists and writing our own responses, scholars in Asian American studies, sociology and feminist studies situated these acts of violence in larger historical, discursive, and social contexts.[2] We sought to counter the narrow, individualized explanations that focused on the motives of the murderer, Robert Aaron Long, particularly his "sexual addiction." Instead, we analyzed the constellation of factors that coalesced into making Asian immigrant women vulnerable targets, not just of these fatal shootings but of everyday harassment and marginalization, especially in service industries such as massage and sex work.

However, in these attempts, many of us were met with frustrating responses. In one interview, a journalist told me she was puzzled by why so many scholars insisted on beginning with the Page Act of 1875, which excluded Chinese women from immigrating based on assumptions that they were engaged in prostitution, as the starting point of the hypersexualization of Asian American women. She asked me to "connect the dots"—did the murderer even know about this history, or was there any evidence that he viewed sexualized images of Asian women before attacking them? I hesitated; would it clarify or cause more confusion to explain that most scholarship, especially in interdisciplinary fields, is less concerned with connecting dots of cause and effect than with mapping wide-ranging intersections, assemblages, and entanglements? Should I reference these scholarly debates and try to apply my own research? What would be the value added of introducing a concept like reproductive exclusion and framing these brutal killings as its most extreme culmination—as the taking of a person's life is the most irrevocable way of excluding them from the right to reproduce life? And would such attempts to make analytical sense of these senseless acts inflict further violence?

The Atlanta killings and the conditions that led to them are not the topic of this chapter, and I hesitate to use them as prologue when they demand much more in-depth treatment.[3] But the dilemmas they present set up the high stakes of the work in which contributors to this volume are engaged, specifically bringing sociology and various interdisciplinary fields together, not just to analyze current events but to respond to them. In terms of my own work, these events and the larger context of rising anti-Asian violence during the COVID-19 pandemic have challenged me to expand my conceptual framework of reproductive exclusion, to make it more accessible, and to engage more fully with issues of illness and disability. My earlier articulation of reproductive exclusion focused on how the control of biological and social reproduction has been utilized to exclude certain groups from immigrating and from claiming full citizenship once they are here. In this chapter, I revisit the framework of reproductive exclusion and expand on it to give more attention to the intersections of race, immigration, gender, sexuality, and disability, highlighting key scholars whose work synthesizes these intersections across the fields of sociology, ethnic studies, and feminist disability studies. Building on examples from my own research, I show how model minority constructions of Asian American "tiger mothers" exclude families and children with disabilities and how Asian American mothers engage in complex negotiations of ongoing structures of reproductive exclusion in their parenting of disabled children. The data draws from a subset of interviews from my larger book project, *Mother Other: Race and Reproductive Politics in Asian America*. Of eighty Asian American mothers who participated in the larger study, seventeen had children who experienced short- or long-term disabilities.

In "Cripping the Welfare Queen," Jina B. Kim articulates a "crip-of-color critique" that shifts attention from disability, as an identity, to disablement, as a mode of analysis. Applying the tools of literary criticism to show how young Black mothers are abandoned by the "basic support systems for maintaining life—public schools, hospitals, housing and social service," she poses the question, "How might disability studies shift if it took up the welfare queen as a central site of inquiry?"[4] Taking up her call, I offer a parallel provocation: "How might sociology and ethnic studies shift if they took up the tiger mother as a central site of inquiry?" If we traced this hyper-competitive Asian American model minority mother figure—not as the embodiment of essentialized Asian cultural norms but as an injunction to reproduce high-achieving, self-sufficient offspring as the price of the ticket for inclusion—how might we better understand the challenges confronting Asian American families with disabled children and their complex negotiations of these challenges? And how might the framework of reproductive exclusion shift attention from presumed pathologies within Asian American families to the conditions of racialized disablement that are imposed upon these families?

Reproductive Exclusion: A Sociological and Ethnic Studies Framework

In an earlier article titled "Reproducing Asian American Studies: Rethinking Asian Exclusion as Reproductive Exclusion," published in the special issue of *Amerasia* on "Rethinking Gendered Citizenship," I introduced the concept of reproductive exclusion to examine "the policing of borders based on acceptable forms of reproduction, and the policing of reproduction of those already within these borders."[5] This framework aimed to integrate "reproduction" as one of the central concepts in studies of gender and sexuality with debates about "exclusion" that are at the core of scholarship on race and immigration:

> Defined narrowly, reproductive exclusion is an analytical framework that identifies control of biological reproduction as a central force shaping state regulation of borders and entry. A more expansive interpretation of reproductive exclusion includes the ongoing social exclusion of certain groups already living within a country, including naturalized and native-born citizens, in order to limit non-normative biological, social, and cultural reproduction, based on constructions of race, gender, sexuality, class, disability, and dependency.[6]

Further, just as reproductive justice has been articulated by Black feminist scholars and activists but has broad theoretical relevance, reproductive exclusion is grounded in Asian American feminist scholarship but is not limited to Asian Americans. At the same time, reproductive exclusion centers Asian Americans as the targets of policies intended to simultaneously restrict reproduction and immigration. While recognizing racialized class animosities as a powerful force driving Chinese exclusion and nativist backlash against immigrants broadly, reproductive exclusion foregrounds recent scholarship that has called for more in-depth examination of the multiple intersections of gender, sexuality, disability, and dependency in shaping Asian exclusion.[7] This body of work seeks to go beyond merely adding disability into Asian American studies, or Asian Americans into disability studies; rather it endeavors to bring these two fields of study into closer inquiry by showing how race and disability are intertwined.

Reproductive exclusion maps the historical continuities between the standards of desirability for immigrants and of able bodies. Scholars have explored these linked histories of US immigration law's exclusions of both Asian Americans and disabled people. Stanley et al. assert, "Both groups have been historically associated with immaturity and vulnerability—the 'underdeveloped' Asian as the White man's burden, the disabled body as society's burden."[8] Two laws in particular, both passed in 1882, demonstrate the linked histories of exclusion based on disability and race. The Chinese Exclusion Act of 1882, following the Page Law of 1875 which banned the entry of unfree laborers and women suspected of engaging in prostitution, was one of the first federal law to limit immigration of a specific national and ethnic group. The 1882 Act to Regulate Immigration, the federal legislation that established a national-level immigration system and bureaucracy, justified exclusion "of any convict, lunatic, idiot, or any person unable to take care of him or herself without becoming a public charge."[9] This notion of "likely to become a public charge" has justified and magnified immigrant exclusion based on both race and disability. As Asian American studies scholar Lisa Sun-Hee Park summarizes:

> Public charge is a political classification used to exclude or deport those immigrants perceived to be or to have the possibility of becoming a burden on the state. Pregnancy has long been categorized as a public burden with respect to low-income immigrant women.[10]

Park further documents how public charge laws were revitalized under the Trump administration to justify family separations at the border, medical deportations of ill or injured immigrants, and threats to deny green cards to those who utilize Medicaid, food stamps, housing subsidies, and other forms of public assistance.[11] The invocation of public charge doctrine across different historical periods provides a vivid illustration of how broad categories of inadmissibility and deportability are linked through seemingly discrete administrative arms of the state, ranging from legislation to policing to social welfare provision; reproductive exclusion provides an analytical tool to lay bare these linkages. The framework of reproductive exclusion connects these broad social forces and synthesizes the work of scholars who work at the intersections of sociology and ethnic studies scholarship to weave together the seemingly disparate strands of research on race, immigration, gender, and disability as they coalesce around notions of the family and reproductive politics.

Regrettably, this cross-fertilization is somewhat lopsided, in my assessment, as more sociologists of Asian America engage with and incorporate Asian American studies critiques than Asian American studies scholars engaging with sociology. Sociology, and the social sciences in general, still occupy a relatively marginalized position in ethnic studies, and particularly in Asian American studies. Nonetheless, various scholars have provided pathbreaking roadmaps to bridge these fields. Most prominently, reproductive exclusion builds on the work of Evelyn Nakano Glenn, whose framework of "the racial division of paid reproductive labor" demonstrates how the social reproduction of White women and families institutionalized the servitude of Black women and extracted low-wage service work from immigrant domestics and nannies.[12] Nurses and domestic workers, many from the Philippines, are valued for their cheap reproductive labor in caring for others but face barriers when seeking to immigrate with and care for their own children and families.[13] Reproductive exclusion draws connections across the various forms of legal and social exclusion of women of color that denigrate their own reproduction and privilege the reproduction of White women.[14] In addition, reproductive exclusion highlights how caring for those who are sick and disabled can result in the disablement of caregivers' bodies.

Reproductive exclusion can also frame scholarship on how public discourses and state apparatuses produce disablement through the welfare system and its evisceration. In her study of how negative perception of Asian refugees fueled welfare reform in the Clinton era, Lynn Fujiwara's *Mothers without Citizenship* brings sociology and ethnic studies together to make sense of the public backlash against Southeast Asian refugees as "welfare abusers" in contrast to the refugees' own sense of betrayal by the US government.[15] Fujiwara grounds these competing discourses in the histories of US wars in Vietnam, Cambodia, and Laos and the CIA's recruitment of Hmong fighters with promises of new lives in the United States. She then contrasts these promises with the marginalization that the Hmong experienced, both by the American public and by state institutions, particularly the cutting off of welfare supports. Seen in this light, the high levels of depression and suicide among Hmong refugees do not inhere in Hmong culture or even in their shared experiences of war and resettlement. Applying the lens of reproductive exclusion, the collective trauma of Hmong refugees becomes visible not just as individual disabilities or cultural propensities but as products of their disablement by unfilled promises and outright abandonment by the US government.

Nadia Kim's book, *Refusing Death: Immigrant Women and the Fight for Environmental Justice in LA*, offers another rich illustration of integrating sociology and ethnic studies, showing how the lens of reproductive exclusion can further illuminate processes of disablement connected to toxic emissions around ports and freeways.[16] Capturing rich ethnographic moments such as the public testimony of workers and residents regarding exposures from a BP oil refinery, Kim documents how participants' rhetorical strategies shifted the burden of proof from community members being tasked with documenting high cancer rates to polluters and regulators having to answer to their actions and lack of accountability. Thus, her study demonstrates the power of Asian and undocumented Latin@ immigrant women connecting discursive frameworks to social conditions, not just to analyze them but to change them.

These examples move beyond what disability scholar Nirmala Erevelles critiques as reductive approaches that "add 'disability' arbitrarily to the expanded sociological trinity of race, class, and gender," rather than showing how racialization and disablement operate in concert.[17] Erevelles's research on the marginalization of students of color in special education programs further adds to understandings of reproductive exclusion by drawing attention to schools as institutions that deny access and resources to families with disabled children. This chapter seeks to build on this body of work that extends disability as an analytical lens rather than simply adding it as another variable. The following illustrations based on interviews and participant observation with Asian

American families raising disabled children show how their parenting struggles reveal ongoing processes of reproductive exclusion, particularly how they must continually contend with racialized and ableist constructions of Asian American tiger mothers.

Reproductive Exclusion and Tiger Mothering: Negotiating the Incommensurability of Disability and Model Minority Status

> As a result of the Wall Street Journal excerpt, the Western parenting world considers Ms. Chua a haughty demoness, a hard-driving task-master of the worst kind. I posit there's an even more extreme variety: The Tiger Special Needs Mother, who also happens to be "Chinese" (Asian).[18]

In her blog post "Tiger Mom: Special Needs Edition," Dianne Dokko Kim chronicles her efforts to raise her autistic son. Noting how Amy Chua's bestselling *Battle Hymn of the Tiger Mother* only briefly mentioned that Chua's sister has Down syndrome and won two gold medals at the Special Olympics, Kim asks, "More than hearing about Ms. Chua's superior/ambivalent parenting methods, or the success stories of her over-achieving children or siblings, that's the story I want to know about." Kim then recounts her own story of pushing her son to master flash cards and stack wooden blocks, to the point that "the therapist would nervously glance up at me as if to ask, 'Should I keep going?' The answer was always Yes." Rather than judging Kim's parenting style—or Chua's—this chapter asks a different question: Why must the answer to the question of whether or not to push Asian American children—whether that be to get into Harvard or to toilet independently—always be yes? And what does it take to be able to say no?

In her essay "Me as a Boy: On Raising an Asian American and Autistic Son" in the special issue of *Amerasia* on "The State of Illness and Disability in Asian America," Kristina Chew articulates how raising her son Charlie, who has autism, has opened her to envisioning new ways of being Asian American that are not contingent on model minority achievement:

> With Charlie, we accept a different kind of life: that he is autistic and that he is severely disabled and that there are limitations on his life and what

he can do. We also learn that there is a whole world of possibilities—that there are diverse and neurodiverse ways of being Asian American.[19]

Where "once upon a time" she "could not have imagined a life without going to college," Chew now recognizes how standards of success based on educational achievement marginalize Charlie and other disabled Asian Americans. While expanding the possibilities of being Asian American beyond entrance into elite colleges, she also shares how her son's diagnosis forces her to let go of aspects of culture that are important to her, such as Chinese language learning, as she makes the necessary choice to not raise son bilingually. "Instead of memorizing rows of Chinese characters, I have tried to figure out his many ways of communicating without words."[20]

Both Kim's blog post and Chew's essay resonate with and frame the interviews that I have conducted with Asian American mothers raising children with disabilities. Following, I present a few examples from my research that illuminate how disability challenges constructions of model minority motherhood and how Asian American mothers contend with these challenges. Many of these women grapple with and alter their expectations for high academic achievement that is the prerequisite for model minority status. Many struggle with how to redefine and adapt cultural identities for their disabled children, particularly with regard to bilingualism, biculturalism, and negotiation of contrasting cultural approaches to health, education, and family relations. Their struggles illuminate how legacies of reproductive exclusion still loom large, even for those who forge alternative parenting approaches, as departure from the imposed standards and expected trajectory of model minority motherhood can both liberate and further marginalize them.

"We're Doing Things to Bring Them Down": Rejecting Model Minority Success

We have been so taught in fear by society, religion. Don't do certain things and you'll be okay, but if you do anything different, you're risking too much. Be a lawyer, be a doctor, but don't be an individual . . . . But when they are sick, you stop worrying about what college they will go to.

Marian, a Chinese American teacher, summarized the impact of her daughter's struggle with depression, saying how she has come to reject standards of Asian American success based on high achievement and material gains. Rather than resisting therapy, which is often what providers assume is the stance of Asian American families, Marian framed her daughter's desire to see a therapist in positive terms as a sign of health.

> I think I had read a book at that point, somewhere in there I think it said you're really healthy if you want to go see a therapist. It's the first sign of healthiness. And we as parents are sort of not 100 percent okay. We're doing things to bring them down, and that's not what we should be doing, and yet even I do that to my own kids.

Marian expressed a desire to destigmatize both mental illness and the process of seeking support through therapy. Further, she acknowledged her own possible role in her daughter's challenges, recognizing mental health challenges within her family of origin, but also situating them within the demands of Asian American model minority success. Both Marian and her brother attended top business schools, but she described her wealthy brother as "obsessive compulsive" and a "miser" whose own daughters' did not want a relationship with him. While articulating the limitations of model minority success, her reference to OCD also reinforced the point that deviation from normative models of health and mental health undermines claims to model minority status. This conceptualizing of disability as a counterpoint to model minority success is both troubling and telling. It potentially reproduces stigma against disabled people, particularly regarding mental illness. At the same time, it indicates a recognition that reproductive exclusion positions disabled bodies—and minds—outside of the Asian American success frame and points to the problematic notion that belonging is contingent on reproduction of model minority families.

"More Familial Involvement with My Daughter's Care": Countering Essentialist Framings of Asian Families as Disabling

> I can't really tell if being Asian American has shaped my parenting of a child with special needs. There's probably more familial involvement with my daughter's care. We are raising out daughter very biculturally, not so much intentionally as out of necessity. We speak to her half in English and half in Chinese, which the speech therapist is against.

Gina, a Wall Street consultant, is raising her daughter, Emma, who has "global developmental delays" in a multigenerational family that includes her own and her husband's parents. Gina's commitment to raising her daughter bilingually was not just a preference but a necessity, as her grandparents, who are the main caregivers when Gina and her husband are at work, only speak Chinese. While disability advocates often focus on the needs of the individual child, Gina took into consideration her larger family caregiving configuration and resources. But ongoing structures of reproductive exclusion that insist on full assimilation subjected her to discriminatory attitudes from teachers and therapists, who saw her speaking to her daughter Chinese as a liability, even a source of additional disablement, rather than as a source of strength.

> [The speech therapist] says she's already speech delayed and it makes it harder for her and harder for other people to understand her. She may be saying something perfectly fine in Chinese but they don't know and they just think she can't talk. But we've more or less insisted because of the family situation—we want her to be able to talk to her grandparents.

Like her choice to raise her daughter bilingually, Gina's desire to utilize various kinds of treatments, including Eastern medicine, at times put her in opposition to her daughter's health-care providers.

> Maybe another aspect of my upbringing that has affected my daughter's care is that I'm more willing to consider alternative therapy like qi gong, acupuncture (more like acupressure—no needles!), herbs, etc. and I'm a little more skeptical that traditional Western medicine holds the answers.

Gina actively sought out alternative treatment modalities for her daughter, which Emma's grandparents are also very involved in providing, but felt that she could not be forthright about this without facing criticism. She struggled to negotiate different views about what was the best possible care for her daughter, while situating this care within her extended family situation and ethnic community.

Gina's case revealed how the specific experiences of many Asian American families differ from the White subjects who are often the assumed subjects of disability studies. Gina and her family struggled to incorporate various healing modalities, including Eastern medicine, which often involved additional expenses and time. In addition, they sought Western medical providers who were supportive of these alternative therapies. Furthermore, at times they had to confront teachers, therapists, and health providers who disagreed with their parenting approaches, particularly raising their child bilingually. Gina prioritized the need for their child to communicate with and forge relationships with important caregivers and family members, but she felt that these efforts were often misread as her being a "pushy tiger mother." Thus, she was subject to disabling racial stereotypes that doubly pathologized her for failing to fit into the normative model minority mold for having a disabled child and for her efforts to raise that child in ways that prioritized her cultural and community ties.

"I Know That She Has Been Treated like an Other": Resisting Reproductive Exclusion

> I know that she has been treated like an "Other" because she has some issues that kind of make her outstanding. You could say deficits or complements; she falls on both sides of the spectrum. She has been diagnosed with ADHD. It gets a lot of attention—it can be frequently negative and frequently rejecting.

Erica articulated an affirmative vision of her child's disability that acknowledges the various forms of exclusion she encounters while refusing to reduce her multiple identities in the pursuit of limited inclusion. She instilled cultural practices such as taking off shoes and greeting elders, which some therapists told her were unrealistic expectations to impose on her daughter but which Erica regarded as "core competencies," explaining:

> It is really important to my mother. I guess some people would say it's a losing battle, I constantly have to remind her. But to me it's like reminding her to bring her lunch or homework, even if I have to do it every day, even if it's a struggle, it's important that she does it. I want her to understand that I'm not the typical all-American person. There are other ways of living and being in this world as well.

Despite pushback from some care providers and other parents in the disability community, Erica was committed to maintaining cultural standards and modeling choices beyond full assimilation for her daughter.

Erica challenged both model minority and ableist standards of achievement and supported her daughter to envision "other ways of living and being," including acknowledging that she did not come from a "typical all-American family." Rather than holding her to expectations dictated by the dominant culture that treated her child as an "Other," Erica focused on giving her child skills and freedom to define her own goals and find pleasure in her own interests.

> What I have been trying to have her do is recognize the pleasure of doing things early. I see her tendencies. She'll wait until the last minute, she's that kind of person. I'll say, 'Well let's finish all of our homework by Wednesday, and then you can have Thursday and Friday off. We could do other things.' So I would tie in incentives to have her learn the pleasure of, the reward of, being done on time.

This encouragement to live in ways that affirm the fullest sense of self included supporting her daughter's exploration of her sexuality. Erica shared a recent conversation where she asked her daughter, "Can you truly own and be proud, and state your sexuality and claim it?" She added:

> I just want her to be secure in who she is. Really. And be able to clearly elucidate her own emotions, what she wants, how she wants, who she wants, and when she wants. Because I think that is the underlying tension in all relationships, in whatever constellation they appear.

Erica thus envisions expanding the possibilities of living at the nexus of race and disability. Reproductive exclusion need not only illuminate the conditions that marginalize mothers and families; it can also be used to equip those mothers and families with the tools necessary to resist reductive and exclusionary categorization and envision alternative and affirmative ways of being.

Discussion: Cripping Asian American Studies and Sociology

What do the above cases tell us about the intersections of race, gender, and disability in the lives of Asian American families raising children with disabilities? And what can the interdisciplinary tools of sociology and Asian American studies contribute? Model minority status is contingent on fulfillment of normative family structures and reproduction, and a disabled child can challenge Asian American families' already precarious claims to belonging in the United States. Reproductive exclusion helps to understand how the image of the model minority child and family assumes physical and emotional health and how these standards are imposed on Asian American families through the linked processes of racialization and ableism.

Yet many Asian American children and parents do not fit into normative models of ability and many Asian American mothers raise their disabled children in complicated and contradictory ways.[21] Many simultaneously challenge model minority discourses while seeking inclusion within these discourses, often facing difficult choices about prioritizing certain identities, needs, and challenges in their child's life while obscuring others. While it is true that immigrants arrive with their own sets of cultural beliefs about disability, these ideologies are rewritten in the US context, and for Asian Americans, the main ideological frame is model minority discourse. Rather than presuming shared roots in Asian cultures, let alone shared notions of disability across these diverse cultures, the lens of reproductive exclusion focuses on collective histories of immigration, racialization, and disablement that have molded whatever common parenting patterns can be observed among Asian Americans. Applying reproductive exclusion specifically to the parenting of disabled children reveals how racialization as the model minority imposes ableist standards but also how parents respond to these normativizing forces in diverse ways.

The history of US immigration law discussed earlier illuminates how practices such as denying or disguising family members' illness or disability that are often attributed simply to the immigrants' ethnic cultures instead have roots in state-sponsored policies of exclusion. For example, the desire of many Asian American families to project a sense of vibrant health and industriousness not only stems from negative cultural views of disability but also responds to directives in US immigration laws that would exclude immigrants if they were to appear otherwise. Thus, the fraught relationship between Asian American communities, families, and disability stems from multiple sources, including but not limited to ethnic culture. Ideologies about disability may reflect homeland cultures, but they are also significantly influenced by migration, settlement, and the contexts of reception into the receiving country. For Asian Americans, model minority standards serve as a powerful force that selects certain groups and emphasizes certain aspects of culture while downplaying or erasing other aspects.[22] Contrary to essentialized beliefs in deeply embedded cultural responses of shame and silence, recent theorizing and empirical research highlights multiple constructions of and responses to disability among Asian Americans.[23]

Reproductive exclusion builds on and resonates with the work of various scholars working at the crossroads of interdisciplinary fields. For example, drawing on literary criticism and psychoanalysis, David Eng and Shinhee Han offer the concepts of "racial melancholia" and "racial dissociation" to identify "distinct psychic mechanisms by which racialized immigrant subjects process problems of discrimination, exclusion, loss, and grief."[24] Whereas racial melancholia refers to histories of racial loss that attach to unresolved mourning for a specific object, racial dissociation results from histories of racial loss that are diffuse, dispersed, often unseen and unacknowledged. These terms help to understand certain longings or attachments, such as for raising bilingual children, as expressed in Chew's essay and in Gina's interview, as instances of racial melancholia, where racial loss congeals around the forfeited object of language. In contrast, the description offered by Marian of her brother as a miser with OCD who is cut off from his children could be seen as an illustration of racial dissociation, where the sense of racial loss is dispersed, unnamed—and hence—unmournable. With both racial melancholia and dissociation, as with reproductive exclusion, the profound impacts on individuals and families are recognized, but these states are located not just within individuals and families but in histories of racialized disablement and the losses imposed by them.

Building on Jasbir Puar's theorizing on "debility," Leah Lakshmi Piepzna-Samarasinha's concept of "crip superpowers," and Kandice Chuh's reimagining of Asian American studies not based on its objects of study but on its mode of critique, Mel Chen calls for feminist, queer, and disability studies to reimagine disability justice to think beyond "the political and cultural specificity of Whiteness and identity within the political-geographic West."[25] This approach resonates with the aim of reproductive exclusion to provide an analytic not only to bridge certain thematic topics, but to explore the productive messiness of working across multiple fields and specifically to foster richer engagements between sociology and ethnic studies.

Conclusion

I began this essay with a discussion of the Atlanta killings as the most extreme form of reproductive exclusion. I end with the above example of Erica as an illustration at the other extreme, of imagining the fullest possibilities for her child and for herself as a mother that embraces the whole range of her wants, pleasures, deficits, and complements. Earlier, I described the challenges of trying to connect the Page Act of 1875, the hypersexualization of Asian women, their vulnerabilities to violence within certain service industries, and how these formed the context for the mass shootings in Atlanta. Along parallel lines, I have drawn connections between the 1882 Chinese Exclusion Act and the Act to Control Immigration (known as the public charge law), to the discourses about Asian bodies as simultaneously racialized and disabled, and how these create standards of model minority motherhood that Asian American mothers must negotiate.

I have mapped out several key issues that emerged in my interviews regarding how Asian American families raising children with disabilities both conform to and disrupt model minority terms of inclusion. Because college attendance, and particularly admission to elite colleges, has become the primary marker of model minority success, illness and disability force parents to fundamentally rethink their approaches to education. Many Asian American families struggle to create and redefine new intersectional identities and parenting approaches that include disability, gender, race, and ethnicity. At the same time, they strive to integrate care for their children within often contrasting frameworks imposed by their own ethnic communities and by the racialization of Asian Americans as model minority subjects. Most parents filter and combine these various influences in their parenting. They are responsive to their child's needs and abilities while also situating these within their family networks, ethnic communities, and the limited terms of model minority inclusion for Asian Americans. In so doing, they illuminate how the dual historical exclusions of race and disability are simultaneously inherited and interrupted in contemporary Asian American families.

In his essay "Illness, Disability and the Beautiful Life," in the special issue of *Amerasia* that I have referred to extensively, James Kyung-Jin Lee asks, "What would it mean for Asian American Studies to imagine its central subject, its imagined body, as a disabled or ill one? What would we need to do intellectually, politically, affectively, to regard this ill or disabled Asian American body and utter, 'it is beautiful'?"[26] Building on these questions, this chapter has explored how the disabled or ill body challenges the notion of the model minority family and child as the central Asian American subject and how Asian American families struggle to raise their children beautifully, in spite of structures of reproductive exclusion that regard them otherwise.

NOTES

1 Kang, "Reproducing Asian American Studies."
2 Dhingra, "Racism Is behind Anti-Asian American Violence"; Ho, "Opinion:"; Kang, "Why Are Perpetrators' Motives Given More Importance?"
3 There are many important theoretical frameworks through which a more in-depth study of the Atlanta murders would engage, such as biopower, necropolitics and precarious life. See, for example Foucault, *The History of Sexuality;* Foucault, *The Will to Knowledge;* Mbembe, *Necropolitics;* Puar, *Terrorist Assemblages;* Butler, *Precarious Life.*
4 Kim, "Cripping the Welfare Queen," 80–81.
5 Kang, "Reproducing Asian American Studies," 1.
6 Ibid.
7 Cheng, *Citizens of Asian America;* Hing, *Defining America through Immigration Policy;* Hsu, *The Good Immigrants;* Park, *Elusive Citizenship;* Wang, "Race, Class, Citizenship"; Wu, *The Color of Success.*

8 Stanley et al., "Enabling Conversations," 77.

9 Daniels and Graham, Debating American Immigration.

10 Park, "Challenging Public Charge Policy," 383.

11 Park, "Four Things You Need to Know."

12 Glenn, "From Servitude to Service Work."

13 Espiritu, *Home Bound*; Guevarra, *Marketing Dreams*; Parreñas, *Servants of Globalization*; Rodriguez, *Migrants for Export*.

14 Chen, *Chinese San Francisco*; Dill, "Fictive Kin"; Lee and Yung, *Angel Island*.

15 Fujiwara, *Mothers without Citizenship*, 54.

16 Kim, *Refusing Death*.

17 Erevelles, "Educating Unruly Bodies."

18 Dokko Kim, "Tiger Mom."

19 Chew, "Me as a Boy," 84.

20 Ibid.

21 He, "Pageant Politics"; Jegatheesan, "Cross-Cultural Issues"; Wang and West, "Asian American Immigrant Parents."

22 Chang, "Asian Americans, Disability, and the Model Minority Myth"; He, "Pageant Politics"; Jegatheesan, "Cross-Cultural Issues"; Wong and Tsang, "When Asian Immigrant Women Speak."

23 Chang, "Asian Americans, Disability, and the Model Minority Myth"; Wu, Chang and Eng *Reconnected*.

24 Eng and Han, *Racial Melancholia, Racial Dissociation*.

25 Chen, "Asian American Speech."

26 Lee, "First-Person Political," xiii.

BIBLIOGRAPHY

Butler, Judith. *Precarious Life: The Powers of Mourning and Violence*. London: Verso, 2006.

Chang, Yoonmee. "Asian Americans, Disability, and the Model Minority Myth." In *Flashpoints for Asian American Studies*, edited by Cathy Schlund-Vials, 241–53. New York: Fordham University Press, 2017.

Chen, Mel. "Asian American Speech, Civic Place, and Future Nondisabled Bodies." *Amerasia Journal* 39, no. 1 (2013): 91–106.

Chen, Yong. *Chinese San Francisco, 1850–1943: A Trans-Pacific Community*. Palo Alto, CA: Stanford University Press, 2002.

Cheng, Cindy I.-Fen. *Citizens of Asian America: Democracy and Race during the Cold War*. New York: New York University Press, 2014.

Chew, Kristina. "Me as a Boy: On Raising an Asian American and Autistic Son." *Amerasia Journal* 39, no. 1 (January 1, 2013): 83–87. https://doi.org/10.17953/amer.39.1.6h32364614448635.

Daniels, Roger, and Otis L. Graham. *Debating American Immigration, 1882–Present*. New York: Rowman & Littlefield, 2001.

Dhingra, Pawan. "Racism Is behind Anti-Asian American Violence, Even When It's Not a Hate Crime." *Conversation*, March 19, 2021. http://theconversation.com.

Dill, Bonnie Thornton. "Fictive Kin, Paper Sons, and Compadrazgo: Women of Color and the Struggle for Family Survival." In *Families in the U.S.: Kinship and Domestic Politics*, edited by Karen V. Hansen and Anita Ilta Garey, 149–69. Philadelphia: Temple University Press, 1994.

Eng, David L., and Shinhee Han. *Racial Melancholia, Racial Dissociation: On the Social and Psychic Lives of Asian Americans*. Durham, NC: Duke University Press, 2019.

Erevelles, Nirmala. *Disability and Difference in Global Contexts: Enabling a Transformative Body Politic*. New York: Palgrave Macmillan, 2011.

———. "Educating Unruly Bodies: Critical Pedagogy, Disability Studies, and the Politics of Schooling." *Educational Theory* 50, no. 1 (2000): 25–47.

Espiritu, Yến Lê. *Home Bound: Filipino American Lives Across Cultures, Communities, and Countries*. Berkeley: University of California Press, 2003.

Foucault, Michel. *The History of Sexuality. Vol. 1, An Introduction*. New York: Pantheon, 1978.

———. *The Will to Knowledge*. Harmondsworth: Penguin, 2006.

Fujiwara, Lynn. *Mothers without Citizenship: Asian Immigrant Families and the Consequences of Welfare Reform*. Minneapolis: University of Minnesota Press, 2008.

Glenn, Evelyn Nakano. "From Servitude to Service Work: Historical Continuities in the Racial Division of Paid Reproductive Labor." *Signs* 18 (1992): 1–43.

Guevarra, Anna Romina. *Marketing Dreams, Manufacturing Heroes: The Transnational Labor Brokering of Filipino Workers*. New Brunswick, NJ: Rutgers University Press, 2009.

He, Fang. "'Golden Lillies' across the Pacific: Footbinding and the American Enforcement of Chinese Exclusion Laws." In *Gendering the Trans-Pacific World*, edited by Catherine Ceniza Choy and Judy Tzu-Chun Wu, 257–83. Boston: Brill, 2017.

Hing, Bill Ong. *Defining America through Immigration Policy*. Philadelphia: Temple University Press, 2004.

Ho, Jennifer. "No F****** Pink Ribbons: A Blog about One Asian American's Anger with Her Breast Cancer." *Amerasia Journal* 39, no. 1 (January 1, 2013): 119–27. https://doi.org/10.17953/amer.39.1.p5n84x1702003496.

———. "Opinion: To Be an Asian Woman in America." CNN, March 17, 2021. www.cnn.com.

Hsu, Madeline Y. *The Good Immigrants: How the Yellow Peril Became the Model Minority*. Princeton, NJ: Princeton University Press, 2017.

Jegatheesan, Brinda. "Cross-Cultural Issues in Parent-Professional Interactions: A Qualitative Study of Perceptions of Asian American Mothers of Children with Developmental Disabilities." *Research and Practice for Persons with Severe Disabilities* 34, no. 3–4 (2009): 123–36.

Kang, Miliann. "Reproducing Asian American Studies: Rethinking Asian Exclusion as Reproductive Exclusion." *Amerasia Journal* 46, no. 2 (December 2, 2020): 136–46. https://doi.org/10.1080/00447471.2020.1840319.

———. "Why Are Perpetrators' Motives Given More Importance Than the Lives They Take?" *Ms.*, March 22, 2021. https://msmagazine.com.

Kim, Diane Dokko. "Tiger Mom: Special Needs Edition." *Dianne Dokko Kim* (blog), January 13, 2013. www.dianedokkokim.com.

Kim, Jina B. "Cripping the Welfare Queen: The Radical Potential of Disability Politics." *Social Text* 39, no. 3 (148) (September 1, 2021): 79–101. https://doi.org/10.1215/01642472-9034390.

Kim, Nadia Y. *Refusing Death: Immigrant Women and the Fight for Environmental Justice in LA*. Stanford, CA: Stanford University Press, 2021.

Lee, Erika, and Judy Yung. *Angel Island: Immigrant Gateway to America*. Oxford: Oxford University Press, 2010.

Lee, James Kyung-Jin. "Illness, Disability, and the Beautiful Life." *Amerasia Journal* 39, no. 1 (January 1, 2013): ix–xvii. https://doi.org/10.17953/amer.39.1.770m7m3413453050.

Mbembe, Achille. *Necropolitics*. Durham, NC: Duke University Press, 2019.

Park, John S. *Elusive Citizenship: Immigration, Asian Americans, and the Paradox of Civil Rights*. New York: New York University Press, 2004.

Park, Lisa Sun-Hee. "Challenging Public Charge Policy: Coalitional Immigrant Community Strategies." *Journal of Asian American Studies* 13, no. 3 (2010): 371–87. https://doi.org/10.1353/jaas.2010.0005.

———. "Four Things You Need to Know about the Border by Lisa Sun-Hee Park." *The Abusable Past* (blog), September 9, 2019. www.radicalhistoryreview.org/.

Parreñas, Rhacel S. *Servants of Globalization: Women, Migration, and Domestic Work*. Stanford, CA: Stanford University Press, 2015.

Puar, Jasbir K. "Prognosis Time: Towards a Geopolitics of Affect, Debility and Capacity." *Women & Performance: A Journal of Feminist Theory* 19, no. 2 (July 1, 2009): 161–72. https://doi.org/10.1080/07407700903034147.

———. *Terrorist Assemblages: Homonationalism in Queer Times*. Durham, NC: Duke University Press Books, 2017.

Rodriguez, Robyn Magalit. *Migrants for Export: How the Philippine State Brokers Labor to the World*. Minneapolis: University of Minnesota Press, 2010.

Song, Min Hyoung. "Communities of Remembrance: Reflections on the Virginia Tech Shootings and Race." *Journal of Asian American Studies* 11, no. 1 (2008): 1–26.

Stanley, Sandra Kumamoto, Tracy Buenavista, Gina Masequesmay, and Laura Uba. "Enabling Conversations: Critical Pedagogy and the Intersections of Race and Disability Studies." *Amerasia Journal* 39, no. 1 (January 1, 2013): 75–82. https://doi.org/10.17953/amer.39.1.m2ur38566510473r.

Wang, Hui-Ting, and Elizabeth A. West. "Asian American Immigrant Parents Supporting Children with Autism: Perceptions of Fathers and Mothers." *International Journal of Whole Schooling* 12, no. 1 (January 1, 2016): 1–21.

Wang, L. Ling-chi. "Race, Class, Citizenship, and Extraterritoriality: Asian Americans and the 1996 Campaign Finance Scandal." *Amerasia Journal* 33, no. 1 (2007): 167–88.

Wong, Yuk-Lin Renita, and A. Ka Tat Tsang. "When Asian Immigrant Women Speak: From Mental Health to Strategies of Being." *American Journal of Orthopsychiatry* 74, no. 4 (October 2004): 456–66. https://doi.org/10.1037/0002-9432.74.4.456.

Wu, Cynthia. *Chang and Eng Reconnected: The Original Siamese Twins in American Culture*. Philadelphia: Temple University Press, 2012.

Wu, Ellen D. *The Color of Success: Asian Americans and the Origins of the Model Minority*. Princeton, NJ: Princeton University Press, 2014.

12

"Can't We All Just Get Along?"

Public Opinion on Race in Los Angeles
Twenty-Five Years after Rodney King

SYLVIA ZAMORA AND NADIA Y. KIM

By the 1980s, nearly 85 percent of immigrants to the United States had origins in Asia, Latin America, or the Caribbean.[1] The growth in these immigrant groups was most pronounced in the nation's largest cities such as Los Angeles, New York, San Francisco, and Miami.[2] As these groups interfaced more and more in economically distressed urban centers like Los Angeles, intergroup tension and conflict arose.[3] These conflicts marked a departure from the social history of US race relations in which groups of color were usually in conflict with White Americans.[4] Yet mass media were quick to cover the developing strain in Asian (namely, Korean) Americans' relations with Black Americans during the period leading up to the 1992 Los Angeles uprising—the focus of this chapter—and sociologists were not as quick to produce empirical investigations of this matter.[5]

By 1992, the year of the historic multiracial uprising that set Los Angeles ablaze for five fateful days, Los Angeles had felt the blunt force of this racial and ethnic shift along with a decade of racialized neoliberal policies. The modern neoliberal era launched by the Reagan administration—including the yawning gap between the rich and poor, law-and-order policies involving the militarized and excessive policing of communities of color, and the swelling of prisons with Black and Brown bodies—radically changed ethno-racial dynamics in Los Angeles.

Despite the growing importance of multiracial and ethnic group dynamics that began fifty years ago, research on race relations in the United States—mainstream sociological theory, methods, and empiricism—continues to be dominated by the Black-White binary paradigm.[6] Much of the sociology of racial attitudes, which tends to draw conclusions based on individual quantitative measures and how these play out in regression models, has focused on White racial attitudes toward Black Americans. While these studies have developed important frameworks for understanding race relations, we argue that racial attitudes survey data, particularly those that center White attitudes, obviate the role of the racial state—both in imperialist and domestic contexts—and of the economic, political, and cultural forces shaping how groups see one another. In this vein, we believe that traditional racial-attitudes research has limited utility for understanding these key inflection points, such as the 1992 urban unrest and the rise of Trumpian White nationalism and (neo)fascism based in racist demagoguery. We propose integrating ethnic and American studies approaches to help address these limitations.

In this chapter, we draw on the critical tools of ethnic and American studies to contextualize descriptive results from public opinion on race relations in Los Angeles following the 1992 uprising (known as the LA riots) and again twenty-five years later during the time of Trump's presidential inauguration in January 2017. In observance of the 1992 LA unrest, the LMU Thomas and Dorothy Leavey Center for the Study of Los Angeles (StudyLA) conducted public opinion surveys of residents in the city of Los Angeles every five years since 1997. The Los Angeles Public Opinion Surveys document the trends in residents' attitudes toward race relations in the city. Each survey included between 600 and 2,404 randomly selected residents from the city of Los Angeles and residents from Los Angeles County who live outside the city of LA. Among the sample, Asian, Black, White, and Latinx people each made up approximately one-quarter of the survey takers, who answered questions offered in multiple languages. Each survey had a unique set of respondents. For this chapter, we focus on the following survey questions posed to Angelenos: whether they believe race relations are improving (or worsening), whether racial/ethnic groups in the city are getting along, and whether they believe another racial unrest like that in 1992 will erupt in LA in the near future.

Our focus on the general state of race relations more broadly is also a departure from traditional race relations survey research, which gauges attitudes toward specific groups and does so by way of "feeling thermometers" (hot-warm-cold) and measures like "easy or hard to get along with" and "discriminatory or not." Rather, analyzing surveys that ask respondents what they think of race relations writ large in the city they live in allows us to move beyond individual group attitudes. Racial attitudes are just as much about social and political relations at the meso-and macro-level as they are about individually held prejudices at the micro level, a point that ethnic and American studies have always underscored and one that we emphasize in this chapter.

The surveys used in this analysis were taken during a time when Angelenos were still reeling from the aftereffects of critical racial forces that begot the LA riots. Yet these moments are often decontextualized or ahistoricized by social scientists who incorporate race as a mere variable rather than as a core theoretical concept.[7] In contrast, as leading ethnic studies scholar Yến Lê Espiritu reminds us, "the central intellectual goal of ethnic studies is to investigate the complex roles played by race and ethnicity in social relations as a way to produce new epistemologies and new data on social power, social institutions, and social identities."[8] In addition, sociology has not followed the lead of American Studies in centering empire, yet we cannot understand the 1992 LA unrest— namely how different racialized groups see each other—without incorporating the imperialist history and related economic context in which their mutual stereotypes emerged.[9] We argue that we must bring the racialized imperialist and neoliberal shifts that spawned the LA uprising and the election of an openly racist White nationalist president—into conversation with more micro-level survey measures. Done effectively, we believe that such engagement expands our understanding not only of public opinion data on race but of "new epistemologies and data" on how race, racism, and power structure the nature of intergroup relations. If we fail to do so, we run the risk of misinterpreting the wealth of survey data available to us.

Lastly, our focus on Los Angeles, an urban metropolis unique in its geographic expanse, residential segregation patterns, highly diversified labor market, and concentration of diverse immigrant groups, serves to underscore the importance of time and place in racial attitudes research. We hope this chapter encourages scholars who report survey results from multiple cities to provide much needed context on those locations rather than glossing over it, as is often done in multicity studies. At the same time, we want to make clear that we do not claim in this piece that historical, structural, and contextual forces like demographic change directly cause patterned racial attitudes and opinions; in addition, determining this relationship is not possible with any existing survey data and is thus beyond the scope of this chapter. What we do argue is that we cannot understand city residents' racial attitudes without examining—and interrelating—the material and discursive dynamics in that city.

Limitations of the Sociology of Racial Attitudes

Sociological research on racial attitudes is predominantly quantitative. Using regression and other models, it tends to examine variables (or indexes of variables) that are found to be significant in predicting the racial attitudes of survey takers, from gender, class, and ethnicity to more complex measures. This reflects a broader trend in sociology as a discipline, which became highly "scientized" in the 1970s.[10] With the advent of computerization, sociologists employed sophisticated survey data using structural equations, log-linear methods, and other complicated models believed to have great explanatory power.[11]

The Chicago school of sociology in the 1920s has long been credited with the birth of modern social scientific research on race relations. Sociologists such as Robert Park, who studied urban Chicago neighborhoods, developed his race relations cycle theory based largely on the experiences of European immigrants. Although not often recognized as the pioneer of the sociology of race relations, W. E. B. Du Bois's groundbreaking study *The Philadelphia Negro* preceded the work of Park and other Chicago sociologists by two decades.[12] In fact, sociologists of color were not included in major sociology departments "in a *meaningful* way" until the 1970s.[13] This is important because as Bonilla-Silva and Tukufu Zuberi remind us, "particular statistical methods' applicability to social problems is determined by the users of social statistics."[14] How social scientists interpret public opinion data on race, therefore, can be highly consequential for the development of social theory and applicability to public policy.

In this section, we briefly review some of the most influential theoretical models in the sociology of racial attitudes that have shaped the field. The *classical prejudice model* focuses on the psychological level of internalized attitudes. It posits that people learn and express negative attitudes about other group members even when controlling for class, other forms of socioeconomic competition, self-interest, and rationality.[15] In a related fashion, Kinder and Sears theorized *symbolic racism* which views prejudice to be a product of abstract, morality-based resentments.[16] Allport proposed the widely recognized intergroup contact theory, which found that increased contact between majority and minority members reduced prejudice between them.[17]

Herbert Blumer's group threat theory has perhaps been the most explored, as he found dominant groups' prejudice to come from their dominant positioning above subordinate groups in the social order.[18] Central to this dominant positioning were the following four sentiments: a feeling of superiority, a feeling that the subordinate race is intrinsically different and alien, a feeling of proprietary claim to certain privileges and advantages, and fear and suspicion that the subordinate race harbors designs on the prerogatives of the dominant race. Although group threat theories like these have enjoyed empirical support, Blumer's theory explains only dominant groups' attitudes toward groups lower on the social ladder.[19] Classic works such as by Bobo and Hutchings have ably documented how group threat theories are applicable to groups of color as well.[20] This use of Blumer was also central to the renowned Multi-City Study of Urban Inequality (MCSUI), which asked group position questions but also other types of racial attitudes measures.

The models of Blumer and Bobo and Hutchings, however, have not sufficiently theorized how group position prejudice relates to immigrants and their attitudes.[21] Racial attitudes are far more complex when involving immigrants and native-born people of color because, unlike examining White attitudes (dominant vs. subordinate outgroups), they come into contact with groups who can be of equal status, subordinate, or superordinate and within more than one socioracial hierarchy.[22] Relying, then, on traditional social science approaches to race relations has been inadequate for understanding prejudicial attitudes and relations among groups of color, especially in regions with large immigrant populations like Los Angeles. Until recently, studies of racial attitudes among US-born people of color, such as African American and Latinx relations or Asian American and Latinx relations, have been relatively few.[23]

At the same time that sociology was aiming for "objectivity" and being "quantified," the United States was undergoing significant social and political transformation that gave rise to revolutionary academic disciplines of ethnic studies, women and gender studies, and African American studies. While sociology took a more conservative turn, feminists and scholars of color criticized their own conservative disciplines for creating "an overly timid and elitist White Protestant male enterprise which tended to reinforce the dominant culture rather than critically analyzing it."[24] Instead, ethnic and American studies were committed to centering empire and imperialism and to the incorporation of women and people of color into "progressive, inclusive, and liberated academic profession[s]."[25]

In this chapter, we draw inspiration from ethnic and American studies to place racial attitudes research in a broader perspective that includes history and macro-political, economic, and cultural forces such as empire—all of which are racialized. Unlike traditional sociology approaches that have emphasized individual quantitative measures and White attitudes, we incorporate ethnic and American studies approaches to help us better understand how patterned responses may align with the broader racialized forces that survey takers have experienced and that continue to swirl around them as they mark their answers.

Contextualizing Racial Attitudes Data

Los Angeles Race Relations in the Era of Rodney King

On April 29, 1992, Angelenos took to the streets in violent protest of the jury acquittal of four White police officers who were accused of using excessive force in the beating of Rodney King, a Black man. In what is arguably the first video of police brutality to go viral, the world had for months prior to the trial watched footage, recorded by a bystander, of the police officers continuously beating King to the ground with batons despite the fact that he was inebriated, unarmed, and not threatening the lives of the officers. The acquittal verdict was met with anger, rage, and frustration by many who never expected that a jury viewing this tape could find the police officers not guilty of excessive force. Decades of disenfranchisement, mistreatment, institutionalized racism, and economic restructuring came to a head and prompted one of the largest and most destructive urban rebellions in the nation's history.

Five years following the historic 1992 uprising, in 1997, the Center for the Study of Los Angeles at Loyola Marymount University surveyed Angelenos to gauge whether they believed the City of Los Angeles had made progress toward improving race relations in the five years since the unrest. Almost half of Angelenos felt fairly optimistic that race relations had improved since the 1992 unrest. The other half, however, believed that the city had stayed the same. There were important differences by race. Latinxs and Asian Americans reported more satisfaction with the progress (54 percent and 57 percent, respectively). African Americans were more divided on the issue, with almost half (48 percent) expressing optimistic views of the racial progress, and the remaining half feeling less optimistic. Similarly, and somewhat surprisingly, far fewer Whites (40 percent) said they believed Angelenos had made progress since the unrest.

However, when asked about the general state of race relations in 1997—as opposed to whether relations had improved in the last five years—a majority of Angelenos (63 percent) said race relations were generally "not good." The results varied to some extent by racial group: African Americans and Latinx groups similarly felt that relations were "not so good" (57 percent and 54 percent, respectively). Asian Americans stood out as the most optimistic group, with 55 percent saying race relations were "good" (versus 39 percent reporting "not good"). Again, Whites by far had the most negative views, with 73 percent saying race relations were "not good." Another noteworthy finding pertained to the views of those who lived in the site of the unrest; whereas one might expect respondents living in the epicenter of the unrest to be most critical of race relations, they were in fact less critical than those living outside the area (54 percent to 61 percent, respectively).

It is perhaps not surprising that overall, a majority of Angelenos in 1997 were less than optimistic about the state of race relations in the city. When one considers the importance of historical shifts, the growing gap between the haves and have-nots from the 1970s onward largely originated in dramatic economic restructuring.[26] Whereas the rest of the central cities in the United States were rusting into the Rustbelt owing to the decline of the manufacturing sector (as it left for the Global South), LA was unique in that its economy remained intensively manufacturing based.[27]

Despite these affirming economic circumstances, the percentage of people in poverty relative to the nonpoor was significantly higher in LA than in the rest of the country, including in the years prior to, during, and after 1992, when the unrest occurred.[28] In 1995, for instance, the difference between LA's percent population below the poverty line and the rest of the country was almost nine points.[29] In addition, Los Angeles is replete with ethnic employment niches that employ a large labor force of "low-skilled" immigrant workers to service the middle and upper classes. Parallel to the double-edged sword of LA's overall economy, the city's ethnic economies have grown dynamically at the same time that these jobs have offered low wages and little opportunity for advancement.[30]

The urban America of the 1980s, especially communities like South LA, also witnessed the racialized and militarized so-called war on drugs. Ardently supported both by the Democratic and Republican Parties in the Reagan years, the drug war also appealed to White Americans' racial antipathies and thwarted the political opposition by Black Americans desperate for solutions to improve their neighborhoods. Instead, Americans witnessed a CIA-orchestrated crack epidemic, severe poverty, police infiltration of drug dealing rings, and harsh sentencing of such rings.[31] The racialization of crack as Black accounted for the 100:1 disparity for crack versus powder cocaine in sentencing for federal drug cases.[32]

Nowhere was this "war" more intense than in Los Angeles, the epicenter of the US crack economy.[33] Police infiltration of the inner city intensified, as the militarized campaigns against drugs and gangs resulted in new and brutal technologies of policing. Historian Donna Murch notes, "By 1992 city sheriffs listed nearly half of the African American men under age twenty-five in Los Angeles County as gang members."[34] The war on drugs exacerbated existing racial disparities, and California arguably led this national trend. By the year 2000, Black and Latinx prisoners were over 64 percent of the total prison population.[35] These racialized images were indelibly seared into Americans' consciousness by the news and shows like Cops that planted themselves in the "ghetto" for middle-class America's consumption. They also shaped the racial attitudes of Angelenos, including immigrant newcomers who arrived with preexisting anti-Black prejudices originating in their home countries.[36]

Many Latinx immigrants moved into South LA and surrounding communities, leading to racial tension with long-time Black residents.[37] Tension and conflict also arose between Asian immigrant, especially ethnically Korean, merchants who replaced Whites as business owners in Black and Latinx communities.[38] Guided in part by American studies' prioritization of US imperialism, Kim also found that to fully understand what shaped mutual Black-Korean prejudice in 1980s and 1990s LA, one must examine the stereotypes that emerged since the US military occupation of South Korea in 1945.[39] The notion of the inscrutable, exotically foreign, feminized, dependent Asian/Korean emerged from US imperialist projects, as did Koreans' stereotypic notions of Black Americans as poorer and less capable than Whites, as Jim Crow military segregation affirmed existing US and Korean skin color hierarchies.[40]

Notably, public opinion on life in LA was already so negative in the months leading up to the uprising that the events of April 1992 did not significantly shift public opinion in a negative direction.[41] A survey taken by UCLA's Institute for Social Science Research before and after the uprising found that an astounding 70 percent of Angelenos felt that Los Angeles had become a "worse place to live" in the years leading up to the uprising.[42] Although we noted a lack of consensus on whether race relations had improved, about half of Angelenos believed that racial groups had gotten along better in the five years after the uprising.

The lack of consensus on the direction of race relations five years post-uprising could also be attributed to the rise—and fall—of the city's first ever multiracial political coalition of mainly White and Black liberals, but also Asian Americans and Latinxs. Referred to as the "Bradley coalition," alluding to African American mayor Tom Bradley, this alliance lasted twenty years (1973–93). But racial politics in the city took a downward turn. The 1992 unrest contributed to Bradley's decision not to seek a sixth term. Instead, Michael Woo, an Asian American city council member, ran for mayor but was defeated by Republican Richard Riordan. By 1997, the coalition had splintered, with Latinxs and Asian Americans voting for Riordan's second term, and Black voters overwhelmingly supporting Democratic candidate Tom Hayden.[43] In the end, differences

in policy preferences and perceived economic competition between racial groups proved insurmountable for a liberal "rainbow" coalition. The
racial future looked bleak; recall that only five years had passed since the
unrest when the 1997 survey was taken. The smoke was barely gone and
the charred remains of hollowed-out stores and of melted and gnarled
metal still blighted the neighborhoods.

*Public Opinion Twenty-Five Years after King: A Growing Awareness
of Structural Racism?*

In commemoration of the twenty-fifth anniversary of the 1992 unrest, in
January 2017, the LMU Leavey Center for the Study of LA asked Angelenos whether they believed that race relations had improved since the
infamous unrest. When asked in 2017 whether LA had seen improvement
in race relations in the previous five years, fewer Angelenos than in 1997
believed that race relations were improving. It is very plausible that in the
five years after the 1992 unrest, any kind of improvement (including no
repeat riots/protests despite concerns that they would erupt) might have
been magnified as signaling "improvement." Asian Americans were most
optimistic in 1997 and showed the biggest decline across time, with only
29 percent saying race relations improved in 2017 compared to 57 percent
feeling the same way following the 1992 unrest. Black and Latinx Angelenos followed a similar trend, with only 29 percent of Black Angelenos and
38 percent of Latinx Angelenos saying relations improved in 2017 (compared to 48 percent of Black Angelenos and 54 percent of Latinxs in 1997).
One could also argue that based on the 2017 question's wording (whether
race relations had "improved" over the past five years), Angelenos generally believed that relations had simply stayed the same; in this way, it
is not necessarily a bad sign. Moreover, LA's demographics had changed
dramatically since the first survey in 1997. As such, there were more immigrant newcomer respondents in the 2017 survey that did not experience
the LA unrest or share the collective memory with longer-term residents.

There is no doubt that at the time Angelenos participated in the 2017
survey, however, the national state of race relations was not looking
good. In fact, the survey was carried out just days before Trump's inauguration as the forty-fifth president of the United States. These data
seem to bear out that Angelenos have different, and perhaps contra-

dicting, opinions about how well groups are getting along interperson-
ally (micro/meso level) versus the general state of race relations more
broadly (macro/structural level). Although Angelenos believing that
race relations had stayed the same between 2012 and 2017 can be inter-
preted as either a glass half full or half empty scenario, it stands in contrast to the overwhelming belief among Angelenos that all groups were
getting along fairly well in the dawn of the Trumpian era.

In fact, Angelenos in 2017 overwhelmingly believed that groups were
getting along fairly well, and these views were at an all-time high.[44]
Asian Americans' optimism of the early 1990s remained, with 79 percent saying groups were getting along, followed by Black (73 percent),
and Latinx Angelenos (72 percent). White Americans were most optimistic, with 81 percent believing groups were getting along, a major
turnaround from their pessimism around the time of the 1992 unrest.
The 2017 results on the "getting along" question show quite a shift from
previous surveys, showing some optimism.[45] Recall that following the
1992 unrest, views were particularly bad (63 percent of Angelenos said
race relations were "not good"). In 2017, however, this number dropped
significantly to 24 percent. Whites expressed the biggest positive change,
from the most cynical views of race relations in 1997 (68 percent saying
they were 'not good') to the most optimistic in 2017.

Angelenos witnessed several unprecedented historical events since
the initial 1997 survey was undertaken. For one, the historic immigrant
mega marches that exploded in Los Angeles and other major cities
across America in 2006 were at the time the largest civil rights protest in
our nation's history.[46] This protest wave was a long time in the making.
Los Angeles—owing to the dramatic growth of its immigration population since the 1980s and 1990s, a long history of pro-immigrant activism,
and its related well-established organizational infrastructure—was ripe
for political eruption.

Other reasons that Mexican and Central American demonstrators
came out in greatest force were linked to America's racialization of these
groups as "illegal" immigrants.[47] It further stands to reason that immigrants from Latin America in particular, but also Asia, the Caribbean,
and Africa who have long faced political exclusion and exploitation in
the service industry, were the ones who would make up the millions
of protestors. Yet although the mega marches were a shining example

of Angelenos working in solidarity to pull off one of the most difficult feats of activism—getting millions of people onto the streets in peaceful protest—they also incited anti-immigrant sentiment and a post-wave state backlash. States introduced and passed draconian immigration laws across the country, and mainstream America's anti-Latinx sentiments intensified in the wake of the marches.[48]

The election of the nation's first Black president, Barack Obama, in 2008, was another major moment of racial and political transformation. Support for President Obama varied significantly by race and political affiliation. Some progressives welcomed Obama's election as a long overdue symbol of the United States' shift toward a postracial society in which race was no longer an obstacle to social mobility.[49] People of color overwhelmingly voted for Obama, perhaps with the hope that his background as a community organizer, his status as the son of an immigrant, and his upbringing in Hawai'i and Indonesia would translate into racially progressive policy changes.[50]

Obama's presidency, however, was marked by both racial progress and repressive policies that disproportionately impacted marginalized communities of color. Although Obama campaigned heavily as an advocate for immigration reform and would later introduce the Deferred Action for Childhood Arrivals (DACA), a move that would earn him as much praise as notoriety, he gained critics among immigrant rights advocates for deporting unprecedented numbers of immigrants prior to introducing DACA.[51] In fact, the Obama administration deported more than three million noncitizens, more than any other presidential administration in US history, earning him the moniker Deporter in Chief.[52] Critics remarked that Obama's deportation policies, specifically the apprehension, detention, and removal of immigrants with no criminal record, including unaccompanied minors and women and children fleeing violence, laid the groundwork for Donald Trump's terrorizing campaign against immigrants.

Interestingly, Obama's election appears to have had a positive effect on White racial attitudes toward Blacks nationally, with the most dramatic shift occurring during his first presidential term between 2004 and 2008 and among registered Democrats.[53] Paradoxically, the racial progress that Obama's election symbolized for some emboldened a nationalist Tea Party that was propped up in part by racists who demonized Obama as undermining so-called American values with his support of immigration reform, universal health care, pro-choice rights, and other progressive policies.

Tea Party racism also set the tone for the rise of Trump in the national political arena and his subsequent election to the presidency in 2017, when the survey data analyzed in this chapter were collected.[54] Trump skillfully harnessed rising White racial resentment by ramping up promotion of his racist and xenophobic rhetoric. As early as 2015, he falsely claimed that Muslims cheered when the World Trade Center collapsed on September 11, 2001, and he called for a "Muslim ban."[55] Soon after, Trump launched his presidential campaign by calling Mexicans "drug dealers, criminals, and rapists" and promoting the building of "the Wall."[56] Of course, these statements were never really about national security; however, they had far-reaching consequences for race relations.

There is a clear correlation between the arrival of Trump on the political scene and racist attitudes and behavior leading to incidents of prejudiced violence.[57] The growth of the Latinx immigrant population across the country, and Los Angeles in particular, could well have led to general anti-Latinx sentiment among some White, and to some degree, Black Angelenos, who in turn could have responded positively to Trump's anti-immigrant rhetoric.[58] With the exception of wealthy areas like Beverly Hills, however, Angelenos decried the election of Trump.[59] In the days following the election, an estimated eight thousand people took to the streets in the heavily Latinx area of MacArthur Park and downtown LA to demand justice for immigrants, women, and people of color in a manner reminiscent of the 2006 immigrant rights march. Given that LA is one of the nation's most diverse cities, it is fair to say that Angelenos were especially attuned to Trump's attacks on people of color and immigrants.

Leading up to this time, Californians—and indeed, the nation—were facing an explosion of video recordings of police misconduct and shootings of unarmed Black persons. In Oakland, the 2009 fatal police shooting of unarmed twenty-two-year-old Oscar Grant at the Fruitvale BART Station was captured on surveillance video and helped put a spotlight on the state's failure to curb police brutality and misconduct since the historic 1992 uprising. In Los Angeles County alone from 2010 to 2014, police shot 375 people, about one person every five days, according to

The Counted, a Guardian US project that tracks deaths at the hands of law enforcement. The report shows that Black Angelenos, who make up 9 percent of the county's population, represented 24 percent of deaths.[60] Indeed, it was frustration over her brother's abuse by police in LA County jails and George Zimmerman's acquittal in the 2012 killing of teenager Trayvon Martin that led young Los Angeles activist Patrisse Cullors to create the hashtag #BlackLivesMatter that would propel the Black Lives Matter movement onto the national scene. Countless local and national cases thereafter solidified BLM as a highly influential movement that forced Los Angeles, and the nation more broadly, to reckon with its historical legacy of brutal police violence against Black and Latinx people.

The Rodney King beating and the acquittal of the four police officers that led to the 1992 uprising are without a doubt etched in the collective memory of Angelenos. As such, the 2017 Leavey Center survey set out to determine whether LA residents believed another unrest was likely to occur in the next five years. The responses show that a majority of Angelenos believed that another unrest was likely to occur in the coming years (and they were right, though the George Floyd protests that erupted in 2020 would not be inner-city groups of color "rioting" but rather much more multiclass and multiracial/-ethnic than anything LA had experienced before). In the immediate years following the 1992 uprising, perhaps not surprisingly, over 65 percent of Angelenos believed riots and disturbances would occur again (they were wrong). This marked the highest number of Angelenos to predict another disturbance.

The 2017 survey, however, was the first time we see an increase in those who predicted another eruption following two decades of steady decline. In fact, with 58 percent of Angelenos in 2017 believing that another unrest was in the cards, this is the first time we see both an increase and a majority consensus since the survey following the 1992 uprising.[61] There are some differences by race; more Black and Latinx Angelenos than White and Asian American Angelenos believe another unrest is possible (68 percent and 65 percent versus 51 percent and 46 percent, respectively).

Here, we offer some context for the seeming contradictions across Angelenos' beliefs that groups are getting along well and the strong likelihood that LA would experience another urban uprising. The survey question asks residents their opinion about the likelihood that another unrest will occur in the coming years. This question is inherently about the future of race relations, and Trump had just been elected with an openly racist platform that gave license to White nationalists to openly discriminate and perpetrate racial violence. Angelenos' prediction that another uprising would occur could very well reflect their—and indeed the nation's—anxiety about Trump and worse things to come. It therefore stands to reason that people believed that another racial unrest was likely.

However, by refocusing on the broader political context of the time, we can see how Angelenos' belief that another unrest was likely could reflect a growing awareness of structural inequality. These Angelenos may believe another unrest is likely not because they think race relations are getting worse, but because they see that the same structural problems that fomented the 1992 unrest remain today: poverty, displacement, residential segregation, over-policing and incarceration in communities of color, lack of accountability by government officials, bias against immigrants, and mass media bias in favor of White America.[62] Economic disparity between Whites and people of color in Los Angeles continues to increase. Kim and Etahad note, "Although the city's unemployment rate last year [2017] was about half of what it was in 1992, the median income of Angelenos, when adjusted for inflation, is lower than it was around the time of the riots. Poverty rates still remain high at 22 percent, comparable with the years preceding the riots."[63]

Sociologist Edward Telles's study of race relations in Brazil introduced a useful theory of race relations that captures a trend similar to what we may be seeing in Los Angeles—the simultaneous coexistence of structural racism and economic exclusion of people of color with high levels of sociability among racial groups, including Whites.[64] Telles refers to this coexistence as horizontal and vertical dimensions of race relations and notes that it is possible to observe positive social interactions among different racial groups alongside glaring structural inequality. Similar to ethnic studies approaches that seek to expose the role of broader racial discourse and structures at play, Telles's theorization helps us understand why Angelenos might say that they get along well with neighbors or coworkers of another race yet also believe that another urban rebellion is likely to occur. We also believe that to the extent that Black, Asian American, and Latinx Angelenos perceive White Angelenos as the group with most power to influence government and policy, then it might be no surprise that quantitative measures may capture perceptions of Whites as a group as discriminatory (vertical relations) while also as easy to get along with on an individual basis (horizontal relations).

We also believe that the high-tech digital age of the 2017 survey era—namely, people's ability to upload photos and videos onto social media—have done much to raise the public's consciousness about systemic racism and the many manifestations of it in the lives of people of color. Greater social media exposure of previously hidden police brutality and outrage, and the move toward police body cams, for example, may have led to the belief among some Angelenos that another urban uprising was on the horizon—and that this time it might bring about real social transformation.

Conclusion: Are We Finally Getting Along?

Since the time of the January 2017 survey, the nation has faced incredible challenges with implications for racial justice and the future of our democracy. The COVID-19 pandemic, the brutal murder of George Floyd, relentless violence against Asian Americans, and mass protests reaffirming that Black Lives Matter have eerily seen the 2017 predictions of another unrest come true. In May 2020, in the midst of the pandemic, over fifty thousand Angelenos flooded the streets of Hollywood in protest over the killing of George Floyd by a Minneapolis police officer who placed his knee on Floyd's neck for nearly nine minutes before he died from lack of oxygen. Reminiscent of the 1992 uprising after the Rodney King verdict, the protests were multiracial.

There were key differences, however. The BLM protests lasted several months, not several days. Instead of targeting communities of color, masked demonstrators marched peacefully in Hollywood and surrounding areas (until outsiders came in and committed violence, looting, and arson). BLM inspired protests and marches by Asian Americans, who suffered thousands of incidents of hate violence over a very short time period. Similarly, Palestinian Americans came out in collective protest over Israel's intensive bombing of their settler colony. When we take a closer look by race, we find that Black and Latinx Angelenos in 2017 were more likely to predict another unrest than other groups but also viewed social relations more positively. In general, we also found this to be true of all LA's groups.

If this is any indication about the future of race relations in multi-racial Los Angeles, we may see growing awareness of systemic and structural inequality together with growing support for racial justice movements and the use of social protest to advance change and a more positive outlook on social relations among Angelenos of all racialized and ethnic groups. Indeed, a recent statewide poll conducted in California in 2020 shows that 55 percent of Californians believe the protests over police killings of Floyd, Ahmaud Arbery, Breonna Taylor, and others have brought people together, not further apart.[65] The same poll shows that White Californians are now much more likely than before the pandemic to say that Black, Latinx, and Asian Americans are discriminated against. The explosion of anti-Asian hate incidents since the onset of the pandemic, for example, seems to have led to greater awareness of the anti-foreigner discrimination often faced by the so-called model minority. In fact, there is greater understanding that precisely because of the model minority trope—they, like China, are doing too well, are too threatening—anti-foreigner racism is ignited.[66] As such, when Angelenos indicate in surveys that they believe another unrest is on the horizon, it may in fact point to a growing awareness of structural racism and even shifting cultural beliefs about the value of protests for bringing about progressive social change.

Overall, the data we analyze in this chapter may reflect Angelenos' understanding of race relations as multidimensional where they express more optimism about Angelenos' ability to relate more positively when engaging face to face or individually, that is, at the micro and meso levels. The relatively pessimistic views regarding Los Angeles's general state of race relations may reflect a broader understanding of systemic racism and other social and political structures that continue to perpetuate racial inequality, one that ethnic and American studies have been underscoring for decades.

As we have argued in this chapter, it is these complex and nuanced interpretations of survey data that are often missing from traditional sociological approaches to racial attitudes. While social scientists have produced a wealth of quantitative data that help us see the bigger picture of race relations, it is imperative that these scholars interpret the numbers within a broader sociohistorical context and use more qualitative data and frameworks in their study of racial attitudes and racism. To this end, we urge quantitative social scientists to engage more closely with related disciplines such as ethnic and American studies to expand our theoretical and empirical understanding of how racism, empire, and power work to create and maintain racial inequity in the US and globally.

NOTES

1 Portes and Rumbaut, *Immigrant America.*
2 Ibid.
3 Cheng and Espiritu, "Korean businesses"; Oliver and Johnson, "Inter-ethnic conflict"; Johnson and Oliver, "Interethnic Minority Conflict"; Portes and Stepick, *City on the Edge.*
4 Takaki, *Strangers from a Different Shore.*
5 Thornton and Shah, "US News Magazine."
6 Telles et al., "Introduction," 1–33. This is not to discredit the fact that countless sociologists have studied other groups of color. The point is that our mainstream sociological concepts, methods, and theoretical models have not given full primacy to the specific forms of racism and racialization that various Latinx, Asian, Indigenous, Middle Eastern, and Muslim ethnics have experienced.
7 Espiritu, "Disciplines Unbound."
8 Ibid., 511.
9 Brückner, "The Critical Place."
10 Long, "Engaging Sociology," 10.
11 Anderson and Massey, "The Sociology of Race."
12 McKee, *Sociology and the Race Problem*; Anderson and Massey, "The Sociology of Race."
13 Bonilla-Silva and Herring, "We'd Love to Hire Them," 180.
14 Bonilla-Silva and Zuberi, *White Logic.*
15 Allport, *The Nature of Prejudice.* Jackman and Muha, "Education and Intergroup Attitudes."
16 Kinder and Sears, "Prejudice and Politics."
17 Allport, *The Nature of Prejudice.*
18 Blumer, "Race Prejudice."
19 Bobo and Kluegel, "Opposition to Race-Targeting"; Scheepers, Gijisberts, and Coenders, "Ethnic Exclusionism"; Wilson, *The Bridge.* Blumer, "Race Prejudice;" Bobo and Kluegel, "Opposition to Race-Targeting." Studies using the group threat approach to examine immigration typically consider dominant group attitudes toward immigrants or immigration rather than the racial attitudes of immigrants (e.g., Scheepers Gijisberts, and Coenders, "Ethnic Exclusionism"). Studies have also focused on whether the relative size of a minority group in an area, a measure of group threat, was associated with dominant groups' attitudes or

political mobilization (Bergesen and Herman, "Immigration, Race, and Riot"; Olzak, *The Dynamics of Ethnic Competition*; Taylor, "How White Attitudes Vary"). As an aside, the geographical unit measured also matters (Oliver and Wong, "Intergroup Prejudice"). The presence of Hispanics and Asians does not always produce the same hostility or stereotypes among Whites as the presence of Blacks (Dixon, "Psychological Reactions to Crime News"; Fox, "The Changing Color of Welfare").

20 Bobo and Hutchings, "Perceptions of Racial."
21 Roth and Kim, "Relocating Prejudice"; Telles et al., "Introduction."
22 Kim, "The Racial Triangulation"; Kim, *Imperial Citizens*.
23 For some examples, see Mindiola, Niemann, and Rodriguez, *Black-Brown Relations*; and Cheng, *The Changs*.
24 Wise, "Paradigm Dramas," 312.
25 Marx, "Thoughts on the Origins."
26 Wilson, *The Truly Disadvantaged*; Kasarda, "Inner-City Concentrated."
27 Hondagneu-Sotelo and Pastor, *South Central Dreams*.
28 Bobo et al., *Prismatic Metropolis*.
29 Ibid.
30 Ibid. And starting in the mid-2000s, Los Angeles also began its last stage of hemorrhaging manufacturing jobs.
31 Murch, "Crack in Los Angeles"
32 Ibid.
33 Ibid.
34 Ibid, xx.
35 Ibid.
36 Kim, *Imperial Citizens*; Zamora, "Racial Remittances."
37 Hondagneu-Sotelo and Pastor, *South Central Dreams*; Baldassare, *The Los Angeles Riots*.
38 Baldassare, *The Los Angeles Riots*.
39 Kim, *Imperial Citizens*.
40 Ibid.
41 Bobo et al., "Public Opinion."
42 Ibid., 108.
43 McClain and Stewart, *"Can We All."*
44 Seventy-five percent of Angelenos in 2017 said groups were getting along "somewhat well" or "very well" compared to fewer than 40 percent in 1997.
45 The 2017 wording of the question changed to "Overall, how would you say that racial and ethnic groups in Los Angeles are getting along these days—very well, somewhat well, somewhat badly, or very badly."
46 Zepeda-Millán, *Latino Mass*.
47 Ibid.
48 Ibid.
49 Barker, *Obama on Our Minds*.

50 Ibid.

51 Truax, *Dreamers*.

52 Ibid.

53 Thompson and Barker, "The Obama Effect."

54 Skocpol and Williamson, *The Tea Party*.

55 Klass, "A Short History."

56 Phillips, "They're Rapists."

57 Williamson and Gelfand, "Trump and Racism."

58 Adamy and Overberg, "Counties That."

59 Vives et al., "8,000 Anti-Trump Marchers."

60 Levin, "Hundreds Dead, No One Charged."

61 Notably, there was a ten-point jump on this measure compared with the 2012 Leavey survey (47 percent vs. 58 percent).

62 Hondagneu-Sotelo and Pastor, *South Central Dreams*

63 Kim and Etehad, "For First Time."

64 Telles, *Race in Another America*.

65 Parvini, "Views on race."

66 Kim, *Imperial Citizens*.

BIBLIOGRAPHY

Adamy, Janet, and Paul Overberg. "Counties That Experienced Rapid Diversification Voted Heavily for Donald Trump." *Wall Street Journal*, November 9, 2016. www.wsj.com.

Allport, Gordon W. *The Nature of Prejudice*. 25th anniversary ed. Reading, MA: Addison-Wesley, 1979.

Almaguer, Tomás. *Racial Fault Lines: The Historical Origins of White Supremacy in California*. Berkeley: University of California Press, 1994.

Anderson, Elijah, and Douglas S. Massey. "The Sociology of Race in the United States." In *Problem of the Century: Racial Stratification in the United States*, edited by Elijah Anderson and Douglas S. Massey, 3–12. New York: Russell Sage Foundation, 2001.

Baldassare, Mark. *The Los Angeles Riots: Lessons for the Urban Future*. Boulder, CO: Westview Press, 1994.

Barker, Lori A. *Obama on Our Minds: The Impact of Obama on the Psyche of America*. Oxford: Oxford University Press, 2016.

Berlet, Chip. "The Roots of Anti-Obama Rhetoric." *Research in Race and Ethnic Relations* 16, (2010): 301–19.

Bergesen, Albert and Max Herman. "Immigration, Race, and Riot: The 1992 Los Angeles Uprising." *American Sociological Review* 63 (1998): 39–54.

Blumer, Herbert. "Race Prejudice as a Sense of Group Position." *Pacific Sociological Review* 1, no. 1 (1958): 3–7.

Bobo, Lawrence, and Vincent Hutchings. "Perceptions of Racial Group Competition: Extending Blumer's Theory of Group Position to a Multiracial Social Context." *American Sociological Review* 61 no. 6 (1996): 951–72.

Bobo, Lawrence, and James Kluegel. "Opposition to Race-Targeting: Self-Interest, Stratification Ideology, or Racial Attitudes?" *American Sociological Review* 58 (1993): 443–64.

Bobo, Lawrence D., Melvin L. Oliver, James H. Johnson Jr., and Abel Valenzuela Jr. *Prismatic Metropolis: Inequality in Los Angeles*. New York: Russell Sage Foundation, 2000.

Bobo, Lawrence, Camille L. Zubrinsky, James H. Johnson Jr., and Melvin L. Oliver. "Public Opinion before and after a Spring of Discontent." In *The Los Angeles Riots: Lessons for the Urban Future*, edited by Mark Baldassare, 103–33. Boulder, CO: Westview, 1994.

Bonilla-Silva, Edwardo, and Cedric Herring. "We'd Love to Hire Them, But . . . The Underrepresentation of Sociologists of Color and Its Implications." *Footnotes* 273: 6–7, 1999.

Bonilla-Silva, Edwardo, and Tukufu Zuberi. *White Logic, White Methods: Racism and Methodology*. Lanham, MD: Rowman & Littlefield, 2008.

Brückner, Martin. "The Critical Place of Empire in Early American Studies." *American Literary History* 15, no. 4 (2003): 809–21.

Chang, Edward T. "Remembering Sa-I-Gu." In *Los Angeles Since 1992: Commemorating the 20th Anniversary of the Uprisings*, edited by Darnell Hunt and David K. Yoo, 31–33. Los Angeles: Asian American Studies Center Press, 2012.

Cheng, Lucie, and Yến Lê Espiritu. "Korean Businesses in Black and Hispanic Neighborhoods: A Study of Intergroup Relations." *Sociological Perspectives* 32, no. 4 (1989): 521–34.

Cheng, Wendy. *The Changs Next Door to the Díazes: Remapping Race in Suburban California*. Minneapolis: University of Minnesota Press, 2013.

Chung, Angie Y. "The Powers that Bind: A Case Study of the Collective Bases of Coalition Building in Post-Civil Unrest Los Angeles." *Urban Affairs Review* 37, no. 2 (2001): 205–26.

Dixon, Travis L. "Psychological Reactions to Crime News Portrayals of Black Criminals: Understanding the Moderating Roles of Prior News Viewing and Stereotype Endorsement." *Communication Monographs* 73, no. 2 (2006): 162–87.

Dubrow, Joshua Kjerulf. "Sociology and American Studies: A Case Study in the Limits of Interdisciplinarity." *American Sociologist* 24, no. 4 (2011): 303–15.

Espiritu, Yến Lê. "Disciplines Unbound: Notes on Sociology and Ethnic Studies." *Contemporary Sociology* 28, no. 5 (1999): 510–14.

Fox, Cybelle. "The Changing Color of Welfare? How Whites' Attitudes toward Latinos Influence Support for Welfare." *American Journal of Sociology* 110, no. 3 (2004): 580–625.

Henley, Jon. "White and Wealthy Votes Gave Victory to Donald Trump, Exit Polls Show." *Guardian*, November 9, 2016. www.theguardian.com.

Hing, Bill Ong. "Deporter-in-Chief: Obama v. Trump." *University of San Francisco Law Research Paper* no. 2019-03.

Hondagneu-Sotelo, Pierrette, and Manuel Pastor. *South Central Dreams: Finding Home and Building Community in South L.A.* New York: New York University Press, 2021.

Jackman, Mary, and Michael Muha. "Education and Intergroup Attitudes: Moral Enlightenment, Superficial Democratic Commitment, or Ideological Refinement?" *American Sociological Review* 49, no. 6 (1984): 751–69.

Johnson, James, Jr., and Melvin Oliver. "Interethnic Minority Conflict in Urban America: The Effects of Economic and Social Dislocations." *Urban Geography* 10, no. 5 (1989): 449–63.

Kaplan, Erin Aubry. "Fire, Then Ice." *Amerasia Journal* 38, no. 1 (2012): 37.

Kasarda, John D. "Inner-City Concentrated Poverty and Neighborhood Distress: 1970 to 1990." *Housing Policy Debate* 4, no. 3 (1993): 253–302.

Kim, Claire J. "The Racial Triangulation of Asian Americans." *Politics and Society* 27, no. 1 (1999): 105–38.

Kim, Nadia. *Imperial Citizens: Koreans and Race from Seoul to LA.* Stanford, CA: Stanford University Press, 2008.

Kim, Victoria, and Melissa Etehad. "For First Time, More L.A. Residents Believe New Riots Likely, New Poll Finds." *Los Angeles Times*, April 26, 2017. www.latimes.com.

Kinder, Donald R., and David O. Sears. "Prejudice and Politics: Symbolic Racism versus Racial Threats to the Good Life." *Journal of Personality and Social Psychology* 40, no. 3 (1981): 414–31.

Klass, Brian. "A Short History of President Trump's Anti-Muslim Bigotry." *Washington Post*, March 15, 2019. www.washingtonpost.com.

Levin, Sam. "Hundreds Dead, No One Charged: The Uphill Battle against Los Angeles Police Killings." *Guardian*, August 24, 2018. www.theguardian.com.

Long, Elizabeth. "Engaging Sociology and Cultural Studies: Disciplinarity and Social Change." In *From Sociology to Cultural Studies*, edited by Elizabeth Long, 1–32. Oxford: Blackwell, 1997.

Marx, Leo. "Thoughts on the Origin and Character of the American Studies Movement." *American Quarterly* 31, no. 3 (1979): 398–401.

McClain, Paula D., and Joseph Stewart Jr. *"Can We All Get Along?": Racial and Ethnic Minorities in American Politics.* Boulder, CO: Westview Press, 2002.

McKee, James. *Sociology and the Race Problem: The Failure of a Perspective.* Chicago: University of Illinois Press, 1993.

Mindiola, Tatcho, Jr., Yolanda Flores Niemann, and Nestor Rodriguez. *Black-Brown Relations and Stereotypes.* Austin: University of Texas Press, 2003.

Murch, Donna. "Crack in Los Angeles: Crisis, Militarization, and Black Response to the Late Twentieth-Century War on Drugs" *Journal of American History* 102, no. 1 (2015): 162–73.

Oliver, Eric J., and Janelle Wong. "Intergroup Prejudice in Multiethnic Settings." *American Journal of Political Science*, 47, no. 4 (2003): 567–82.

Oliver, Melvin, and James Johnson Jr. "Inter-ethnic Conflict in an Urban Ghetto." *Research in Social Movements, Conflicts and Change* 6 (1984): 57–94.

Olzak, Susan. *The Dynamics of Ethnic Competition & Conflict.* Stanford, CA: Stanford University Press, 1992.

Parker, Christopher S., and Matt A. Barreto. *Change They Can't Believe In: The Tea Party and Reactionary Politics in America.* Princeton, NJ: Princeton University Press, 2013.

Parvini, Sarah. "Views on Race Relations in State Alter Dramatically as More White People See Reality of Discrimination, Survey Shows." *Los Angeles Times*, July 14, 2020. www.latimes.com.

Phillips, Amber. "'They're Rapists.' President Trump's Campaign Launch Speech Two Years Later, Annotated." *Washington Post*, June 16, 2017. www.washingtonpost.com/.

Portes, Alejandro, and Rubén G. Rumbaut. *Immigrant America: A Portrait.* Berkeley: University of California Press, 2014.

Portes, Alejandro, and Alex Stepick. *City on the Edge: The Transformation of Miami.* Berkeley: University of California Press, 1993.

Roth, Wendy, and Nadia Kim. "Relocating Prejudice: A Transnational Approach to Understanding Immigrants' Racial Attitudes." *International Migration Review* 47, no. 2 (2013): 330–73.

Scheepers, Peer, Mérove Gijisberts, and Marcel Coenders. "Ethnic Exclusionism in European Countries: Public Opposition to Civil Rights for Legal Migrants as a Response to Perceived Ethnic Threat." *European Sociological Review* 18, no. 1 (2002): 17–34.

Skocpol, Theda, and Vanessa Williamson. *The Tea Party and the Remaking of Republican Conservatism.* New York: Oxford University Press, 2012.

Takaki, Ronald. *Strangers from a Different Shore: A History of Asian Americans.* New York: Penguin, 1998.

Taylor, Marylee C. "How White Attitudes Vary with the Racial Composition of Local Populations: Numbers Count." *American Sociological Association*, 63, no. 4 (1998): 512–35.

Telles, Edward E. *Race in Another America: The Significance of Skin Color in Brazil.* Princeton, NJ: Princeton University Press, 2004.

Telles, Edward, Gaspar Rivera-Salgado, Mark Q. Sawyer, and Sylvia Zamora. Introduction to *Just Neighbors? Research on African American and Latino Relations in the United States*, edited by Edward Telles, Mark Q. Sawyer, and Gaspar Rivera-Salgado, 1–33. New York: Russell Sage Foundation, 2011.

Thompson, Curtis A., and Lori A. Barker. "The Obama Effect on Racial Attitudes: A Review of the Research." In *Obama on Our Minds: The Impact of Obama on the Psyche of America*, edited by Lori A. Barker, 109–40. Oxford: Oxford University Press, 2016.

Thornton, Michael C., and Hemant Shah. "US News Magazine Images of Black-Asian American Relationships, 1980–1992." *Communication Review* 1, no. 4 (1996): 497–519.

Truax, Eileen. *Dreamers: An Immigrant Generation's Fight for Their American Dream.* Boston: Beacon Press, 2015.

Vives, Ruben, Deborah Netburn, Soumya Karlamangla, and Esmeralda Bermudez. "8,000 Anti-Trump Marchers Flood Downtown Los Angeles; Many Fear Immigration Policies." *Los Angeles Times*, November 12, 2016. www.latimes.com.

Willer, Robb, Matthew Feinberg, and Rachel Wetts. "Threats to Racial Status Promote Tea Party Support among White Americans." Social Science Research Council, April 28, 2016. https://papers.ssrn.com.

Williamson, Vanessa. "What the Tea Party Tells Us about the Trump Presidency." Brookings, November 6, 2016. www.brookings.edu.

Williamson, Vanessa, and Isabella Gelfand. "Trump and Racism: What Do the Data Say?" Brookings, August 14, 2019. www.brookings.edu/.

Wilson, William Julius. *The Bridge over the Racial Divide: Rising Inequality and Coalition Politics*. Berkeley: University of California Press, 2001.

———. *The Truly Disadvantaged: The Inner City, the Underclass, and Public Policy*. Chicago: University of Chicago Press, 1987.

Wise, Gene. "'Paradigm Dramas' in American Studies: A Cultural and Institutional History of the Movement." *American Quarterly* 31, no. 3 (1979): 293–337.

Zamora, Sylvia. "Racial Remittances: The Effect of Migration on Racial Ideologies in Mexico and the United States." *Sociology of Race and Ethnicity* 12, no. 4 (2016): 466–81.

Zepeda-Millán, Chris. *Latino Mass Mobilization: Immigration, Racialization, and Activism*. New York: Cambridge University Press, 2017.

13

Mana as Sacred Space

A Talanoa of Tongan American College Students in a Pacific Studies Learning Community Classroom

ESITELI HAFOKA AND FINAUSINA TEISA PAEA TOVO

Those are families and generations and oceans that prayed for you all to be in this very space. So, of course, it's different. There's actual Mana in here. There's praise poured into this room. God is in this presence every single day. And not to say that God isn't with us in our math classes or in our psychology classes, but this space has been intentionally prayed for. And when you pray intentionally for something, God sees it. God does and performs His work every single day in this space.
—Kalisi

In the United States, federal laws explicitly enforce the separation of church and state, but what does it mean when a public community college like the College of the Bay Area (CBA) accommodates sacred space-making for Tongan American Mana Students (TAMS)? While some religious leaders and academic scholars may argue that this space might better be defined as auspicious at best, for TAMS, religious and secular meaning-making are constantly negotiated in this space. While to the Tongan American students, Mana spaces do not support sectarian or denominational beliefs: "Native peoples live out their own religious identities. . . . They take an outside religious idea . . . and mold it into a practice that reflects their own reality."[1] These words by religious studies scholar Angela Tarango ring true for the Tongan American students. When they navigate academics, they use Mana education spaces to reimagine previously established histories by adding cultural context, including cultural religious beliefs, for relevancy to the students' own Tongan American faith practices.

The major sections of our chapter first define what the sacred means to Tongans, including these students, by introducing *angafakafonua* (the way of the land or Tongan culture) as Tongan epistemology. We also draw attention to one of College of the Bay Area's culturally sustaining learning communities, Mana, and present the three *talanoa* (informal talking) sessions we conducted during which students chose religious language and ideas to describe their experiences. We follow this presentation with an analysis of the *talanoas* to construct recommendations for educators to thoroughly meet the needs of their Tongan American students. Finally, we are both first-generation Tongan American college students and, as such, understand the TAMS-related issues that are voiced in this chapter. We accessed our own experiences as first-generation community college transfers as instruments for this research.

Context and Background

The Enrollment Decline in Higher Education

The Great Recession of 2007–09 led to a dramatic spike in community college enrollment.[2] Since then, reports have revealed a decline in community college enrollment since 2010, with 2014–17 representing the peak of that decline. Alarmingly, a National Student Clearinghouse Research Center (NSCRC) report highlighted that at most, 39 percent of all community college students earned a credential, while the US Department of Education official graduation rate is 25 percent.[3] By 2017, the NSCRC revealed a decline of 1.8 percent, or 275,000 students, compared to the previous spring, which that implied for the seventh year in a row, community college enrollment had declined in thirty-four out of fifty states in the United States. During the 2016–17 academic year, the total Native Hawaiian and Pacific Islander (NHPI) enrollment was 67,845, a 17 percent decline compared to 2012–13 when the number was 81,956.[4] The proportion of NHPI adults who have not enrolled in any postsecondary education is especially high among the following ethnic subgroups: Samoans (58 percent), Tongans (57 percent), Native Hawaiians (53 percent), and Guamanians or Chamorros (49 percent). Because there is little qualitative literature on the NHPI community in the

United States—perhaps none on the California community colleges—these numbers are often not met with a culturally responsive approach to support the decline. As the breadth of data continues to grow, it is vital that institutions are aware of the ongoing trends related to the decline in enrollment. Further, it will be necessary to look at disaggregated data to uncover the decline in enrollment for hyper-marginalized groups like TAMS.

Although the NHPI community is seen as new to the academic discussion of enrollment decline, when NHPI students choose US higher education as a pathway, data show that they do not stay. For instance, the American Community Survey showed that the national bachelor's degree attainment rate was 29.1 percent, which was greater than the bachelor's degree attainment rate for Native Hawaiians (20.5 percent), Guamanians or CHamorus (18.6 percent), Samoans (13.4 percent), and Tongans (12.3 percent).[5]

Mana Learning Community

To account for these broader trends and those at College of the Bay Area, the Mana Learning Community is the first Pacific studies learning community in the state of California and was created at the College of the Bay Area. As the first of its kind, Mana Learning Community is a transition support program focused on intensive retention strategies for student success throughout their academic journey in college. As part of the California Student Equity Plan, the Mana Learning Community was created and adopted a cohort-style model to guide students on a clear pathway to achieve success while offering a specialized curriculum leading to a certificate in critical Pacific and Oceania studies and to provide an enveloping and supportive community. In the 2013–14 academic year, data analysis at CBA confirmed that NHPI students represented 2.4 percent of all students at CBA, roughly mirroring their participation rate in Bay Area County public schools (2.2 percent) and presence in San Mateo County (2 percent; San Mateo County, California Department of Education, 2015). NHPI students at CBA demonstrated the lowest course completion rates and high withdrawal rates (60.6 percent and 17.3 percent, respectively), which was similar to African American and Latinx students at CBA.

Gap in Literature

Historians and Pacific Island (PI) studies scholars Vicente Diaz and Hokulani Aikau (a contributor to this volume) have argued that the categories of race and religion, in their Chamorro and Kanaka Maoli contexts, respectively, are complex and intertwined as determinants of colonization responsible for producing precarious contemporary challenges to autonomy in Guåhan (Guam) and Hawai'i.[6] Despite their invaluable contribution to both fields, the historical framework that guides their research could be expanded to include intersections with the fields of education and religious studies that take seriously the implications of migration and settler colonialism for second-generation Tongan American students who have a faith practice. Grounding in the field of religious studies pushes the intersection of race and religion in history and PI studies beyond the colonial context to investigate the formative role of religion on racial identity and epistemology, which are always in flux. Other scholars, like Halaevalu Vakalahi, in the field of PI studies have tackled histories of Tongan national public schools and detailed tertiary school-aged Tongan academic achievements in North America and Hawai'i, but scholars in the Pacific have yet to broach theoretical and practical measures to address the challenges for Tongan American students in the US context.[7]

Purpose of Study/Research Questions

Our chapter's goals are three-fold: to use the *talanoa* framework to voice the emotional, social, and academic encounters of NHPI students in higher education given their very small (and declining) numbers in college; to center NHPI voices in qualitative data; and to inform staff and faculty of validating opportunities within these academic spaces to engage with NHPI student communities. By weaving together all three goals, we aim to increase awareness of the NHPI student population and to highlight culturally sustaining programs that currently serve NHPI students in two-year colleges. Working with the Mana Learning Community students and alumni, a retention program, we addressed the following questions to guide this qualitative study: What are the experiences of NHPI students in community college? In what ways does their

Oceania identity affect their academic journey? How does the Mana program at the community college foster NHPI students' academic/cultural identity? Upon collecting data, this study borrowed Pacific research methodologies that included processes that centered collective practices. Through a privileging of the power of transactionality and decentralizing the Eurocentric notions of college success, this research challenges educators and college educators to take proactive steps to ensure the fortitude, perseverance, and resilience of the people of the Pacific, who need to be featured in curricula, research, policy, and praxis.

Data and Method

Talanoa Method

Our methodological approach is primarily based on Timote Vaioleti's "*talanoa* method," which conducts research on students who engage with assigned readings from Oceanic scholars in Socratic-style seminars.[8] Introduced by Sitiveni Halapua as a method to talk openly from the heart, the *talanoa* method was applied to political settings and then further developed as a research methodology in education by Timote Vaioleti.[9] *Talanoa* has been defined as unconcealed storytelling, a curious dialogue that is a social rather than individual phenomenon, and as talking critically yet harmoniously.[10] Vaioleti identified *talanoa* as nonlinear and responsive, which leads to more authentic knowledge under the use of appropriate researchers. *Talanoa a Mana* (conversations of Mana) is then a method that expanded *talanoa* to an academic research context inside the classroom using many different forms of *talanoa*, such as face-to-face dialogue, written class assignments, course reading requirements, and written reflections.[11]

Inspired by Django Paris's culturally sustaining pedagogy, *talanoa a Mana* allows the data to introduce a culturally sustaining pedagogy as a teaching tool that requires classroom structure and implementation to be more than responsive to the cultural experiences and practices of young people.[12] Paris stated that supporting young people in sustaining "the cultural and linguistic competence of their communities while simultaneously offering access to dominant cultural competence" requires educators to pedagogically respond to students' realities and acknowledge their systems of knowledge.[13] To this point, *talanoa a Mana* served this study in two ways: 1) it allowed NHPI students to connect and critically engage with culturally responsive articles and activities, and 2) completing these assignments directly affected students' overall grades. *Talanoa a Mana* was specifically designed as a guide to incorporate a mixture of different research strategies and classroom pedagogical approaches to accommodate further academic research and classroom structure and praxis. Although *talanoa* as a research approach centers discussions and collects data through its oral depictions of engagement, there is no current research in which classrooms (research settings) were designed with what Paris called young people in mind.

Selection Process of Participants

We recruited participants based on self-selection by the Mana generation-five (gen-five) students, the fifth cohort of the Mana program (fall 2019), who were in their first semester in the program. Thirty-five gen-five students agreed to participate, and two opted out for personal reasons. In addition to these thirty-five gen-five students, ten Mana alumni (who are students from previous cohorts) agreed to also join the *talanoa*, thereby expanding the conversation using their encounters at their respective four-year universities as a comparison. The age of the Mana participants ranged from eighteen to twenty-two years, with seventeen participants identified as females, twenty identified as males, and three identified as nonbinary gender-conforming. The *talanoa* sessions were divided into pre- and post-*talanoa* dialogue, drawing connections between both parts to highlight personal thoughts and written reflections as a consequence of the face-to-face discussions. One of the complex components of the *talanoa* method is establishing a sense of security in the dynamic created between researcher and community (in this case, NHPI students in college) in face-to-face discussions; this security is established through the cultural protocol of an oral contract, called village voices, that is mutually agreed on by both researcher and community members. We uploaded all videos, recordings, and notes into a Google shared drive. All data were stored in a password-secured drive and organized through an Excel database.

Theoretical Background

Navigating Formal Institutions of Learning

Although multiple education theories address the NHPI experience in education, those theories, which focus on general student outcomes in college settings, expand on Tinto's claim that college students must change their behavior habits for a successful transition. Tinto's student departure theory emphasizes the legitimacy of shedding old connections to find success in a new institution.[14] This idea provokes tension in a community like NHPI, who operate in the opposite manner. In fact, asking for NHPI students to shed the old community would mean shedding parts of themselves, permanently disconnecting them from their homes and realities. For NHPI students, this is out of the question. Even when NHPI students explore behavior habits individually, they are still drawing connections between themselves and the collective they subscribe to at home. Tongan American students' status as first-generation college students places them at a disadvantage due to their understanding of college and institutional expectations, often hindering academic success. During the first year in college, most NHPI students must navigate through new transitions alone, which discourages them from moving forward and for some ultimately contributed to their early departure.

To complicate the problem of being a first-generation college student even further, research has shown that NHPI students' efforts to balance Pasifika cultural expectations with mainstream American cultural expectations have negatively impacted their ability to persist through their first year in college.[15] Wolfgramm-Foliaki's qualitative study involved NHPI first-generation college students at a four-year university and used the *talanoa* method; she found that family and community were central to NHPI students and their educational journey; hence, both elements needed to be part of any support initiatives and curriculum development for students. Because of this disconnected understanding, the curriculum and programming at universities did not adequately respond to the NHPI student community.[16] Wolfgramm-Foliaki's qualitative study illustrated the relationships between and among multicultural education, critical pedagogy, and learning communities as bridges for creating spaces for students academically. These studies also validated

Tinto's argument that open access does not equate to equity or opportunity, and in Wolfgramm-Foliaki's particular study, there needed to be more discussion on how to respond to NHPI students. NHPI students will continue to lag behind their non-NHPI peers if institutions do not create intentional pathways within their curriculum that respond to and reflect the cultural capital and experiences of NHPI students.[17]

Angafakafonua and Sacred Space

Tongan identity-making is rooted in *angafakafonua*, which combines the words *anga* (affect or manner), *faka* (of/of the), and *fonua* (land, body, womb, people). Though some scholars have defined *angafakafonua* as the Tongan way or the way of the land, we authors prefer to think of *angafakafonua* as a process. We define the process of *angafakafonua* as governing Tongan social relations in various social contexts. Tongans acknowledge these social relations by performing, and thus fulfilling, *fatongia* (cultural duty). This performance of *fatongia* requires, first, an evaluation of social relationships at any major life event, and second, a fulfillment of *fatongia* based on finite tasks which are dispensed according to the imbalance of social power that the relationship produces. For instance, at a funeral, the deceased's father's sister presides as the *fahu*, the highest social rank in the Tongan family unit, whereas the deceased's mother's brother is relegated to cooking and cleaning for the event. Each person involved in the funeral evaluates their familial connection to the deceased and then fulfills their *fatongia* at the event. Dualistic in nature, *angafakafonua*, as a process, balances *'eiki* (high social rank) and *tu'a* (low social rank) to constitute both high and low social status to every Tongan individual. While English translations of these concepts merely approach a Tongan import, it is a constellation of the Tongan conceptual practice of *angafakafonua*.

While TAMS' definitions of concepts like *angafakafonua*, faith, family, and *fatongia* inscribe boundaries that distinguish each separate yet related concept, our understanding of *angafakafonua* blurs the boundaries and, instead, views the concepts as strands of *angafakafonua*. As parts that make up the whole, a strand of *angafakafonua*, like the sacred, is both a part of *angafakafonua* and the whole of *angafakafonua*. Another concept that shapes TAMS understanding of the world, the *kāinga* framework, establishes the type of working relationships TAMS have experienced growing up. Larger than a nuclear family but smaller than a village, the *kāinga* framework includes individuals who are distantly related and typically work together to fulfill broader family *fatongia*. For TAMS, faith cannot be understood outside the context of *kāinga*, and *kāinga* is unintelligible outside the context of the politics of power. TAMS' modus operandi mobilizes a *kāinga* framework that situates the individual within a larger student network of individuals drawn together in education networks. By the time TAMS begin formal schooling at the age of five, they have been exposed to funerals, birthdays, weddings, and church events of their siblings, parents, aunts, uncles, grand-parents, grand-aunts, or grand-uncles. At these events, TAMS absorb new families, learn and participate in cultural traditions and practices, and learn and recite oral histories and genealogies. These experiences shape and construct the lens with which TAMS see the world and themselves and how they fare in school.

This intimate relationship between TAMS communities in the United States and their spirituality sustains cultural heritage. Tongan epistemology and Christianity are tightly woven, and many of the Tongan rituals and protocols are often held at church halls and during church gatherings and are performed during Christian milestones (e.g., Easter and Christmas).[18] This serves two purposes for Tongan communities in the diaspora: diaspora Tongans can practice their spirituality while connecting to each other, and Tongans in the United States can continue to practice Tongan rituals and traditions and speak the language to sustain their Tongan identity. This is the very essence of their existence and culture, their faith, and their God. As a result, many Mana students understand their spirituality as it continues to be fostered through their *kāinga* relationships, the *fatongia* that comes with it, and the act of *tauhi vā* (nurturing relationships) to sustain this. Thus, acknowledgement then becomes a mandatory protocol.

Throughout the latter half of the nineteenth to the early twentieth century, scholars like Émile Durkheim developed theoretical formulations regarding the concept of the sacred to understood how humans understand their world which. For Durkheim, the Aborigines in Australia served as a prime example of the most primitive religious groups holding the most primitive beliefs among humankind.[19] In his theory, sacred and profane stood at opposite ends of a spectrum that formulaically defined all aspects of primitive life. He rigidly defined the sacred as things that were set apart and forbidden, whereas the profane represented the opposite, that which was accessible to everyone and not set apart.[20] Educational spaces like the Mana classroom, according to Durkheimian definitions, are classified as profane. Later in the century, Mircea Eliade removed rigid Durkheimian constraints, adding nuance to sacred spatial discourse.[21] Whereas Durkheim's dichotomy cemented sacred objects and spaces as permanently so, Eliade claimed that objects within a sacred space are simultaneously unchanged yet transformed, stating, "By manifesting the sacred, any object becomes *something else*, yet it continues to remain *itself*, for it continues to participate in its surrounding cosmic milieu."[22] From this description, then, groups like the Tongan students imbue the Mana classroom with sacredness.

Since the 1980s, scholars of religion have agreed that these basic Durkheimian concepts, among others, fail to capture expanding definitions of religion, like *lived religion*, a term coined by David Hall.[23] Onaje Woodbine claims that street basketball *is* religion for streetballers in Boston's notorious Roxbury neighborhood.[24] For Woodbine, "the central problems and structures of inner-city life are displayed, renegotiated, and reimagined on the court."[25] Furthermore, he puts forward Nancy Ammerman's foundational example of lived religion, in which she argues, "Scholars of lived religion acknowledge that religious phenomena such as ritual practice, healing, transcendent experience, spiritual encounters, and prayer occur in places and times that exist apart from the control of recognized experts and religious authorities."[26] For the Tongan students, this can happen in college.

Findings and Analysis

Talanoa a Mana was organized through storytelling narratives, written responses to articles, and reflections that are combined and formed into a collective of academic pathways that emerged from an analysis of NHPI students' interactions rooted in the theory of *angafakafonua* as Tongan epistemology and our Talanoa method. In this section, we spotlight TAMS' lived experiences as part of a larger *talanoa* that included Mana students, alumni, and educators. By this point in the semester, students had already read Epeli Hauʻofaʻs foundational article, "Our Sea of Islands," and his collection of works in *We Are the Ocean*, which students responded to and discussed in their writing assignments and class discussions.[27] To prime our first *talanoa*, we assigned selections from Onaje Woodbine's *Black Gods of the Asphalt: Religion, Hip-Hop, and Street Basketball*, to introduce students to the field of religious studies and the ongoing conversation about religion, race, and lived religion in the field. As TAMS embarked on their college journey, their responses to the articles, assignments and projects revealed a culturally specific identity with which Mana educators responded to with culturally sustaining pedagogy.

Mana spaces not only fulfilled a sense of *angafakafonua* for TAMS but also provided safety, which fostered a vulnerability typically hidden deep beneath a tough exterior. The consistency of answers from the TAMS in the written reflections they submitted the day before our *talanoa* lead us to believe that Mana spaces engender and stimulate salient learning communities with which TAMS can approach successful educational outcomes. Students were divided into groups, and each group elected a member to write their group's thoughts about the readings on the white board at the front of the classroom. Their thoughts formed the basis for our discussion, and what originally began as a discussion of American religions literature pivoted to a discussion on sacred space.

Tonga American Mana Student (TAMS) Profile

In "Pacific Islander Students Caught between a Rock and a Hard Space?," Halaevalu Vakalahi found that because institutions are unaware of duo-culture, Pacific Islander students feel a chasm between home and school.[28] Tomasi Filimoehala, a first-year business major, expressed the difference between two educational spaces, Mana and non-Mana, by using his name as an example of how something often valued as a connecting factor in the Tongan culture is not validated as an identity outside of the Tongan context:

> For my other classes, they don't give me a voice. In English and math, you just sit there for an hour or two and shut up. They don't get my respect because they don't even know my name. How am I supposed to respect you when you don't know my name?

The class's emphatic applause validated his input; it was as if everyone in that room had encountered a similar experience. Tomasi's experience highlights a missed opportunity for instructors to engage students in the curriculum and in the classroom setting. Further, this experience makes us wonder about other missed opportunities in instructors' daily encounters when they fail to "see" the students, or their name. Thus, Tomasi weaves together his respect (*faka'apa'apa*, one of the four golden pillars), his name (genealogical connection to the space and others in the space), and his engagement with his education experiences.

Kalisi sat in the corner of the classroom listening to each student share their experience about Mana classrooms as sacred. As a Mana alumnus currently attending a four-year university, Kalisi felt inspired to share with the class how Mana education spaces affected her own educational outcome, proclaiming, rather than explaining, the distinct sacred nature of Mana:

> In a Mana class, there was just a different sense of empowerment behind the things you said. So we understood that everything you said had a weight to it. No matter if our experiences were different—if it was from a different side of the bay or out of state, if you were from different denominations and practiced our culture differently—we all learned that at the end of the day, we are ocean. . . . There is no boundary when it comes to everyone in this room, because in this very room, I see my brothers' and sisters' faces; I see my mom and dad's faces. And that's why Mana has a lot to do with education, is to understand that how I treat my education is how I treat my family, how I treat my faith and how I treat my God.

For a moment, it was as if the room conceptually shifted into a living room or worship hall as Kalisi weaved two principal institutions in her life: faith and education. This transformation highlights the way *anga-fakafonua* as Tongan epistemology establishes and reifies connections between various facets of TAMS' lives. Kalisi reconciled her academic journey by using Mana courses as a platform to reflect on the way TAMS connect, relate and acknowledge differences as a uniting factor. Like the ocean, this unity transforms small movements into larger movements, connecting ideas in new ways, as if education acts as a function of TAMS' *angafakafonua*. Kalisi further characterized the sacredness in

the Mana space, claiming that the program is "founded on that very belief that God is greater than everything." TAMS used a variety of ways to
communicate how and why the space was sacred, claiming, for the most
part, that the space was purposely made sacred by former students and
the residual effects of that sacralization continue to reinforce sacredness
for current TAMS and other non-TAMS in Mana spaces. TAMS also
reflected on how Mana spaces felt immediately unique upon passing
through the threshold of the space:

Ano, a junior and a second-year social sciences major and one of
many talented Mana athletes, detailed the leveling effects of the Mana
classroom and how regardless of dissimilarities, individuals in the space
understood that the rules for the outside world did not apply in the space:

> I realized that there was a sense of family in the classroom that was only
> offered for the Pacific Islanders. There was a sense of air that was differ-
> ent, like a transcendence. Ocean air and transcendence, like Mana, the
> energy and that feeling of that space being really sacred. For us. By us. For
> our future. And the sense of our culture is being instilled in us that way,
> too, because the class is already a sense of community with our culture
> because we are living and breathing our culture. We are our traditional
> past lives with each other, from generations before.

For Ano, the space was brand new, familiar, and sacred as a product of
their own work and, even more important, for their own benefit. For
Ano and first-year students, the unique Mana education space with
culturally sustaining curriculum is one they have never encountered.
At the same time, it is familiar because the core tenets of the *fā kavei
koula* (four golden pillars, which include *tauhi vā, faka'apa'apa* [respect],
loto tō [humility], and *mamahi'ime'a* [passion for one's beliefs]) are
acknowledged, encouraged, and cultivated in the space and enforced
through village voices. Although Ano's phrasing specifies culture and
not *angafakafonua*, we know that his definition of culture aligns with
our characterization of the process of *angafakafonua* because he chose
ocean, transcendence, and sacred to describe the air and energy in the
Mana education space.

Mele, a sophomore TAMS majoring in communication, recalled an
instance that impacted her approach to education: "I remember one

time we had a speaker series with a Sāmoan professor from UCLA on systematic racism and leadership. He was talking about how his mom taught him about the 'three Fs,'—faith, family, and fa'a Samoa—which helped him to navigate oppressive spaces in academia." The Sāmoan professor's Sefa Aina experience resonated with Mele's own experiences; her family's model of *angafakafonua* mitigated her ability to navigate oppressive academic spaces. For Aina, the three Fs are ranked in order of importance. However, for Mele, rather than listing the Fs in order, she collapsed the first two Fs into the third, *angafakafonua*. Aina's anecdote reassured Mele that her understanding and practice of *angafakafonua* could potentially leverage success in academia rather than result in academic failure. For a descendent of wayfinders who used the stars to navigate the largest body of water in the world, we see Mele's interpretation of *angafakafonua* as a constellation that guides TAMS through the troubled waters of higher education.

TAMS further identify the ways in which Mana spaces foster and sustain *angafakafonua*. Mele shared that Mana spaces "build a community where it's a safe space . . . where everyone will feel comfortable here." This comfort level and safety are byproducts of the way Mana educators attune the space to accommodate *angafakafonua*, such as village voices, which securely privilege the four golden pillars of *angafakafonua*. Jessie, a first-year undeclared major, also related his experience of belonging in the Mana classroom, claiming, "You have a spiritual being in you. You want to be able to stand up to that, even though it's hard. In pop culture, they teach you to just follow along with the ride, but nobody teaches you how to be yourself." Mana education spaces embolden TAMS like Jessie to reject a subscription to the status quo and instead tap into their internal spiritual beings to find academic success.

Carson, another Mana alumnus who successfully transferred to a four-year university majoring in Pacific studies, shared his ethereal take on his Mana experience, claiming, "I didn't understand how to articulate validation until I walked into a Mana classroom. I felt like my ancestors meant for me to be there." It was as if their intentions, which directed him beyond time and space, were only manifested as he contacted the space. Would Carson have otherwise known that his ancestors intended for him to find a Mana space if he had not had contact with it? For Carson, Jessie, and the other TAMS, *angafakafonua* provided the vocabulary to validate their presence in higher education. Moreover, *angafakafonua* articulated cultural values like spirituality and the sacred that are often abandoned by students at the threshold of most public-school classroom spaces.

Despite the positive outcomes of TAMS' mobilization of *angafakafonua* in education spaces, portions of the process of *angafakafonua*, particularly the emphasis on evaluating social relationships, presented challenges to TAMS. These challenges manifest as behaviors, which are practiced in their home environments that often contradicted normal campus routines. An apt example is Vivian, who shared, "When I face adversity in school now, I just keep remembering *Koe otua mo Tonga ko Hoku Tofi'a* [God and Tonga are my inheritance] and think of my grandma."

Vivian, a first-year TAMS majoring in ethnic studies and Pacific Islander studies, returned to the United States a few months before fall semester began. Although Vivian was born in the United States, she was raised in Tonga with her maternal grandmother. Vivian's parents sent her to stay with her grandmother while they both worked around the clock as casino housekeepers to purchase their family's first home. After seventeen years of living abroad with her grandmother, Vivian completed her final year at a public secondary school in Tonga before moving back to her new family home in East Palo Alto, California. When asked about her motivation to pursue college, she proclaimed, "We do everything for God and our families. My grandma said we would be lost in the dark without it. She said God and prayer was the *maama* [light]. Being so far away from my grandma made me long for her presence."

Vivian's educational experiences in Tonga weaved together staple concepts from her Tongan upbringing that centered Tongan rituals, traditions, and values. Yet this weaving felt more like an entanglement. Vivian's *angafakafonua* clashed with the education system she encountered at the California community college that expounded US rituals, traditions, and values that aligned with university and college academic culture situated within a system of meritocracy and White supremacy. Vivian's grandmother taught her that speaking out and asking questions in class was rude and disrespectful, which points to the imbalance of power between authoritative instructor and student acknowledged in *angafakafonua*. In an academic space in which intellectual curiosity or vulnerability are supported and fostered, TAMS' upbringing informs their conflation of intellectual curiosity with questioning authority, resulting in closed mouths and thus no one being fed. Malia, a first year at CBA, characterized this struggle as having jigsaw puzzle pieces dumped on their laps—just the pieces—without the handy picture on the box to guide them in assembling the pieces to create a beautiful picture.

Forging New Pathways

> This may not be a church-church but it's still a group of people that come together with the same purpose, or cause, I guess. In Mana—it's like . . . you can be yourself and not have to look over your shoulder because it's all genuine love in here. Nobody's praying for your downfall; we all want to see each other succeed and do well in Mana.
> —Carson

Carson ended his explanation by expressing how his educational journey is an opportunity from the "man above." As TAMS negotiate the disharmony between Mana and non-Mana space, they also confront the intimidating task of finding a way within and through the educational journey for themselves and those who come after them. TAMS recognize and appreciate these specialized education spaces, as evidenced by increased matriculation rates of TAMS to four-year universities.

But what of those TAMS who graduated and transferred to four-year universities? We spoke to two TAMS, Kalisi and Carson, who voiced several grave concerns about life after Mana. First, they were most concerned with finding spaces like Mana on their new university campuses. Unfortunately, because Mana is an inaugural program at CBA, similar programs are still unavailable at the university level. However, Mana graduates at four-year universities excitedly express their passion for creating Mana spaces in their new environments. As products of these spaces, TAMS are privy to a wealth of knowledge regarding the creation of Mana spaces. In this section, we will explore the potential ripple effects of Mana across other American education spaces outside of College of the Bay Area. In the direction of future research, we ask ourselves the following questions: Is there a formula for creating Mana education spaces? If space becomes sacred through manifestations of the sacred by its inhabitants, is it necessary for TAMS to imbue future Mana spaces with the sacred or can these spaces exist without the sacred contents from CBA?

Carson relayed to us the formula for creating Mana spaces outside of CBA:

> Creating a Mana space at [my] current university requires a self-sustaining staff who can utilize necessary university resources. Second, proper representation in these intimidating academic and administrative spaces ensures that they're [TAMS] being looked after in ways that parallel their previous Mana experiences. Third, establishing a trusting relationship between Mana staff and students increases TAMS' self-confidence and, ultimately, their academic success and degree attainment.

According to Carson, these are the ingredients for Mana success away from CBA. Once the above three ingredients for the formula are established, Carson concludes that what exists is "the space, the workshops, even cohorts, to create the classrooms where our students feel vulnerable and open to sharing and soaking in the material so that we can create hopefully future leaders to come back and take over these positions to just recreate."

After interviewing Carson, we realized that while he detailed the formula for Mana outside of CBA, he overlooked his own role as a TAMS from CBA; his role might represent a necessary component for the institutionalization of a sacred Mana education space at his new campus. Carson, as well as other TAMS, might serve as conduits of the sacred from CBA's Mana space to their new education spaces. We question whether the introduction of Mana outside of CBA without a former CBA TAMS to imbue the space with the sacred could work. We have yet to see whether the answer to the above question will yield positive results, particularly as other community colleges in the same state as CBA have instituted Mana programs on their campuses. We look forward to further research that addresses these issues, knowing the answers contain valuable insight for those who study both sacred and education spaces.

NOTES

1 Angela Tarango, *Choosing the Jesus Way: American Indian Pentecostals and the Fight for the Indigenous Principle* (Chapel Hill: University of North Carolina Press, 2014).
2 Jolanta Juszkiewicz, "Trends in Community College Enrollment and Completion Data," American Association of Community Colleges, 2015, www.aacc.nche.edu/.

3 National Student Clearinghouse Research Center, *Term Enrollment Estimates: Fall 2016*, https://nscresearchcenter.org.

4 Robert Teranishi, Anna Le, Gutierrez, Rose Ann Eborda, Rikka Venturanza, Inoke Hafoka, Demeturie Toso-Lafaele Gogue, and Lavinia Uluave, *Native Hawaiians and Pacific Islanders in Higher Education, Los Angeles, CA*, APIA Scholars, 2019, https://apiascholars.org.

5 US Census Bureau, *2011–2013 American Community Survey 3-Year National Bachelor's Degree Attainment*, 2013, SAS data file, www2.census.gov.

6 Hokulani Aikau, *A Chosen People, A Promised Land: Mormonism and Race in Hawai'i*, (Minneapolis: University of Minnesota Press, 2012); Vicente Diaz, *Repositioning the Missionary: Rewriting the Histories of Colonialism, Native Catholicism, and Indigeneity in Guam* (Honolulu: University of Hawai'i Press, 2010).

7 Halaevalu F. Ofahengaue Vakalahi, "Pacific Islander American Students: Caught between a Rock and a Hard Place?" *Children and Youth Services Review* 31, no. 12 (2009): 1258–63.

8 Sitiveni Halapua and Pago Pago, "Talanoa in Building Democracy and Governance," in *A Paper Prepared for the Conference of Future Leaders of the Pacific*, Pago Pago, American Samoa, February 2013, 4–7.

9 Timote Vaioleti, "Talanoa Research Methodology: A Developing Position on Pacific Research," *Waikato Journal of Education* 12, no. 21–34 (2006). doi:10.15663/wje.v12i1.296.

10 David Fa'avae, Alison Jones, and Linitā Manu'atu, "Talanoa'i 'A e Talanoa—Talking about Talanoa: Some Dilemmas of a Novice Researcher," *AlterNative: An International Journal of Indigenous Peoples* 12, no. 2 (2016): 138–50; Trisia Farrelly and Unaisi Nabobo-Baba, "Talanoa as Empathic Research," in *International Development Conference* 12 (2012); Tevita O. Ka'ili, *Marking Indigeneity: The Tongan Art of Sociospatial Relations* (Tucson: University of Arizona Press, 2017).

11 Finausina Tovo, "Talanoa A Mana: Validating Oceania Voices in a Pacific Studies Learning Community," PhD diss., San Francisco State University, 2020.

12 Django Paris, "Culturally Sustaining Pedagogy: A Needed Change in Stance, Terminology, and Practice," *Educational Researcher* 41, no. 3 (2012): 93–97.

13 Ibid.

14 Vincent Tinto, "Dropout from Higher Education: A Theoretical Synthesis of Recent Research," *Review of Educational Research* 45, no. 1 (1975): 89–125; *Leaving College: Rethinking the Causes and Cures of Student Attrition* (Chicago: University of Chicago Press: 1987); "Building community," *Liberal Education* 79, no. 4 (1993): 16–21.

15 Denise L. Uehara, Jonathan Chugen, and Vidalino Staley Raatior, "Perceptions of Pacific Islander Students in Higher Education," *Journal of Diversity in Higher Education* 11, no. 2 (2018): 182–91.

16 Ema Wolfgramm-Foliaki, "'Do Not Assume We Know': Perspectives of Pacific Island First in the Family Students," in *Culturally Responsive Leadership in Higher Education* (New York: Routledge, 2015), 123–35.

17 Ibid.

18 In the first draft of Tonga's new code of governance, the Vava'u Codes of 1850 and 1862, Tongans were given the freedom to practice any religion. However, King Tupou's Christian conversion and his reevaluation of the Indigenous Tongan religion, which led to the destruction of Indigenous temples and the abuse of Tongan hieratics, illustrated the superiority of Christian beliefs and practices over Indigenous Tongan ones. See Sione Latukefu, *Church and State in Tonga: The Wesleyan Methodist Missionaries and Political Development, 1822–1875* (Honolulu: University Press of Hawai'i, 1974).

19 Émile Durkheim, *The Elementary Forms of Religious Life* (New York: Free Press, 1995).

20 For Durkheim, modern religious forms evolved from this primitive example, which represented the most basic religious concepts: souls, spirits, gods, cults, and rites. He believed comparisons for religions worldwide should be drawn from these basic concepts.

21 Mircea Eliade, *The Sacred and the Profane: The Nature of Religion* (New York: Harper & Row, 1959).

22 Ibid., 12.

23 David Hall, *Lived Religion in America: Toward a History of Practice* (Princeton, NJ: Princeton University Press, 1997).

24 Onaje Woodbine, *Black Gods of the Asphalt: Religion, Hip-Hop, and Street Basketball* (New York: Columbia University Press, 2016), 7. Woodbine claims street basketball is religion for streetballers in Boston's notorious Roxbury neighborhood. For Woodbine, "the central problems and structures of inner-city life are displayed, renegotiated, and reimagined on the court."

25 Ibid., 9.

26 Nancy Ammerman, "Lived Religion," in *Emerging Trends in the Social and Behavioral Sciences: An Interdisciplinary, Searchable, and Linkable Resource* (Hoboken, NJ: Wiley Online Library, 2015), 1–8.

27 Epeli Hau'ofa, "Our Sea of Islands," *Contemporary Pacific* 6, no. 1 (Spring 1994), 147–61; *We Are the Ocean* (Honolulu: University of Hawai'i Press, 2008).

28 Vakalahi, "Pacific Islander American Students."

14

Unsettling the Settler Colonial Triptych

Visioning AlterNative Futures with Octavia E. Butler's Wild Seed

HŌKŪLANI K. AIKAU

She flew as a large bird for a while.[1]

My flight to escape colonial reality was a flight into Nish-
naabewin. It was a returning, in the present, to myself. It
was an unfolding of a different present. It was freedom as a
way of being as a constellation of relationship, freedom as
world making, freedom as a practice. It was biiskabiyang.[2]

Freedom is not a destination or an event. It is a structure and a way
of being that must be worked at day after day, generation after generation. Freedom is having the space and opportunity to live one's
authentic life and be one's authentic self. In ʻōlelo Hawaiʻi, the Hawaiian language, the term that comes to mind that resonates with the
notions of freedom expressed in the epigraphs is ea. Ea is both a noun
and a verb.[3] It is often defined as sovereignty, rule, independence and
is used in the context of political governance (see also Das Gupta, this
volume).[4] When we consider other definitions, such as life, air, breath,
and its verb tense to rise, go up, raise, ea bridges scales from that of
the political status of nations to the individual at the level of bodily
sovereignty and independence.[5] It is life, the air we breathe, and the
ability to determine for one's self the present and future for them and
their kin. Octavia E. Butler's novel *Wild Seed* is a kind of imaginative
itinerary that simultaneously attends to structures of power, oppression, liberation, and freedom. As a dystopic novel, Butler consistently
reminds the reader that we must be ever diligent if we are going to
seek freedom and remain free.

Indeed, movement, migration, taking flight are themes throughout the novel. The first epigraph describes Anyanwu's escape from the abusive, authoritarian control of Doro. As a large bird, her flight path toward healing and reconnecting with her sovereign self took her to the ocean, where she became a dolphin. Among the sociality of dolphins, with their gentle touch and acceptance, she begins the healing process and unlearns the habit of submission. There she begins to vision and plan for an alternative future. The second quote is from Leanne Betasamosake Simpson reflecting on the time she spent with elders, on the land, and how those years were her "first flight path out of settler colonialism" and toward biiskabiyang, "the process of returning to ourselves, a reengagement with the things we have left behind, a reemergence, an unfolding from the inside out."[6] This essay is not a literary critique of the novel. Rather, it is a meditation on flight paths out of settler colonialism, White supremacy, domination, and oppression. A flight path must attend to the past, present, and futures. How can the classroom be a site where students learn to take flight? How do we create conditions where an unfolding of a different present and futures can be imagined and nurtured? This essay demonstrates how bringing literary analysis and social science frameworks together with speculative and visionary fiction methods invites students into a practice of visioning freedom and new world making.

As an Indigenous professor, I find it increasingly necessary to challenge the bifurcation between struggles against Native genocide and for anti-Black racism. Setter colonial studies has made important contributions to understanding how land, labor, and capital structurally function to perpetuate Native dispossession and erasure, the enslavement of Africans through chattel slavery, and White supremacy and the perniciousness of anti-Black racism. And while the native-slave-settler triptych is a useful analytic, these categories are far too often aligned with identity positions that are considered distinct and separate. This framing is an overly simplistic rendering of the structures of power and oppression in the United States. Additionally, it is a structure organized to prevent alliances from forming across the panels of the triptych, and thus it maintains the hegemony of White supremacy, heteropatriarchy, and settler colonialism. As a pedagogue committed to curating transformative classroom experiences that challenge these and other bifurcations, I come to the novel in the guise of a pedagogical exercise to demonstrate how Butler opens up possibilities for unsettling the settler colonial triptych of native-slave-settler and for creatively reimagining alternative futures.

The Novel

Literary scholars recognize Butler as one of the leading Black science fiction (SF) authors whose work is widely lauded for pushing readers to consider race, gender, slavery, and the body beyond dominant ways of thinking. Literary scholar Ingrid Thaler situates *Wild Seed*, the prequal to the *Patternmaster* series, within the tradition of Black Atlantic speculative fiction.[7] She argues that as a historiographic speculative novel, *Wild Seed* uses historical references not to rewrite the past but to provide the reader with enough historical context to make the fantastic storyline of Doro and Anyanwu, two immortal characters in dialectical struggle over freedom and the future, more plausible. Equally important, Butler presents the reader with a version of the past that makes the power dynamics between Doro and Anyanwu explicit while also attending to the violence their relationship enacts on those around them who are not nearly as powerful. In doing so, the reader is not allowed to retreat to a space of utopian refuge or to a place of innocence but is constantly reminded that Doro's power is eternal and inescapable. I applaud Butler's ability to insist that the reader not place agency above or outside of structure. The intersection of sociology and American studies is most pedagogically and powerfully seen when social and political theory intersect with cultural analysis of material culture. My approach to reading/teaching *Wild Seed* is intended to assist students to critically and creatively vision an otherwise to power and oppression.

Relocations and Mutual Recognition

> Writing prompt #1: Tell Mohawk Girl's story. Create an alternative storyline where Mohawk Girl does not disappear from the novel but becomes an ally or accomplice with Anyanwu.[8]

Wild Seed begins in 1690 on the western coast of Africa in what is today known as Nigeria and follows Anyanwu's journey from her homeland to the "new world." The middle-passage narrative is told from Anyanwu's point of view as she learns about Doro's breeding project, his successes, and his failures. While she cautiously and willingly leaves her Igbo village and travels to the Americas, Butler is quite explicit about what is at stake for Anyanwu and her people if she does not go with Doro. Butler establishes the relationship between Doro and his people as a covenant, an agreement between a god and his people. He establishes obedience through fear, authoritarian paternalism, and his god-like ability to wear the skin of other humans. At issue are the moral and ethical dilemmas Anyanwu must face if she is to continue to keep her descendants safe from Doro's breeding project and the violence Doro's children enact on one another and on those around them. Butler creates a kind of moral equation in the first part of the novel where Anyanwu is framed as a person who honors her covenants, and Doro, in contrast, demands total obedience but does not feel the need to honor his commitments to his people.

Butler uses book 1 to draw the reader's attention to the kinds of covenants Doro has with Anyanwu and his people—a presumption of mutual consent through contract or a relationship of commitment between a god and his people. This first writing prompt goes beyond the relationship of commitment between Doro, Anyanwu, and his people to that between Anyanwu and the Mohawk girl she meets at dinner on her first night at Wheatley, Doro's most successful settlement in upstate New York.

In terms of the overall narrative arc of the novel, the welcome dinner is a plot device that serves two purposes: first, the dialogue at the dinner situates the reader within the historical period; second, it allows Anyanwu to proclaim a covenant to her future children. The scene is structured around Sarah's daughter-in-law, the young, shy Indian, a Mohawk. Butler writes, "The girl was slender and olive-skinned, black-haired and dark-eyed and even to Anyanwu's eyes, very beautiful." The dialogue during dinner instructs the reader that thirty years prior, Indians had twice attacked Wheatley, and Doro had "showed" himself to the Indians, who were so frightened they did not bother Wheatley again. More recently, Sarah, Doro's housekeeper and daughter-in-law, reports Praying Indians and their French allies had attacked nearby British settlements. In response to the heated discussion about Indians, the Mohawk girl smiles and whispers, "My people could tell them what powerful spirits live here." The rest of the table laughs.[9]

It is during this discussion of settler-Native relations that Anyanwu wonders "whether the Mohawk girl would have preferred to forget who she was as the conversation turned to talk of war with Indians." It is also during this conversation that she resolves to make sure her children do not become fully assimilated into the new world. "It would be good for the children of their [Doro and Anyanwu] marriage to know her world as well as Doro's—to be aware of a place where blackness was not a mark of slavery. She resolved to make her homeland live for them whether Doro permitted her to show it to them or not. She resolved not to let them forget who they were."[10] As the story of Anyanwu's life in Wheatley progresses, the reader learns that she works hard to live up to this covenant. She gives all of her children both English and Ibo names and in their home, and she speaks to her children in her Native language. She, too, refuses to adopt an English name, that is, until the end of the novel, when she moves her family to California, where she adopts the European name Emma. "She had heard that it meant grandmother or ancestress, and this amused her. She became Emma Anyanwu."[11]

As Robyn D. G. Kelley argues, "The Atlantic Slave Trade rips Africans from their homeland and deposits them in territories undergoing settlement and dispossession, but renaming severs any relationship to their land and Indigenous communities."[12] Being more than three hundred years old, Anyanwu has called many villages and tribes home and is the mother, grandmother, great-grandmother, great-great-great-grandmother to many descendants. She is keenly aware that Blackness in the new world is devalued and associated with slavery. When she decides to raise her children to know where they come from, she is making a refusal. "Refusal," Audra Simpson explains, "is about no longer granting states and hegemons [in the context of the novel, Doro] the prerogative to set the terms under which their authority will be contested."[13] Throughout the novel, the reader witnesses Anyanwu enacting refusal, that is, "the very deliberate, willful, intentional actions that people were making in the face of the expectation that they consent to their own elimination as a people, that they consent to having their land taken, their lives controlled, and their stories told for them."[14] Anyanwu will come to know in very emotional, personal, and costly ways the full impact of Doro's power and authority to make life and make death. And she will refuse his power and authority in the only ways she knows how, through shape-shifting and by manipulating her own immortality.

The story of Anyanwu's first dinner in Wheatley is a good example of how Africans "were relocated to Native lands among Native populations in the 'New World.'"[15] It also illustrates how African Indigeneity persists as it establishes Anyanwu's commitment to maintain her Indigeneity—her language, history, and cultural practices—even as she vows to learn the ways of the English and the Dutch. The scene emphasizes how African peoples were cognizant of and sympathetic to the experiences of Native peoples. And it is a troubling scene because Anyanwu fails to see how similar she and the Mohawk girl may be. If we extend African Indigeneity beyond the Middle Passage, as Kelley suggests, and if we read the novel as both an Afro-futurist *and* an Indigenous-futurist text, then we co-create new possibilities for what Leanne Simpson calls "a constellation of co-resistance and freedom." To achieve this objective, she argues, "we need to be willing to take on White supremacy, gender violence, heteropatriarchy, and anti-Blackness within our [Indigenous] movement. We need to be willing to develop personal relationships with other communities of co-resisters beyond White allies."[16] As Butler does so well, in returning to the past, we have an opportunity to reinterpret, understand, and live into the present differently.

Indeed, this very minor scene in the novel is illustrative of a larger debate between settler colonial studies and Black studies about the persistence of African Indigeneity beyond the Middle Passage. In the introduction to "Body and Soul," the *American Quarterly* forum that honored Patrick Wolfe's contribution to American studies and settler colonial studies, Njoroge summarizes Wolfe's project as "inextricably interwoven with the dispossession of people and the creation of 'others.'"[17] Njoroge goes on to write, "For Wolfe's purposes, the rise of European capitalism and imperialism, the territorial and existential erasure of Indigenous peoples, the enslavement, physical estrangement, and bodily dispossession of the African are all different moments in the movement of the structures of race and racialization."[18] Through punctuation and prepositions, Indigenous peoples and Africans become relegated to separate, distinct panels in the settler colonial mural of history. In contrast, Kelley argues that the separation of Indigeneity from Africans is a consequence of Wolfe "not incorporating more of the globe in his studies," specifically not taking European colonization and decolonization *in* Africa seriously.[19] Kelley has two problems with Wolfe's framing: "First, it presumes that Indigenous people exist only in the Americas and Australasia. African Indigeneity is erased in this formulation because, through linguistic sleight of hand, Africans are turned into Black Americans." Not only is Wolfe guilty of this "linguistic sleight of hand," it mirrors dominant narratives about the triangle trade, slavery, colonization, and the formation of the US and American national identity. If African Indigeneity is acknowledged at all, it is stripped during the Middle Passage to transform Indigenous peoples into slaves. But what would it mean to hold onto the idea that folks from the African continent are Indigenous peoples displaced and dispossessed from their lands, peoples who also suffered the logics of elimination? Kelley draws on the work of Cedric J. Robinson, another intellectual, who passed in 2016, to punctuate the limits and erasures of Wolfe's framework. Robinson writes (as quoted by Kelley):

> The cargoes of laborers also contained African cultures, critical mixes and admixtures of language and thought, of cosmology and metaphysics, of habits, beliefs, and morality. These are the actual terms of their humanity. These cargoes, then, did not consist of intellectual isolates or decultured Blacks—men, women, and children separated from their previous universe. African labor brought the past with it, a past that had produced it and settled on it the first elements of consciousness and comprehension.[20]

What might it mean to our theorizing and thinking about the racial and gender logics of settler colonization in the United States to consider "slaves" and "cargo" as displaced Indigenous peoples? How might our thinking about the meanings of Indigenous, Native, settler, White, Black need to change to make space for this reality? Through the Anyanwu character, Butler provides one illustration of Robinson's point. She is a woman who not only brings her "language and thought, of cosmology and metaphysics, of habits, beliefs, and morality" with her to Doro's world—to the Americas; she draws on the knowledge she has acquired over generations of learning and living to resist and refuse Doro's control of her body and the future of her descendants.

When, as Kelley offers, African Indigeneity is allowed to persist beyond the middle passage, what it reveals are how logics of elimination and enslavement are not conditions aligned with only one group or another. Rather, the novel makes visible how expropriation and exploitation, land and labor, dispossession and displacement are structural conditions under colonialism and authoritarian fascist regimes that impact all beings, albeit in different ways.[21] Indeed, as Doro's most powerful "wild seed," Anyanwu is afforded more latitude and agency in comparison to those of his people who do not have the value she has for his breeding project, and yet she too is unfree and subject to enslavement and bodily control. Butler brings the reader's attention back to the messiness of structure and agency. She does not allow the reader the relief or hope that freewill, choice, or escape is possible. Rather, as a dystopic novel, she maintains that one's choices are always already constrained by the structures and external forces we operate within and that operate on our bodies. For example, early in the novel, the reader learns, along with Anyanwu, that when she transforms her body into animals, Doro cannot sense her; she becomes invisible to him. Butler allows the reader a moment of hope in the awareness that she could become a dolphin or bird and swim or fly away. Even as the reader is presented with this option and despite her vast power, as long as Doro holds her children and descendants hostage, she will acquiesce to his authority.

Through the interaction between Anyanwu and the Mohawk girl, we see played out on the page how the eliminatory project targeting Indigenous Africans was not the same as the genocidal and, later, assimilatory project targeting Native Americans, and yet both are part and parcel of eliminatory logics. Again, Kelley is instructive on this point; chattel slavery as a structure "[eliminated] the culture, identity, and consciousness while preserving the body for labor."[22] In the novel, the Mohawk girl and Anyanwu's bodies are essential to Doro's project, and as long as he gets what he wants, he does not care about eliminating the culture, identity, and consciousness of his "people." In part, his disinterest in differences according to race, nation, or tribe are subordinate to a person's breeding potential—to their reproductive value. And even in this moment of mutual recognition—the Indigenous African seeing similarities with the Indigenous North American—Butler does not provide the Mohawk girl the same level of agency to refuse elimination and assimilation that is afforded to Anyanwu. Rather, Anyanwu wonders if the Mohawk girl will reject her Indianness and consent to elimination. Here then is a moment in the novel when an alliance between two displaced and dispossessed Indigenous women could be formed, and yet Butler retreats; Anyanwu's story continues while the Mohawk girl vanishes.

What I find provocative about this scene is how Butler relies on this Native character to draw the reader's attention to Anyanwu's Indigeneity and Indigenous notions of relationality—relationship to ancestors, language, culture, and land. In drawing out this connection, Butler opens up the possibility for a political alliance to form between these two Indigenous women as allies or coconspirators, an alliance that at its core is about trying to protect individual and collective relationships to Indigenous ancestors, languages, cultures, and lands. And while there is a moment for mutual recognition between two Indigenous women, Butler just as quickly closes down the possibility and the Mohawk girl is eliminated from the story never to appear again.

Joint Action and Visioning an AlterNative Future

> Writing prompt #2: Butler ends the novel with Anyanwu making peace with Doro and preparing to move her family to California. Write a short story that tells the story of Anyanwu's family in California that integrates the lessons of visiting, understanding, joint action, and treaty.

Political theorists Noomi Matthiesen and Jacob Klitmøller, drawing on Hannah Arendt's theory for moral action, argue that moral action derived through visiting and understanding is important but not sufficient on its own, in part because visiting and understanding do not tell us what to *do*. Thinking with Arendt's theory for moral action, they write, "Action is constituted by a doubleness: the singular beginning of a unique subject *and* the joint enterprise of seeing an activity through."[23] For Arendt, visiting and understanding are necessary preconditions for joint action because we can never know the other, and as such, taking action is a continual cycle of visiting, understanding, thinking, and action. While Matthiesen and Klitmøller, with Arendt, are working at the level of the individual, scaling this model up to ever larger spheres proves difficult. I couple Leanne Simpson's notion of treaty with Arendt as a way to think about joint action as more than a process between individuals. A relational theory of treaty, as Simpson posits, opens up possibilities for joint action emerging toward constellations of co-resistance.[24] Unlike treaty as contract that presumes certainty, Simpson's model is a process that people must engage in moment to moment, day after day, generation after generation.

Leanne Simpson, in *Dancing on our Turtle's Back*, asserts that treaty is a relationship based on sharing and mutual benefit. The relationship that is created from treaty must maintain balance and work toward balance.[25] Creating this balance takes patience and persistence to ensure the relationship for the long term. Finally, treaty must be supported by family, community, and nation. To be sure, treaty between Doro and Anyanwu is not possible earlier in the novel, because Doro is not interested in balance. He sees others as either contributing to his breeding program or as useless; he has no hesitation slaughtering a breeder whose reproductive use has ended. It is not until he is confronted with the reality that Anyanwu will not submit to him and would rather die than continue living under his control that he is forced to visit and understand Anyanwu as more than wild seed.

While the novel is dystopic, the future is both open ended and hopeful as Anyanwu and Doro make peace in advance of moving her family to California. In their analysis of Black discourses and understandings of Indian Territory in the nineteenth and early twentieth centuries, Tiya Miles and Sharon P. Holland, in *Crossing Waters, Crossing Worlds: The African Diaspora in Indian Country*, contend that Native Americans are both necessary and peripheral to Black notions of freedom associated with Indian Territory. They explain that the geographical imaginary created by Blacks seeking freedom worked to render Indians necessary "because it was the Indian presence that differentiated Indian Territory from the states, and it was also the complex history between Indians and their former black slaves that opened the door for African American settlement; they were peripheral because blacks located Native people at the margins of their new communities."[26] Indeed, we see this representational pattern reproduced in the novel from the Mohawk girl, who functions as a plot device to express Anyanwu's Indigeneity to Thomas, whose death marks the depth of Doro's evil. By book 3, Native characters are fully eliminated from the novel—and from the series.[27] This writing prompt, invites students to do their own visioning forward. To take inspiration from Butler and vision an alterNative future, one where Indigeneity is not peripheral or vanishing but central or foundational to the futures.

As is the case with Butler's dystopic approach in the *Patternmaster* series, hope is not allowed to persist for long. *Mind of My Mind*, the second chronological novel in the series, picks up the story of Doro and Anyanwu in 2010, one 150 years after Anyanwu decides to leave Louisiana and relocate her family to California. As per their treaty, both Doro and Anyanwu have continued their respective breeding/family-making projects. As the novel opens, we learn that the city of Forsyth has become home to both Doro's and Anyanwu's descendants. The two families have lived in relative peace; however, Butler does not allow the reader to dwell in the utopia of peace; *Wild Seed* is a dystopian SF novel, and Butler's version of how this story can end is cataclysmic. In Butler's future, issues associated with the Native-slave-setter triptych are irrelevant to larger concerns about the very future of humanity. In this future, the Patternists—Doro's race of more-than-humans—grow so powerful that they turn humans into slaves. The *Patternmaster Series* ends in a postapocalyptic future where an alien virus transforms a portion of the human population into powerful hybrid beings who come to dominate the North American continent. In this future, a different triptych of power emerges; humans are enslaved, and the superhuman Patternists wage war against the human-alien hybrid Clayarks for control over the future.

Closing Thoughts

By approaching the novel as an Indigenous text, my goal was to reconsider the Native-slave-settler triptych from a relational framework that acknowledges Native peoples' claims, prior occupancy, sovereignty, and nationhood on the lands we now consider to be the United States, while also acknowledging the continuance of African Indigeneity despite enslavement, removal, and dispossession from their homelands on the African continent. My reading of *Wild Seed* sought to demonstrate how African Indigeneity persists, even as it is contrasted with "Indians," who are often figured as plot devices in the novel. I demonstrated how the categories that constitute the triptych continue to have explanatory value for describing how hetero-patriarchal capitalism structures these identity positions as always already in contestation with each other. My intention was to blur the boundaries of these categories to demonstrate how the violence of colonialism, which requires death and replacement, is not our only option.

The writing prompts are not just about visioning futures and itineraries that produce flight paths out of the colonial, racist, sexist, ableist presents into otherwise futures. I also see them as providing students with insights into how to be good ancestors themselves. As John Hausdoerffer, Brooke Parry Hecht, Melissa Nelson, and Katherine Kassouf Cummings assert in the introduction to their edited volume, *What Kind of Ancestor Do You Want to Be?*, we are all ancestors. "Even if we never are remembered or never have children. The question [what kind of ancestor do you want to be?] deepens our awareness of the roots and reach of all of our actions and non-actions. In every moment, whether we like it or not and whether we know it or not, we are advancing values and influencing systems that will continue long past our lifetimes."[28] In asking this question, the editors invite the reader to consider their own transformation or evolution from child into adulthood and into becoming an ancestor. They contend, "Being a good ancestor means understanding how to handle power, when to hold it, when to hand it over, and how to transform it. Just as our bodies, the fundamental sources of our power, will be transformed when breathing ends, so we can begin to practice being ancestors today by recognizing how we want to transform the power—the life force—we've been given."[29] Indeed, the juxtaposition between Doro, who is unambiguously a terrible ancestor, and Anyanwu, who strives to be a good ancestor, offers many lessons. As the novel concludes, Doro and Anyanwu make peace, and in this process, another lesson for how to vision an otherwise future unfolds.

The writing prompts provide students with an opportunity to devise a flight path out of the confines of settler colonialism. Arendt's notion of visiting and understanding provide an alterNative framework for helping students to "[develop] their own voice and ability to take responsibility."[30] The novel provides illustrative examples of how to engage in joint action. And the writing/creative assignments are an invitation for students to take the insights and lessons of the past and reconfigure them and remember them differently to envision other ways of being and alterNative futures. They have an opportunity to take flight not as a move to innocence but toward moral action.

NOTES

1 Octavia E. Butler, *Wild Seed* (New York: Popular Library, 1980), 196.
2 Leanne Betasamosake Simpson, *As We Have Always Done: Indigenous Freedom through Radical Resistance* (Minneapolis: University of Minnesota Press, 2017), 18.
3 I do not italicize Native Hawaiian terms.
4 For the full definition, see Mary Kawena Pukui and Samual H. Elbert, *Hawaiian Dictionary: Revised and Enlarged Edition* (Honolulu: University of Hawaiʻi Press, 1986).
5 For a fuller discussion of the meaning of each, see the introduction to Noelani Goodyear-Kaopua, Ikaika Hussey, and Erin Kahunawaikaʻala Wright, eds., *A Nation Rising: Hawaiian Movements for Life, Land, and Sovereignty* (Durham, NC: Duke University Press, 2014).
6 Simpson, *As We Have Always Done*, 17.
7 In an interview, Butler describes *Wild Seed* as a *science* fiction novel because the character Anyanwu is grappling with medical science. Randall Kenan, "An Interview with Octavia E. Butler," *Callaloo* 14, no. 2 (1991): 495–504, doi:10.2307/2931654.k.
8 For discussion about the difference between allies and accomplices see Indigenous Action, "Accomplices Not Allies: Abolishing the Ally Industrial Complex," May 4, 2014, www.Indigenousaction.org.
9 Butler, *Wild Seed*, 115.
10 Ibid., 114.
11 Ibid., 278.
12 Robin D. G. Kelley, "The Rest of Us: Rethinking Settler and Native," *American Quarterly* 69, no. 2 (June 26, 2017): 268, doi:10.1353/aq.2017.0020.
13 Audra Simpson, "Consent's Revenge," *Cultural Anthropology* 31, no. 3 (August 18, 2016): 326–33, doi:10.14506/ca31.3.02.
14 Ibid., 327–28.
15 Tiya Miles and Sharon P. Holland, "Introduction: Crossing Waters, Crossing Worlds," in *Crossing Waters, Crossing Worlds: The African Diaspora in Indian Country* (Durham, NC: Duke University Press, 2006), 3.
16 Simpson, *As We Have Always Done*, 231.
17 Cynthia G. Franklin, Njoroge, and Suzanna Reiss, "Tracing the Settler's Tools: A Forum on Patrick Wolfe's Life and Legacy," *American Quarterly* 69, no. 2 (June 26, 2017): 239, doi:10.1353/aq.2017.0017.
18 Ibid.
19 Kelley, "The Rest of Us," 268.
20 Robinson quoted in Kelley, "The Rest of Us," 269.

21 I am responding here to Wolfe's claim that settler colonialism mobilizes structures of race that align land with Native Americans and Aboriginal Australians and labor with Blacks in the United States. While I agree that the dominant discourses of racial triangulation that centers land in the relationship between Native Americans and settlers and labor in the relationship between settler colonialism and Blacks—people of African descent—my purpose in this essay is to acknowledge the hegemony of this framework while also recognizing how it erases histories of Native enslavement for labor and Black dispossession from land. Patrick Wolfe, "Land, Labor, and Difference: Elementary Structures of Race," *American Historical Review* 106, no. 3 (June 2001): 866–905, doi:10.2307/2692330.

22 Kelley, "The Rest of Us," 268.

23 Ibid., 195.

24 For a thorough discussion of a constellation of co-resistance see Simpson, *As We Have Always Done*.

25 In *Dancing*, Simpson theorizes breastfeeding and childrearing as treaty. I realize that the contexts are different; however, I am extending Simpson's insights to the novel because her purpose was to go beyond legal notions of treaty to consider how treaty is about relationality, sharing, and mutual benefit. She argues that treaty is not possible where there is no balance within the relationship. See pages 106–8.

26 Miles and Holland, "Introduction: Crossing Waters, Crossing Worlds," 7.

27 To be sure, Anyanwu's move to California in the 1850s does not map exactly with this larger geographical imaginary describe by Miles and Holland who identify Indian territory was Oklahoma. But again, the specific facts are secondary to the gesture Butler makes toward reality; it is enough of a gesture to help the reader make the connection between California and Indian territory. As Miles and Holland also note, making the association of Indian Territory with the West elides how the eastern part of the north American continent is also Indian territory.

28 John Hausdoerffer, Brooke Parry Hecht, Melissa K. Nelson, and Katherine Kassouf Cummings, *What Kind of Ancestor Do You Want to Be?* (Chicago: University of Chicago Press, 2021).

29 Ibid.

30 Noomi Matthiesen and Jacob Klitmøller, "Encountering the Stranger: Hannah Arendt and the Shortcomings of Empathy as a Moral Compass," *Theory and Psychology* 29, no 2 (March 1, 2019): 196.

15

Creating Intuitively

The Art and Flow of Intuitive Social Science

BRITTANY FRIEDMAN AND MICHAEL L. WALKER

During the 1980s through the 1990s, the overhead projector was a staple in classrooms. This was an especially useful tool in math and geography classes. A problem would be written in black; the proper algebraic formula might be written in blue, a wrong step in solving it written in red, and the correct steps written in green. Each color was on a different transparency, each of which could be overlaid or removed to ensure students followed along with how to solve the problem. Geography teachers used separate transparencies for land and water features, adding layer upon transparency layer to provide new information about a given region. The whole point was to focus one's attention on processual steps and/or important characteristics—that is, to explain.

We have the same mandate in sociology, and we have our own transparencies: gender, race, class, age, groups, social exchange, and so forth. Most of us specialize in one or two transparencies, and good scholars produce work that focuses our attention on neglected aspects of a given social circumstance. The best use of transparencies in social science is not chauvinistic in preferring one overlay or another, and the worst instances are when scholars overlook the relevancy of other layers of information and explanation. Our goal should not be to show that gender was missed or that "*A-ha!* Group identities are once again at play!" any more than a geography teacher should be trying to show that hills really matter most. Are water features more important than rocky formations? The question is silly, but sociology has a tradition of such questions, hierarchically organizing transparencies of information when our charge is to consider as much information as is possible and necessary to better explain what is happening and why.

In the coming pages, we make our pitch for what we call an intuitive social science: an ontological, epistemological, and methodological stance that takes seriously sentiment and mood through sensing transparencies (touch, taste, sight, sound, and smell) married to imagination and intuition as heuristics. The social world is, after all, sensed and not merely cognitively constructed. Intuition and imagination can help us uncover mood and patterned social realities. Mood often dictates social behavior; and sentiment can inform the truthfulness of a study. Indeed, sentiment and mood are elemental contributions to knowledge, not novelties to be trotted out for more poetic writing. We begin with an analysis of why intuitive research tends to be devalued. As we will show, the standard form of much sociological work (questions posed, research design, method, and a mechanical style of presenting arguments) has roots in positivism and Victorian philosophies that pit formality in zerosum diametric opposition to sentiment and mood as scientific elements. Philosophies of race and racism, we shall see, are woven throughout the preference for mechanical writing and against intuitive social science. Still, there are examples of intuitive social science, and we intend to highlight the tenets thereof.

From Positivism and Postpositivism to Intuitive Social Science

The critiques of positivism are legion.[1] There are more disagreements and variants concerning positivism than there is consensus on the philosophy's contemporary meaning, but some throughlines include beliefs that sociology can and should be value free, objective, and unemotional.[2] Leading critiques of positivism emerged within the postpositivism movement, led by feminists, women of color intersectionality scholars, and scholars of race and ethnicity.[3] For example, feminist philosopher Sandra Harding's "strong objectivity" recognized the lack of bias recognition, humanness, and emotionality among positivists, which as a scientific process was institutionalized and legitimated by elite White men who formulated positivism as a sexist and racist approach to science.[4] The groundbreaking contributions from postpositivism proposed that scholars commit to the difficult work of acknowledging that the social location of the researcher shapes questions, methods, analyses, and results, while remaining in pursuit of objective findings.[5] We build on the postpositivism movement to advance a step further, by centering a key point we feel is missing from their calls for a new process beyond positivism.

We propose an intuitive social science to argue that it is the centering of intuition and imagination to the process of research design, analyses, and data presentation that is crucial to producing findings and writing that accurately reflect the social location of the researcher and the researched, while instilling within the reader a connection to both.

An intuitive social science builds on the critique that scholars operating in a positivist tradition tend to approach social science in a mechanical (unemotional and "ghostly") manner.[6] Specifically, the research design, writing, and professional presentations in sociology are stripped of emotion, and instead of being an affected participant within, and an observer or investigator of, social phenomena, the scholar is apparitional, floating through social scenes between and beyond the "participants." The researcher is at once there and not there.

The text may be full of theoretical insights and useful concepts packaged in writing that, in the extreme, "kill[s] the person" and leaves only forces, properties, and variables to do the job of explaining social life.[7] To be sure, whether a researcher analyzes and writes through a positive process or an intuitive one is partly a matter of the author's goals for the reader. As much as it is a philosophy of science, positivism is simultaneously a style of questioning, method, and data presentation, one that is mechanical in its focus to convince the reader of the scholar's professionalism, expertise, reliability, and objectivity. Positivism demands lack of emotion and lack of humanness of the researcher and the researched, to provoke the reader to feel trust in the researcher and their findings, privileging a researcher who now appears devoid of a social location. Positivism celebrates and centers this false belief that social science is best performed by robots who lack intuitive knowing as the baseline for their ontological (realities studied), epistemological (knowledge of reality), and methodological (strategy for truth(s) seeking) scaffolding as social scientists. Researchers analyzing and writing through an intuitive process, on the other hand, have as one of their many goals the provocation of a feeling of humanness for readers. Whichever style one chooses, the researcher is making ontological, epistemological, and methodological decisions. Does network structure matter here? Do race relations factor into what we are seeing? Is this a matter of relative social status? Did mood constrain how a given social interaction unfolded? Was the setting troubling, invigorating, arousing, or dangerous for the researcher?[8] What questions could not be pursued in this context? Each question implies a decision as to whether a new transparency will add information towards the goal of 1) informing credentialism by provoking dry shallow realities *or instead*, 2) provoking humanness to inform patterned social realities. We suggest an intuitive social science offers us a chance to fully explore the latter.

Let us consider two examples of positive writing that are, perhaps, not usually thought of as such: sociologist Erving Goffman's *Asylums* and sociologist W. E. B. Du Bois's *The Philadelphia Negro*.[9] In Goffman's view, the point of participant observation is to experientially subject oneself "to the set of contingencies that play upon a set of individuals, so that you can physically and ecologically penetrate their circle of response to their social situation, or their work situation, or their ethnic situation or whatever."[10] Indeed, he set for himself that very goal in *Asylums*: "to learn about the social world of the hospital inmate, as this world is subjectively experienced by him."[11] No doubt, *Asylums* is a sociological classic and important study that resonates today in part *because* Goffman was concerned with capturing subjective experiences. Still, Goffman is a ghost in his study. While brilliant in his harrowing descriptions of life in a mental health hospital, his diction is distant and expository without sentiment.

These are, we contend, epistemological and methodological decisions by Goffman. *Asylums* is full of wonderfully generative theoretical nuggets. We learn of a social world from an organizational and institutional perspective, in terms of "career," and through a dozen or so other transparencies. Each adds to the knowledge of the subjective experience of the mental health patient. We do not, however, get a sense of how Goffman felt about the patients he encountered, the hospital itself, or the staff, and we learn little of how mood was emplaced or how mood contributed to social behavior. Goffman is there and not there, telling us, without the emotional content that would trigger a similar or related feeling in the reader, that patients expressed certain attitudes about being restricted to a mental health hospital. We can, therefore, read, "Among inmates in many total institutions there is a strong feeling that time spent in the establishment is time wasted or destroyed or taken from one's life" and easily come away feeling no particular way about it.[12] And if one feels something, it is likely because of one's own level of empathy for the patients rather than the processual choices made by the scholar. The quoted sentence is explanatory and passionless in its description of what is surely a deeply emotional experience for patients. Rather than *express* to us how lives are destroyed using emotive devices to convey social facts, the text simply *states* that destruction has occurred as a declaration. *Asylums*, while brilliant in its theorizing and substantive contribution, is an example of how it is quite possible to be concerned with subjective experience while ignoring the researcher's own feelings about the matter—all while talking (mechanically) about the feelings of the patients.

Du Bois wrote *The Philadelphia Negro* in a similarly positive voice.[13] This sociological classic is a study wed to positive tenets that presents the state of the union for African Americans in Philadelphia during the 1890s. Covering broad-view matters like federal initiatives, city planning, styles of social organization, and the start of chattel slavery in the United States to matters of basic social living like food, drink, and family life, *The Philadelphia Negro* is a catholic examination of a people in time. Du Bois provided statistics on education, commentary on race relations and how racism constrained participation in labor markets for African Americans, rates of marriage, divorce, and widowing; he gave us descriptions of housing and city conditions—of patterns of crime. All this he presented with restrained adjectival writing. History, institutions, organizations, interpersonal relations: Du Bois delivered a complete study, and yet the heart of the book largely ignores emotional life and mood, and there are sparingly few sentimental statements in the text. On his observations of several saloons in the Seventh Ward between 8:00 p.m. and 10:00 p.m. on Saturdays, Du Bois wrote:

> It was impractical to make this count simultaneously or to cover the whole ward, but eight or ten [saloons] were watched each night. The results are a rough measurement of the drinking habits in this ward. . . . Of those entering these saloons at this time a part carried away liquor— mostly beer in tin buckets. . . . The observers stationed near these saloons saw, in the two hours they were there, 79 drunken persons.[14]

Following these points and an interesting series of raw observational data entries, Du Bois offered an assessment of the potential economic impact of drinking. And while there is some sense of mood in those data entries, the final product, *The Philadelphia Negro*, is stripped of the place-time shared feelings between participants and also Du Bois, or an assessment thereof. We might imagine the music, police-citizen interactions, whether it was cold or warm, whether there was a sense of danger or tension in the air, or whether the moods were generally celebratory. We can imagine almost anything we want from the analyses Du Bois included, but imagining is a task he left to us because he decided neither to convey his sentiments nor to imprint within readers a feeling one way or another.

Control versus Expressiveness

To this point, we have contended that approaches to knowledge-seeking are a matter of epistemological stance—that social scientific "facts" do not exist outside of what one argues is knowledge.[15] Positivism is but one such knowledge style and also an ontological and methodological stance (altogether positive processes), and there are certain transparencies—that is, analytical perspectives—that are considered necessarily outside of a positive tradition. The usual character of positive processes is one of emotional distance—distance from the subjective lives of the participants, from the mood that sets social behavior on one path or another, from authorial sentiment, and from imagination. These distances are part of a pageantry meant to project scientific objectivity. Put another way, positive processes are designed to demonstrate emotional restraint as a virtue rather than expressiveness with the understanding that the latter is somehow unscientific, irrational, and something better suited for the arts instead of the cool and collected scientist who is swayed by "facts" and not "feelings."

It should be noted, however, that emotional restraint versus expressiveness belongs to a debate that is much larger (and older) than disagreements about positivism in social science.[16] In many social arenas, we find value systems that disparage and discredit people who are expressive while valorizing demonstrations of emotional control. The degree to which restraint is favored varies, but in the worlds of politics, sports, medicine, and corporate business (among others), we find professionalism defined, in part, by one's ability to control emotional expressions.[17] Just as often, our society is steeped in emotional restraint that has been racialized and gendered as an ideological component of the civility and human progress embodied by White men.[18]

Often in a not so hidden manner, normative arguments against expressiveness include beliefs about what it means to be civilized, masculine, and White.[19] Generally, the more expressive a person is, the more feminine, the less civilized or evolved, the wilder (i.e., the less self-regulated), and the less European and respectable the person is thought to be. Indeed, the more expressive, the less likely one is to be taken seriously. Thus, during the early 1800s through the early 1900s, when Victorian culture dominated White American society, Black people were generally thought of as the "female" of the races.[20] In "Lecture VII" of his well-received text, *Lectures on Man*, evolutionary biologist Charles Darwin's contemporary and adherent, zoologist and geologist Carl Vogt, contrasted Black people with Germans specifically and White people more generally. The chapter is a bit like descending into a filthy pseudo-scientific White male fantasy that draws intersections between women, children, Black people, and animals to glorify White masculine domination. Some of the highlights include:

> The grown up Negro partakes, as regards his intellectual faculties, of the nature of the child, the female, and the senile White. He manifests a propensity to pleasure, music, dancing, physical enjoyments, and imitation, while his inconstancy of impressions and all the feelings are those of the child. . . . The Negro resembles the female in his love to children, his family, and his cabin. . . . In his native country . . . we may boldly assert that the whole race has, neither in the past nor in the present, performed anything tending to the progress of humanity or worthy of preservation.[21]

This is a remarkable—if not all too common at the time—mode of thinking. What can be said about what should have been massive cognitive turmoil from holding all these ideas in one's mind at once? On the one hand, the United States had descended into civil war over chattel slavery and the institutionalized horrors that White folk visited upon Black bodies, minds, and spirits. The genocidal brutality of Manifest Destiny was in full swing, and the criminal destruction of African nations had long been underway and would continue. The social Darwinist needed only to find an honest mirror to see uncivilized feeders on unbridled passions. But we can make a strong argument that social Darwinists and other racists understood very well that they were peddling junk theories, for if it were not so, there would be no need to erect laws and support domestic terrorism to keep Black people from competing fairly against any other race.

On the other hand, while Vogt laid bare the social Darwinist claim that Black people (like women, it was argued) are genetically predisposed to the arts and emotional expression, the implicit counterclaim is that White men are not. And to assert that an emotionally repressed apparently rhythmless people are better suited for world domination is best understood as an aspiration born in envy of what is thought to be missing from their own genetic code. The notion calls to mind a quote from composer and jazz pianist Duke Ellington after a 1944 tax levied against clubs with dancing transformed jazz from a harmonious blend of music and dance to the sit-down easy listening that it is most known as today: "I think people who don't dance, or who never did dance, don't really understand the beat.... I know musicians who don't and never did dance, and they have difficulty communicating."[22] Ellington's humorous anecdote reverses the typical relationship between expressiveness and intelligence where creative expressiveness means poor cognitive capacities.

And this is the larger point: the sticky residue of Victorian ideals and social Darwinism yet remains in American culture. It is evident in the recurring Hollywood trope of the Black entertaining fool.[23] It was part of the leading discourse of the uplift movement, which mobilized the same race-gender admixture of intelligence, self-restraint, and civility found among social Darwinists.[24] It has been a theme in professional sports—especially in class-privileged and exclusionary sports like golf and tennis, where emotional restraint is built into rules of decorum. Thus, Arthur Ashe was held as a model of gentility against the likes of Jimmy Connors, and Serena Williams became the object of ridicule for arguing with an official during her 2018 US Open match against Naomi Osaka.[25] And it has long been a subject in football, a rougher sport, where Black athletes have been lionized for athleticism while being funneled away from the quarterback position (a supposedly thinking man's position) or graded on a slant for being as dangerous with their running as they are with throwing.[26]

In sum, then, positive processes foster fruit from the tree with roots in the politics of respectability, masculine civility, and racial hierarchy in ways that tend to place a higher valuation on emotional restraint relative to expressiveness and that set intelligence in zero-sum opposition to creative evocativeness. Our lane, however, is a social scientific one, and for all its virtues, the epistemological lifeblood of a positive social science leaves out information crucial to the fulfillment of a sociological mandate: to explain. To a stack of transparencies that include social exchange, race, gender, and power, to name some—each contributing a form of knowledge to researchers studying a given social topography, as it were—we propose mood, sentiment, imagination, and intuition as social scientific knowledge transparencies that inform as much as they evoke. We propose an intuitive social science. Such a social science is processual—it informs the definition of realities, strategies for undertaking a quest for knowledge, and the resulting data presentation—creating a finished product that evokes mood and feelings from the reader.

Toward an Intuitive Social Science

It is, we believe, a common refrain shared among scholars that sociologists cannot write very well or that we do not write in an interesting way.[27] Few would argue with the latter statement. Who among us has not had our initial excitement dashed from our hearts when a researcher droned through incredible data in a manner that seemed designed to evoke the color beige? The problem, as we see it, is more than a matter of writing with precision, typing a metaphor or two, or even telling a better story. It is about rethinking knowledge itself and tapping into a more emotive and sentimental process of data collection and analysis and thus into a more expressive style of data presentation.

We are not the first to make this kind of call. Anthropologist Renato Rosaldo's *Culture & Truth* is an anthropological standard bearer with applicability across social scientific disciplines and is closest to what we mean by an intuitive social science. Among the methodological and writing charges he set for social scientists is the value of using personal emotion to interrogate social surroundings, the need to put culture in action—to think processually, and to use language and narratives that are congruent between the author and participants.[28] Sociologist Andrew Abbott echoes much of Rosaldo's interests with the exception that Abbott actively urges against "narrative" as explanation. The writer should instead be concerned with the emotional content of a situation and evoke feelings within the reader while focusing attention on "momentaneity"—social circumstance in a moment in time—without trying to explain. The goal is to convey mood, to analytically encircle an event and all its complexities without feeling compelled to explain it as an example of something else.[29]

Sociologist Michael L. Walker's "organic ethnography" shares elements with Abbott and Rosaldo; however, he did not abandon "narrative" in Abbott's terms, and his method involves toggling between the peculiar and the familiar to draw connections beyond the subject of his study and broader sociological interests.[30] Sociologist Loïc Wacquant's description of an "enactive ethnography" intersects the methods described by Walker, Abbott, and Rosaldo with yet another difference: Wacquant's focus on the epistemological gains reaped from the *doing* of the fieldwork is disconnected from the presentation of those gains in writing.[31] Finally, sociologist Reuben Miller similarly exhorts us to learn through our bodies and to not separate the soul from the body in our social scientific method. Going further, he invites us to embrace proximity as a "gift" that can teach us more about our participants and their social circumstances than could ever be gained by remaining emotionally detached.[32]

With Abbott as the exception, each of the aforementioned scholars makes the argument that the "subject/object divide that animates much of our social scientific inquiry is artificial."[33] In one way or another, each invites us to pay close attention to mood and sentiment, to include within our knapsack of analytical transparencies those that provoke readers to feelings while maintaining rigorous analysis. But we do not advocate provocation for provocation's sake. Readers should be provoked toward a better understanding of the subject of analysis through the senses and the soul.[34] We encourage scholars to ground the content of their analyses in what humans (not variables) experience. Put the action back into the bodies of people. Do not abandon abstractions but tether them to a sensed reality, one that is recognizable as a human condition. Reject the false dichotomy between creative expressiveness and rationalism, the sensual and the logical, subjective and objective. There is a symbiotic relationship between the rational mind and emotion that cannot be undone without sacrificing an understanding of what sets the stage for how social behavior will unfold. This is the very justification of social psychological theories of emotions. We know that emotion, cognition, and behavior are braided together.[35]

In the next subsections, we sketch the contours of an intuitive social science. It is intuition that governs the ability to understand social processes, discover applicable abstract theory, and connect both creatively to reach knowledge points. We introduce what we mean by mood, sentiment, imagination, and intuition, weaving examples of the outcome of intuitive work throughout. Finally, we offer concluding thoughts and a template for moving forward with intuitive research.

Mood and Sentiment

> When I examine myself and my methods of thought I come to the conclusion that the gift of fantasy has meant more to me than my talent for absorbing positive knowledge.
> —Albert Einstein, Nobel laureate in physics[36]

In any given social situation, race, ethnicity, gender, class, age, and relative social status transparencies *might* matter. One is hard pressed, however, to imagine a social situation in which *mood*, the place-time temporary state of feeling and thinking shared among social actors, can be ignored without losing something in the analysis. Consider the following passages from sociologist Michael Walker:

> I was in the dayroom when six prisoners returned to the housing unit from in-custody court appearances. Apparently, their respective cases had not been adjudicated, so the prisoners went about life in the housing unit until their next scheduled court appearance.
>
> I was in the dayroom when six prisoners of various ethnicities returned to the housing unit from in-custody court appearances. Often called "court bodies" by deputies, the prisoners had been gone for most of the day, and they looked tired on the way to their respective cells. Once rested, they would resume usual social interactions.

I was zombie-ing through a game of checkers with Herc when the slider opened and all eyes turned toward the sally port. I hadn't noticed how noisy it was until the din settled just then. The "court bodies," as deputies called them, were tottering in. It was nearly 5:00 p.m., and they had been gone since 2:30 a.m. They looked emaciated—robbed of normal sociability—the five or six of them. As usual, their legs shuffled their bodies straightaway to their cells, skipping the never-guaranteed chance to shower, use a phone, or hang out. None of us troubled them about what had happened. There were a few "what up" head gestures, but we kept our questions to ourselves: Did you get to eat? Who did you see? When do you go back to court? What happened? Were there fights? Who was involved? All of that would come out eventually. In the meantime, the court bodies retreated to their respective cells for chrysalis and, hours later, they would emerge again as jail residents. Anyhow, the moment passed, and my partner in opposition to tedium was looking down, waiting on me to take my turn. We picked up where we left off, thrusting round plastic pieces at each other without strategies.[37]

Each passage conveys the same basic information: prisoners—that is, "jail residents"—returned to a housing unit following in-custody court appearances. That is in the first passage overlayed with the number of prisoners and that their cases had been continued for one reason or another. However, the stripped down, just-some-of-the-facts description in the first passage is deceptively simple. We are left with the sense that prisoners walked back into the housing unit and immediately returned to the normal flow of social behavior. The second passage suggests otherwise. We learn that "the prisoners had been gone for most of the day, that prisoners with in-custody court appearances were called 'court bodies,' and that they looked tired on the way to their respective cells." Thus, we get a transparency that adds information missing in the first passage: temporality. We also get a sense of why it might be that the returning prisoners did not immediately rejoin the flow of interaction in the housing unit. They were tired after being gone all day. The third passage provides more information than the first two, and not just because it is longer. We are given a more specific timespan than the second passage's "most of the day." Most significantly, the passage gives us mood. That the action temporarily paused when the prisoners returned indicates the importance of their return. Instead of telling us that the prisoners "went about life in the housing unit" or that "they looked tired on the way to their respective cells," we are given an image of "emaciated" bodies being "shuffled" by the will of their legs into a housing unit that was, until that very moment, loud with cacophonic conversations and noises. The sudden quiet and questions that filled the minds of those in the housing unit help to convey the mood while the sharp return to a game of checkers helps to convey the author's *sentiment* or *emotional stance toward a situation*.[38] He is not unaffected by the goings on, but the whole scene is bookended by the painful dullness of life in the housing unit.

More than just adding information, the three passages indicate different ontologies, epistemologies, and methodologies that led to their creation. The second passage is fundamentally the same as the first—both presenting a decidedly unemotional view of the moment. Both treat sentiment and mood as irrelevant knowledge. The third passage, however, is sentimental and impassioned, giving us emotional insight into more than just prisoners returning to a housing unit.

Imagination

> For after the jazzman has learned the fundamentals of his instrument and the traditional techniques of jazz—the intonations, the mute work, manipulation of the timbre, the body of traditional styles—he must then find himself, must be reborn, must find, as it were, his soul. All this through achieving that subtle identification between his instrument and his deepest drives which will allow him to express his own unique ideas and his own unique voice.
>
> —Ralph Ellison, National Book Award winner in fiction[39]

If fortunate, graduate students survive graduate training having gained an understanding of their specialties without sacrificing imagination on the altar of the god of false objectivity. Imagination has little to do with the impossible mandate to find something original to say—especially since so many "new ideas" are merely unread refurbished ideas updated for a new concept marketplace. On this point, the goal should be, as Abbott stated in a tongue-in-cheek way, "to say something interesting— perhaps even true—about social life."[40] Such is the goal of imagination:

the invention of an inventive way of sensing, understanding, and explaining the social world. To use one's imagination is to recognize that social theories are often imaginary social worlds rendered linguistically.[41] There is no actual magic in social theory. The magic is in the intuitive nudges that lead us to create said theory. The magic is as much about what we believe or what rings true as it is in whatever evidence can be marshaled in support of a theory. Most "theories" are either untestable or will never be "tested," anyhow. Given this, it can be helpful to think of social theory as an imaginary world. For instance, no one bumps into the micro-interactional plane or is stumped to get around macro-interactional "structures." These are imaginative analytical tools that we use to create an image of the way society might work. There are others. We may conceive of a "field" of social worlds.[42] We can imagine social dimensions with forces and variables intersecting and interacting to produce a "geometry" of social outcomes—none of which even requires humans.[43] Indeed, there is no such thing as "up" or "down" in the universe, but that does not stop us from imagining there to be a proper orientation of the Earth in space. In each instance, we build from imagination to understand and explain.

To a very large degree, critical theories take imagination more seriously than many other sociological perspectives. What is critical in critical theory? The point is to subject the assumptions of a method, perspective, or analysis to an exacting interrogation to reveal and replace systems of domination with emancipatory modes of social science.[44] Arguably, critical race theorists have been more committed than others to employing imagination in their scholarship. See, for instance, legal scholar Derrick Bell's *The Space Traders*.[45] Part science fiction, part intuition, and full imaginative social science, *The Space Traders* is (among other things) a revealing narrative about the staying power of racism.

In fact, Bell often used allegory as a method that permits a creative flow of social scientific ideas. Musicians and artists speak of this feeling often—a creative flow—and if you look at their public interviews, scholars in the natural sciences such as physics, chemistry, and medicine speak of the joy they feel when engaged in the deeply intuitive process known as research. As social scientists, we shy away from this admission, not because we do not feel it as we engage in our work but because we fear it goes against our institutional credibility and our disciplines' explicit and subconscious desire to apply techniques from the natural sciences to the social world. And we interpret this desire as rationally dominated, but in the words of Nobel laureate physicist Albert Einstein himself and other well-known leaders of the natural sciences, "fantasy," "imagination," "magic," and thus intuition, are the building blocks that shape what pioneering natural scientists believe to be possible and drive their method for discovering the world through experiments. When we stifle this imaginative joy from publicly emerging within our knowledge quest and methods, we transfer this practice to our students, punishing them if we perceive they are unable to strictly adhere to the tenets of positivism and its claims at subverting the subjective.

However, natural scientists themselves admit to straying far away from the full tenets of positivism when undertaking the creative process of research—meaning, the scientific method allows room for and works best when intuition is allowed to emerge as a guide along each step rather than falsely being suppressed within the creator, who is then unable to innovate beyond anything they've ever known. When we come up with ideas we have never heard of or seen before or revamp ideas into a new arrangement, it is our intuition—our creative power—that makes this possible, not simply our rational power that is inherently obsessed with the past as opposed to the present. Mind-seated knowledge is multifaceted and flows from every corner of the psyche and body until it makes its way out of our minds and onto a page in the form of a prospectus for research. The current emphasis on positivism as a method to undertake our investigations creates corners around possibility that cage the very hearts that we need to fully make sense of what we sense around us.

Intuition

> The function of art is to do more than tell it like it is—it's to imagine what is possible.
> —bell hooks, winner of the American Book Award[46]

Intuition is variously called a "gut feeling," "an instinct," "Spidey-sense" (for those familiar with Spiderman), and "raised hairs" on one's nape. The physician listens to a patient's narrative with its conflicting indicators, follows the appropriate diagnostic protocol to a particular end, but on a "hunch" from years of experiential wisdom and practice sends the patient to a specialist not indicated by the protocol, where it is learned that, despite the protocol, her intuition was correct. The ethnographer is relieved about new lines of inquiry after getting an incredible response to a question she asked because she *got the sense* that she should ask a participant one—last—question. Intuition is a heuristic that relies on personal experience and circumstantial attunement to discover a next step in terms of method, analysis, theory, and/or writing.

In general, sociologists feel compelled to offer a rational explanation for every methodological and analytical decision made. In many cases, that pressure is proper, but intuition is not opposed to rationality. Mainstream sociologists tend to hinge research on the rational in favor of respectability—to be taken seriously as scientists. This is a failure to reconcile the intuitive with the rational as dually structuring our creative process and is based on fears of scientific illegitimacy and irrelevancy. However, the false distinction between intuition and rationality is a distortion of the creative process because, in fact, it is our intuition that often guides how we make decisions along the way, particularly when it comes to how and when we begin our quest for discovery. Intuition requires no effort except releasing the fear of the unknown and instead celebrating it. Surrendering. What is intuition but an imagining of what could be? With respect to the scientific discovery of knowledge, intuition is a recognition of wonder in a future possibility that reconciles the contextual clues and facts in our present with the courage to leave room for surprise. Once the intuitive downloads are received, it is then up to the discoverer to ground this magic into the material reality that lay before us through decision-making. It is a cyclical process of constant freefall surrender followed by grounded application that produce knowledge and allow us to create an ordered rendering of the world.

Intuitive nudges come to our minds like a ping, either out of nowhere when we are dreaming or at the gym, and in the middle of reading previous literature or workshopping our research with colleagues. For many, our best innovations come when the rational mind is quiet. As Guggenheim Fellow Anne Lamott writes:

> You get your intuition back when you make space for it, when you stop the chattering of the rational mind. The rational mind doesn't nourish

you. You assume that it gives you the truth, because the rational mind is the golden calf that this culture worships, but this is not true. Rationality squeezes out much that is rich and juicy and fascinating.[47]

Some scholars even carry a small notebook with them everywhere to write down intuition-inspired epiphanies that can be integrated into their research once they get back to their lab or desk—and many do not call this intuition but will simply say something akin to, "When it is quiet and I'm not trying to think, ideas just flow to me." Oftentimes, when we are at a crossroads, big or small, intuitive nudges come to us, leading us to choose a particular position. Rather than a one-sided process of rational decision-making, the creative process of research is a cyclical relationship between intuition and rationality. However, it is our intuition that ultimately sparks change and innovation when faced with puzzles in our work. For example, when unable to choose a topic, questioning our field sites, unsure of our methods, workshopping our ideas with colleagues, or reviewing previous literature, these are all steps in the creative process that require us to listen to ourselves to make final judgment calls on how to operationalize rationality. When asked whether his discoveries were the result of intuition or rationality, Einstein replied "Both. . . . I sometimes feel I am right, but do not know it . . . . I'm enough of an artist to draw freely on my imagination, which I think is more important than knowledge. Knowledge is limited. Imagination encircles the world."[48] Einstein went on to further explain that "certainly we should take care not to make the intellect our god; it has, of course, powerful muscles, but no personality. It cannot lead, it can only serve; and it is not fastidious in its choice of a leader."[49] As we cling to the legacy of positivism in sociology, we simultaneously stifle innovation and ignore the reality that intuition and rationality co-produce the creative processes of our research endeavors when it comes to decisions about and execution of method, style, and data presentation.

Intentionally Intuitive

It may seem like cheating to be imaginative and intuitive and to use transparencies of sentiment and mood when doing ethnography. After all, the author should know a setting's mood and be able to express sentiment based upon having been there. But how does one capture and convey mood without having been there? An intuitive social science works when the researcher is intentional about intuition and imagination. Below is an exemplary excerpt from sociologist Brittany Friedman:

> We are all haunted. One way or another the ghosts find us. It is easier for them to uncover our whereabouts when we live in a cage, when there is nowhere else to be. In 1965, Hugo "Yogi Bear" Pinell was sentenced three years to life. Ghosts surrounded him. He did not know he would spend a lifetime in darkness. No one imagines they will live for forty-five years in solitary confinement. Because if you knew, if they warned you, the panic might set in. Soon after, either hopeless paralysis or survival could follow, and they wouldn't want to take a chance on the latter. The gates at San Quentin State Prison brought the sea breeze closer, though it was, and continues to be, "little more than a warehouse of human flesh." The frigid water did not appear welcoming. It did not look like home. But where was home, anyhow? Hugo knew the dark waters owned him and that now was not the time to feel. Now was not the time to fear. But he couldn't contain the surge, the crisis brewing, raging. Even adults are afraid of the dark. Many at San Quentin will tell you, you should be.[50]

In the simplest terms, the excerpt describes Hugo Pinell's entry to solitary confinement. More than that, the texts respond to the question, What does it *feel* like to be held in solitary confinement? The answer is not just a statement of fact. It is a provocation of emotion—of action. "Because if you knew . . . the panic might set in." The first excerpt gives us a sense of the uncertainty that surrounds restriction to solitary confinement. But, we learn, this is a useful uncertainty—a functional uncertainty that helps to stave off what would likely be panic. Expectation is a form of protection in the sense that through expectation, we create a workable plan for a thing. If one expects to be in solitary for just a little while, one drafts a plan for that. If you learn you will be in solitary confinement for forty-five years, the timespan is unfathomable. A plan cannot be constructed for the innumerable unknowns that come with forty-five years of solitary confinement, and that realization is surely panic inducing. Note the imaginative turn in the excerpt. "We are all haunted. One way or another the ghosts find us." We share in Hugo's predicament, not to the same degree but on a basic human level we can intuit what it means to be beleaguered by past wrongs and fears—our "ghosts." And when do they find us? In our most acutely vulnerable moments—in literal darkness. We learn of all this not through direct quotes from Hugo but from the intuitive wisdom of careful scholarship and the effective use of imagination.

We are also asked to turn our attention to what it felt like to be there. It was cold. Dark. Isolating. There is an interesting play on the meaning of "home." Home is not where we live—not exactly. That is both obvious and simultaneously insightful. Prisoners make a home of their cells while pining for the day that they are released and can go *home*. The issue of home is sandwiched between water metaphors: "the sea breeze"; the "frigid water"; "the dark waters"; and "the surge." "Home" was certainly not those new cold, dark waters surging at Hugo.

Final Thoughts

> There's a contract that I make between myself, the author, and the reader. I have to figure out how to give the reader certain powers of recognition, or his own knowledge, his own feelings, but I provide them, so we're working together.
> —Toni Morrison, Nobel laureate in literature[51]

The goal of this chapter was to trace the outline of an intuitive social science. Our efforts here are preliminary but, we hope, generative in calling for a process that centers intuition and imagination. The central components of intuitive research marry discovery with ontology and epistemology to produce approaches to research design, analysis, and data presentations (whether writing or oratory) that lean into expressiveness—that unbridle humanness. We also advocate for mood and sentiment as transparencies of knowledge worthy of analysis throughout the research process. What sets a situational mood? What ruins mood? How is mood emplaced? How does sentiment contour the presentation of data? These questions invite researchers to use and interrogate the use of intuitive scientific components. We have only hinted at how a complete intuitive research project might unfold. Future intuitive scientific research should lay out how scholars use intuition, mood, imagination, and sentiment to dream up questions, design research, and analyze and present data.

NOTES

1 Smith, *Decolonizing Methodologies: Research and Indigenous Peoples*, 216–20.
2 Abrutyn, "Positivism."
3 For an example, see Collins, *Black Feminist Thought*.
4 Harding, "Strong Objectivity," 332.
5 Reed, "Social Theory," 665.
6 For a discussion of the complexities of social life that positivist approaches fail to fully grasp see Gordon, *Ghostly Matters*
7 Black, "Dreams of a Pure Sociology," 362.
8 See Contreras, "The Broken Ethnographer," 167.
9 Goffman, *Asylums*; Du Bois, *The Philadelphia Negro*.
10 Goffman, "On Field Work," 125.
11 Goffman, *Asylums*, ix.
12 Ibid., 67.
13 As an aside, compare this to Du Bois's other works to see a stark contrast. Yet this work is discussed much more in the discipline of sociology while other works are privileged in disciplines within the humanities.
14 Du Bois, *The Philadelphia Negro*, 278.
15 See Smith, *Decolonizing Methodologies*; and Collins, *Black Feminist Thought*.
16 Kendi, *Stamped from The Beginning*, 15–30, 79–91.
17 See Hall, "Professionalization and Bureaucratization"; McCabe, Reddick, and Demir, "Municipal Professional"; Wynd, "Current Factors."
18 See Bederman, *Manliness & Civilization*; Evetts, "The Sociological Analysis of Professionalism"; Strawbridge, "Darwin and Victorian Social Values"; Young, *Middle-Class Culture in the Nineteenth Century*.
19 See Young, *Middle-Class Culture in the Nineteenth Century*.
20 See Bederman, *Manliness and Civilization*; and Gould, *The Mismeasure of Man*.
21 Vogt, *Lectures on Man*, 192.
22 Malone, *Steppin' on the Blues*, 93.
23 Ibid., 115.
24 See Gaines, *Uplifting the Race*; Higginbotham, *Righteous Discontent*.
25 See Thomas, "The Quiet Militant"; Abad-Santos, "Serena Williams's US Open Fight."
26 See Mercurio and Filak, "Roughing the Passer"; Niven, "Race, Quarterbacks, and the Media."
27 See Abbott, "Against Narrative"; Becker, "Above All, Write with Precision"; Erikson, "On Sociological Writing."
28 See Rosaldo, *Culture and Truth*.
29 See Abbott, "Against Narrative."
30 Walker, *Indefinite*, 17–20.
31 See Wacquant, "For a Sociology of Flesh and Blood."
32 Miller, *Halfway Home*, 295–97.

33 Ibid., 296.
34 See Miller, *Halfway Home*, 283–97; Rosaldo, *Culture and Truth*; and Walker, *Indefinite*, 17–20.
35 Turner and Stets, *The Sociology of Emotions*, 1–23.
36 See Clark, *Einstein*; Einstein, *Out of My Later Years*; Konnikova, "Reclaiming the Sacred Gift."
37 Walker, *Indefinite*, 129.
38 See also Abbott's discussion of "stance" in "Against Narrative."
39 See Ellison, *Shadow and Act*.
40 Abbott, *Methods of Discovery*, 4.
41 For a truly singular study of fantasy, see Caughey, *Imaginary Social Worlds*.
42 For the formulation of field theory, see Bourdieu, *Distinction*.
43 See Black, *Moral Time*.
44 See Zuberi, "Critical Race Theory of Society."
45 See Bell, *Faces at the Bottom of the Well*.
46 See hooks, *Outlaw Culture*.
47 See Lamott, *Bird by Bird*.
48 See Einstein, *Out of My Later Years*; Konnikova, "Reclaiming the Sacred Gift.".
49 See Einstein, *Out of My Later Years*.
50 See Friedman, *Born in Blood*
51 See Akṣapāda, *Living Toni Morrison*.

BIBLIOGRAPHY

Abad-Santos, Alex. "Serena Williams's US Open Fight with Umpire Carlos Ramos, Explained." *Vox*, September 10, 2018.
Abbott, Andrew. "Against Narrative: A Preface to Lyrical Sociology." *Sociological Theory* 25, no. 1 (2007): 67–99.
———. *Methods of Discovery: Heuristics for the Social Sciences*. New York: W. W. Norton, 2004.
Abrutyn, Seth. "Positivism." In *Oxford Bibliographies in Sociology*, edited by Lynette Spillman. Oxford: Oxford University Press, 2022. Article published September 30, 2013. doi:10.1093/obo/9780199756384-0142.
Akṣapāda. *Living Toni Morrison: 425 Wise & Uplifting Verses of America's Beloved That You Should Read* (self-pub., 2019).
Becker, Howard S. "Above All, Write with Precision." *Sociological Inquiry* 78, no. 3 (2008): 412–16.
Bederman, Gail. *Manliness & Civilization: A Cultural History of Gender and Race in the United States, 1880–1917*. Chicago: University of Chicago Press, 1995.
Bell, Derrick. *Faces at the Bottom of the Well: The Permanence of Racism*. New York: Basic Books, 1992.
Black, Donald. "Dreams of a Pure Sociology." *Sociological Theory* 18, no. 3 (2000): 343–67.
———. *Moral Time*. New York: Oxford University Press, 2011.

Bourdieu, Pierre. *Distinction: A Critique of the Judgement of Tastes*. New York: Routledge, 2010.

Caughey, John L. *Imaginary Social Worlds*. Lincoln: University of Nebraska Press, 1984.

Clark, Ronald W. *Einstein: The Life and Times*. New York: Harper Collins, 1984.

Collins, Patricia Hill. *Black Feminist Thought: Knowledge, Consciousness, and the Politics of Empowerment*. New York: Routledge, 2008.

Contreras, Randol. "The Broken Ethnographer: Lessons from an Almost Hero." *Qualitative Sociology* 42 (2019): 161–79.

Du Bois, W. E. B. *The Philadelphia Negro: A Social Study*. Philadelphia: University of Pennsylvania Press, 1899. Reprint, Eastford, CT: Martino Fine Books, 2004.

Einstein, Albert. *Out of My Later Years: The Scientist, Philosopher, and Man Portrayed through His Own Words*. New York: Philosophical Library/Open Road Publishing, 2011.

Ellison, Ralph. *Shadow and Act*. New York: Vintage, 1964.

Erikson, Kai. "On Sociological Writing." *Sociological Inquiry* 78, no. 3 (2008): 399–411.

Evetts, Julia. "The Sociological Analysis of Professionalism: Occupational Change in the Modern World." *International Sociology* 18, no. 2 (2003): 395–415.

Friedman, Brittany. *Born in Blood: Death Work, White Power, and the Rise of the Black Guerilla Family* (tentative title). Chapel Hill: University of North Carolina Press, forthcoming.

Gaines, Kevin K. *Uplifting the Race: Black Leadership, Politics, and Culture in the Twentieth Century*. Chapel Hill: University of North Carolina Press, 1996.

Goffman, Erving. *Asylums: Essays on the Social Situation of Mental Patients and Other Inmates*. New York: Anchor Books, 1961.

———. "On Field Work." *Journal of Contemporary Ethnography* 18 (1989): 123–32.

Gordon, Avery F. *Ghostly Matters: Haunting and the Sociological Imagination*. Minneapolis: University of Minnesota Press, 1997.

Gould, Stephen Jay. *The Mismeasure of Man*. New York: W. W. Norton, 1996.

Hall, Richard H. "Professionalization and Bureaucratization." *American Sociological Review* 33, no. 1 (1968): 92–104.

Harding, Sandra. "Strong Objectivity: A Response to the New Objectivity Question." *Synthese* 103, no. 3 (September 1995): 331–49.

Higginbotham, Evelyn Brooks. *Righteous Discontent: The Women's Movement in the Black Baptist Church 1880–1920*. Cambridge, MA: Harvard University Press, 1993.

hooks, bell. *Outlaw Culture: Resisting Representations*. New York: Routledge, 1994.

Kendi, Ibrahim X. *Stamped from The Beginning: The Definitive History of Racist Ideas in America*. New York: Nation Books, 2016.

Konnikova, Maria. "Reclaiming the Sacred Gift: A Postscript on Humanities and Science." *Scientific American. Literally Psyched* (blog), August 16, 2012. https://blogs.scientificamerican.com.

Lamott, Anne. *Bird by Bird: Some Instructions on Writing and Life*. New York: Anchor Books, 1995.

Malone, Jacqui. *Steppin' on the Blues: The Visible Rhythms of African American Dance*. Urbana: University of Illinois Press, 1996.

McCabe, Barbara Coyle, Christopher G. Reddick, and Tansu Demir. "Municipal Professional: More than Just a Job in Government?" *American Review of Public Administration* 47, no. 8 (2017): 867–80.

Mercurio, Eugenio, and Vincent F. Filak. "Roughing the Passer: The Framing of Black and White Quarterbacks prior to the NFL Draft." *Howard Journal of Communication* 21, no. 1 (2010): 56–71.

Miller, Reuben Jonathan. *Halfway Home: Race, Punishment, and the Afterlife of Mass Incarceration*. New York: Little, Brown, 2021.

Niven, David. "Race, Quarterbacks, and the Media: Testing the Rush Limbaugh Hypothesis." *Journal of Black Studies* 33, no.5 (2005): 684–94.

Reed, Issac. "Social Theory, Post-Post-Positivism and the Question of Interpretation." *International Sociology* 23, no. 5 (September 2008): 665–75.

Rosaldo, Renato. *Culture and Truth: The Remaking of Social Analysis*. Boston: Beacon Press, 1989.

Smith, Linda Tuhiwai. *Decolonizing Methodologies: Research and Indigenous Peoples*. New York: Zed Books, 2021.

Strawbridge, Sheelagh. "Darwin and Victorian Social Values." In *In Search of Victorian Values: Aspects of Nineteenth Century Thought and Society*, edited by E. M. Sigsworth, 102–15. New York: Manchester University Press, 1988.

Thomas, Damion. "'The Quiet Militant': Arthur Ashe and Black Athletic Activism." In *Out of the Shadows: A Biographical History of African American Athletes*, edited by D. K. Wiggins, 279–300. Fayetteville: University of Arkansas Press, 2006.

Turner, Jonathan H., and Jan E. Stets. *The Sociology of Emotions*. Cambridge, UK: Cambridge University Press, 2005.

Vogt, Carl. *Lectures on Man: Place in Creation, and the History of the Earth*. London: Longman, Green, Longman, and Roberts, 1864. Reprinted Charleston, MA: Acme Bookbinding, 2003.

Wacquant, Loic. "For a Sociology of Flesh and Blood." *Qualitative Sociology* 38, no. 1 (2015): 1–11.

Walker, Michael L. *Indefinite: Doing Time in Jail*. New York: Oxford University Press, 2022.

Wynd, Christine A. "Current Factors Contributing to Professionalism in Nursing." *Journal of Professional Nursing* 19, no. 5 (2003): 251–61.

Young, Linda. *Middle-Class Culture in the Nineteenth Century*. New York: Palgrave MacMillan, 2003.

Zuberi, Tukufu. "Critical Race Theory of Society." *Connecticut Law Review* 43, no. 5 (2011): 1573–91.

16

On the Margins of Sociology and Grounded in Chicana/o Latina/o Studies

Cross-Generational Reflections on (Un)Disciplining

LAURA E. ENRIQUEZ AND GILDA L. OCHOA

Sociology was one of the first academic spaces that provided us with language, frameworks, and methodologies for understanding contemporary issues and communities. A generation apart, we came to sociology as undergraduate students because of our commitments to better understand areas with which we are personally connected, in particular Latina/o/x communities, race and racism, immigration, and education.[1] We pursued PhDs in sociology and conducted research to answer critical questions about inequality and advance social justice for our communities. However, at pivotal moments in graduate school at UCLA and during our careers in academia, our positionalities, research questions, methodological approaches, and social change work have been overlooked, dismissed, and outright disparaged.

Fortunately, generations before us offered models of how to persist in sociology and created spaces that helped sustain us in academia. While such scholars were often invisible in the courses we took, sociology has a significant legacy of early community-engaged and critical sociologists, including W. E. B. Du Bois, Ida B. Wells-Barnett, Jane Addams, and C. Wright Mills. There is also an important lineage of Chicana/o/x and Latina/o/x sociologists, beginning with Julian Samora, who earned his PhD in 1953. Samora completed foundational work on border studies, Mexican American politics, and health that was used to inform policy through the Mexican American Legal Defense Fund and established the Mexican American Graduate Studies Program at the University of Notre Dame in 1971.[2] Together, the approaches of these early sociologists extend into the groundbreaking work of contemporary sociologists, including the dynamic Latina/o Sociology section, which gained official recognition at the 1993 American Sociological Association (ASA) meetings—and recent ASA presidents such as Patricia Hill Collins, Evelyn Nakano Glenn, Eduardo Bonilla-Silva, Mary Romero, Aldon Morris, and Cecilia Menjívar.[3] Despite these legacies, we, like community-engaged scholars before us, have at crucial times been forced to seek supportive academic spaces outside of sociology, including within Chicana/o/x Latina/o/x studies.

With its origins in community, transdisciplinarity, and commitment to transformative change, Chicana/o/x Latina/o/x studies (CLS) has been an important site of sustenance and resistance.[4] CLS offers crucial context on the specific histories and experiences of Mexican Americans and Latinas/os/xs more generally, critical lenses on society, and a purpose rooted in community and transformation. Existing on the periphery of academia and with its own fraught patterns of exclusion, CLS has nonetheless allowed for more holistic and imaginative approaches.

Drawing on our experiences moving between and within sociology and CLS, in this chapter, we use cross-generational storytelling to unpack what we have observed as the limits, overlaps and possibilities of the sociology and CLS we know. In the tradition of Chicana and Latina feminists, such storytelling is a way to push back against master narratives that have devalued and rejected our ways of knowing.[5] It "engenders a process of survival, healing, and transformation for the individual, their community, and the larger society."[6] Our cross-generational approach allows us to reflect on our shared experiences and note some of the changes we have observed within these two academic arenas, as well as within the three academic institutions we have moved among and between at different times—UC Irvine, Pomona College, and UCLA. Together, we reflect on the limits of the normative epistemological and methodological expectations that remain within sociology that fuel marginalization and hinder knowledge construction, we offer ways of enhancing sociology by learning from CLS, and we share how drawing on select approaches from sociology while working within CLS has enabled us to more fully thrive and do the work we are committed to. As such, this chapter adds to long-standing debates about the social construction of knowledge and the roles of social science theories and methodologies in justifying and perpetuating inequalities.[7]

Seeing Parts of Ourselves: The Power of the Sociological
Imagination in the Hands of Scholars of Color

We were drawn to sociology because we saw ourselves and society
reflected in the curriculum, even if only partially. Sociology classes
provided a language and a lens to better understand our own lived
experiences. Growing up as the daughter of a Nicaraguan immigrant
and a second-generation Italian American from New York, Gilda saw
first-hand the impacts of an assimilationist imperative, colorism, and
language discrimination in her family when she was admonished by her
Nicaraguan grandmother for staying in the sun and was taught only
English by her father in an attempt to shield her from the racist assaults
he experienced. For her, sociology enhanced her understanding of the
larger processes shaping such dynamics. She was formally introduced to
sociology as a first-year college student at UC Santa Cruz and continued
to study it as her undergraduate major at UC Irvine. Sitting in lecture
halls, she heard, for the first time in a classroom setting, some of her
experiences come to life through rich descriptions, films, and discussions about race, class, and gender.

Laura's introduction to sociology was through Gilda. We first met in
2004—almost twenty years after Gilda began college. Laura was a first-
year college student and attended Gilda's faculty lecture during welcome
week. We introduced ourselves and quickly realized that we grew up
minutes from each other but a generation apart. The one-hour talk drew
Laura into the power of sociology to contextualize one's experience and
prompted her to take Gilda's seminar on Los Angeles Communities later
that year. The class exposed her to books about the areas she grew up
in, providing a lens to understand power and inequality that she had
witnessed but did not have language for. For the final paper, Gilda encouraged Laura to develop her own research project based on interviewing family members about their migration experiences to Los Angeles.
This was a unique opportunity to center her and her family's experiences
related to immigration, racism, and assimilation and to make sense of
them in the context of the literature. In a later class, she read Gilda's
book, *Becoming Neighbors in a Mexican American Community*, which
examined intra-ethnic dynamics in the area they grew up in. Reading
about the effects of California's anti-immigrant Proposition 187 in the

early 1990s and racial dynamics locally helped Laura understand the structures that prompted her family to speak only English to her and her cousins when they were growing up.[8] It offered an opportunity to heal and come to terms with her limited Spanish language.

For us, sociology offers a unique opportunity to understand individual experiences within the context of US society. C. Wright Mills's *The Sociological Imagination* was one of the key texts linking micro and macro inequities and contextualizing individual experiences and experiential knowledge.[9] It is precisely this sociological lens that enabled us to better see, understand, and excavate our own experiences and the experiences of our families and communities. Mills was one of few early White male sociologists who advanced critical forms of sociology, likely contributing to why we resonated with his work over that of other prominent White male theorists.[10] His work is considered canonical, ensuring its assignment in most sociology courses and facilitating our ability to see parts of ourselves in mainstream sociology courses.

However, for us, it has largely been women of color sociologists who have embodied a way of applying one's sociological imagination to uplift marginalized communities and theorize power and inequality. Gilda remembers the publication of Patricia Hill Collins's *Black Feminist Thought* as an influential theoretical framework when she was beginning graduate school at UCLA and struggling with the Eurocentric masculinist theories that predominated in the required courses. Collins's text centered Black women as producers of knowledge rather than as objects of study.[11] She showed how knowledge is a sociopolitical construct and linked knowledge construction to the perpetuation of race, class, and gender hierarchies. Mary Romero's *Maid in the USA* launched a critique of capitalism by unpacking the micro-level impacts of systems of power and inequality on the lives of Mexican American domestic workers, while also highlighting the role of individual agency.[12] For Laura, theories of intersectionality have informed her understanding of interlocking systems of oppression that jointly construct the emergence of power and inequality. Early on, she found examples of this type of work in Nancy Lopez's *Hopeful Girls, Troubled Boys*, Angela Valenzuela's *Subtractive Schooling*, and Pierrette Hondagneu-Sotelo's *Domestica*.[13] Such texts centered the voices of community members and traced the structural sources of race, class, and gender inequalities. Notably, these role models were working at the intersections of multiple arenas of study, traversing among sociology, CLS, ethnic studies, women's studies, and education.

Becoming the Problem: The Marginalized Sociology of Scholars of Color

Despite our love for these texts, it quickly became apparent that they belonged to a marginalized sociology. For the most part, they were not assigned in our required sociology undergraduate and graduate courses. Instead, Gilda remembers seeking out theory by women of color in the company of her peers during graduate school in the 1990s. While taking a feminist theory class, they approached the sociology professor to question why the only inclusion of women of color were three articles by Black feminists reserved for the last week of class, to which the professor replied, "Women of color aren't doing theory." When Gilda and her colleagues countered by citing theories of the flesh, such as in *This Bridge Called My Back* and *Black Feminist Thought*, they were told they could fix the problem by recommending readings.[14]

This pushback was common throughout graduate school when we tried to bring in the critical sociological theories, readings, and approaches inspiring us. The methods courses, taught entirely by symbolic interactionists, tended to dismiss the salience of power, race, class, and gender. For example, when Gilda brought *Maid in the USA* into a two-quarter qualitative research class, the professor criticized Romero's macro-structural analysis of power based on her interviews about everyday interactions between White employers and Mexican American domestic workers.[15] Similarly, in her own research, Gilda was chastised for including race in her field note observations. Students were instructed to focus on micro-level interactions only, as though how people interact and move through the world are unrelated to race and larger structures of power. Then, while completing her dissertation, one of Gilda's committee members whose work focuses on race critiqued her community study on La Puente as "too anthropological." The implication was that her work was more descriptive than theoretical and that she spent too much time immersing herself and organizing with the community as opposed to studying them.

A generation later, research by scholars who wrote about our communities remained largely absent in Laura's graduate courses. The sociology she had come to know as an undergraduate through Gilda's classes, the sociology that valued her experiences and perspectives, was relegated to a week on race/ethnicity in her graduate proseminar. Immigration classes were shockingly divorced from discussions of race. Women of color remained absent, and work like *Black Feminist Thought* went unassigned, despite Patricia Hill Collins being a prolific scholar and elected ASA president the year Laura started graduate school. Instead, because in her required theory class she critiqued a reading for not sufficiently accounting for the experiences of marginalized individuals, Laura was called "the problem with sociology" and "the reason why there is no more grand theory." The professor aspired to reify universalist theories with the idea that such theory could explain all types of social interactions. Laura was astounded by the idea that race and gender were somehow less important or unnecessary to consider when her own experiences and research had made it crystal clear that such intersectional social locations matter deeply to social interactions.

Labeling individual people a problem is part of a larger phenomenon through which structural inequities are erased, one that W. E. B. Du Bois also queries in *The Souls of Black Folk*, asking, "How does it feel to be a problem?"[16] Indeed, these moments capture the persisting structural and social violence that has been perpetrated within sociological spaces by sidelining the study of race and intersectionality, which is often authored by scholars of color. They are examples of everyday experiences that contribute to a larger pattern of marginalization and how the discipline erases sociologists who aspire to an "engaged sociology aimed at change for a better world."[17] A case in point is the erasure of early critical sociologists such as Du Bois and Jane Addams.[18] Mary Romero's 2020 ASA presidential address argues that "sociology has, from its inception, been engaged in social justice."[19] Her critical reading of the discipline's history elevates the contributions of some of the founders who have been "ignored, isolated, and marginalized" as part of efforts to advance a hegemonic narrative of seemingly "value-free objective sociology." Such efforts to write out marginalized scholars and more critical approaches is by no means unique to sociology but occurs across disciplines and throughout academia. What makes sociology unique, however, is how this erasure contradicts its claim to focusing on human behavior, society, and contemporary issues.

Despite being advanced by prominent sociologists and recent ASA presidents, including Bonilla-Silva and Romero, a social justice–oriented sociology that centers marginalized communities remains largely absent from what is deemed as the core of the discipline.[20] Likewise, even though the Latina/o Sociology section within the ASA is thriving, it remains mostly unknown to sociologists outside of this field.[21] The reclamation of these histories and voices are an important lifeline, offering evidence of the type of sociology we have come to know and love and that more accurately represents society and people's social locations. Like Mills's *Sociological Imagination*, we can hold them up to defend the value of our work to sociology. Yet hegemonic sociology persists, and these daily and institutionalized instances of social and structural exclusion serve to protect it, reflecting how individual ASA presidents alone are insufficient for transforming the discipline.

Often, these everyday instances went unnoticed and unexamined by many of our sociology colleagues. Rather, most absorbed and espoused the hegemonic notions of sociology that we were increasingly pushing against. In graduate school, it was only a few of our peers, often those who also occupied marginalized social locations, who shared our critiques of sociology and offered a knowing glance when such moments manifested. We rolled our eyes together or mapped out strategic responses. In the earlier example, when Laura was called "the problem with sociology" by her theory professor, none of her classmates recognized the problematic nature of this dismissal. Searching around the room for a glimmer of understanding, she was met with blank stares. The moment passed unchallenged. However, she was able to find validation when recounting the incident to another Latina graduate student a few cohorts ahead of her. Such relationships have fortified us as we have participated in building a sociology that thrives on the margins.

Fortifying Sociology on the Margins

While we found traces of the sociology we aspired to in the literature, our ability to carry out this kind of sociology has been heavily influenced by a lineage of sociologists, often people of color, who have worked on the margins of sociology with intentionality to disrupt its norms. bell hooks writes that margins are "much more than a site of deprivation" but "the site of radical possibility, a space of resistance . . . a site one stays in, clings to even because it nourishes one's capacity to resist. It offers to one the possibility of radical perspective from which to see and create, to imagine alternatives."[22] On the margins, we identified mentors and peers who were doing research that uplifted marginalized communities, countered problematic narratives, critiqued structural inequality, and pursued social justice. They eschewed objectivity and embraced their subjectivities, often leaning into the power of studying, teaching, and serving those like themselves. Their very presence and survival in the academy showed us that there was a place for us there.

For us, one of the most critical embodiments of how to be a sociologist who values social justice and marginalized communities has been our graduate advisor, Dr. Vilma Ortiz. Vilma joined the UCLA Department of Sociology in 1988 as the first and only Latina in the department. Gilda was one of her first students when she began in 1990. Almost two decades later, Gilda sent Laura off to UCLA to be advised by Vilma as well. Her constant and continued presence enabled us to thrive during and after our graduate training, guiding us as we developed our own ways of approaching sociology.

Gilda saw Vilma as a model. Searching for ways to act on her personal and political commitments within academia, Gilda watched as Vilma moved between and among multiple spaces—sociology, women's studies, and Chicana/o studies. Vilma advocated for students in department meetings, and she had a strong public presence. Vilma spoke at demonstrations in support of establishing a Chicana/o studies department, and as one of the few Latina professors at UCLA, she was also an outspoken critic of narrow nationalism and sexism. Outside of the public eye, Vilma built a community of students who worked as research assistants on the groundbreaking Mexican American Study Project. Meeting with students regularly, Vilma encouraged students to bring their whole selves into academia and to follow their own research and career paths—even when they did not align with departmental expectations of becoming R1 university professors.

Vilma has made it her mission to plant seeds, to send her students off to inspire others, and continue to make space for this work in academia. Gilda was one of her first students, and she, in turn, inspired Laura.

As an undergraduate, Laura worked with Gilda as a research assistant for her project interviewing students at a local high school. The research idea came from school officials' concerns about educational disparities at the school and eventually resulted in the book *Academic Profiling*.[23] Participating in the project allowed Laura to witness the intentional development of a research project that interrogated social inequities and informed policies and practices to address them. It reinforced the idea that research should have a larger social justice purpose. The project was also collaborative, with Gilda including Laura in early project discussions with administrators and staff. Along with two other undergraduate students, Laura worked alongside Gilda to conduct interviews and participant observations. All team members were encouraged to draw on their own experiences to inform their approach and analysis. For Laura, this meant focusing on understanding the experiences of students who were enrolled in the International Baccalaureate program, which she had also completed in high school.[24] There were staggering racial disparities with only one Latina enrolled in the program, a reality that was also true of Laura's experience at another school. Laura drew on this to inform several conversations and an interview with the Latina student. These conversations were never encouraged to be distant or to aim for objectivity but rather were semi-therapeutic conversations punctuated with laughter and anger as they learned from each other about the racial dynamics of the school. This initial experience created the foundation for Laura's approach to sociological research, one that aspires to promote social change and values collaboration, experiential knowledge, and subjectivity and as a result enables informants to speak freely and candidly.

For Laura, graduate school was a rude awakening to the fact that she and her approach to research were going to be undervalued and overlooked. This was made instantly visible in her being awarded one of the lowest funding packages of her cohort. And it was Vilma, in their first meeting, who refused to allow this to happen. She turned instantly to her computer, firing off an email to the chair that resulted in Laura being awarded additional funds. Vilma also encouraged Laura to pursue research projects that aligned with her social justice values and stemmed from her experiential knowledge. Such support did not exist in the larger program that sought to train students to pursue objectivity (or at best manage their subjectivity), encouraged the development of strategic, rather than authentic, relationships with community members, and devalued implications for policy and practice. If not for Gilda's early lessons and Vilma's reinforcement of these values, it would have been much harder for Laura to hold fast to her vision of what sociology could be.

Importantly, we found spaces of like-minded people who would fortify us in our mission. For Gilda, this was through friendship with other graduate students of color, participation in women's studies and CLS, and the formation of a women of color campus group: Voices. For Laura, such spaces were available in the form of Vilma's research group. The growth of the number of underrepresented students of color, particularly Latinas and women of color, admitted to the UCLA sociology department resulted in Vilma advising twelve students when Laura was enrolled. Vilma created a weekly research group meeting of her graduate students, composed exclusively of women of color studying race and immigration, with whom Laura engaged for much of her graduate school tenure. The group created an important counter-space to mainstream sociology where Laura and her peers could find validation and support for their work and well-being. They validated alternative ways of doing sociology that were centered in marginalized communities, valued working closely with community members, and sought to unpack and address social inequalities. This space taught Laura that she had accomplices in our collective mission to advance our version of sociology.

Vilma created a safe space within sociology that allowed us to be ourselves. Her work has been carried on and reinforced by many others who imparted lessons that allowed us to persist in the face of the racist, sexist, and other toxic aspects of academia. We could draw on this lineage of strength and resistance to sustain our work. We grew, and continue to grow, into our own version of sociology, one that we later realized drew from central tenants of CLS.

Called to Chicana/o Latina/o Studies' Commitment to Community and Action

From its inception, activism, community, and transformation have been central to CLS. Chicana/o studies was created through struggle.

During the 1960s' activist movements, organizers outlined the objectives of Chicano studies in *El Plan de Santa Bárbara* in April 1969.[25] In it, they centered research, teaching, and public service in the interest of Chicano communities. *El Plan* advocated for Chicano liberation and research for social change by "provid[ing] action-oriented analysis of conditions" along with "politically educating the Chicano community."[26] This activist and critical approach to society has shaped the culture of CLS classrooms even when this history was not always made explicit.

As undergraduate students twenty and thirty-five years after *El Plan*, we sought classes focusing on Chicanas/os and Latinas/os because they centered curriculum relevant to our lives and still missing in most other courses. The course assignments also tended to be applied, encouraging us to engage in qualitative research in local communities and to write about our families. While the course options were limited because of a lack of institutional investment in CLS, these initial classes helped inspire our research interests and passion for advanced study.[27] However, it was in graduate school for Gilda and then when both of us were professors that at crucial junctures, we were explicitly called to CLS. For us, these pivotal moments highlight the strengths of CLS, especially in relation to some of our negative experiences in sociology.

Gilda was drawn to CLS early in her PhD program as she struggled with the Eurocentric curriculum and with the often disconnected, objectifying approaches in sociology. At the time, UCLA lacked an undergraduate and graduate CLS department.[28] Fortunately, Gilda's master's and dissertation work on Mexicanas' migration experiences and Mexicana/o-Mexican American relationships helped her become a teaching assistant in undergraduate classes taught by Vilma Ortiz on Chicanas/os in contemporary society and Chicanas and Latinas. These classes focused on areas common in sociology, such as identity, race and racism, labor, immigration, media, and family. However, rather than engage with the topics and readings in abstract ways typical of graduate-level sociology classes, students drew from their experiences and the sociopolitical context. There was a feeling of urgency and relevancy to what was discussed. This ethos encouraged students and instructors to bring their whole selves into the classroom in a more dynamic, collectivist, and community-centered way.

These courses also did not avoid analyses of power, capitalism, racism, and sexism. Instead, they began with an understanding of inequality rooted in larger systems and not individual groups, as was often the case in sociology in the early 1990s when ethnicity-based or assimilationist paradigms based on southern and eastern European immigrants still framed the literature. CLS offered what Emma Pérez refers to as *un sitio y un lengua*—a space and a language that "rejects colonial ideology and the by-products of colonialism and capitalist patriarchy—sexism, racism, homophobia, etc."[29]

The intellectual and personal affirmation Gilda experienced as a teaching assistant in both CLS and women's studies helped foster her community-centered and social-change approach to research and teaching. She also began to develop a stronger voice and sense of belonging as a graduate student despite feeling that she was on the periphery of sociology. Based on these experiences, Gilda searched for tenure-track jobs in joint appointments where she hoped she could draw on the strengths of both sociology and CLS. She accepted a tenure-track position at Pomona College in CLS and sociology, where she also affiliated with women's studies.

With time, it became clearer that Gilda's commitments to local communities and her overall approach aligns more closely with CLS. During an early review, she was reprimanded by the chair of the sociology department as "gutsy" and chastised with "how dare you" for publishing in one of the oldest women's studies journals with what she perceived as a small *n* of eighteen participants. Reflecting the hegemony of quantitative research in sociology, the number of participants were valued over the process of building authentic relationships and centering community voices, which are so prized in CLS. Likewise, while Gilda was sometimes praised in sociology, in other instances, the messages were that her approach was narrow and activist. Such disciplinary constraints in sociology assume that there is one audience and one way to research and write. Fortunately, CLS facilitates Gilda's work, as it did while she was in graduate school, and offers justification for why she merges her research, teaching, organizing, and living. Just as importantly, CLS colleagues have modeled counterapproaches to positivist dictates and created a space of belonging that enabled Gilda to do the type of research and teaching relevant for the communities and students with whom she works.

On the other hand, Laura was steeped in a CLS community throughout her undergraduate and graduate education, but she did not realize it.
She took cross-listed undergraduate courses with Gilda and other professors with joint appointments in CLS and ethnic studies departments.
However, this institutional setup prevented her from realizing that she
was experiencing a CLS curriculum. In graduate school, she enjoyed the
supportive space created by her Latina peers in Vilma's research group.
Their critical perspectives, social justice aims, and collaborative ethos
reflected an underlying commitment to CLS tenets, but they all were
being trained as sociologists. By grounding herself in these spaces, Laura
felt that she could carve out a space for herself in sociology. She did not
feel pulled toward CLS in the ways Gilda had. Rather, Laura was called
to CLS when she accepted a tenure-track job in the Department of Chi-
cano/Latino Studies at UC Irvine.

Laura started fully identifying with CLS as a second-year assistant
professor when her department chair suggested she teach the department's graduate level course, Theoretical Issues in Chicana/o-Latina/o
Studies, which is the cornerstone of its graduate emphasis curriculum.
Needing to familiarize herself with what she thought was a new discipline for her, Laura spent a lot of time reading and trying to figure out
what CLS was. While much was new, she quickly realized that her prior
cross-listed coursework and interdisciplinary reading on Chicana/o/
Latina/o communities had constituted a hidden CLS curriculum. In
familiarizing herself with seminal texts like *El Plan de Aztlan* and *El
Plan de Santa Bárbara* from 1969, she began to realize that her way of
being a sociologist and approaching research were rooted in core values
shared by CLS. These were lessons she had learned before, but now she
could anchor them in a scholarly approach and tradition. In particular, *El Plan de Santa Bárbara* critiqued academia and blurred the binary
constructions of college and community. Its emphasis on doing research
to positively impact communities stuck with her and guided subsequent
framings of her ongoing research projects, along with her commitment
to providing professional development for students from marginalized
groups to be able to research their own communities.

Laura also found that her position in a CLS department has created a greater sense of liberty. At sociology conferences and in reviewer
comments, Laura was urged to make her work "more sociological" by

engaging with noted sociological theorists like Michel Foucault or Erving Goffman. While meant to be helpful, this emphasis on framing research around the literature can detract from and obscure the voices of participants, especially in the case of Laura's research, where little sociology literature centers the lives and experiences of undocumented immigrants and mixed status families. While there are times in which such sociological connections can be meaningfully made, Laura does not feel compelled to make them at all times. Rather, she has embraced her position in CLS to design research studies in accordance with community needs and her research questions, without the constraints of abiding by sociological approaches and theories. Further, her community-centered approach to research, which includes partnerships with undocumented student services, research teams composed of students from undocumented and mixed-status families, and public-facing writing, has been valued as both research *and* service by her CLS colleagues.

Despite its transformative power, CLS has not been immune to institutional constraints and internal dynamics limiting knowledge, thought, and research. Academic hierarchies and epistemological racism devaluing CLS have resulted in still limited classes, faculty hired in joint appointments with ties to traditional disciplines, and few CLS graduate programs. As a product of larger society and fighting to exist within historically White institutions, Chicano studies has not always accounted for the diversity within Chicana/o/x and Latina/o/x communities.[30] Some CLS faculty and spaces have reinforced the sexism, heterosexism, anti-Blackness, and other forms of exclusion and erasure within academia.[31] This includes ignoring the foundational roles, experiences, and frameworks of feminists, women, Black, Indigenous, and LGBTQ+ community members, and until the past ten to fifteen years, Central Americans were rarely discussed. At times, such narrow constrictions of who belongs has also forced us to grapple with our place in what was initially Chicano studies.[32]

As in sociology, feminists of color have been instrumental in creating spaces that challenge static constructions of identity, ways of being, and approaches to work.[33] Their naming of exclusionary practices within academia and emphasis on both/and frameworks centering race, class, gender, *and* sexuality offered necessary context, inspiration, and counternarratives, enabling us to persist in academia from graduate school to the present. This scholarship complicated the facile binary constructions we experienced and instead allowed us to better embrace the messiness that comes with more nuanced both/and worldviews.

Moving from Discipline to Approach

Both sociology and CLS have been disciplined by the academy, pushed to conform to positivist notions of objective scientific inquiry, and in the case of CLS, weakly supported with few institutional resources. The disciplining—or building and maintaining of these fields of study—has helped to place value in a mainstream sociology that centers objectivity and an institutionalized version of CLS that maintains Western academic traditions while studying Chicana/o/x Latina/o/x populations.[34] Individuals who do not subscribe to these values and approaches may be disciplined or punished to compel them to subscribe to these academic norms.

Much is lost when we confine ourselves to narrow disciplinary expectations. Disciplinary boundaries reduce the kinds of knowledge and methods that we have access to. Disciplining pushes people out and harms those of us who stay. Because CLS is understood as an inter-/ multi- and sometimes trans-disciplinary project, it offers us space to participate in the academy in ways that are meaningful for us. We have not always been fully situated in any discipline. Instead we have built our own academic toolbox that has enabled us to carry out the work we aspire to do. We draw methods, theories, and inspiration from critical sociology and CLS, but we also find useful frameworks and approaches in a range of other disciplines and interdisciplinary fields. Moving beyond disciplines has been an agentic process wherein we are able to move in the academy and between our two primary disciplinary affiliations on our own terms. Thus, we call for a move away from disciplines. Eliminating, or at least blurring, narrow disciplinary lines will enhance what we know and open up greater spaces of belonging.

Rather than an adherence to disciplinary perspectives, we have been guided by a critical, community based, social justice approach that centers our core values rather than disciplinary perspectives. This approach is characterized by four core values:

1. *An intention of listening and learning from and with community.*
   Our work has been motivated by our personal experiences and
   community connections. We have centered community interests
   by building long-term relationships and collaborations with community members. We listen deeply to build authentic relationships
   and connections, regardless of whether they last only the hour or
   two we spend with an interviewee or the years we spend with community members.

2. *A practice of centering individuals and their stories while placing
   them in structural contexts.* We believe in the power of stories to
   foster connections, empathy, and understanding. Our work has
   consisted primarily of interviews where we listen deeply and learn
   from the experiential knowledge that community members offer.
   We then situate these within structural inequalities to push back
   against the individualization and deficit orientations that obscure
   power and reproduce inequities.

3. *A valuing of nuanced and intersectional perspectives.* We recognize
   the multidimensionality of people and power structures and seek
   to convey the complexity of experiences and social inequalities.
   We push back on binary conceptions as Western constructs that
   perpetuate hierarchies. Instead, we heed Patricia Hill Collins's call
   for a both/and mode of analysis that aids the acknowledgment of
   interlocking systems of oppression and enables coalition building
   to combat them.[35]

4. *A commitment to creating opportunities for healing and change.* We
   approach our work with a purpose and intention of identifying
   ways to redress the inequalities we are describing. We recognize
   that our interviews, surveys, and other forms of data collection will
   help us understand the processes that create inequality, but this
   can also evoke painful memories for participants; we are committed to making sure that these tears have a purpose beyond our own
   professional advancement. We aspire to create opportunities for
   participants to heal and self-reflect during the interview process.
   We put our research into practice through direct action, collaborations with community partners, and policy recommendations, and
   we aim to engage multiple audiences through workshops, speeches,
   talks, poetry, opinion pieces, policy briefs, resolutions, journal

articles, and books. We see the potential for change by supporting members of marginalized communities to become the next generation of scholars doing work for and with their own communities.

This approach has guided our way of being in academia. It grounds our research, teaching, and service. Importantly, it also lives outside of disciplinary boundaries and thus has been an implicit act of resistance in the face of academic disciplining.

Aspects of our approach can be found in, and have been inspired by, the critical sociologists we discussed earlier and the core tenets of CLS. However, these people-centered values were instilled in us by our families and communities long before we came to academia. CLS, ethnic studies, and women's studies scholars have since offered us a language to understand these early lessons and spaces to enact them. In the words of Dolores Delgado Bernal, our approach is the result of the "pedagogies of the home" or the family and community lessons on how to make sense of and negotiate an unequal world.[36] bell hooks teaches us that the "world of women talk" in our homes can ignite our voices and teach us to "talk back."[37]

This knowledge pushes us to question whether such an approach is unique to critical sociology or CLS. Indeed, such critical, community based, social justice approaches can be found in the work of scholars from other disciplines as well. Thus, we have drawn on our lived experiences to talk back, to call for the liberation of such approaches from a disciplinary home. It is an approach available *both* to sociology *and* CLS and beyond.

Conclusion

It has been made clear to us that our sociology is perceived as an attack on mainstream sociology. We see that these attacks reflect similar narratives around competing for resources that have served to reinforce power structures of White supremacy, patriarchy, heteronormativity, and nativism. They are attempts to put us in our place, to demand allegiance to the mainstream—to sit down, shut up, and stop being a problem. Called to talk back, we seek to infiltrate sociology on our own terms. In these spaces, we do the work that is needed to push back on a version of sociology that has at best erased and at worst deeply harmed our communities. Our presence and voices resist a fundamental injustice that has excluded people and ways of knowing. Working in the margins has been a "site of radical possibility" where we have found a purposeful approach to scholarship that is urgent and valuable.[38] But this work takes a toll on us and our well-being, pushing us away, or forcing us to pull back, so we can muster energy for the next fight.

These instances force us to find places where we can thrive. CLS has offered us this space because its values align with our critical, community based, social justice approach. But life in the borderlands betwixt and between disciplines is difficult. In Gloria Anzaldúa's borderlands imaginary, the "border *es una herida abierta* where the Third World grates against the first and bleeds."[39] We find ourselves in the borderlands of academia, "a vague and undetermined place created by the emotional residue of an unnatural boundary."[40] For us, power structures have created an unnatural boundary of binary choices. Inspired by critical scholars before us, we reject these choices and instead choose our own path through academia by grounding ourselves in our core values.

In reflecting on our stories here, we have learned from ourselves and one another while also naming the structural processes at work and engaging in healing. In sharing our stories, we hope to hold space for additional learning, healing, and empowerment. As others have done for us, we offer our approach to aid us in the move toward an undisciplined world. We are committed to cheering, supporting, and ultimately getting out of the way as new generations of scholars expand our thinking and methodologies for the good of self, communities, and the creation of knowledge.

NOTES

1 Knowing the politics of terms and the heterogeneity among Latinas/os/xs, when referring to people and earlier time periods, we use terms to reflect historical contexts and in accordance with how people define themselves. When referring generally to Latina/o/x communities in our current period, we use Latina/o/x to be as inclusive as possible and to disrupt gender binaries.

2 Pulido, Driscoll de Alvarado, and Samora, *Moving beyond Borders*.

3 Zinn and Mirandé, "Latino/a Sociology"; Romero, "Notes from the Chair."

4 While names of programs and departments have changed over time and continue to be in flux, we use Chicano studies when referring to earlier programs and

Chicana/o/x Latina/o/x studies (CLS) in the contemporary period to reflect the current names used within academia and by students.

5 See Moraga and Anzaldúa, *This Bridge Called My Back*; Latina Feminist Group, *Telling to Live*; Trujillo, *Living Chicana Theory*.

6 Facio, "Writing and Working in the Borderlands."

7 See Aguirre, "Teaching Chicano Sociology"; Zinn, "Sociological Theory in Emergent Chicano Perspectives"; Barrera, *Race and Class in the Southwest*; Collins, *Black Feminist Thought*; Go, "Decolonizing Sociology"; Gonzalez, *Chicano Education in the Era of Segregation*; Mirandé, "A New Paradigm for Social Science."

8 Ochoa, *Becoming Neighbors in a Mexican American Community*.

9 Mills, *The Sociological Imagination*.

10 Romero, "Sociology Engaged in Social Justice."

11 Collins, *Black Feminist Thought*.

12 Romero, *Maid in the USA*.

13 Hondagneu-Sotelo, *Domestica*; Lopez, *Hopeful Girls, Troubled Boys*; Valenzuela, *Subtractive Schooling*.

14 Collins, *Black Feminist Thought*; Moraga and Anzaldúa, *This Bridge Called My Back*.

15 Romero, *Maid in the USA*.

16 Du Bois, *The Souls of Black Folk*, 1.

17 Romero, "Sociology Engaged in Social Justice," 3.

18 Deegan, *Jane Addams*; Morris, *The Scholar Denied*.

19 Romero, "Sociology Engaged in Social Justice."

20 Romero, "'Reflections'"; See also Bonilla-Silva, "Feeling Race"; Romero, "Sociology Engaged in Social Justice."

21 Zinn and Mirandé, "Latino/a Sociology," 304–5.

22 hooks, "Choosing the Margin," 20.

23 Ochoa, *Academic Profiling*.

24 The International Baccalaureate program is an honors program started in international schools geared toward the children of diplomats that now exists in public schools around the world.

25 Chicano Coordinating Council on Higher Education, *El Plan de Santa Bárbara*.

26 Ibid., 78

27 From 1987 to 1990, while Gilda was an undergraduate student at UC Irvine, there was no Chicana/o Latina/o studies major or department. Thus, Gilda took classes in what was called comparative cultures.

28 After decades of struggle, a Chicana and Chicano Studies Department was established at UCLA in 2005. In 2010, the MA/PhD graduate program was approved. See https://chavez.ucla.edu/about/history/.

29 Pérez, "Sexuality and Discourse," 47–48.

30 Soldatenko, "Constructing Chicana and Chicano Studies."

31 Blackwell, *Chicana Power!*; Rojas Durazo, *The Imperial University*.

32 Ochoa and Enriquez, "Contested Belongings."

33 Blackwell, *Chicana Power!*
34 Glenn, "Whose Public Sociology?"; Soldatenko, *Chicano Studies.*
35 Collins, *Black Feminist Thought.*
36 Delgado Bernal, "Learning and Living Pedagogies of Home."
37 hooks, *Talking Back.*
38 hooks, "Choosing the Margin," 20.
39 Anzaldúa, *Borderlands/La Frontera*, 25.
40 Ibid.

BIBLIOGRAPHY

Aguirre, Adalberto, Jr. "Teaching Chicano Sociology: A Response to the Academic Stock-Story about Ethnic Studies Classes." *Teaching Sociology* 27 (July 1999): 264–273.

Anzaldúa, Gloria. *Borderlands/La Frontera: The New Mestiza.* 2nd ed. San Francisco: Aunt Lute Books, 1999.

Barrera, Mario. *Race and Class in the Southwest.* Notre Dame, IN: Notre Dame University Press, 1979.

Blackwell, Maylei. *Chicana Power! Contested Histories of Feminism in the Chicano Movement.* Austin: University of Texas Press, 2011.

Bonilla-Silva, Eduardo. "Feeling Race: Theorizing the Racial Economy of Emotions." *American Sociological Review* 84, no. 1 (January 2019): 1–25.

Chicano Coordinating Council on Higher Education. *El Plan de Santa Bárbara.* Oakland, CA: La Causa Publications, 1969. http://mechadeucdavis.weebly.com.

Collins, Patricia Hill. *Black Feminist Thought: Knowledge, Consciousness and the Politics of Empowerment.* Boston: Routledge, 1990.

Deegan, Mary Jo. *Jane Addams and the Men of the Chicago School, 1892–1918.* New Brunswick, NJ: Transaction Books, 1988.

Delgado Bernal, Dolores. "Learning and Living Pedagogies of Home: The Mestiza Consciousness of Chicana Studies." In *Chicana/Latina Education in Everyday Life: Feminista Perspectives on Pedagogy and Epistemology*, edited by Dolores Delgado Bernal, C. Alejandra Elenes, Francisca E. Godinez, and Sofia Villenas, 113–32. Albany: State University of New York Press, 2006.

Du Bois, W. E. B. *The Souls of Black Folk.* New York: Bantam, 1989.

Durazo, Ana Clarissa Rojas. "Decolonizing Chicano Studies in the Shadows of the University's 'Heteropatriarchal' Order," In *The Imperial University: Academic Repression and Scholarly Dissent*, edited by Piya Chatterjee and Sunaina Maira, 187–214. Minneapolis: University of Minnesota Press, 2014.

Enriquez, Laura E. *Of Love and Papers: How Immigration Policy Affects Romance and Family.* Berkeley: University of California Press, 2020.

Facio, Elisa Linda. "Writing and Working in the Borderlands: The Implications of Anzaldúan Thought for Chicana Feminist Sociology." *Chicana/Latina Studies* 10 (Fall 2010): 62–82.

Glenn, Evelyn Nakano. "Whose Public Sociology?" In *Public Sociology,* edited by Dan Clawson, Robert Zussman, Joya Misra, Naomi Gerstel, and Randall Stokes, 213–30. Berkeley: University of California Press, 2007.

Go, Julian. "Decolonizing Sociology: Epistemic Inequality and Sociological Thought." *Social Problems* 64, no. 2 (2017): 194–99.

Gonzalez, Gilbert. *Chicano Education in the Era of Segregation.* Philadelphia: Balch Institute Press, 1990.

Hondagneu-Sotelo, Pierrette. *Domestica: Immigrant Workers Cleaning and Caring in the Shadows of Affluence.* Berkeley: University of California Press, 2007.

hooks, bell. "Choosing the Margin as a Space of Radical Openness." *Framework: The Journal of Cinema and Media* 36 (1989): 15–23.

Latina Feminist Group. *Talking Back: Thinking Feminist, Thinking Black.* Boston: South End Press, 1989.

———. *Telling to Live: Latina Feminist Testimonios.* Durham, NC: Duke University Press, 2001.

Lopez, Nancy. *Hopeful Girls, Troubled Boys: Race and Gender Disparity in Urban Education.* New York: Routledge, 2003.

Mills, C. Wright. *The Sociological Imagination.* New York: Oxford University Press, 1959.

Mirandé, Alfredo. "A New Paradigm for Social Science." *Pacific Sociological Review* 21, no. 3 (July 1978): 293–312.

Moraga, Cherríe, and Gloria Anzaldúa, eds. *This Bridge Called My Back: Writings by Radical Women of Color.* New York: Kitchen Table Press, 1981.

Morris, Aldon D. *The Scholar Denied: W. E .B. Du Bois and the Birth of Modern Sociology.* Berkeley: University of California Press, 2015.

Ochoa, Gilda L. *Academic Profiling: Latinos, Asian Americans and the Achievement Gap.* Minneapolis: University of Minnesota Press, 2013.

———. *Becoming Neighbors in a Mexican American Community: Power, Conflict and Solidarity.* Austin: University of Texas Press, 2004.

Ochoa, Gilda L., and Laura E. Enriquez. "Contested Belongings in Sociology and CLS." Presentation at the annual conference of the *American Sociological Association,* August 6–10, 2021.

Pérez, Emma. "Sexuality and Discourse: Notes from a Chicana Survivor." In *Chicana Critical Issues: Mujeres Activas en Letras y Cambio Social,* edited by Norma Alarcón, Rafaela Castro, Emma Pérez, Beatriz M. Pesquera, Adaljiza Sosa Riddell, and Patricia Zavella, 159–94. Berkeley, CA: Third Woman Press, 1993.

Pulido, Alberto López, Barbara Driscoll de Alvarado, and Carmen Samora, eds. *Moving Beyond Borders: Julian Samora and the Establishment of Latino Studies.* Urbana: University of Illinois Press, 2009.

Romero, Mary. *Maid in the USA.* New York: Routledge, 1992.

———. "Notes from the Chair." *Notas: The Newsletter of the Section of Latina and Latino Sociology American Sociological Association* 2, no. 1 (October 1993): 1–2.

———. "Reflections on 'The Department is Very Male, Very White, Very Old, and Very Conservative': The Functioning of the Hidden Curriculum in Graduate Sociology Departments." *Social Problems* 64, no. 3 (May 2017): 212–18.

———. "Sociology Engaged in Social Justice." *American Sociological Review* 85, no 1 (2020): 1–30.

Soldatenko, Michael. *Chicano Studies: The Genesis of a Discipline.* Tucson: University of Arizona Press, 2009.

———. "Constructing Chicana and Chicano Studies: 1993 UCLA Conscious Students of Color Protest." In *Latino Los Angeles: Transformations, Communities, and Activism,* edited by Enrique C. Ochoa and Gilda L. Ochoa, 246–77. Tucson: University of Arizona Press, 2005.

Trujillo, Carla, ed. *Living Chicana Theory.* Berkeley, CA: Third Woman Press, 1998.

Valenzuela, Angela. *Subtractive Schooling: U.S.-Mexican Youth and the Politics of Caring.* Albany: State University of New York Press, 1999.

Zinn, Maxine Baca. "Sociological Theory in Emergent Chicano Perspectives." *Pacific Sociological Review* 24, no. 2 (April 1981): 255–72.

Zinn, Maxine Baca, and Alfredo Mirandé. "Latino/a Sociology: Toward a New Paradigm." *Sociology of Race and Ethnicity* 7, no. 3 (2021): 304–17.

ACKNOWLEDGMENTS

The first tip of the hat goes to Pawan Dhingra, my very capable coeditor. Without his sharp mind, tireless diligence, and sense of humor, this volume would not have come to pass—or at least would not have been as fun to complete. Of course, hats off to all our contributors who wrote such brilliant, beautiful essays and did so under historic pandemic duress. I am so grateful for their patience with all our edits and emails when they likely just wanted to focus on their health and that of their loved ones—or just get through what was already piled high on their desks. Editor Ilene Kalish has been an enthusiastic supporter from the start, and for that we are so thankful, especially for her keen eye and thoughtful critique that refined the volume to sophisticated heights. We are thrilled that our anthology is an NYU Press imprint. I must thank Lara Ullrich for invaluable research and library assistance (good luck in grad school!), my remaining students for inspiring me, and my LMU Asian and Asian American studies colleagues, along with Miliann Kang, Tom Romero, and Ric Noguchi, for their support and good cheer during this project. Finally, I must thank my nearest and dearest for all their sincere "How Are You's?" and kind gestures over the past two years, those who kept me going under the weight of exhaustion: Taybi, Kitani, C. Benny, Hamp, Nina, Tati, and my mother and the rest of my familia. Here I hold up, with love, my father Kim Bock-ki, uncle Kim Duk-ki (keun abuji), aunts Kim Haeyoung and Kim Haeja (jageun gomo deul), and mother-in-law Dao Tran, none of whom are still with us to grab my face and tell me how proud they are of their Youngna-ssi. Whether I must move beyond dimensions or boundaries to do so, it is to them that I dedicate this book.

—Nadia Y. Kim

My sincere thanks goes to Nadia Kim. I appreciate her invitation to join her in this journey that we hope advances the multiple fields we are invested in. She has been a prime partner committed to producing the best book possible. There are many scholars who have played a critical role in my intellectual growth, which has led me to this book, the co-crafting of the introduction, and my personal chapter. Some of these guiding lights are authors in this volume; others have been acknowledged in my other books and remain central to my development. The broader professional circles in which I have been part of, both formal and informal, have given me a setting in which to share ideas and learn new ways of thinking. I also appreciate each of my colleagues in American studies at Amherst College; they warmly welcomed me as I entered the college and have been model scholars/teachers. Both Nadia and I thank Freeden Blume Oeur for his thoughtful feedback on the book prospectus. I also thank our editor at New York University Press, Ilene Kalish. This is my second time working with Ilene, and I could not ask for a better partner and advocate for this book. My family and friends are so tied up in my professional well-being, often in hidden ways, that I cannot imagine having completed this work without them. Charu has been a constant presence and force for goodness in my life. Talvin and Amitav are breaking their own boundaries as they grow. My parents still surprise me to this day. I remain inspired by those around me.

—Pawan Dhingra

HŌKŪLANI K. AIKAU (KANAKA 'ŌIWI) is Professor of Indigenous Governance at the University of Victoria. She is the author of *A Chosen People, A Promised Land: Mormonism and Race in Hawai'i* and co-editor of *Detours: A Decolonial Guide to Hawai'i.*

BEN CARRINGTON is Associate Professor of Sociology and Journalism in the Annenberg School at the University of Southern California. He is the author of *Race, Sport and Politics: The Sporting Black Diaspora.*

MONISHA DAS GUPTA is Professor in the Departments of Ethnic Studies and Women's Gender and Sexuality Studies at the University of Hawai'i at Mānoa. She is the author of the award-winning book *Unruly Immigrants: Rights, Activism, and Transnational South Asian Politics in the United States.*

LAURA E. ENRIQUEZ is Associate Professor of Chicano/Latino Studies at the University of California, Irvine. She is the author of the award-winning book *Of Love and Papers: How Immigration Policy Affects Romance and Family,* and principle investigator of the Undocumented Student Equity Project and the UC Collaborative to Promote Immigrant and Student Equity.

KEVIN ESCUDERO is Assistant Professor of American Studies and Ethnic Studies and affiliated faculty member in the Sociology Department at Brown University. He is the author of *Organizing while Undocumented: Immigrant Youth's Political Activism under the Law.*

YẾN LÊ ESPIRITU is Distinguished Professor of Ethnic Studies at the University of California, San Diego. She is the author of *Body Counts: The Vietnam War and Militarized Refuge(es)* and *Home Bound: Filipino*

American Lives across Cultures, Communities, and Countries. She is also a founding member of the Critical Refugee Studies Collective.

BRITTANY FRIEDMAN is Assistant Professor of Sociology at the University of Southern California. She is an Access to Justice Faculty Scholar of the American Bar Foundation and JPB Foundation and a (De)Racing National Security and Policing Fellow at the Center for Security, Race and Rights. She has a forthcoming book titled *Born in Blood.*

ESITELI HAFOKA is a PhD candidate in the Religious Studies Department at Stanford University. Esiteli's dissertation surveys historical narratives, ethnographies, social media, and personal interviews to argue that religion is essential to understanding Tongan collective identity in America. Esiteli's research reveals the ways Tongans navigate their racial identity in America through a religious epistemology and how, for Tongan Americans, religion and race are co-constitutional.

MELISSA HORNER (MÉTIS/ANISHINAABE) is a PhD candidate in Sociology at the University of Missouri. Her research interests cohere around exploring how Native peoples navigate and heal the effects of intergenerational historical trauma caused by past and ongoing settler colonialism. She pursues her research and doctoral degree as a Health Policy Research Scholar for the Robert Wood Johnson Foundation.

MILIANN KANG is Professor of Women, Gender, Sexuality Studies and affiliated faculty in Sociology and Asian/Asian American Studies at the University of Massachusetts, Amherst. She is the author of *The Managed Hand: Race, Gender and the Body in Beauty Service Work* and is completing her next book, *Mother Other: Race and Reproductive Politics in Asian America.*

SUNAINA MAIRA is Professor of Asian American Studies at the University of California, Davis. She is the author of five monographs, including *The 9/11 Generation: Youth, Rights, and Solidarity in the War on Terror* and *Missing: Youth, Citizenship, and Empire After 9/11.*

GILDA L. OCHOA is Professor of Chicana/o-Latina/o Studies at Pomona College. She is the author of *Academic Profiling: Latinos, Asian Americans, and the Achievement Gap, Becoming Neighbors in a Mexican American Community,* and *Learning from Latino Teachers.*

YVONNE P. SHERWOOD is Assistant Professor of Sociology at the University of Toronto, Mississauga. Her research has been published in *American Indian Culture and Research Journal* and *Fourth World Journal.* She is Spokane and Coeur d'Alene and was raised on the Yakama Nation Reservation in what is currently known as Washington State.

ERICH STEINMAN is Professor of Sociology at Pitzer College. His research has been published in the *American Journal of Sociology, Sociology of Race and Ethnicity,* and *Ethnic and Racial Studies.*

FINAUSINA TEISA PAEA TOVO is Program Coordinator and faculty for the Mana Learning Community at the College of San Mateo. She is of Tongan, Niuean, and Samoan ancestry and was born in East Palo Alto, California. She received her EdD from San Francisco State University with the completion of her dissertation, titled "Talanoa a Mana: Validating Oceania Voices in a Pacific Studies Learning Community," in May 2020.

SALVADOR VIDAL-ORTIZ is Associate Professor of Sociology at American University. He co-authored *Race and Sexuality;* and has co-edited several books: *The Sexuality of Migration: Border Crossings and Mexican Immigrant Men, Queer Brown Voices: Personal Narratives of Latina/o LGBT Activism,* and *Travar el Saber: Educación de Personas Trans y Travestis en Argentina.*

MICHAEL L. WALKER is Beverly and Richard Fink Professor in Liberal Arts in the Department of Sociology at the University of Minnesota-Twin Cities. He is the author of *Indefinite: Doing Time in Jail.*

SYLVIA ZAMORA is Assistant Professor of Sociology at Loyola Marymount University. She is the author of *Racial Baggage: Mexican Immigrants and Race Across the Border.*

ABOUT THE EDITORS

NADIA Y. KIM is Professor of Asian and Asian American Studies and affiliated faculty in Sociology at Loyola Marymount University. The author of multi-award-winning *Imperial Citizens: Koreans and Race from Seoul to LA* and of multi-award-winning *Refusing Death: Immigrant Women and the Fight for Environmental Justice in LA*, her work has appeared on public radio, the *Washington Post*, and the *Chronicle of Higher Education*.

PAWAN DHINGRA is Associate Provost and Associate Dean of the Faculty and is the Aliki Perroti and Seth Frank '55 Professor of US Immigration Studies at Amherst College. He is President of the Association for Asian American Studies. He is also an award-winning author and teacher who has written for the *New York Times*, *CNN*, and other venues. His most recent book is *Hyper Education: Why Good Schools, Good Grades, and Good Behavior Are Not Enough*.

INDEX

Page numbers in italics indicates Photos.

constitutional law, Indigenous justice and, 129–30

Contemporary Cultural Studies (CCCS), Hall, S., and, 189–90; *Policing the Crisis* project of, 191

control, intuitive social science compared to expressiveness in, 307–10

Corbin, Carlyle, 89

corporatization, U.S. empire use of, 6

Costs of War project, on September 11, 2001, 28

Council of American-Islamic Relations (CAIR), 47; ARC and, 46

counterterrorism policies: FBI and anti-Muslim/Arab, 50–51; Yemeni Americans impacted by, 42, 44, 50

COVID-19 pandemic: anti-Asian violence during, 223; Black and Brown community on mask mandate, 53–54; Yemen fatality rate from, 45; Yemeni American small business owners during, 42–59, 53

Crenshaw, Kimberle, 14n1

crip-of-color critique, of Kim, J., 223

"Cripping the Welfare Queen" (Kim, J.), 223–24

crip superpowers, Piepzna-Samarasinha on, 236

critical immigration studies, 21

critical Indigenous studies (CIS): settler colonialism studies and, 143; on sovereignty concepts, 144–45, 148

critical race studies, 14n1

Crossing Waters, Crossing Worlds (Miles and Holland), 297

Cudworth, Erica, 143

Cullors, Patrisse, 255

cultural duty. *See fatongia*

cultural identity, sociology concept of, 30–31

cultural loss, IHT from, 165

cultural studies, 7, 8, 12; criticism of, 191; on discourse and centered power, 190;

Gilroy on, 191–92; Hall, S., on, 183, 189–92, 200n30; on popular culture, 190

Cultural Studies 1983 (Hall), 190

culture, 22–24; USAmerican power, 212

Culture & Truth (Rosaldo), 310–11

Current Population Surveys, data for immigration studies, 29

DACA. *See* Deferred Action for Childhood Arrivals

Dancing on our Turtle's Back (Simpson, L.), 297, 301n25

Darwin, Charles, 308

data: driven approach to sociology of migration, 29; INS for immigration studies, 29, 38n40; Los Angeles racial attitudes, 247–51, 252; for Mana as sacred space study, 273–74; NHPI qualitative, 272; quantitative, 29, 245; sociology of migration driven approach, 29

Dear Science (McKittrick), 13

debility, Puar on, 236

Debord, Guy, 127–28; on spectacle of capitalism, 131

DeBruyen, Lemyra, 165

debwewin (truth) teaching, of Anishinaabe people, 170

decolonization: Guåhan Social Studies curriculum on colonization and, 82–98; Guam Commission on Decolonization education mandate on, 82, 99n21; layered approach to colonization impact, 84, 98; theory, 27

Deferred Action for Childhood Arrivals (DACA), of Obama, 253

Deloria, Philip, 114–15

deportation: anti-deportation activism, 142, 145; of Arab and Muslim Americans, 44, 49; Obama policies of, 253; U.S. nation-state sovereignty and deportation and, 145

Kelley, Robyn D. G.: on African Americans slave trade, 292; on African Indigeneity, 293–95; on *Wild Seed*, 292, 293
Keystone XL Pipeline, 133
Kim, Dianne Dokko, 228
Kim, Jina B., 223–24
Kim, Nadia, 227
King, Martin Luther, Jr., 193
King, Rodney: LA riot and beating of, 247; White police officers' acquittal for beating of, 247, 255
Klitmøller, Jacob, 296
knowledge, ethnic studies use of, 6
Know Your Rights workshops, for Yemeni Americans, 48
Kristof, Nicholas, 62, 77
Kumisón i Fino' CHamoru yan i Fina'nå'guen i Historiata yan i Lina'la'i Taotao Tåno' (Commission on CHamoru language and the teaching of the history and culture of the Indigenous people of Guam), 94, 98n2
Kuper, Kenneth Gofigan, 89

Lamott, Anne, 317–18
land-centered concept, of Indigenous sovereignty, 144–46; Goeman on, 143; settler colonialism and land dispossession, 143
LA riots. *See* Los Angeles uprising
Latina/o sociology section, of ASA, 326, 331
Lawrence, Brenda, 126
Leavey survey. *See* Thomas and Dorothy Leavey Center for the Study of Los Angeles
Lectures on Man (Darwin), 308
Lee, James Kyung-Jin, 237
legislation: Act to Regulate Immigration, 225, 236; Chinese Exclusion Act, 225, 236; DACA, 253; Immigration Act (1924), 67; Immigration Act (1990), 67; Immigration and Naturalization Act,

66–67; Johnson-Reed Act, 26; National Environmental Policy Act, 133; Naturalization Act (1790), 26; Organic Act of Guam, 87, 88; Page Act, 222, 236
Leong, Karen, 154
life, breath, sovereignty. *See* ea
lifeworld of Indigenous justice, 129–30
lived religion: Ammerman example of, 278; of Hall, D., 278; Woodbine on, 278
Long, Robert Aaron, 222
Lopez, Nancy, 328
Lorde, Audre, 205, 207
Los Angeles, public opinion on race, 258–59; Angelenos survey questions, 243–44; Bradley coalition racial alliance, 250; ethno-racial dynamics change, 242; on future unrest disturbances, 255–56; Latinx and Black communities, 250; Los Angeles Public Opinion Surveys, 243–45; Obama presidency and, 253–54; racial attitudes data for, 247–51, 252; racial justice movements, 258; StudyLA on, 243–45, 251, 255; survey of 2017, 251–52; Tea Party racism and, 253–54; Trump impact on, 254; twenty-five years after LA riots, 251–57
Los Angeles Public Opinion Surveys, 243–45
Los Angeles uprising (LA riots) (1992), 242; description of, 247; neoliberal shift impact on, 244; poverty impact on, 249; racialized imperialism impact on, 244; twenty-five years after, 251–57; UCLA Institute for Social Science Research on, 250; war on drugs and, 249
Lowe, Lisa, 23

Maid in the USA (Romero), 328, 329
Makah Nation, of Washington State: course on tribal perspectives of, 106; White conflict with, 105
"Making Sense of Culture" (Patterson), 195